GRAHAM GREENE

GARLAND REFERENCE LIBRARY
OF THE HUMANITIES
(VOL. 173)

GRAHAM GREENE
A *Bibliography*
and Guide to Research

R.A. Wobbe

GARLAND PUBLISHING, INC. • NEW YORK & LONDON
1979

Library of Congress Cataloging in Publication Data

Wobbe, R   A
   Graham Greene, a bibliography and guide to research.

   (Garland reference library of the humanities ; v. 173)
   Includes indexes.
   1. Greene, Graham, 1904–   —Bibliography.   I. Title.
Z8368.987.W64   [PR6013.R44]   016.828'9'1209
ISBN 0-8240-9760-2   78-68307

Printed on acid-free, 250-year-life paper
Manufactured in the United States of America

to Stirley

CONTENTS

List of Illustrations ix

Introduction xi

Acknowledgments xv

A: Books and Pamphlets by Graham Greene
First Editions 3
Later Editions 185

B: Books with Contributions by Graham Greene 197

C: Contributions to Newspapers and Periodicals 205
Film Criticism 272

D: Miscellanea 291
Manuscripts, Typescripts, Letters, etc. 293
Films Written or Produced (Wholly or in Part)
by Graham Greene 320

E: A Bibliography of Works about Graham Greene 321
Books 323
Theses and Dissertations 326
Bibliographies 337
Articles 338
References to Greene in Books 389

F: Graham Greene's Radio and Television Broadcasts
and Film Appearances 405

G: Published or Broadcast Interviews with Graham Greene 413

Index
Works by Greene 419
Works Reviewed by Greene 427

ILLUSTRATIONS

following page 195:

1. *The Berkhamstedian*, March 1922
   contains Greene's fable "The Tyranny of Realism" (C2)

2. *The Oxford Outlook*, November 1923
   contains Greene's story "The New House" (C14) and his
   poems "At the Theatre" (C15) and "The Coming" (C16)

3. *Babbling April*, Blackwell, 1925 (A1)

4. *The Man Within*, Heinemann, 1929 (A2a)

5. *The Man Within*, Doubleday, 1929 (A2b)

6. *The Name of Action*, Heinemann, 1930 (A3a)

7. *Rumour at Nightfall*, Heinemann, 1931 (A4a)

8. Bindings for 1st English Editions of
   The Name of Action, 1930 (A3a)
   Rumour at Nightfall, 1931 (A4a)

9. Dust jackets for
   British Dramatists, 1942 (A17)
   The Name of Action, 1930 (A3a)
   Rumour at Nightfall, 1931 (A4a)

10. *The Old School*, Cape, 1934 (A7)

11. *England Made Me*, Heinemann, 1935 (A8a)

12. *England Made Me*, Doubleday, 1935 (A8b)

13. *The Bear Fell Free*, Grayson & Grayson, 1935 (A9)

14. Endpapers of *The Bear Fell Free*, 1935 (A9)

15. *The Basement Room*, Cresset Press, 1935 (A10)

16. *Journey Without Maps*, Heinemann, 1936 (A11a)
    Frontispiece and title-page

17. *The Lawless Roads*, Longmans, Green and Co., 1939 (A14a)
    Frontispiece and title-page

18. *The Labyrinthine Ways*, Viking, 1940 (A16b)

19. *Why Do I Write?* Percival Marshall, 1948 (A22)

20. *The Lost Childhood*, Eyre & Spottiswoode, 1951 (A26)

21. *Introductions to Three Novels*, Norstedts, 1962 (A44)
    Front cover of wrapper

22. *Victorian Detective Fiction*, Bodley Head, 1966 (A49)

INTRODUCTION

This book is at least partly the result of chance meetings and common interests, but it is especially the result of a continuing curiosity to know more about England's most prominent living novelist. I had been a reader of Graham Greene for four or five years before I went to the University of Iowa. At Iowa I met David Pryce-Jones, who had then only recently published his own book on Greene, and a subsequent conversation stimulated my interest in Greene's style, which critics had been hard-pressed to define. When I went to the University of Exeter in 1968 I met Florian Shaskey, who introduced me to the methods of bibliographic research and inspired an interest in the book as an object of significance beyond its literary value. At Exeter I also met K.W. Salter and Professor Moelwyn Merchant, both of whom were excellent guides to the intricate traditions and paths confronting a reader new to the analysis of religion in fiction.

My research on Greene tended to branch in three directions, though all were related. My earlier thrust toward stylistic inquiry began to be paralleled by investigations into both biographical and, of necessity, bibliographical details. At that time no published list of criticism on Greene seemed complete. Lists of his first editions were available, but no attempt had been made to sort out Greene's extensive periodical contributions. At Berkhamsted, the public school Greene had attended and of which his father had been headmaster, I found literary traces of Greene the adolescent and had the distinct impression that this was a view of the writer few others had seen. Research at Oxford left much the same impression.

In 1974, with most of the research finished for my original study, I turned toward a bibliographical inquiry; there was still a vacuum. The broad audience attracted to Greene's work had no single-volume source of bibliographic information. The collector needed a plan. The student needed obscure information. Another reader followed a vague trail, looking for a novel or forgotten collection which could not be found in the local library's card index.

This bibliography and research guide is a result of that original inquiry and aims at a remedy including not only bringing the lists up to date but also much new information about Graham Greene, his work and his critics.

The arrangement of works departs somewhat from the standard bibliographical format, especially in Section A, because Greene's popularity has led to a very large number of reprints, both in English and in translation. With this in mind, Section A contains descriptions of the first English and American editions of books and pamphlets written by Greene, works written in collaboration with others and works edited by him. Reprints are listed in a subsection following the first-edition descriptions, but because they are so numerous, translations have been omitted entirely. Section B lists the first printings of books and pamphlets containing contributions by Greene. Section C lists Greene's contributions to press and periodicals and supplies a separate list of film criticism. Section D lists manuscripts and typescripts in collections and those of Greene's screenplays which have been produced. Section E is a bibliography of works about Greene. Sections F and G list published and broadcast interviews with Greene and his involvement with radio and television.

The terminal date for all sections is December 1977. Though it has been possible to include a few items which came to my notice early in 1978, the sections should not be considered complete for that year.

These lists will be of interest to both the casual reader and the scholar because they graphically demonstrate the range of Greene's interests and describe a career which divides into five distinct periods: Greene's formal education; his journalism while learning the writer's trade; his life during the war and in government service; his connections with publishing and reporting from the "Third World"; and, finally, a more relaxed but nonetheless fertile period. It is a story that might only be surpassed by a full-fledged biography. There is substance and reality as one examines in their contexts the products of Greene's long, impressive career.

Finally, it is worth repeating that I originally came to this project not as a bibliographer but as a critic. I appreciate the scholar's problems and needs and hope that this bibliography has taken care of much groundwork that dogs the heels not only of the novice researcher on Greene but of the veteran as well. In the same light, I know that errors may exist in this book, though I have tried to catch them. Any corrections or additions are certainly welcomed.

Spring Hill Mountain
South Charleston, West Virginia
December 1978

ACKNOWLEDGMENTS

My largest debt is to my wife, Stirley, who has labored beside me throughout this project.

Mary Hogue of the Reference Department of the West Virginia Library Commission has helped far more than one could have expected, and I also wish to thank the staff of the West Virginia Library Commission. In addition, I am grateful for the much-needed support of the West Virginia College of Graduate Studies.

Many others have helped either directly or indirectly with the gathering of information, and I would like to thank the following persons for their aid: Dr. Judy Adamson, Dawson College, Quebec; Ellen S. Dunlap, Humanities Research Center; Sue Forrest, Sylvia Newman and the staff of the library of the West Virginia College of Graduate Studies; Barry Guthary, Reference Librarian, Harvard College Library; Nancy Herb, Department of Special Collections, Hofstra University Library; Jacqueline Kavanaugh, BBC Written Archives Centre; George McWhorter, Rare Book Collections, University of Louisville Library; Katherine Moore and Nancy C. Little, M. Knoedler & Co., Inc.; Dr. Gene Phillips, Loyola University of Chicago; Libby Scobell, Michele Koplove and Marilyn Bushey of the West Virginia State College Library; Peter Van Wingen, Rare Book and Special Collection Departments of the Library of Congress. Also, Jill Benson, *Life Magazine*; Shirley Connell, *Vogue*; Paulette S. Gaudet, *Playboy*; Adele Hoening, *Esquire*; L. Langley-Kemp, Eyre Methuen Ltd.; Peter LeBeck, Samuel French, Inc.; Judith Newman, *Cosmopolitan*; Carl R. Reed, University of Pittsburgh; Ragnar Svanström, Norstedts; Roy Wandelmaier, Doubleday & Company; *Harper's Magazine*; *Ellery Queen's Mystery Magazine*; *Alfred Hitchcock's Mystery Magazine*.

There are others who have been very helpful whose names I do not have and whom I therefore cannot thank personally, but I do wish to express my gratitude to the staffs of the institutions and companies which follow: Berkhamsted School Library; Bodleian Library; British Library; Newspaper Library at Colindale; Library of Congress; Bell, Book and Radmall Booksellers; Bertram Rota Booksellers; Bernard Quaritch Booksellers; Blackwells of Oxford; University of Exeter Library; Exeter Public Library; Bristol University Library.

I must thank also all the libraries who lent copies of books, checked information and responded to questions. They are: Bluefield State College Library; Boston Public Library; Bowdoin College Library; California State Library; Duke University Library; Florida State University Library; Harvard University Library; Indiana University Library; Joint University Libraries (Nashville); Kanawha County Public Library (West Virginia); Kansas State University Library; Kent State University Library; LaSalle College Library; Library of Congress; Marshall University Library; Miami University Library; New York Public Library; Notre Dame University Library; Oberlin College Library; Ohio County Public Library (West Virginia); Ohio State University Library; Ohio University Library; Princeton University Library; Southern Illinois University Library; Stanford University Library; University of Alabama Library; University of Florida Library; University of Illinois Library; University of Iowa Library; University of Kentucky Library; University of Miami Library; University of Michigan Library (Ann Arbor); University of North Carolina Library; University of Oklahoma Library; University of Pittsburgh Library; University of South Carolina Library; University of Southern California Library; University of Tennessee Library; University of Virginia Library; West Liberty State College Library; West Virginia State College Library; West Virginia University Library; Villanova University Library.

Finally, I owe much to those who broke the ground on the subject of this project and whose names are recorded elsewhere in this book. I realize that the gratitude must be spread thinly, but it is nonetheless warmly felt.

GRAHAM GREENE

A

BOOKS AND PAMPHLETS BY GRAHAM GREENE

This section describes first editions of works written or edited by Greene either alone or in collaboration with others. First editions are defined as first printings in English. In those exceptional cases where the only printing is in another language, they are considered first editions. The compiler has attempted, when possible, to see multiple copies of each item. Two items in the section have not been seen and these are specifically noted as such. Reprintings are listed at the end of this section.

Collations. If on occasion a notation such as $X/X*^{8/8}$ is used, it refers to an 8vo in sixteens with $X*_1$ standing for X_9.

Number of copies. Information referring to the number of copies, if it has been graciously provided or is otherwise indicated, will be given in the notes.

Dust jackets. When dust jackets have been seen, their descriptions follow *Price* and publishing date. If dust jackets are not described, it is still likely that they exist.

Notes. Details which do not fit into the general format of this section are given in the notes. Information is most often of a bibliographical, historical or biographical nature, but because this list may well be used by a wide variety of researchers and advisors, some critical comments have been added (though only where they have seemed necessary).

This list is arranged chronologically.

A1   BABBLING APRIL   1925

First Edition

BABBLING APRIL / BY GRAHAM GREENE / OXFORD: BASIL BLACKWELL /
1925

Collation: [A]^4 B-C^8, 20 leaves.

Pagination: p. [i] title-page; p. [ii] printing notice;
p. [iii] quotation; p. [iv] dedication; p. [v] acknowledge-
ments; p. [vi] blank; p. [vii] CONTENTS; p. [viii] blank;
pp. 1-32 text.

Printing: Caslon, 11 pt., printed in Great Britain at the
Shakespeare Head Press, Stratford-Upon-Avon.

12.5 x 19 cm., white paper, with all edges untrimmed; bound
in gray paper over boards with the title, author and a small
leaf device printed in blue ink on the cover and also on the
spine.

Price: 4s. 6d. Published in April 1925 in a gray paper dust
jacket with the front cover having the title, author and leaf
device (repeating the cover of the binding) at the head and
the publisher and price at the tail in black; the back cover
carries advertisements for *Oxford Poetry 1924*, edited by
Harold Acton and Peter Quennell, and *Eighty Poems: An Anthology* edited by L.A.G. Strong.

Dedication: To my father and mother

Contents: Sensations -- 1. The Coming -- 2. Atmosphere --
3. The Back Porch -- 4. At the Theatre -- 7. Small Talk --
8. Stupidity -- 9. 1930 -- 10. Apres vous -- 11. I Shall
Be Happy -- 12. If You Were Dead -- 13. Sonnet -- 14. The
Godly Distance -- 15. Before Breakfast -- 16. The Banbury
Road, 12 P.M. -- 17. Death and Cosmetics -- 18. Old Age of a
Georgian -- 19. The Librarian -- 20. Fears -- 21. Paradisal
Tea -- 22. Paint and Wood -- 23. Sonnet -- 24. The Old
Clipper -- 25. On a Walking Tour -- 26. Selfdom -- 27. Step-
ping Stones -- 28. Apologia -- 29. The Judgement -- 30.
Childishness -- 31. The Gamble -- 32.

Notes: The copy examined is in the rare book collection of
the Library of Congress (PR6013/.R44B3). Other copies have
been examined at the Bodleian Library, Oxford, and at the

British Library. The booksellers, Blackwells of Oxford, report in their catalogue #858 another copy with a dust jacket.
Blackwells also reports that a printing of 500 copies was
planned but that only 300 or so were ever issued.

The poems in *Babbling April* had appeared previously in
the following periodicals: *The Golden Hind*, *The Weekly Westminster*, *The Westminster Gazette*, *The Decachord*, *Oxford Poetry*, *The Oxford Outlook*, *The Oxford Chronicle*, *The Cherwell*.

The recto of the second leaf carries the following quo-
tation: "It is not enough that yearly, down this hill, /
April / Comes like an idiot, babbling and strewing flowers."
-- EDNA ST. VINCENT MILLAY.

Poems in *Babbling April* are not dated, but some idea of
the order of composition can be gained by consulting Section
C of this bibliography.

The dust jacket advertisements include *Oxford Poetry 1924*
edited by Harold Acton and Peter Quennell. This volume con-
tained "Paint and Wood" and "Childishness," both of which
Greene collected in *Babbling April*. As for the editions of
Oxford Poetry 1924, Greene had known Peter Quennell at Berkhamsted and Quennell followed him to Oxford, a term or two
later than Greene. According to Evelyn Waugh, Greene and
Harold Acton were not to become friends until some years
after their Oxford days, though they certainly had already
crossed paths by this time (see Evelyn Waugh's *A Little
Learning*).

Greene's few references either to *Babbling April* or to
the poems are all disparaging. He remarks in *A Sort of Life*
that he knew he could never be a good poet. He is bothered
by the sentimentality and pessimism of the poems. Neither
the book nor any of the poems have been reprinted.

A2   THE MAN WITHIN   1929

a. *First Edition*

THE MAN WITHIN / BY / GRAHAM GREENE / [small device] /
"There's another man within me / that's angry with me." /
SIR THOMAS BROWNE. / [publisher's device] / [rule] / LONDON:
WILLIAM HEINEMANN LTD.

Collation: [A]^8 B-Y^8, 184 leaves.

Pagination: pp. [i-ii] blank; p. [iii] half-title; p. [iv]
publisher's advertisement; p. [v] title-page; p. [vi] publication and printing notices; p. [vii] dedication and quotation; p. [viii] blank; p. [ix] CONTENTS; p. [x] blank;
p. [xi] PART I; p. [xii] blank; pp. 1-131 text of part one,
with chapter headings on pp. 1, 15, 40, 66, 99; p. [132]
blank; p. [133] PART II; p. [134] blank; pp. 135-282 text of
part two, with chapter headings on pp. 135, 163, 189, 249;
p. [283] PART III; p. [284] blank; pp. 285-354 text of part
three, with chapter headings on pp. 285, 326; pp. [355-356]
blank.

Printing: Caslon, 12 pt., printed in Great Britain at the
Windmill Press, Kingswood, Surrey.

12 x 18.5 cm., white paper, with all edges trimmed; bound in
black cloth over boards with the title, author and publisher
between ruled lines stamped in gold on the spine and a windmill device blind stamped at the right tail of the back cover.

Price: 7s. 6d. Published in June 1929.

Dedication: For Vivienne my wife in wonder

"As common chests encasing wares of price, / Are borne with
tenderness through halls of state, / For what they cover, so
the poor device / Of homely wording I could tolerate, / Knowing its unadornment held as freight, / The sweetest image
outside Paradise." -- THOMAS HARDY

Contents: Part I -- 1. Part II -- 132. Part III -- 280.

Notes: The copy examined is in the British Library (NN 15537).
    Greene himself puts the number of copies in the first
printing at 2,500, although the novel sold more than 8,000
copies (*A Sort of Life*). Evidently the book's popularity

grew rather quickly; by February 1930 it resided two numbers
beneath J.B. Priestley's two-volume *The Good Companions* on
the Tauchnitz list. The Tauchnitz edition has not been seen,
but it is number 4917.

The first English edition is the only novel of Greene's
to contain an advertisement within the book for novels by
other authors. The following books are listed on p. [iv] of
the preliminaries as "New and Recent Fiction": *The Painted
Face* by Oliver Onions; *The Perfect Murder Case* by Christopher
Bush; *Indiana Jane* by Cecil Roberts; *Six Mrs. Greenes* by Lorna
Rea; *Nile Gold* by John Knittel; *Cats in the Isle of Man* by
Daisy Fellows.

In later editions the dedication is shortened to: "For
Vivienne" and the quotation from Hardy's poem is removed.

Though *The Man Within* was Greene's first published novel,
it was actually his third in order of composition. At Oxford
his first attempt at a novel was "the unhappy history of a
black child born to white parents." Heinemann rejected
Greene's offer of the novel and it was never published. His
second attempt, called *The Episode*, was about a young ideal-
ist caught up in a disappointing revolution and was submitted to Heinemann in July 1926. Though the publisher rejected the novel in this form, it was eventually published
by them as *Rumour at Nightfall* (1931).

The Man Within was begun in 1926 as Greene recuperated
in hospital from an appendicitis operation. Upon completion
he submitted the novel to both Heinemann and The Bodley Head.
Charles Evans of Heinemann accepted the book, and it was an
almost immediate success. S.P.B. Mais said in *The Daily
Telegraph*: "a book impregnated with beauty, subtle in con-
struction, in dramatic tension comparable with the best
chapters of *Treasure Island*. It is a first novel of such
perfect poise and accomplishment that one trembles for the
future of the young author." In a letter to Robert Nichols,
dated 17 February 1930 (it seems just after the Tauchnitz
publication) Aldous Huxley compared the book to Virginia
Woolf's *To the Lighthouse* and thought *The Man Within* the much
better of the two: "It's the difference between something
full and something empty, between a writer who has a close
physical contact with reality and one who is a thousand miles
away and only has a telescope to look, remotely, at the world."

In an "Author's Note" to the Library Edition, Greene
describes an attempt to revise the novel as a failure; "the
story remained just as embarrassingly romantic, the style as
derivative...." So the revision was dropped in favor of the
original text, which has been reprinted without any important
changes.

b. *First American Edition* (1929)

THE / MAN / WITHIN/ BY GRAHAM GREENE / [in green: publisher's device] / *"There's another man within me / that's angry with me."* / *Sir Thomas Browne.* / DOUBLEDAY, DORAN & COMPANY, INC. / GARDEN CITY, NEW YORK / *MCMXXIX* [entire title-page surrounded by ruled octagon of three lines in green]

Collation: [1]^{10} $^{(8+2)}$ [2]-[20]^8, 162 leaves.

Pagination: pp. [i-ii] blank; p. [iii] half-title; p. [iv] note on author; p. [v] title-page; p. [vi] copyright, publisher and printing notices; p. [1] PART I; p. [2] blank; pp. 3-118 text of part one, with chapter headings on pp. 3, 15, 37, 60, 90; p. [119] PART II; p. [120] blank; pp. 121-251 text of part two, with chapter headings on pp. 121, 146, 168, 221; p. [252] blank; p. [253] PART III; p. [254] blank; pp. 255-316 text of part three, with chapter headings on pp. 255 and 292; pp. [317-318] blank.

Printing: Garamond, 11 pt., printed in the U.S.A. at The Country Life Press.

13 x 18.9 cm., white paper, top and bottom edges trimmed, top edges colored green; bound in green cloth over boards with a darker green cloth for the spine with the title, author and publisher stamped in gold on the spine; green endpapers.

Price: $2.50. Published in October 1929 in a white dust jacket with the following printed in blue: the front cover carrying the title and author bordered by a rectangle of double lines of small triangles; the spine carrying a double line of triangles above the title above the author above the price above another double line of triangles; and the back cover carrying advertisements for other books published by Heinemann.

Notes: The copy examined is in the library of the University of Louisville. This copy has green endpapers. The half-title and title-page form one conjugate leaf which is sewn or tipped in after the first leaf of section [1].
     This edition differs from the English edition in that it has no dedication, and the author is introduced by means of a short essay (unsigned) on the half-title verso. This mentions that *The Man Within* went into "two editions" in England "before publication."

A3   THE NAME OF ACTION   1930

a. *First Edition*

THE / NAME / OF ACTION / *by* / Graham Greene / ".*and lose the
name of action.*" / Hamlet / [publisher's device] / LONDON /
WILLIAM HEINEMANN LTD

Collation: [A]^8 B–W^8 X/X*$^{2/8}$, 178 leaves.

Pagination: pp. [i–ii] blank; p. [iii] half-title; p. [iv]
author's advertisement; p. [v] title-page; p. [vi] publication and printing notices; p. [vii] dedication; p. [viii]
blank; p. [ix] quotation and disclaimer; p. [x] blank;
p. [1] PART I; p. [2] blank; pp. 3–150 text of part one,
with chapter headings on pp. 3, 21, 54, 97, 129; p. [151]
PART II; p. [152] blank; pp. 153–274 text of part two, with
chapter headings on pp. 153, 175, 197, 240; p. [275] PART III;
p. [276] blank; pp. 277–344 text of part three, with chapter
headings on pp. 277, 302; pp. [345–346] blank.

Printing: Caslon Old Face, 12 pt., printed in Great Britain
at the Windmill Press, Kingswood, Surrey.

12 x 18.5 cm., white paper, with all edges trimmed; bound in
dark blue cloth over boards with the title, author and publisher stamped in gold on the spine; a windmill device is blind
stamped at the right tail of the back cover.

Price: 7s. 6d. Published in October 1930 in a yellow dust
jacket with the title in red followed by the author in black
and the notation: "Author of THE MAN WITHIN." The back
cover of the dust jacket has extracts of three reviews of
The Man Within. The inside back cover carries advertisements.
The spine carries the price.

Dedication: For Vivienne

"Thou art so truth, that thoughts of thee suffice, / To make
dreams truths; and fables histories." -- JOHN DONNE

Notes: The copies examined are in the collection of the compiler and the Library of Congress (PZ3/.G8319/Nam).
      The number of copies printed is unknown. Assuming that
Greene's estimate of the first printing of *The Man Within* is
accurate and noting his remark that the first printing of all
his books up to and including *The Power and the Glory* was

rarely more than 3,500 copies, a conservative estimate would
be at least 2,500 but probably not more than 3,000. Greene
reports that *The Name of Action* sold barely more than 2,000
copies.

The last page of text (344) has at the bottom the following dates: "March, 1929 - July, 1930" which, no doubt, is a
reference to the period of the book's composition.

Page [ix] of the preliminaries carries the following
quotation from T.S. Eliot's "The Hollow Men": "Between the
idea / And the reality / Between the motion / And the act /
Falls the Shadow / *For Thine is the Kingdom* / Between the
conception / And the creation / Between the emotion / And the
response / Falls the Shadow." The lines clearly have a special significance for Greene; they are parodied later in *It's
a Battlefield* when Greene describes the life of a factory
girl.

Greene remarks that the title for *The Name of Action*,
suggested to him by Clemence Dane, is the only part of the
novel he approves of. His failure with the novel, he says,
is due to his not yet knowing that excitement "is a situation,
a single event. It musn't be wrapped up in thoughts, similes
and metaphors." He adds that this failure might have led him
down the path taken by Charles Morgan and Lawrence Durrell.
But the fact that the book did so poorly saved him (*A Sort
of Life*).

Greene has withdrawn *The Name of Action* from the body of
his work, and no other editions, other than the American, or
reprints exist.

An autograph manuscript in the Humanities Research
Center is inscribed "For Vivienne 1930 October 15."

b. *First American Edition* (1931)

THE / NAME OF ACTION / *Graham Greene* / AUTHOR OF "THE MAN /
WITHIN" / [in red: publisher's device] / ".*and lose the name
of action*." HAMLET / [in red: rule] / *Doubleday*, *Doran &
Company*, *Inc.* / *Garden City*, *New York* / MCMXXXI

Collation: [1]$^{(8+1)}$ [2]-[20]^8, 161 leaves.

Pagination: p. [1] half-title; p. [ii] blank; p. [iii] title-
page; p. [iv] printing, copyright and publishing notices;
p. [v] dedication; p. [vi] blank; p. [vii] quotation;
p. [viii] blank; p. [ix] disclaimer; p. [x] blank; p. [1]
PART I; p. [2] blank; pp. 3-135 text of part one, with

chapter headings on pp. 3, 19, 49, 88, 117; p. [136] blank;
p. [137] PART II; p. [138] blank; pp. 139-248 text of part
two, with chapter headings on pp. 139, 159, 179, 218; p. [249]
PART III; p. [250] blank; pp. 251-312 text of part three,
with chapter headings on pp. 251, 274.

Printing: Garamond, 12 pt., printed in the U.S.A. at The
Country Life Press, Garden City, New York.

13 x 19 cm., white paper, top and bottom edges trimmed, top
edges colored red; bound in black cloth over boards with the
title, author and publisher stamped in gold down the spine;
a leopard device is blind stamped on the front cover.

Price: $2.50.   Published in March 1931.

Dedication: as first English edition.

Notes: The copy examined is in the Library of Congress
(PZ3/.G8319/Nam/2).   The title-page of this copy has been
tipped in between leaves one and two.
     The Doubleday Company has said that no record survives
of either the number of copies printed or the number of
copies sold.   Greene remarks that the sales for the American
edition were "disastrous."   If the disaster was anywhere near
that of the American edition of *Rumour at Nightfall* in the
next year, *The Name of Action* probably sold barely more than
a thousand copies.
     The verso of the title-page of this copy carries the
date of receipt of copyright copies as February 19, 1931.
This copy also has red endpapers.

A4   RUMOUR AT NIGHTFALL   1931

a. *First Edition*

[in red:] *Rumour at* / [in red:] *Nightfall* / *by* / *Graham Greene* / [in red: publisher's device] / *London* / *William Heinemann Ltd*

Collation: [A]^8 B–F^8 [G]^8 H–S^8 T^{10}, 154 leaves.

Pagination: p. [i] half-title; p. [ii] author's advertisement; p. [iii] title-page; p. [iv] publication and printing notices; p. [v] dedication; p. [vi] blank; p. [vii] quotation; p. [viii] blank; p. 1 RUMOUR AT NIGHTFALL / PART I; pp. 1–91 text of part one; p. 92 PART II; pp. 92–234 text of part two; p. 235 PART III; pp. 235–300 text of part three.

Printing: Imprint, 11 pt., printed in Great Britain at the Windmill Press, Kingswood, Surrey.

12 x 18.5 cm., white paper with all edges trimmed; bound in red cloth over boards with the title, author and publisher stamped in gold on the spine; a star design is blind stamped in the right corner at the head of the front cover, and one line of the design runs to the left corner of the tail; a windmill device is blind stamped at the right tail of the back cover.

Price: 7s. 6d. Published in November 1931 in a dust jacket having a blue and green cover with title, author and "Author of 'The Man Within'" in white; title, author and publisher are in blue on a white spine with the price and publisher's device in green; on the back cover are reviews of *The Man Within* in blue with a green border on white.

Dedication: For my father and mother in gratitude

Notes: The copies examined are in the collection of the compiler and the Library of Congress (PZ3/.G8319/Ru).
     Considering the low sales volume of *The Name of Action*, it is unlikely that the publisher would order more than 2,500 copies for the first printing of *Rumour at Nightfall*. In this light it is perhaps significant that the jacket carries no reviews of *The Name of Action*. In fact, the back cover of the jacket is a reprint of the jacket for *The Name of Action*. *Rumour at Nightfall* sold only 1,200 copies, 800 less than *The Name of Action*.

   Page [vii] of the preliminaries carries the following
quotation from Thomas Traherne: "O ye that stand upon the
brink, / Whom I so near me through the chink / With wonder
see: What faces there, / Whose feet, whose bodies do ye
wear? / I my companions see / In you, another me. / They
seemèd others, but are we; / Our second selves those shadows
be."

   If one detects that the confusion of identity is the
most significant theme in *Rumour at Nightfall*, Greene pro-
vides at least a partial explanation when he says that Conrad
was the influence, in fact, the Conrad of *The Arrow of Gold*,
Conrad under the influence of Henry James (*A Sort of Life*).
Most of the confusion in the novel results from experimentation with the multiple points of view of the dual protagonists,
the intense introspection and self-analysis, and the psycho-
logical parallels of character. Yet one might easily justify
this novel as a necessary step toward *The Power and the Glory*
with its priest-lieutenant relationship.

   An autograph manuscript in the Humanities Research Center is dated: 1930 September–1931 April 27.

b. *First American Edition* (1932)

RUMOUR AT NIGHTFALL / Graham Greene / [rule] / [in red:
publisher's device] / Doubleday, Doran & Company, Inc. /
Garden City 1932 New York

Collation: $[1]^{8+1}$ $[2]-[18]^{8}$ $[19]^{4}$ $[20]^{8}$, 157 leaves.

Pagination: pp. [i-ii] blank; p. [iii] half-title; p. [iv]
author's advertisement; p. [v] title-page; p. [vi] printing,
copyright and publishing notices; p. [vii] dedication;
p. [viii] blank; p. [ix] quotation; p. [x] blank; p. [xi]
PART I; p. [xii] blank; pp. [1]-90 text of part one; p. [91]
PART II; p. [92] blank; pp. 93-231 text of part two; p. [232]
blank; p. [233] PART III; p. [234] blank; pp. 235-299 text
of part three; pp. [300-302] blank.

Printing: Garamond, 12 pt., printed in the U.S.A. at The
Country Life Press, Garden City, New York.

13 x 19 cm., white paper, with top and bottom edges trimmed,
top edges colored red; bound in black cloth over boards with
the spine in red cloth having a printed herringbone pattern
in black and the author, title and publisher negatively
printed on a black panel.

Price: $2.50.   Published in May 1932.

Dedication: as first English edition.

Notes: The copy examined is in the Library of Congress
(PZ3/.G8319/Ru/2).
   The title-page of this copy has been tipped in between
leaves two and three.
   The verso of the title-page of this copy carries the
date of receipt of copyright copies as January 25, 1932.
This copy also has red endpapers.
   The Doubleday Company reports no record of the number of
copies printed, but they record the number of copies sold at
1,018.

a. *First Edition*

[double rule] / STAMBOUL TRAIN / BY / GRAHAM GREENE / [double
rule] / [publisher's device] / LONDON / WILLIAM HEINEMANN LTD /
[double rule]

Collation: [A]^8 B-U^8, 152 leaves.

Pagination: pp. [i-ii] blank; p. [iii] half-title; p. [iv]
author's advertisement; p. [v] title-page; p. [vi] publication and printing notices; p. [vii] dedication; p. [viii]
blank; p. [ix] quotation; p. [x] blank; p. [xi] CONTENTS;
p. [xii] blank; p. [1] PART ONE / OSTEND; p. [2] blank;
pp. 3-37 text of part one, with numbered divisions on pp. 3
and 14; p. [38] blank; p. [39] PART TWO / COLOGNE; p. [40]
blank; pp. 41-106 text of part two, with numbered divisions
on pp. 41 and 98; p. [107] PART THREE / VIENNA; p. [108]
blank; pp. 109-175 text of part three, with numbered divisions on pp. 99, 135, 147; p. [176] blank; p. [177] PART
FOUR / SUBOTICA; p. [178] blank; pp. 179-276 text of part
four, with numbered divisions on pp. 179, 189, 216, 247;
p. [277] PART FIVE / CONSTANTINOPLE; p. [278] blank; pp. 279-
307 text of part five; p. [308] blank.

Printing: Old Style, 11 pt., printed in Great Britain at the
Windmill Press.

11.7 x 17.8 cm., white paper, with all edges trimmed; bound
in black cloth over boards with the title over a mosque device, and the author and publisher stamped in gold on the
spine; a windmill device is blind stamped at the right tail
of the back cover.

Price: 7s. 6d. Published in December 1932.

Dedication: For Vivien Candace with all my love

Contents: Part One: Ostend -- 3. Part Two: Cologne -- 41.
Part Three: Vienna -- 109. Part Four: Subotica -- 179.
Part Five: Constantinople -- 279.

Notes: The copies examined are in the collection of the compiler and the Library of Congress (PZ3/.G8319).
    Concerning the number of copies, one might extrapolate
from given information and place the number for the first
printing at around 13,000 copies. The lack of success of both

The Name of Action and *Rumour at Nightfall* would suggest that
a large printing would have been highly imprudent. However,
the book was chosen by the Book Society which, as Greene says
in *A Sort of Life*, almost guaranteed a sale of 10,000 copies.
Greene also relates a conversation with Charles Evans concerning J.B. Priestley's threat of a libel action if certain
lines in the then undistributed book were not changed. At
that time 13,000 copies had already been printed and bound,
and altered pages had to be substituted. Priestley had seen
a review copy when he demanded the changes, and so it is possible that a few copies without the alterations mentioned in
A Sort of Life may still exist. The book went through
several printings. One copy in the compiler's possession indicates that in December 1932 and January 1933 there were
three "editions," though the printer seems to have meant
three impressions. In this copy the notice on the verso of
the title-page lists "FIRST PUBLISHED DECEMBER 1932 / SECOND
EDITION DECEMBER 1932 / THIRD EDITION JANUARY 1933." This
"third edition," save for the printing notice, is practically
indistinguishable from the first printing, but it measures
slightly larger all around, being 12.1 x 18.4 cm. The binding is also slightly taller and wider. Another small difference is that at the bottom of page 140 of the first impression at the end of the last line is a colon that has
slipped downward about half a letter's height. In the third
impression the colon has been repaired.

Page [ix] of the preliminaries carries a quotation from
George Santayana: "Everything in nature is lyrical in its
ideal essence; tragic in its fate, and comic in its
existence."

Greene writes that he chose to do another adventure
story perhaps to get away from the influence of the Conrad
of *The Arrow of Gold*. He had already learned how difficult
it was to bring life to physical action. He wrote *Stamboul
Train*, he says, while Honneger's *Pacific 231* played on the
gramophone. Under financial pressure because of his contract
and the sense of failure resulting from the two previous
novels and Heinemann's rejection of his biography of Lord
Rochester, the novel was finished and mailed to Heinemann's
by August 4.

Though originally published as a novel, Greene later
categorized *Stamboul Train* as an "entertainment." He is obviously not happy with a book that he sees so full of the
sense of failure and despair; it is the one of his books he
finds almost impossible to reread because he sees in it the
anxieties of that bleak period of this life. Yet the old
socialist schoolteacher, Dr. Czinner, Myatt, the callous and
fearful dealer in currants, and the chorus girl, who gives

pity but never receives any in return, come to life much more
readily for the reader because of that same grim sense of
doom.

The film rights to *Stamboul Train* were sold to Twentieth Century-Fox for £1,500.

An autograph manuscript in the Humanities Research Center
dated "1932 January 2" carries the following possible titles
on the title-page: "The Orient Express" and "Snow on the
Line."

b. *First American Edition* (1933)

Orient Express / BY GRAHAM GREENE / [device] / *1933* / [rule] /
Doubleday, *Doran & Company*, *Inc.* / GARDEN CITY, NEW YORK

Collation: [1] - [20]^8, 160 leaves.

Pagination: p. [i] half-title; p. [ii] author's advertisement;
p. [iii] title-page; p. [iv] printing, copyright and publishing notices; p. [v] dedication; p. [vi] blank; p. [vii] quotation; p. [viii] blank; p. [ix] CONTENTS; p. [x] blank;
p. [1] PART ONE / OSTEND; p. [2] blank; pp. 3-38 text of part
one, with a numbered division on p. 14; p. [39] PART TWO /
COLOGNE; p. [40] blank; pp. 41-108 text of part two, with a
numbered division on p. 100; p. [109] PART THREE / VIENNA;
p. [110] blank; pp. 111-178 text of part three, with numbered divisions on pp. 137 and 149; p. [179] PART FOUR /
SUBOTICA; p. [180] blank; pp. 181-278 text of part four,
with numbered divisions on pp. 191, 218, 249; p. [279] PART
FIVE / CONSTANTINOPLE; p. [280] blank; pp. 281-310 text of
part five.

Printing: Garamond, 12 pt., printed in the U.S.A. at The
Country Life Press, Garden City, New York.

13 x 19 cm., white paper, with top and bottom edges trimmed,
top edges colored red; bound in red cloth over boards with
the title and author at the head of the spine and a long device representing a train on tracks starting beneath the
author on the spine and running across the front cover to
the right tail; the publisher is stamped at the bottom of the
spine; all printing on the binding is in black.

Price: $2.00. Published in March 1933.

Dedication: as first English edition.

Contents: Part One: Ostend -- 3. Part Two: Cologne -- 41.
Part Three: Vienna -- 111. Part Four: Subotica -- 181.
Part Five: Constantinople -- 281.

Notes: The copy examined is in the Library of Congress
(PZ3/.G8319/Or/2). The verso of the title-page of this copy
carries the date of receipt of copyright copies as March 17,
1933.
    The Doubleday Company reports no record of the number of
copies printed, but they record the number of copies sold at
4,334.

A6   IT'S A BATTLEFIELD   1934

a. *First Edition*

GRAHAM GREENE / [double rule] / IT'S A / BATTLEFIELD /
[publisher's device] / [double rule] / LONDON / WILLIAM
HEINEMANN LTD

Collation: [A]^8 B-S^8, 144 leaves.

Pagination: pp. [i-ii] blank; p. [iii] half-title; p. [iv]
author's advertisement; p. [v] title-page; p. [vi] publication and printing notices; p. [vii] dedication; p. [viii]
AUTHOR'S NOTE; p. [ix] quotation; p. [x] blank; pp. 1-275
text, with numbered division headings on pp. 1, 24, 114, 177,
246, and unnumbered divisions on pp. 29, 37, 42, 68, 75, 78,
92, 98, 124, 143, 172, 181, 189, 210, 220, 232, 262, 296;
pp. [276-278] blank.

Printing: Old Style, 11 pt., printed in Great Britain at The
Windmill Press, Kingswood, Surrey.

12 x 18.5 cm., white paper, with all edges trimmed; bound in
black cloth over boards with the title separated from the
author by a device at the head and the publisher at the tail
of the spine, all stamped in gold, and a windmill device
blind stamped at the right tail of the back cover.

Price: 7s. 6d.   Published in February 1934.

Dedication: For David and Anne in London, and for Nils and
Ingeborg in Oslo

Notes: The copies examined are in the collection of the compiler and the Library of Congress (PZ3/.G8319/It).
    In the "Introduction" to *It's a Battlefield* first pub-
lished in a revised American edition (Viking, 1962) and later
reprinted in The Collected Edition, Greene described subsequent revisions of the text of the first edition. He removed
the whole scene involving the mad murderer of the Salvation
Army, and he tinkered with the meeting of the Communist Party
branch attended by Mr. Surrogate. The edition in which the
mad murderer scene is cut is the Penguin, 1940. This scene
seems to have been mostly restored in all later editions,
including later Penguins. A comparison of the first English
edition with the Viking, 1962 (which seems to contain the
final text) indicates that the following lines having to do

with the Communist Party meeting in the first English edition
have been removed in the Viking, 1962 edition and later:
p. 48, line 3 - p. 52, line 2; p. 54, line 8 - p. 55, line 21;
p. 56, lines 4-9, line 29; p. 58, lines 1-2, lines 22-27,
line 29; p. 59, lines 4-17; p. 60, lines 25-29; p. 62, lines
24-25. It should also be noted that the Commissioner retains
that rank only in the first edition. In later editions he
has been demoted to Assistant Commissioner.

On page [viii] Greene makes the usual disclaimer regarding persons, places and so on, but adds that regarding Scotland Yard, there is no need for a disclaimer, because he has
"committed the initial absurdity of allowing a Government to
appoint a Commissioner of Police with experience of police
work."

Page [ix] carries the following quotation from Alexander
Kinglake: "In so far as the battlefield presented itself to
the bare eyesight of men, it had no entirety, no length, no
breadth, no depth, no size, no shape, and was made up of
nothing except small numberless circlets commensurate with
such ranges of vision as the mist might allow at each spot....
In such conditions, each separate gathering of English sol-
diery went on fighting its own little battle in happy and
advantageous ignorance of the general state of the action;
nay, even very often in ignorance of the fact that any great
conflict was raging."

In his "Introduction" Greene mentions that when he began
It's a Battlefield, his fourth novel, *Stamboul Train*, was
still in manuscript, there was little money left from the
publisher's advances, and he and his wife were expecting a
child. Under the circumstances, one can understand how he
felt that the act of beginning *It's a Battlefield* was "self-
destructive." He reminds the reader that the book was not a
popular entertainment and that, in fact, it has been read
less than any of his novels. Those select few who have had
the pleasure know that this book begins to show the writer
who is so influenced by the cinema that one often can almost
see the film emerging as the book is read. V.S. Pritchett in
The Spectator (February 9, 1934, p. 206) was the first reviewer to see that "the most notable thing about *It's a
Battlefield* ... is its ingenious use of cinema technique.
Each character is a cameraman and the shot taken reveals not
only what he sees, but how it mingles with the thoughts tick-
ing by in his own life." Pritchett goes on to add that
Greene is considerably more than a visual artist, though.
There is also "his humanity, his subtle moral sense and his
patient, supple and startling intuition of human character."

There are several influences that have found their way
into *It's a Battlefield* that Greene describes in his

"Introduction." One that he mentions in *A Sort of Life* is
his recuperation from the appendectomy. Not only did he be-
gin *The Man Within* at this time, but the familiarity with
hospitals and dying patients picked up during his recovery is
used to superb advantage as Conrad lies dying in the ward at
the novel's end. But other allusions and influences abound
in the novel. There is, for example, the language of Eliot,
the themes of Huxley's *Brave New World* and the imagery of
René Clair's *A Nous la Liberté* in Greene's account of the
match factory and the prison. Of course, there is also the
overriding image of significance in many of Greene's novels
and stories of the thirties. But in this novel, image becomes symbol and finally the controlling theme.

The manuscript in the Humanities Research Center is
dated September 13, 1932–August 4, 1933.

b. *First American Edition* (1934)

Graham Greene / IT'S A BATTLEFIELD / [publisher's device] /
1934 / [rule] / *Doubleday, Doran & Company, Inc.* / GARDEN
CITY, NEW YORK

Collation: [1]-[20]^8, 160 leaves.

Pagination: pp. [i-ii] blank; p. [iii] half-title; p. [iv]
author's advertisement; p. [v] title-page; p. [vi] printing,
copyright and publishing notices; p. [vii] dedication;
p. [viii] blank; p. [ix] AUTHOR'S NOTE; p. [x] blank; p. [xi]
quotation; p. [xii] blank; p. [xiii] fly-title; p. [xiv]
blank; pp. [1]-304 text, with numbered division headings on
pp. [1], 26, 126, 196, 272, and unnumbered divisions on pp.
31, 40, 46, 75, 82, 86, 101, 108, 137, 158, 190, 201, 209,
233, 243, 257, 290, 297; pp. [305-306] blank.

Printing: Garamond, 12 pt., printed in the U.S.A. at The
Country Life Press, Garden City, New York.

13.2 x 19 cm., white paper, with top edge colored black, all
others untrimmed; bound in brown cloth over boards with title,
author and publisher printed on the spine in black with alternating oblique ruling decorations above and below the
title.

Price: $2.50. Published in March 1934 in a dust jacket which
is predominantly white on black with the cover carrying the
title and author in white above a photo of a man in full dress

standing above a reclining woman; the spine carries the title, author and photo with the publisher beneath; the back cover carries the author's photo with comments about Greene.

Dedication: as first English edition.

Notes: The copy examined is in the British Library (x.989/ 12252). Another copy examined is in the Library of Congress (PZ3/.G8319/It/2). The verso of the title-page of this copy carries the date of receipt of copyright copies as April 5, 1934. Another copy seen at the University of Louisville has the dust jacket described.

The Doubleday Company reports no record of the number of copies printed, but they record the number of copies sold at 1,960.

A7   THE OLD SCHOOL   1934

First Edition

The / OLD SCHOOL / Essays / by Divers Hands / Edited by /
GRAHAM GREENE / [publisher's device] / Jonathan Cape / Thirty
Bedford Square / London

Collation: [A]^8 B-Q^8, 128 leaves.

Pagination: p. [1] half-title; p. [2] blank; p. [3] title-
page; p. [4] publishing and printing notices; pp. 5-6 CON-
TENTS; pp. 7-8 PREFACE; pp. 9-20 HONOUR / (GRESHAM'S SCHOOL,
HOLT) / BY W. H. AUDEN; pp. 21-33 GRAMMAR SCHOOL / (KETTERING)
/ BY H. E. BATES; pp. 35-44 HOT-WATER-BOTTLE LOVE / (CHELTEN-
HAM LADIES COLLEGE) / BY THEODORA BENSON; pp. 45-59 THE MUL-
BERRY TREE / (DOWNE HOUSE) / BY ELIZABETH BOWEN; p. [60]
blank; pp. 61-72 MORE FRANK THAN BUCHMAN / (ST. PAUL'S) / BY
ARTHUR CALDER-MARSHALL; pp. 73-84 LANGY ROAD / (A SALFORD
COUNCIL SCHOOL) / BY WALTER GREENWOOD; pp. 85-102, THE CON-
FORMER / (HARROW) / BY L. P. HARTLEY; pp. 103-120 PITY THE
PEDAGOGUE / (WELLINGTON) / BY HAROLD NICHOLSON; pp. 121-130
AN IRISH SCHOOLING / (CORK) / BY SEÁN O'FAOLÁIN; pp. 131-146
THE GOTHIC ARCH / (RUGBY) / BY WILLIAM PLOMER; pp. 147-162
THE WAT'RY GLADE / (ETON) / BY ANTHONY POWELL; pp. 163-172
THE NOTIONAL MANNER / (WINCHESTER) / BY J. N. RICHARDS;
pp. 173-184 POTTING SHED OF THE ENGLISH ROSE / (SHERBORNE) /
BY E. ARNOT ROBERTSON; pp. 185-198 DAY BOY / (UNIVERSITY
COLLEGE SCHOOL) / BY STEPHEN SPENDER; pp. 199-214 INDIAN
INNOCENCE LTD. / (MALVERN) / BY DEREK VERSCHOYLE; pp. 215-228
PIONEERS / (BEDALES) / BY E. L. GRANT WATSON; pp. 229-246 A
CHILD OF THE FIVE WOUNDS / (LIPPINGTON) / BY ANTONIA WHITE,
with numbered divisions on pp. 229, 230, 233, 236, 238, 240,
242, 243, 245; pp. 247-256 THE LAST WORD / (BERKHAMSTED) /
BY GRAHAM GREENE.

Printing: Baskerville, 12 pt., printed in Great Britain in
the city of Oxford at the Alden Press.

13.5 x 20 cm., white paper, with top and fore edges trimmed;
bound in black cloth over boards with the title stamped in
blue at the top of the cover and with title, author and
publisher stamped in blue on the spine.

Price: 7s 6d. Published on July 23, 1934.

Contents: Preface -- 7. Honour (Gresham's School, Holt) by
W. H. Auden -- 9. Grammar School (Kettering) by H.E. Bates --
21. Hot-Water-Bottle Love (Cheltenham Ladies' College) by
Theodora Benson -- 35. The Mulberry Tree (Downe House) by
Elizabeth Bowen -- 45. More Than Buchman (St. Paul's) by
Arthur Calder-Marshall -- 61. Langy Road (Langworthy Road
Council School, Salford) by Walter Greenwood -- 73. The
Conformer (Harrow) by L.P. Hartley -- 85. Pity the Pedagogue
(Wellington) by Harold Nicholson -- 103. An Irish Schooling
(Lancasterian School, Cork) by Seán O'Faoláin -- 121. The
Gothic Arch (Rugby) by William Plomer -- 131. The Wat'ry
Glade (Eton) by Anthony Powell -- 147. The Notional Manner
(Winchester) by J. N. Richards -- 163. Potting Shed of the
English Rose (Sherborne) by E. Arnot Robertson -- 173. Day
Boy (University College School) by Stephen Spender -- 185.
Indian Innocence, Ltd. (Malvern) by Derek Verschoyle -- 199.
Pioneers (Bedales) by E.L. Grant Watson -- 215. A Child of
the Five Wounds ('Lippington') by Antonia White -- 229. The
Last Word (Berkhamsted) by Graham Greene -- 247.

Notes: The copy examined is in the British Library (08364
ff 52).
    The first impression was of 1,517 copies.
    In "The Last Word," his own contribution to this collec-
tion of school memoirs, Greene explains that the book is the
result of an attempt to understand why it is that a man
"should feel more loyal to a school which is paid to teach
him than to a butcher who is paid to feed him...." It is
significant that Greene's long-standing interest in childhood and its effects should find its first literary expression, outside of fiction, in a book on the subject of schools
and schooling.

a. *First Edition*

ENGLAND MADE ME / *A NOVEL* / BY / GRAHAM GREENE / [small device] / [publisher's device] / [rule] / WILLIAM HEINEMANN LTD / LONDON :: TORONTO

Collation: $[A]^8$ $B-T^8$ $U/U*^{2/8}$, 162 leaves.

Pagination: pp. [i-ii] blank; p. [iii] half-title; p. [iv] author's advertisement; p. [v] title-page; p. [vi] publication and printing notices; p. [vii] dedication; p. [viii] blank; p. [ix] quotation; p. [x] disclaimer; p. 1 PART I / 1; pp. 1-42 text of part one, with numbered division headings on pp. 1, 14, 23; p. 43 PART II / 1; pp. 43-94 text of part two, with numbered division headings on pp. 43, 53, 69, 87; p. 95 PART III / 1; pp. 95-168 text of part three, with numbered division headings on pp. 95, 105, 120, 132, 164; p. 169 PART IV / 1; pp. 169-220 text of part four, with numbered division headings on pp. 169, 194, 200; p. 221 PART V / 1; pp. 221-267 text of part five, with numbered division headings on pp. 221, 234, 240, 250; p. 268 PART VI / 1; pp. 268-304 text of part six, with numbered division headings on pp. 268, 284, 290; p. 305 PART VII; pp. 305-314 text of part seven.

Printing: Baskerville, 11 pt., printed in Great Britain at the Windmill Press, Kingswood, Surrey.

12 x 18.5 cm., white paper, with all edges trimmed; bound in red cloth over boards with the title, author and publisher stamped in gold on the spine and a windmill device blind stamped at the right tail of the back cover.

Price: 7s. 6d. Published in June 1935.

Dedication: To Vivien with ten years love 1925-1935

Notes: The copies examined are in the British Library (N.N. 24142) and the Library of Congress (PZ3/.G8319/En).
     Page [ix] of the preliminaries carries the quotation: "All the world owes me a living." -- Walt Disney (*The Grasshopper and the Ants*).
     William Plomer very favorably reviewed *England Made Me* for *The Spectator* (June 28, 1935, p. 1116) and compared

Greene's dialogue with Hemingway's ("as neat ... and much less monotonous"). Other comparisons are to Virginia Woolf and W.H. Auden.

One detects in Greene's "Introduction" to this novel, first published in *Adam International* in 1966, a sense of irony and surprise in retrospect that the power figure around which most of the novel's plot revolves, Eric Krogh, was impossible to bring to life, despite the fact that he was based on the mysterious financier Ivar Kreugar who Greene enjoyed comparing to Uncle Ponderevo in Wells' *Tono Bungay* ("Gold Bricks," *The Spectator*, March 3, 1933, p. 308). Adding to the irony is the minor character Minty who emerges relatively late in the novel, put there as a plot device, but who comes so thoroughly to life that he threatens to get out of hand.

The manuscript in the Humanities Research Center is dated November 16, 1933, and carries the alternate titles: "The Shipwrecked" and "The Ex-Patriots," this last being deleted.

b. *First American Edition* (1935)

GRAHAM GREENE / *England Made Me* / A Novel / [publisher's device] / *Garden City New York* / Doubleday, Doran & Company, Inc. / 1935

Collation: [1]-[20]^8, 160 leaves.

Pagination: p. [i] advertisement; p. [ii] blank; p. [iii] half-title; p. [iv] author's advertisement; p. [v] title-page; p. [vi] printing and copyright notices; p. [vii] dedication; p. [viii] blank; p. [ix] disclaimer; p. [x] blank; p. [xi] quotation; p. [xii] blank; p. [xiii] fly-title; p. [xiv] blank; p. [1] PART I; pp. [1]-39 text of part one, with unnumbered division headings on pp. 14 and 22; p. 42 PART II; pp. 42-91 text of part two, with unnumbered division headings on pp. 51, 67, 84; p. 92 PART III; pp. 92-163 text of part three, with unnumbered division headings on pp. 102, 117, 129, 160; p. 164 PART IV; pp. 164-213 text of part four, with unnumbered division headings on pp. 188 and 194; p. 214 PART V; pp. 214-259 text of part five, with unnumbered division headings on pp. 226, 233, 243; p. 260 PART VI; pp. 260-295 text of part six, with unnumbered division headings on pp. 276 and 281; p. 296 PART VII; pp. 296-305 text of part seven; p. [306] blank.

Printing: Garamond, 12 pt., printed in the U.S.A. at The
Country Life Press, Garden City, New York.

14 x 20 cm., white paper, with top and bottom edges trimmed,
top edges colored green; bound in green cloth over boards
with vertical wavy lines running the length of the spine
stamped in gold and the author, title and publisher negatively stamped on a central panel of gold on the spine.

Price: $2.50.   Published in September 1935

Dedication: as first English edition.

Notes: The copy examined is in the Library of Congress
(PZ3/.G8319/En/2).   The verso of the title-page of this copy
carries the date of receipt of copyright copies as
September 16, 1935.

   The Doubleday Company reports no record of the number of
copies printed, but they record the number of copies sold
at 2,102.

First Edition

THE GRAYSON BOOKS / Edited by *JOHN HACKNEY* / [double rule] /
The / *Bear Fell* / *Free* / [device] / Graham / Greene / [double
rule] / GRAYSON & GRAYSON / LONDON: MDCCCCXXXV

Collation: [A]-[B]^4 C-E^4, 20 leaves.

Pagination: pp. [1-2] blank; p [3] half-title; p. [4] blank;
p. [5] [notice of number of copies printed and for sale,
number of this copy, and author's signature]; p. [6] blank;
p. [7] title-page; p. [8] blank; p. [9] quotation; pp. [10-
11] blank; p. [12] illustration; pp. [13-30] text; pp. [31-
32] blank; p. [33] author's advertisement; p. [34] blank;
p. [35] illustrator's notice; p. [36] blank; p. [37] colophon;
pp. [38-40] blank.

Printing: Walbaum, 14 pt., printed in Great Britain by The
Garden City Press Ltd., Letchworth, Herts.

14 x 22 cm., white paper, with top edges trimmed; bound in
dark olive green cloth over boards with the cover carrying
the author's name in a rectangle above a stylized airplane
pierced by oblique arrows above the title printed in descend-
ing steps above a wavy line, all stamped in gold; the title
and author are stamped in gold on the spine (see *Notes*).

Price: 10s. 6d. Published in June 1935 in a buff dust jacket
printed in blue with title and author along the spine and the
cover having Grayson Books, title and author, Pan playing
pipes, a typewriter and radio antenna all bordered on the
left and right by pillars with the editor's name at the
bottom.

Notes: The copy collated is in the British Library (10651WP).
Another copy having the dust jacket described has been seen
at Bell, Book and Radmall, 80 Long Acre, London, WC2E 9N6.
Two other copies have been seen at the University of Louisville. The unnumbered copy in the British Library is bound
in black cloth with an unmarked cover and the title and author
stamped in gold on the spine.
285 copies were printed; 250 of these were numbered and
signed by the author and were for sale.
The endpapers of this volume are very unusual (see
plate). They carry a design of the author's initials, "GG,"

topped by a five-pointed rosette which in turn is topped by
crossed lightning bolts, all of this printed in red on a
cream-colored semi-glossy paper.

The illustration on page [12] facing the first page of
the text is by Joy Lloyd.

The colophon on page [37] is as follows: The Grayson
Books *edited by* John Hackney *are published by* Grayson & Grayson Ltd., Curzon Street, Mayfair London, *and printed* and *made
by* The Garden City Press Ltd., Letchworth, Herts. *AD*
MDCCCCXXXV.

Page [9] carries the following quotation: "Events do
not happen; we come across them." -- Weyl.

To the compiler's knowledge, Greene has never referred
to the text of *The Bear Fell Free*. One critic has remarked
that the story is an attempt to "impress the intellectuals."
What is more obvious, especially to a reader of *England Made
Me*, is its relationship to the novel. Both works make extensive use of stream-of-consciousness techniques, though in
the novel they are much more coherent. The narrative of *The
Bear Fell Free* is almost surrealistic, resulting in an insis-
tent tone which is irritating.

Of most interest, certainly, is the similarity between
the story's main character, Tony Farrell, and the protagonist
of *England Made Me*, Anthony Farrant. Farrell is a charmer,
always eager to impress, and like Anthony, he too becomes a
victim both of his own standards and his associates' betrayal.
Whatever the relationship of this story to *England Made Me*, and
the signs of experimentation are too obvious to ignore, the
story is unlike any other story Greene had written at the
time or would write later.

A facsimile reprint of this volume is available from the
Folcroft Press, Folcroft, Pennsylvania.

A10   THE BASEMENT ROOM   1935

First Edition

Graham Greene / [double rule] / THE BASEMENT / ROOM / *and
other stories* / THE CRESSET PRESS LIMITED / 11 FITZROY SQUARE /
LONDON

Collation: [A]^8 B-L^8, 88 leaves.

Pagination: pp. [a-b] blank; p. [i] half-title; p. [ii]
blank; p. [iii] title-page; p. [iv] publication notice; p. [v]
dedication; p. [vi] blank; p. vii CONTENTS; p. [viii] blank;
p. [1] THE BASEMENT ROOM; p. [2] blank; pp. 3-52 text, with
numbered divisions on pp. 3, 13, 23, 32, 42; p. [53] THE END
OF THE PARTY; p. [54] blank; pp. 55-72 text; p. [73] I SPY;
p. [74] blank; pp. 75-80 text; p. [81] BROTHER; p. [82]
blank; pp. 83-97 text; p. [98] blank; p. [99] JUBILEE;
p. [100] blank; pp. 101-112 text; p. [113] A CHANCE FOR MR.
LEVER; p. [114] blank; pp. 115-144 text; p. [145] PROOF POSI-
TIVE; p. [146] blank; pp. 147-154 text; p. [155] A DAY SAVED;
p. [156] blank; pp. 157-[165] text; p. [165] colophon;
p. [166] blank.

Printing: Baskerville, 11 pt., printed in Great Britain by
Butler-Tanner Ltd., Frome and London.

11 x 18.5 cm., white paper, with all edges trimmed; bound in
green cloth over boards with title, author and publisher
stamped in gold on the spine.

Price: 3s. 6d. Published in November 1935.

Dedication: To Charles Evans

Contents: The Basement Room -- 3. The End of the Party --
55. I Spy -- 75. Brother -- 83. Jubilee -- 101. A Chance
for Mr. Lever -- 115. Proof Positive -- 147. A Day Saved --
157.

Notes: The copy examined is in the British Library (12626 V
41).
       The book is dedicated to Charles Evans, managing director
and chairman of W.H. Heinemann. Evans had written personally
to Greene upon the ultimate rejection of the second novel he
had submitted. The letter encouraged Greene to write one
more book, which, being *The Man Within*, was accepted by

Heinemann. Greene refers to Evans' reputation both as a dis-
coverer of young writers and a "remarkable publisher."

The story "A Day Saved" was written for radio. The story
was read by Harcourt Williams over the BBC National Service
on June 22, 1934.

Greene's first collection of short stories should have
been a notable event in the world of publishing but, his
reputation being that of a novelist, little seems to have
been made of the book's appearance. Greene himself, according to the "Introduction" in *Collected Stories*, was uneasy
with the short story form. Though he had written stories almost since his childhood, he was more at home with the novel.
Writing a short story was more an escape from the novelist's
world. Clearly, Greene became a short story writer without
realizing that his novelist's craft could support the more
rigorous form. And the stories in this collection need no
apology. Two of them, the title story and "A Chance for Mr.
Lever," are masterpieces, and the collection marks the first
appearance since his adolescence of the nightmare world of
childhood the reader knows so well.

a. *First Edition*

JOURNEY / WITHOUT MAPS / BY / GRAHAM GREENE / [small device]
/ [publisher's device] / WILLIAM HEINEMANN LTD. / LONDON ::
TORONTO

Collation: $[A]^{10}$ $B-T^{8}$, 154 leaves.

Pagination: p. [i] half-title; p. [ii] author's advertisement;
frontispiece, with blank back, p. [iii] title-page; p. [iv]
publication and printing notices; p. [v] dedication; p. [vi]
blank; p. [vii] CONTENTS; p. [viii] blank; p. ix-x ILLUSTRA-
TIONS; p. [xi] quotations; p. [xii] blank; p. [1] PART I;
p. [2] blank; pp. 3-80 text of part one; p. 3 CHAPTER I /
THE WAY TO AFRICA / HARVEST FESTIVAL; pp. 3-13 text of chapter
one, with division headings on p. 3 HARVEST FESTIVAL, p. 5
BLUE BOOK, p. 11 VIA LIVERPOOL; p. 14 CHAPTER II / THE CARGO
SHIP / MADEIRA; pp. 14-31 text of chapter two, with division
headings on p. 14 MADEIRA, p. 19 BALLYHOO, p. 22 LAS PALMAS,
p. 24 GRAVEYARD, p. 25 DAKAR, p. 28 THE SHAPE OF AFRICA;
p. 32 CHAPTER III / THE HOME FROM HOME / FREETOWN; pp. 32-80
text of chapter three, with division headings on p. 32 FREE-
TOWN, p. 38 THE CITY BAR, p. 42 SIGNED ARONSTEIN, p. 50 PA
OAKLEY, p. 53 UP TO RAILHEAD, p. 59 BORDER TOWN, pp. 66 FREE-
DOM TO TRAVEL, p. 71 TO THE FRONTIER, p. 74 THE WAY BACK;
p. [81] PART II; p. [82] blank; pp. 83-192 text of part two;
p. 83 CHAPTER I / WESTERN LIBERIA / THE FOREST EDGE; pp. 83-
113 text of chapter one, with division headings on p. 83 THE
FOREST EDGE, p. 90 SUNDAY IN BOLAHUN, p. 94 A CHIEF'S FUNERAL,
p. 97 THE LIBERIAN 'DEVILS,' p. 100 THE MASKED BLACKSMITH,
p. 103 MUSIC AT NIGHT, p. 110 NEW COUNTRY; p. 114 CHAPTER II
/ HIS EXCELLENCY THE PRESIDENT / "BOSS OF THE WHOLE SHOW";
pp. 114-145 text of chapter two, with division headings on
p. 114 "BOSS OF THE WHOLE SHOW," p. 121 HOSPITALITY IN
KPANGBLAMAI, p. 130 THE PRIMITIVE; p. 146 CHAPTER III / INTO
BUZIE COUNTRY / THE HORRIBLE VILLAGE; pp. 146-166 text of
chapter three, with division headings on p. 146 THE HORRIBLE
VILLAGE, p. 149 RATS, p. 151 BUZIE COUNTRY, p. 154 THE BIG
BUSH DEVIL, p. 162 KINDNESS IN A CORNER; p. 167 CHAPTER IV /
BLACK MONTPARNASSE / THE CARRIERS' STRIKE; pp. 167-192 text
of chapter four, with division headings on p. 167 THE CAR-
RIERS' STRIKE, p. 174 BAMAKAMA, p. 177 GALAYE, p. 180 THE
DEAD FOREST, p. 184 RAIN IN THE AIR, p. 186 CAFÉ BAR;
p. [193] PART III; p. [194] blank; pp. 195-296 text of part

three; p. 195 CHAPTER I / MISSION STATION / THE LOWLANDS;
pp. 195-210 text of chapter one, with division headings on
p. 195 THE LOWLANDS, p. 198 LIBERIAN COMMISSIONER, p. 200
THE SECRET SOCIETIES, p. 205 A SACRED WATERFALL, p. 209
MYTHOLOGY; p. 211 CHAPTER II / "CIVILISED MAN" / FULL MOON;
pp. 211-231 text of chapter two, with division headings on
p. 211 FULL MOON, p. 213 STEVE DUNBAR, p. 218 THE TAX-
GATHERER, p. 224 "ALL HAIL, LIBERIA, HAIL!," p. 228 TAPPEE
TA; p. 232 CHAPTER III / THE DICTATOR OF GRAND BASSA / BLACK
MERCENARY; pp. 232-247 text of chapter three, with division
headings on p. 232 BLACK MERCENARY, p. 243 VICTORIAN SUNDAY;
p. 248 CHAPTER IV / THE LAST LAP / A TOUCH OF FEVER; pp. 248-
266 text of chapter four, with division headings on p. 248
A TOUCH OF FEVER, p. 251 THE EDGE OF "CIVILISATION," p. 255
THE DETECTIVE OF DARNDO, p. 259 GRAND BASSA, p. 264 THE SEEDY
LEVEL; p. 267 CHAPTER V / POSTSCRIPT IN MONROVIA / A BOATLOAD
OF POLITICIANS; pp. 267-296 text of chapter five, with divi-
sion headings on p. 267 A BOATLOAD OF POLITICIANS, p. 271
MONROVIA, p. 276 THE EXILES, p. 282 POLITICS, p. 286 A CABI-
NET MINISTER, p. 290 FLOREAT COLLEGIUM LIBERIA / BY R.T.D.,
p. 292 RETURN.

Printing: Baskerville, 12 pt., printed in Great Britain at
the Windmill Press, Kingswood, Surrey.

13.5 x 21.5 cm., white paper, with all edges trimmed; bound
in yellow cloth over boards with title, author and publisher
stamped on the spine, and broad lines ruled between author
and publisher, all in brown, with a windmill device blind
stamped at the right tail of the back cover; a map of the
region bordered in African figures, all in brown, serves for
endpapers.

Price: 15s. Published in May 1936.

Dedication: To My Wife
            "I carry you like a passport everywhere."
                    -- William Plomer: *"Visiting the Caves."*

Contents: Part One: Chapter I. The Way to Africa -- 3.
Chapter II. The Cargo Ship -- 14. Chapter III. The Home
from Home -- 32. Part Two: Chapter I. Western Liberia --
83. Chapter II. His Excellency the President -- 114.
Chapter III. Into Buzie Country -- 146. Chapter IV. Black
Montparnasse -- 167. Part Three: Chapter I. Mission Sta-
tion -- 195. Chapter II. "Civilised Man" -- 211. Chapter
III. The Dictator of Grand Bassa -- 232. Chapter IV. The
Last Lap -- 248. Chapter V. Postscript in Monrovia -- 267.

Illustrations: Masked Blacksmith -- *frontispiece.* Dakar:
The French Corner -- facing page 24. Freetown: The English
Corner -- 36. The Edge of the Forest -- 84. Sunday in Bola-
hun -- 84. Pagan Mosambolqhun -- 96. A Chief's Funeral --
100. At Tailahun: Le Roi est mort, vive le Roi -- 104. A
Dance in Bolahun -- 104. The Devil at the Funeral -- 112.
Bolahun Market Place -- 124. Kpangblamai: The Lower and the
Higher Nature -- 124. The Buzie Devil at Kpangblamai -- 128.
Duogobmai: The Horrible Village -- 140. Nicoboozu -- 152.
Into Zigita -- 160. The Big Bush Devil's Hut -- 160. Black
Montparnasse -- 168. Crossing the St. Paul -- 180. The
Chief's Daughter of Djicke -- 180. Galaye: The Ceaseless
Watch -- 192. A Rest by the St. John -- facing page 192.
Mark and Monkey -- 200. Peyi: The Louse Hunter -- 216. Bush
Village -- 220. The Hops Devils of Sacrepie -- 220. Mr.
and Mrs. Nelson of Baplai -- 224. The New Road -- 236. The
Old Prisoner of Tappee -- 244. Bassa Town: The Edge of
Civilisation -- 256. The Hot-house Way to Grand Bassa -- 264.

Notes: The copy examined is in the British Library (010093
ee 41).
    The decorated endpapers representing a map of Liberia
and bordering countries though reduced in size may be seen in
the "Uniform Edition" (1950) along with sixteen of the original thirty-one photographs by the author.
    Page [xi] carries two quotations which follow: " 'O do
you imagine,' said fearer to farer, / 'That dust will delay
on your path to the pass, / Your diligent looking discover
the lacking / Your footsteps feel from granite to grass?'" --
W.H. Auden.
    "The life of an individual is in many respects like a
child's dissected map. If I could live a hundred years,
keeping my intelligence to the last, I feel as if I could put
the pieces together until they made a properly connected
whole. As it is, I, like all others, find a certain number
of connected fragments, and a larger number of disjointed
pieces, which I might in time place in their natural connec-
tion. Many of these pieces seem fragmentary, but would in
time show themselves as essential parts of the whole. What
strikes me very forcibly is the arbitrary and as it were ac-
cidental way in which the lines of the junction appear to run
irregularly among the fragments. With every decade I find
some new pieces coming into place. Blanks which have been
left in former years find their complement among the undistributed fragments. If I could look back on the whole, as we
look at the child's map when it is put together, I feel that
I should have my whole life intelligently laid out before
me...." -- Oliver Wendell Holmes.

The author's advertisement on page [ii] of the preliminaries makes no mention of either *The Name of Action* or *Rumour
at Nightfall*. This is the first of Greene's books which does
not carry these titles on the advertisement and an indication,
perhaps, that the author's suppression of them is more or
less complete by this time.

Journey Without Maps is the first of Greene's travel
books and his first published work of this nature, his biography of Rochester not to be published until 1974. Several
critics (especially John Atkins and Gwen Boardman) have suggested that Greene's trip to Liberia and the resulting travel
book mark a change both in his mind and his fiction. He had
gone to Africa to search out the reality of an image which
for him had always been important. He talks of how the word
"Africa" evokes qualities both of darkness and of the "inex-
plicable," and he seems to sense that this journey is not
just back into time, back to beginnings, but back to a place
(before "centuries of cerebration") where elemental power
exists without modern sophisticated trappings. One hears
echoes of Lawrence in this. When Greene compares the African
manifestations of that power with his dreams in the short
section called "Mythology" (p. 209), he suggests that evil
united with power is more a quality of civilization.

Greene was accompanied by his cousin who has also written an account of the trip (see Barbara Greene's *Land Be-
nighted*, London, Geoffrey Bles, 1938).

b. *First American Edition* (1936)

Journey / Without Maps / GRAHAM GREENE / [publisher's device]
/ Garden City   New York / DOUBLEDAY, DORAN & COMPANY, INC. /
1936.

Collation: [1]-[20]^8, 160 leaves.

Pagination: p. [i] half-title; p. [ii] author's advertisement;
p. [iii] title-page; p. [iv] printing, copyright and publishing notices; p. [v] dedication; p. [vi] blank; p. [vii] quotations; p. [viii] blank; p. ix CONTENTS; p. [x] blank;
p. [1] PART I; p. [2] blank; pp. 3-85 text of part one, p. 3
CHAPTER I / THE WAY TO AFRICA / HARVEST FESTIVAL; pp. 3-14
text of chapter one, with division headings on p. 3 HARVEST
FESTIVAL, p. 6 BLUE BOOK, p. 12 VIA LIVERPOOL; p. 15 CHAPTER
II / THE CARGO SHIP / MADEIRA; pp. 15-33 text of chapter two,
with division headings on p. 15 MADEIRA, p. 20 BALLYHOO,

p. 23 LAS PALMAS, p. 25 GRAVEYARD, p. 27 DAKAR, p. 30 THE
SHAPE OF AFRICA; p. 34 CHAPTER II / THE HOME FROM HOME /
FREETOWN; pp. 34-85 text of chapter three, with division
headings on p. 34 FREETOWN, p. 37 FASHIONABLE WEDDING AT ST.
GEORGE'S CATHEDRAL, p. 41 THE CITY BAR, p. 45 SIGNED ARON-
STEIN, p. 53 PA OAKLEY, p. 57 UP TO RAILHEAD, p. 63 BORDER
TOWN, p. 70 FREEDOM TO TRAVEL, p. 75 TO THE FRONTIER, p. 79
THE WAY BACK; p. [86] blank; p. [87] PART II; p. [88] blank;
pp. 89-202 text of part two; p. 89 CHAPTER 1 / WESTERN LIBE-
RIA / THE FOREST EDGE; pp. 89-120 text of chapter one, with
division headings on p. 89 THE FOREST EDGE, p. 97 SUNDAY IN
BOLAHUN, p. 100 A CHIEF'S FUNERAL, p. 104 THE LIBERIAN DEVILS,
p. 106 THE MASKED BLACKSMITH, p. 109 MUSIC AT NIGHT, p. 117
NEW COUNTRY; p. 121 CHAPTER II / HIS EXCELLENCY / "BOSS OF
THE WHOLE SHOW"; pp. 121-153 text of chapter two, with divi-
sion headings on p. 121 "BOSS OF THE WHOLE SHOW," p. 129
HOSPITALITY IN KPANGBLAMAI, p. 138 THE PRIMITIVE; p. 154
CHAPTER III / INTO BUZIE COUNTRY / THE HORRIBLE VILLAGE;
pp. 154-175 text of chapter three, with division headings on
p. 154 THE HORRIBLE VILLAGE, p. 157 RATS, p. 160 BUZIE
COUNTRY, p. 163 THE BIG BUSH DEVIL, p. 171 KINDNESS IN A
CORNER; p. 176 CHAPTER IV / BLACK MONTPARNASSE / THE CAR-
RIERS' STRIKE; pp. 176-202 text of chapter four, with division
headings on p. 176 THE CARRIERS' STRIKE, p. 183 BAMAKAMA,
p. 186 GALAYE, p. 189 THE DEAD FOREST, p. 194 RAIN IN THE
AIR, p. 196 CAFÉ BAR; p. [203] PART III; p. [204] blank;
pp. 205-310 text of part three; p. 205 CHAPTER I / MISSION
STATION / THE LOWLANDS; pp. 205-221 text of chapter one,
with division headings on p. 205 THE LOWLANDS, p. 208 LIBE-
RIAN COMMISSIONER, p. 210 THE SECRET SOCIETIES, p. 216 A
SACRED WATERFALL, p. 220 MYTHOLOGY; p. 222 CHAPTER II /
"CIVILISED MAN" / FULL MOON; pp. 222-242 text of chapter two,
with division headings on p. 222 FULL MOON, p. 224 STEVE
DUNBAR, p. 230 THE TAX-GATHERER, p. 235 "ALL HAIL, LIBERIA,
HAIL!," p. 240 TAPPEE TA; p. 243 CHAPTER III / THE DICTATOR
OF GRAND BASSA / BLACK MERCENARY; pp. 243-259 text of chapter
three, with division headings on p. 243 BLACK MERCENARY,
p. 254 VICTORIAN SUNDAY; p. 260 CHAPTER IV / THE LAST LAP /
A TOUCH OF FEVER; pp. 260-279 text of chapter four, with di-
vision headings on p. 260 A TOUCH OF FEVER, p. 263 THE EDGE
OF 'CIVILISATION,' p. 268 THE DETECTIVE OF DARNDO, p. 272
GRAND BASSA, p. 276 THE SEEDY LADY; p. 280 CHAPTER V /
POSTSCRIPT IN MONROVIA / A BOATLOAD OF POLITICIANS; pp. 280-
310 text of chapter five, with division headings on p. 280
A BOATLOAD OF POLITICIANS, p. 284 MONROVIA, p. 289 THE EXILES,
p. 296 POLITICS, p. 300 A CABINET MINISTER, p. 303 THE PRESS,
p. 305 FLOREAT COLLEGIUM LIBERIA / BY R.T.D., p. 307 RETURN.

Printing: Garamond, 11 pt., printed in the U.S.A. at The
Country Life Press, Garden City, New York.

13.8 x 20 cm., white paper, with top edges trimmed, top edges
colored brown; bound in black cloth over boards with a native
figure blind stamped on the front cover and the author,
title and publisher stamped in gold in a panel on the spine
with decorative panels above and below stamped in gold.

Price: $2.75. Published in November 1936 in a dust jacket
with the front cover having the title and author in white
over a jungle and natives on a raft in olive and gold; the
spine carries the title, author and publisher over the same
jungle; the back cover carries a comment about the author in
black on white.

Dedication: as first English edition.

Contents: Part One: I. The Way to Africa -- 3. II. The
Cargo Ship -- 15. III. The Home from Home -- 34. Part Two:
I. Western Liberia -- 89. II. His Excellency the President --
121. III. Into Buzie Country -- 154. IV. Black Montparnasse
-- 176. Part Three: I. Mission Station -- 205. II. "Civilised Man" -- 222. III. The Dictator of Grand Bassa -- 243.
IV. The Last Lap -- 260. V. Postscript in Monrovia -- 280.

Notes: The copy examined is in the Library of Congress
(DT626/.G7/1936a/2). The verso of the title-page of this
copy carries the date of receipt of copyright copies as
November 9, 1936. Another copy with the dust jacket described has been seen at the University of Louisville.
    The Doubleday Company reports no record of the number of
copies printed, but they record the number of copies sold at
2,200.
    This edition differs from the English edition mainly in
that it lacks the photographic illustrations. It has, however, endpapers that seem identical to those in the English
edition.

A12   A GUN FOR SALE   1936

a. *First Edition*

A GUN FOR SALE / AN ENTERTAINMENT / BY / GRAHAM GREENE /
[small device] / [publisher's device] / [rule] / WILLIAM
HEINEMANN LTD / LONDON :: TORONTO

Collation: [A]^8 B-R^8, 136 leaves.

Pagination: pp. [i-ii] blank; p. [iii] half-title; p. [iv]
author's advertisement; p. [v] title-page; p. [vi] publication
and printing notices; p. [vii] fly-title; p. [viii] blank;
pp. 1-261 text, with chapter headings on pp. 1, 31, 90, 120
161, 186, 194, 239, and numbered division headings on pp. 1,
6, 11, 22, 25, 28, 31, 43, 50, 67, 86, 90, 98, 110, 117, 120,
140, 143, 158, 161, 179, 186, 190, 194, 210, 239, 244, 247,
250, 255; pp. [262-264] blank.

Printing: Baskerville, 11 pt., printed in Great Britain at
the Windmill Press, Kingswood, Surrey.

13 x 19 cm., white paper, with all edges trimmed; bound in
slick finished red cloth over boards with the title, author
and publisher stamped in gold on the spine and a windmill device
blind stamped at the right tail of the back cover.

Price: 7s. 6d. Published in July 1936.

Notes: The copy examined is in the British Library (N.N.25916).
     The binding is slightly unusual for one of Greene's books
of this period in that the type used for stamping the author
and publisher on the spine is a modern sans-serif face. It
should also be noted that this same type appears once again
on the spine of *Brighton Rock*.
     The book carries no dedication or epigraph.
     In his review for *The Spectator*, William Plomer notes
Greene's background by that time as a film critic and how, as
a novelist, Greene has been indebted to the cinema. He goes
on to the effect that Greene has beaten the "scenario-writers
at their own game" because this thriller "reads very much as
a quick firing gangster film looks and sounds."
     Even more significant than the novelist's technique is
the character Raven. He is of a new breed of thriller characters. He is a coldly professional killer who commits out-
rageous violence as if it were no more than a logical move on
a gameboard. He is the harbinger of the atrocities of the
next decade. An emotional cripple who kills for a living, he

is a further step along the line from Grünlich, the thief,
and the army officer who orders Czinner's face shot away in
Stamboul Train by way of Fred Hall, Krogh's thug in *England
Made Me*, to the anonymous killers in *The Confidential Agent*
and *The Ministry of Fear*.

Film rights to *A Gun for Sale* were purchased by Paramount for £2,500.

b. *First American Edition* (1936)

GRAHAM GREENE / *This Gun for Hire* / [publisher's device] /
[rule] / DOUBLEDAY, DORAN & COMPANY, INC. / *Garden City* 1936
New York

Collation: [1]-[19]^8, 152 leaves.

Pagination: p. [i] advertisement; p. [ii] blank; p. [iii]
half-title; p. [iv] author's advertisement; p. [v] title-
page; p. [vi] printing, copyright and publication notices;
p. [vii] fly-title; p. [viii] blank; pp. [1]-293 text, with
chapter headings on pp. [1], 35, 101, 134, 181, 200, 217,
268, and numbered division headings on pp. 7, 12, 25, 28, 31,
48, 57, 75, 97, 110, 124, 131, 156, 160, 177, 201, 213, 235,
274, 277, 280, 286; pp. [294-296] blank.

Printing: Garamond, 11 pt., printed in the U.S.A. at The
Country Life Press, Garden City, New York.

13 x 19 cm., white paper, with top and bottom edges trimmed,
top edges colored green; bound in ivory cloth over boards
with the title, author and publisher stamped in black on
the spine.

Price: $2.00. Published in June 1936.

Notes: The copies examined are in the library of West Virginia University (823/G32t) and the Library of Congress
(PZ3/.G8319/Th).

The verso of the title-page of the Library of Congress
copy carries the date of receipt of the copyright copies as
June 24, 1936.

The Doubleday Company reports no record of the number
of copies printed, but they record the number of copies sold
at 2,100.

a. *First Edition*

BRIGHTON ROCK / A NOVEL / BY / GRAHAM GREENE / [small device]
/ [publisher's device] / [rule] / WILLIAM HEINEMANN LTD /
LONDON :: TORONTO

Collation: [A]^8 B-Y^8, 184 leaves.

Pagination: p. [i] half-title; p. [ii] author's advertisement;
p. [iii] title-page; p. [iv] publication and printing notices;
p. [v] quotation; p. [vi] blank; p. [1] PART ONE; p. [2]
blank; pp. 3-58 text of part one, with chapter headings on
pp. 3, 26, 37; p. [59] PART TWO; p. [60] blank; pp. 61-92
text of part two, with chapter headings on pp. 61 and 82;
p. [93] PART THREE; p. [94] blank; pp. 95-137 text of part
three, with chapter headings on pp. 95, 112, 119, 132;
p. [138] blank; p. [139] PART FOUR; p. [140] blank; pp. 141-
182 text of part four, with chapter headings on pp. 141, 171,
175; p. [183] PART FIVE; p. [184] blank; pp. 185-219 text of
part five, with chapter headings on pp. 185, 195, 202, 208,
212, 218; p. [220] blank; p. [221] PART SIX; p. [222] blank;
pp. 223-272 text of part six, with chapter headings on pp. 223
and 238; p. [273] PART SEVEN; p. [274] blank; pp. 275-361
text of part seven, with chapter headings on pp. 275, 291,
300, 309, 313, 322, 326, 338, 346, 355, 358; p. [362] blank.

Printing: Baskerville, 11 pt., printed in Great Britain at
the Windmill Press, Kingswood, Surrey.

12.5 x 19 cm., white paper, with all edges trimmed; bound
in red cloth over boards with the title, author and publisher
stamped in gold on the spine in sans-serif type and a windmill
device blind stamped at the right tail of the back cover;
tan endpapers.

Price: 7s. 6d. Published in July 1938.

Notes: The copy examined is in the British Library
(N.N. 29069).
      The typeface used for stamping the spine is the same
sans-serif face used on the spine of *A Gun for Sale.*
      Though the number of copies printed is undisclosed,
Greene says that about 8,000 copies were sold at the time.
      Page [v] of the preliminaries carries the following epi-
graph: "This were a fine reign; / To do ill and not hear of

it again." -- *The Witch of Edmonton*. [by Rowley, Dekker and
Ford, 1658].

In his "Introduction" which first appeared in the Collected Edition, Greene remarks that the novel was written
under circumstances not unlike those surrounding his earlier
books. He was still not out of debt to the publisher and his
novels were not yet bringing in enough money to live on. Besides reviewing for *The Spectator,* he wrote his second screenplay, an adaptation of Galsworthy's story "The First and the
Last," and for six months he edited with John Marks his ill-
fated magazine *Night and Day* (the demise of the magazine because of a libel action brought by Shirley Temple is fairly
well documented in Greene's *Collected Film Criticism*).

The author bemoans the fact that the novel began as a
detective story, part of which still survives in the first
few pages. He says that if he were to revise the novel now,
though he has no plans to, he would start the novel with
Part Two. The one influence Greene himself sees in a few
lines of description in the novel is that of Beatrix Potter.

b. *First American Edition* (1938)

Graham Greene / BRIGHTON ROCK / *An Entertainment* / [double
rule] / *New York* / THE VIKING PRESS / *1938*

Collation: [1]-[23]^8, 184 leaves.

Pagination: p. [i] half-title; p. [ii] author's advertisement;
p. [iii] title-page; p. [iv] publishing, printing, copyright
and Canadian distribution notices; p. [v] quotation; p. [vi]
blank; p. [vii] author's note and editor's note; p. [viii]
blank; p. [1] PART ONE; p. [2] blank; pp. 3-58 text of part
one, with chapter headings on pp. 3, 26, 37; p. [59] PART
TWO; p. [60] blank; pp. 61-93 text of part two, with chapter
headings on pp. 61 and 82; p. [94] blank; p. [95] PART THREE;
p. [96] blank; pp. 97-138 text of part three, with chapter
headings on pp. 97, 114, 121, 133; p. [139] PART FOUR;
p. [140] blank; pp. 141-183 text of part four, with chapter
headings on pp. 141, 172, 175; p. [184] blank; p. [185] PART
FIVE; p. [186] blank; pp. 187-219 text of part five, with
chapter headings on pp. 187, 197, 203, 209, 212, 218; p. [220]
blank; p. [221] PART SIX; p. [222] blank; pp. 223-273 text
of part six, with chapter headings on pp. 223 and 238;
p. [274] blank; p. [275] PART SEVEN; p. [276] blank; pp. 277-
358 text of part seven, with chapter headings on pp. 277, 293,

301, 309, 313, 321, 325, 337, 344, 352, 355; pp. [359-360] blank.

Printing: a modern face similar to Walbaum, 11 pt., printed in the U.S.A.

13.3 x 20.2 cm., white paper, with all edges trimmed, top edges colored black; bound in red cloth over boards with a strip of black cloth running horizontally across both covers and spine at the head. The front cover has a wide and a narrow rule stamped in silver at the join between the red and black cloth as does the spine. The title is stamped in silver on the black on the spine. The author and publisher are stamped in silver on the red on the spine.

Price: $2.50. Published in June 1938 in a predominantly blue dust jacket with the cover having the title in orange above a large gramophone which is above "an entertainment by Graham Greene"; the spine carries the title and author in white on a black panel with the publisher below in white on a black panel; the back cover carries advertisements for *Brighton Rock*.

Notes: The copy examined is in the Library of Congress (PZ3/.G8319/Br). The verso of the title-page in this copy carries the date of the receipt of the copyright copies as June 25, 1938. The copy having the dust jacket described is at the University of Louisville.

This edition contains a note by the author explaining that the character Hale, though not based upon an actual newspaperman, is involved in a treasure hunt which certain newspapers organize at the seaside.

This is the first of Greene's earlier novels not to be published in the U.S.A. by Doubleday. His association with Viking continued through the sixties. Simon and Schuster then became his American publishers.

A14   THE LAWLESS ROADS   1939

a. *First Edition*

THE LAWLESS ROADS / *A MEXICAN JOURNEY* / *by* / GRAHAM GREENE /
With Ten Illustrations / LONGMANS, GREEN AND CO. / LONDON
[device] NEW YORK [device] TORONTO

Collation: [A]^8 B-S^8 T/T*$^{2/8}$, 154 leaves.

Pagination: p. [1] half-title; p. [2] author's advertisement;
frontispiece with blank back, IN CHIAPAS; p. [3] title-page;
p. [4] publishing, publication and printing notices; p. 5
AUTHOR'S NOTE; p. 6 quotations; p. 7 CONTENTS; p. 8 ILLUS-
TRATIONS; p. 9 PROLOGUE / 1 / THE ANARCHISTS; pp. 9-20 text
of prologue, with division headings on p. 9, 1 / THE ANAR-
CHISTS, p. 17, 2 / THE FAITH, p. 20, 3 / (no title); p. 21
CHAPTER I / THE BORDER / ACROSS THE RIVER; pp. 21-37 text of
chapter one, with division headings on p. 21 ACROSS THE
RIVER, p. 25 BIOGRAPHY, p. 26 SAN ANTONIO, p. 27 CATHOLIC
ACTION, p. 30 FREAK SHOW, p. 32 LAREDO; p. 38 CHAPTER II /
THE REBEL STATE / A GOOD OLD MAN; pp. 38-78 text of chapter
two, with division headings on p. 38 A GOOD OLD MAN, p. 42
MONTERREY, p. 48 SAN LUIS POTOSÍ, p. 52 SUNDAY LUNCH, p. 55
COCK-FIGHT, p. 58 TOUR OF THE CATACOMBS, p. 60 THE PHILOSO-
PHER, p. 61 A DAY AT THE GENERAL'S, p. 75 TO MEXICO CITY;
p. 79 CHAPTER III / NOTES IN MEXICO CITY / ANATOMY; pp. 79-
114 text of chapter three, with division headings on p. 79
ANATOMY, p. 82 PLANS, p. 84 CINEMA, p. 84 ALL BOYS TOGETHER,
p. 85 NUN'S BABIES, p. 86 FRESCOES, p. 88 "SUFFER LITTLE
CHILDREN," p. 93 FUN AT NIGHT, p. 98 SUNDAY, p. 101 NO GOLD-
DIGGER, p. 101 THE OLD FRIEND, p. 102 COOK'S TOUR, p. 105
MEXICAN BISHOP, p. 107, 1997, p. 108 GUADALUPE; p. 115
CHAPTER IV / TO THE COAST / JOURNEY DOWNHILL; pp. 115-126
text of chapter four, with division headings on p. 115 JOUR-
NEY DOWNHILL, p. 118 ORIZABA, p. 121 SAINT'S NIGHT, p. 123
THE MORNING AFTER, p. 124 TO VERA CRUZ; p. 127 CHAPTER V /
VOYAGE IN THE DARK / "*AS GOOD A SPORT* ..."; pp. 127-145 text
of chapter five, with division headings on p. 127 "*AS GOOD A
SPORT* ...," p. 134 THE GULF, p. 136 EL FRONTERA, p. 140 THE
RIVER; p. 146 CHAPTER VI / THE GODLESS STATE / GARRIDO'S
CAPITAL; pp. 146-172 text of chapter six, with division head-
ings on p. 146 GARRIDO'S CAPITAL, p. 149 A DAY IN THE BEAUTI-
FUL CITY, p. 155 A VICTORIAN ADVENTURER, p. 161 TABASCAN
SUNDAY, p. 164 A DENTIST'S LIFE, p. 167 TROLLOPE IN MEXICO;
p. 173 CHAPTER VII / INTO CHIAPAS / SALTO DE AGUA; pp. 173-

197 text of chapter seven, with division headings on p. 173
SALTO DE AGUA, p. 178 THE LONG RIDE, p. 185 VISITING THE
RUINS, p. 190 SIGHT OF PARADISE, p. 193 NIGHT ON THE PLAIN;
p. 198 CHAPTER VIII / A VILLAGE IN CHIAPAS / THE EXILE; pp.
198-218 text of chapter eight, with division headings on
p. 198 THE EXILE, p. 206 ALAS! FOR TROY, p. 209 MISS BOWEN
AND THE RAT, p. 211 MASS BAPTISM, p. 213 UNHOLY BIRTH,
p. 215 CLAUSTROPHOBIA, p. 216 THE RAIN; p. 219 CHAPTER IX /
ACROSS THE MOUNTAINS TO LAS CASAS / "THE LUCK OF THE ROAD,"
pp. 219-232 text of chapter nine, with division headings on
p. 223 ARCTIC NIGHT, p. 227 A GROVE OF CROSSES, p. 230 THE
HIDDEN CITY; p. 233 CHAPTER X / HOLY WEEK / FIRST VIEW OF LAS
CASAS; pp. 233-263 text of chapter ten, with division head-
ings on p. 233 FIRST VIEW OF LAS CASAS, p. 235 THE MASS HOUSE,
p. 237 POLITICS, p. 241 HOLY THURSDAY, p. 244 THE BROTHER OF
JUDAS, p. 244, 242 SISSIES, p. 246 GOOD FRIDAY, p. 249 SAN
MIGUELITO, p. 253 FERIA DE PRIMAVERA, p. 256 IN SEARCH OF A
MIRACLE, p. 261 THE LAST OF CHIAPAS; p. 264 CHAPTER XI /
RETURN TO THE CITY / MEXICAN AIRMAN; pp. 264-291 text of chap-
ter eleven, with division headings on p. 264 MEXICAN AIRMAN,
p. 266 OAXACA, p. 268 MITLA, p. 270 TRAIN JOURNEY, p. 273
PUEBLA, p. 273 THE HIDDEN CONVENT, p. 277 BACK AGAIN, p. 281
OLD THREADS, p. 282 ART AND CRAFT, p. 285 ALL QUIET, p. 288
GOOD-BYE; p. 292 EPILOGUE / 1 / THE BLIND EYE; pp. 292-306
text of epilogue / 1 /, with division headings on p. 292 THE
BLIND EYE, p. 296 ATLANTIC, p. 297 THE ESCAPIST, p. 303
ETCETERA; pp. 304-306 text of epilogue / 2 /, A STATE OF
MIND; pp. [307-308] blank.

Printing: Baskerville, 12 pt., printed in Great Britain by
Western Printing Services Ltd., Bristol.

14 x 22 cm., white paper, all edges trimmed; bound in red
cloth over boards with the title, author and publisher stamped
in gold on the spine; the illustrated endpapers are decorated
with a map of Chiapas and Tabasco in Mexico, printed blue on
yellow.

Price: 10s. 6d. Published in March 1939.

Contents: Prologue -- 9. I. The Border -- 21. II. The Rebel
State -- 38. III. Notes in Mexico City -- 79. IV. To the
Coast -- 115. V. Voyage in the Dark -- 127. VI. The Godless
State -- 146. VII. Into Chiapas -- 173. VIII. A Village in
Chiapas -- 198. IX. Across the Mountains to Las Casas --
219. X. Holy Week -- 233. XI. Return to the City -- 264.
Epilogue -- 292.

Illustrations: In Chiapas -- frontispiece. Indian Dictator
-- 64 (this and the following page numbers are for pages
facing the illustration). The Conquest -- 104. Entrance to
Tabasco -- 136. Atlantic Liner -- 136. The Capital of Tabasco -- 150. A Dictator's Signature -- 160. The Ruins of
Palenque -- 186. Yajalon -- 210. Street Scene -- 210.
Map of Mexico -- Endpapers.

Notes: The copy examined is in the British Library (01049/b7).
     The acknowledgment at the bottom of page 8 indicates
that the photographs reproduced in this edition were all
taken by the author except for the one titled "Indian Dictator." The illustrations in this book seem to vary from edition to edition, but it is clear that the first edition is
illustrated almost entirely by the author's own photographs.
The same cannot be said for other editions. Some portions
of the book had already appeared in *The Spectator*, *The Tablet*, the *New Statesman* and the *Evening Standard*.
     Page 6 carries three epigraphs which follow: "What made
the change? The hills and towers / Stand otherwise than they
should stand, / And without fear the lawless roads, / Ran
wrong through all the land." *Edwin Muir* . -- "Man's like the
earth, his hair like grasse is grown, / His veins the rivers
are, his heart the stone." *Wit's Recreations, 1640* . --
"To consider the world in its length and breadth, its various
history, the many races of man, their starts, their fortunes,
their mutual alienation, their conflicts; and then their
ways, habits, governments, forms of worship; their enter-
prises -- their aimless courses, their random achievements
and requirements, the impotent conclusion of long-standing
facts, the tokens so faint and broken, of a super-intending
design, the blind evolution of what turn out to be great
powers or truth, the progress of things, as if from unreason-
ing elements, not towards final causes, the greatness and
littleness of man, his far-reaching aims, his short duration,
the curtain hung over his futurity, the disappointments of
life, the defeat of good, the success of evil, physical pain,
mental anguish, the prevalence and intensity of sin, the per-
vading idolatries, the corruptions, the dreary hopeless ir-
religion, that condition of the whole race, so fearfully yet
exactly described in the Apostle's words, 'having no hope
and without God in the world' -- all this is a vision to
dizzy and appal; and inflicts upon the mind the sense of a
profound mystery, which is absolutely beyond human solution.
     "What shall be said to this heart-piercing, reason-
bewildering fact? I can only answer, that either there is no
Creator, or this living society of men is in a true sense
discarded from His Presence ... *if* there be a God, *since*

there is a God, the human race is implicated in some terrible
aboriginal calamity." *Cardinal Newman.*

This edition carries an "Author's Note" on page 5 which
reminds the reader that the substance of the book is largely
made up of subjective responses to a small part of Mexico at
one point in time, that his conclusions may well be proved
wrong and that time changes situations. In a "Note" to the
third edition (dated 1950) Greene remarks that it may seem
that he "dwells too much on a religious situation" which is
liable to change. But his excuse is that he was commissioned
to do just such a book. He also points out that the source
for *The Power and the Glory* can be found in the section called
"Frontera" and in succeeding pages.

Much of the material of the story "Across the Bridge"
can be found in Chapter I of *The Lawless Roads*, particularly
the descriptions of the border country.

The first page of the manuscript in the Humanities Research Center indicates that the book was originally titled
"Anthology."

b. *First American Edition* (1939)

Another Mexico / Graham Greene / [photograph of Monastery of
San Agustín Acolman] / New York • THE VIKING PRESS • 1939

Collation: [1]-[18]^8, 144 leaves.

Pagination: p. [i] half-title; p. [ii] author's advertisement;
p. [iii] title-page; p. [iv] copyright, printing, distribution and publication notices; p. [v] AUTHOR'S NOTE; p. [vi]
quotations; p. [vii] CONTENTS; p. [viii] blank; p. [ix]
ILLUSTRATIONS; p. [x] blank; p. 1 PROLOGUE /1/ THE ANARCHISTS;
pp. 1-12 text of prologue, with division headings on p. 1,
1/ THE ANARCHISTS, p. 9, 2/ THE FAITH, p. 12, 3/ (no title);
p. 13 CHAPTER I / THE BORDER / ACROSS THE RIVER; pp. 13-28
text of chapter one, with division headings on p. 13 ACROSS
THE RIVER, p. 17 BIOGRAPHY, p. 18 SAN ANTONIO, p. 19 CATHOLIC
ACTION, p. 21 FREAK SHOW, p. 23 LAREDO; p. 29 CHAPTER II /
THE REBEL STATE / A GOOD OLD MAN; pp. 29-67 text of chapter
two, with division headings on p. 29 A GOOD OLD MAN, p. 33
MONTERREY, p. 38 SAN LUIS POTOSÍ, p. 42 SUNDAY LUNCH, p. 45
COCK-FIGHT, p. 48 TOUR OF THE CATACOMBS, p. 50 THE PHILOSO-
PHER, p. 51 A DAY AT THE GENERAL'S, p. 64 TO MEXICO CITY;
p. 68 CHAPTER III / NOTES IN MEXICO CITY / ANATOMY; pp. 68-
101 text of chapter three, with division headings on p. 68
ANATOMY, p. 70 PLANS, p. 72 CINEMA, p. 73 ALL BOYS TOGETHER,

p. 74 NUN'S BABIES, p. 75 FRESCOES, p. 77 "SUFFER LITTLE
CHILDREN," p. 82 FUN AT NIGHT, p. 86 SUNDAY, p. 88 NO GOLD-
DIGGER, p. 89 THE OLD FRIEND, p. 90 COOK'S TOUR, p. 93 MEXI-
CAN BISHOP, p. 94, 1997, p. 95 GUADALUPE; p. 102 CHAPTER IV /
TO THE COAST / JOURNEY DOWNHILL; pp. 102-112 text of chapter
four, with division headings on p. 102 JOURNEY DOWNHILL,
p. 105 ORIZABA, p. 108 SAINT'S NIGHT, p. 109 THE MORNING
AFTER, p. 110 TO VERACRUZ; p. 113 CHAPTER V / VOYAGE IN THE
DARK / "AS GOOD A SPORT ...," pp. 113-129 text of chapter
five, with division headings on p. 113 "AS GOOD A SPORT ...,"
p. 120 THE GULF, p. 122 FRONTERA, p. 125 THE RIVER; p. 130
CHAPTER VI / THE GODLESS STATE / GARRIDO'S CAPITAL; pp. 130-
154 text of chapter six, with division headings on p. 130
GARRIDO'S CAPITAL, p. 133 A DAY IN THE BEAUTIFUL CITY, p. 138
A VICTORIAN ADVENTURER, p. 144 TABASCAN SUNDAY, p. 147 A DEN-
TIST'S LIFE, p. 150 TROLLOPE IN MEXICO; p. 155 CHAPTER VII
/ INTO CHIAPAS / SALTO DE AGUA; pp. 155-178 text of chapter
seven, with division headings on p. 155 SALTO DE AGUA, p. 160
THE LONG RIDE, p. 166 VISITING THE RUINS, p. 170 SIGHT OF
PARADISE, p. 174 NIGHT ON THE PLAIN; p. 179 CHAPTER VIII /
A VILLAGE IN CHIAPAS / THE EXILE; pp. 179-197 text of chapter
eight, with division headings on p. 179 THE EXILE, p. 186
ALAS, FOR TROY!, p. 189 MISS BOWEN AND THE RAT, p. 191 MASS
BAPTISM, p. 193 UNHOLY BIRTH, p. 195 CLAUSTROPHOBIA, p. 196
THE RAIN; p. 198 CHAPTER IX / ACROSS THE MOUNTAINS TO LAS
CASAS / "THE LUCK OF THE ROAD"; pp. 198-210 text of chapter
nine, with division headings on p. 198 "THE LUCK OF THE ROAD,"
p. 201 ARCTIC NIGHT, p. 205 A GROVE OF CROSSES, p. 208 THE
HIDDEN CITY; p. 211 CHAPTER X / HOLY WEEK / FIRST VIEW OF LAS
CASAS; pp. 211-239 text of chapter ten, with division head-
ings on p. 211 FIRST VIEW OF LAS CASAS, p. 213 THE MASS HOUSE,
p. 215 POLITICS, p. 219 HOLY THURSDAY, p. 221 THE BROTHER OF
JUDAS, p. 221, 242 SISSIES, p. 223 GOOD FRIDAY, p. 226 SAN
MIGUELITO, p. 230 FERIA DE PRIMAVERA, p. 232 IN SEARCH OF A
MIRACLE, p. 237 THE LAST OF CHIAPAS; p. 240 CHAPTER XI /
RETURN TO THE CITY / MEXICAN AIRMAN; pp. 240-265 text of
chapter eleven, with division headings on p. 240 MEXICAN AIR-
MAN, p. 242 OAXACA, p. 244 MITLA, p. 245 TRAIN JOURNEY,
p. 248 PUEBLA, p. 249 THE HIDDEN CONVENT, p. 252 BACK AGAIN,
p. 256 OLD THREADS, p. 257 ARTS AND CRAFTS, p. 260 ALL QUIET,
p. 262 GOOD-BYE; p. 266 EPILOGUE /1/ THE BLIND EYE; pp. 266-
277 text of epilogue /1/, with division headings on p. 266
THE BLIND EYE, p. 270 ATLANTIC, p. 271 THE ESCAPIST, p. 276
ETCETERA; pp. 277-279 text of epilogue /2/ A STATE OF MIND;
p. [280] blank.

Printing: Modern, 11 pt., printed in the U.S.A.

14 x 21.5 cm., white paper, all edges trimmed; bound in light
brown cloth over boards with the title, author and publisher

stamped in dark brown on the spine; illustrated endpapers are decorated with map of Chiapas and Tabasco in Mexico, printed in dark brown on cream paper.

Price: $3.00. Published in June 1939.

Illustrations: Monastery of San Agustín Acolman, near Mexico City -- *title-page*. The Bishop's Palace, Monterrey -- *facing page* 36. El Carmen, at San Luis Potosí -- 37. Indian Dictator, Cedillo -- 102. Atlantic Liner -- 103. The Capital of Tabasco -- 130. A Dictator's Signature -- 131. Salto de Agua, on the Edge of Chiapas -- 152. The Ruins of Palenque -- 153. Yajalon, in Northern Chiapas -- 182. Street Scene -- 183. La Merced, at Las Casas -- 232. Interior of Santo Domingo, Las Casas -- 232. Santo Domingo, at Oaxaca -- 233. La Soledad, at Oaxaca -- 248. The Hidden Convent of Santa Monica, Puebla -- 249.

Notes: The copy examined is in the library of West Virginia University (823/G832an).

A comparison between this edition and the English indicates that this edition contains eight illustrations which are not found in the English edition. There are also two illustrations in the English edition which are not found in the American edition. There is no information indicating the source of the photographs.

a. *First Edition*

THE / CONFIDENTIAL AGENT / AN ENTERTAINMENT BY / GRAHAM
GREENE / [publisher's device] / [rule] / WILLIAM HEINEMANN
LTD / LONDON :: TORONTO

Collation: [A]^8 B-S^8 T^4, 148 leaves.

Pagination: pp. [i-ii] blank; p. [iii] half-title; p. [iv]
author's advertisement; p. [v] title-page; p. [vi] publication and printing notices; p. [vii] CONTENTS; p. [viii] blank;
p. [1] PART ONE / THE HUNTED; p. [2] blank; pp. 3-149 text of
part one, with chapter headings on pp. 3, 46, 98, 134;
p. [150] blank; p. [151] PART TWO / THE HUNTER; p. [152]
blank; pp. 153-208 text of part two, with chapter headings on
pp. 153, 187, 199; p. [209] PART THREE / THE LAST SHOT;
p. [210] blank; pp. 211-251 text of part three, with chapter
headings on pp. 211 and 246; p. [252] blank; p. [253] PART
FOUR / THE END; p. [254] blank; pp. 255-286 text of part four,
with chapter headings on pp. 255 and 277; p. [287] publisher's
questionnaire; p. [288] blank.

Printing: Baskerville, 11 pt., printed in Great Britain at
the Windmill Press, Kingswood, Surrey.

13 x 19 cm., white paper, all edges trimmed; bound in blue
cloth over boards with the title, author and publisher stamped
in red on the spine and a windmill device stamped in red at
the right tail of the back cover.

Price: 7s. 6d. Published in September 1939 in a dust jacket
which is predominantly white with printing in black; the front
cover carries the title, a letter with attached thumb print
and passport photo above the author's name, described as the
author of *Brighton Rock*; the spine carries the title, author,
price and publisher with narrow horizontal lines between in
red and gray; the back cover carries comments about Greene by
William Plomer, V.S. Pritchett, Ezra Pound and Richard Church.

Contents: Part One: The Hunted -- 3. Part Two: The Hunter
-- 153. Part Three: The Last Shot -- 211. Part Four: The
End -- 255.

Notes: The copy examined is in the British Library (N.N.
30965). Another copy, with the dust jacket described, has
been seen at the University of Louisville.

Page [287] carries a long advertisement by the publisher requesting readers of this book to write to Heinemann if the book was enjoyable, to communicate their wishes and tastes concerning other books. The address given is William Heinemann Ltd., The Windmill Press, Kingswood, Tadworth, Surrey.

The Confidential Agent was written during the Spanish Civil War and Greene, according to Rayner Heppenstall, was a rather reluctant Franco supporter. Though he seems to have taken no active part in the argument, his brother Herbert (see *Secret Agent in Spain*, London: Robert Hale, 1938) made three trips to Spain as an agent-courier. His brother's adventures may have supplied useful information. In particular a "motor accident" which hospitalized Herbert with head injuries and delayed the publication of *Secret Agent in Spain* in January of 1938 has the ring of an episode occurring in the early pages of *The Confidential Agent*. In *The Spy's Bedside Book* Greene quotes his brother's description of the incident.

The Confidential Agent was written in 1938 in six weeks' time while Greene was also at work on *The Power and the Glory*. Experience indicated that an "entertainment" would bring in more money than a novel; with the war coming on, military service his occupation in the near future, and a growing family to support, there seemed an urgent need to produce a more saleable book than *The Power and the Glory* promised to be. As he describes in his "Introduction" in the Collected Edition, he rented a studio in Mecklenburgh Square (mostly blown up during the blitz) and wrote the entertainment in the mornings and *The Power and the Glory* in the afternoons. The writing of the entertainment went quickly, he relates, "because I was not struggling with my own technical problems...." He was "to all intents ghosting" the novel for Ford Madox Ford who was to die in a year's time. The autograph manuscript of the novel at the Humanities Research Center also suggests that the idea of publishing the novel under a pen name must have crossed Greene's mind. The title-page of the manuscript carries the following words which have been deleted: "An entertainment by Henry Gough." Greene's Christian name is Henry.

b. *First American Edition* (1939)

THE / CONFIDENTIAL / AGENT / *An Entertainment* / GRAHAM GREENE
/ [double rule] / NEW YORK • THE VIKING PRESS • MCMXXXIX

Collation: $[1]-[18]^{6/10}$ $[19]^{2+1}$ $[20]^{8}$, 155 leaves.

Pagination: p. [i] half-title; p. [ii] author's advertisement;
p. [iii] title-page; p. [iv] copyright, printing and publishing notices; p. [v] CONTENTS; p. [vi] blank; p. [1] PART ONE /
THE HUNTED; p. [2] blank; pp. 3-157 text of part one, with
chapter headings on pp. 3, 48, 103, 141; p. [158] blank;
p. [159] PART TWO / THE HUNTER; p. [160] blank; pp. 161-219
text of part two, with chapter headings on pp. 161, 197, 210;
p. [220] blank; p. [221] PART THREE / THE LAST SHOT; p. [222]
blank; pp. 223-266 text of part three, with chapter headings
on pp. 223 and 260; p. [267] PART FOUR / THE END; p. [268]
blank; pp. 269-302 text of part four, with chapter headings
on pp. 269 and 292; pp. [303-304] blank.

Printing: a modern face similar to Walbaum, 11 pt., printed
in the U.S.A.

12.5 x 19 cm., white paper, all edges trimmed, top edges
colored yellow; bound in gray cloth over boards with a stylized robot-like figure stamped in black on the cover and the
author, title and publisher stamped in black on the spine
with orange disks stamped above the author and beneath the
title.

Price: $2.00. Published in October 1939 in a dust jacket,
the front cover of which has the title in white and yellow
over a shadowy figure in black and white (similar in shape
to the figure on the front cover of the binding) with the
author's name in shaded script, a yellow ball at the upper
right and an orange ball at the lower left; the spine carries
the title in script, a yellow ball, the author in script and
the publisher on a scroll; the back cover carries an advertisement for *The Confidential Agent* and is printed black on
white and bordered in orange.

Contents: Part One: The Hunted -- 3. Part Two: The Hunter
-- 161. Part Three: The Last Shot -- 223. Part Four: The
End -- 269.

Notes: The copy examined is in the Library of Congress
(PZ3/.G8319/Co). Another copy with the dust jacket described
was seen at the University of Louisville.

a. *First Edition*

THE POWER AND / THE GLORY / BY / GRAHAM GREENE / [publisher's device] / [rule] / WILLIAM HEINEMANN LTD / LONDON :: TORONTO

Collation: $[A]^8$ $B-S^8$, 144 leaves.

Pagination: p. [i] half-title; p. [ii] author's advertisement; p. [iii] title-page; p. [iv] publication and printing notices; p. [v] dedication; p. [vi] quotation and AUTHOR'S NOTE; p. [1] PART I; p. [2] blank; pp. 3-70 text of part one; p. 3 CHAPTER I / THE PORT; p. 20 CHAPTER II / THE CAPITAL; p. 35 CHAPTER III / THE RIVER; p. 54 CHAPTER IV / THE BY-STANDERS; p. [71] PART II; p. [72] blank; pp. 73-199 text of part two, with chapter headings on pp. 73, 128, 152, 176; p. [200] blank; p. [201] PART III; p. [202] blank; pp. 203-264 text of part three, with chapter headings on pp. 203, 230, 239, 254; p. [265] PART IV; p. [266] blank; pp. 267-280 text of part four; pp. [281-282] blank.

Printing: Baskerville, 11 pt., printed in Great Britain at The Windmill Press, Kingswood, Surrey.

12.5 x 19 cm., white paper, all edges trimmed; bound in yellow cloth over boards with the title, a rule, author and publisher in red on the spine, and a windmill device stamped in red at the right tail of the back cover.

Price: 8s. 3d. Published in March 1940 in a dust jacket which is predominantly purple having a front cover with the title and "a novel by Graham Greene" in a decorated border in a white panel; the spine is similar to the cover except that the title and author are separated by a small device and the publisher is at the tail; the back cover carries in black on white comments about Greene by Hugh Walpole, V.S. Pritchett, Seán O'Faoláin and Richard Church.

Dedication: For Gervase

Notes: The copies examined are in the British Library (N.N. 31394) and the Library of Congress (PZ3/.G8319/Po). Another copy, with the dust jacket described, has been seen at the University of Louisville. A copy in the compiler's possession is a "second printing," though the month of the

second printing (March) is the same month as that of the
first printing. In his "Introduction" to the novel, first
printed in *Introductions to Three Novels* (Stockholm, Norstedt, 1962) and in the Time Inc. Reading Program Special
Edition of *The Power and the Glory* (1962) and later reprinted
in the Collected Edition, Greene mentions a "first edition"
of *The Power and the Glory* of 3,500 copies, though in *A Sort
of Life*, he uses the same figure for the "first printing" of
The Power and the Glory.

In an "Author's Note" on page [vi] of the preliminaries
Greene says that the novel is based "on the situation in one
of the states in Mexico rather more than ten years ago."
Actually the priest's trek across Tabasco and Chiapas is very
much like the trip Greene described in *The Lawless Roads*.
R.W.B. Lewis and Peter J. Conn trace the parallels in a note
at the beginning of their edition of *The Power and the Glory*
(New York, Viking Critical Library Edition, 1970).

The epigraph for the novel, on page [vi], is a quotation
from Dryden: "Th' inclosure narrow'd; the sagacious power /
Of hounds and death drew near every hour."

The Power and the Glory was first issued in the United
States as *The Labyrinthine Ways* and only later published
under its original title.

In his "Introduction" Greene says that this was the only
novel that he had ever "written to a thesis," a story in
which the reader could distinguish between the priest, as a
man, and his office.

Unaccountably, the four chapters of Part I all carry
titles, but these seem to be the only ones.

Greene was awarded the Hawthornden Prize in 1941 for
this novel.

b. *First American Edition* (1940)

GRAHAM GREENE / THE / LABYRINTHINE / WAYS / NEW / YORK [the
words "New York" are bordered on the top and sides by two
scroll devices] / 1940 · THE VIKING PRESS

Collation: [1]-[19]^8, 152 leaves.

Pagination: p. [1] half-title; p. [2] author's advertisement;
p. [3] title-page; p. [4] copyright, printing and publishing
notices; p. [5] dedication; p. [6] blank; p. [7] part I;
p. [8] blank; pp. [9]-78 text of part one, with chapter headings on pp. [9], [26], [41], [61]; p. [79] part II; p. [80]
blank; p. [81]-214 text of part two, with chapter headings

on pp. [81], [139], [165], [190]; p. [215] part III; p. [216]
blank; pp. [217]-284 text of part three, with chapter headings
on pp. [217], [246], [256], [273]; p. [285] part IV; p. [286]
blank; pp. [287]-301 text of part four, with a chapter heading
on p. [287]; pp. [302-304] blank.

Printing: Scotch Roman, 11 pt., printed in the U.S.A. at the
American Book-Stratford Press.

13.5 x 20.3 cm., white paper, all edges trimmed, top edges
colored green; bound in yellow cloth over boards with the
author's initial (bordered by the same scroll device as on
the title-page) and the title at the head of the cover and
the author's name (bordered top and bottom by scrolls), the
title and the publisher on the spine and the author's initial
and scroll border at the right head of the back cover; all
printing is in black.

Price: $2.50. Published in March 1940.

Dedication: To Vivien with dearest love

Notes: The copy examined is in the Library of Congress
(PZ3/.G8319/Lab). The verso of the title-page carries the
date of receipt of copyright copies as March 15, 1940.
     Whereas the English edition is dedicated to Gervase,
this edition is dedicated to Greene's wife, Vivien.
     This edition contains no author's note, nor does it
carry the chapter titles of Part One that exist in the English
edition.

A17   BRITISH DRAMATISTS   1942

First Edition

BRITISH / DRAMATISTS / [rule] / GRAHAM GREENE / [rule] /
WITH / *8 PLATES IN COLOUR* / AND / *26 ILLUSTRATIONS IN* /
BLACK & WHITE / [publisher's device] / WILLIAM COLLINS OF
LONDON / MCMXXXXII

Collation: [A]^4 B^8 C-E^4, 24 leaves.

Pagination: p. [1] half-title; p. [2] a note by the general
editor; p. [3] title-page; p. [4] publishing and printing
notices; pp. [5-6] LIST OF ILLUSTRATIONS; pp. 7-[48] text.

Printing: Plantin, 10 pt., printed in Great Britain by
William Brown and Co., Ltd., London.

16 x 22 cm., white paper, all edges trimmed; bound in brown
paper-covered boards with the title, a figure representing
the Elizabethan stage and the author's name on the cover surrounded by a printed border; the title and the author are
on the spine.

Price: 4s. 6d. Published in September 1942 in a dust jacket
printed with colors and type identical to that of the boards,
and also carrying advertisements on the back cover.

Illustrations: [Plates in Colour] "A Scene from *Venice Pre-
served: A Tragedy* by Thomas Otway," David Garrick as "Jaffier"
and Mrs. Cibber as "Belvidera," oil painting by John Zoffany
-- facing page 8. "John Dryden 1631-1700," oil painting by
James Maubert -- facing page 9. "William Congreve 1670-1729,"
oil painting by Sir Godfrey Kneller -- facing page 24.
"Oliver Goldsmith 1728-1774," oil painting: Studio of Sir
Joshua Reynolds -- facing page 25. "Richard Brinsley Sheridan 1751 -1816," pastel by John Russell, 1788 -- facing page
32. "Oscar Wilde 1856-1900," caricature by "Ape" from
Vanity Fair, May 24th, 1884 -- facing page 33. "Sir Arthur
Pinero," oil painting by Joseph Mordecai -- facing page 40.
"George Bernard Shaw," oil painting by Augustus John --
facing page 41. [Black and White Illustrations] "Man, Surrounded by the Virtues, Receives the Message From Death,"
illumination from Thomas Chaundler's *Liber Apologeticus* --
11. "Interior of the Swan Theatre, 1596," contemporary drawing by John de Witt -- 13. "The Globe Theatre, Southwark,
c. 1612," engraving from Wilkinson's *Theatrum Illustrata* --

14. "Inside the Red Bull Playhouse, Clerkenwell," frontispiece from *Kirkman's Drolls*, 1672 — 15. "William Shakespeare, 1564-1616," frontispiece to the first folio edition,
1623, engraved by Martin Droeshout — 17. "A Scene From *The
Taming of the Shrew*," engraving from the first illustrated
edition of Shakespeare, edited by N. Rowe, 1709 — 18.
"Scene From *A Midsummer Night's Dream*," engraving from the
first illustrated edition of Shakespeare, edited by N. Rowe,
1709 — 19. "Ben Jonson 1573(?)-1637," panel after Gerard
Honthorst — 21. "Illustration to the Dramatic Works of Beau-
mont and Fletcher," water colour by M. Rooker, 1743-1801 —
23. "Interior of the Duke's Theatre, Lincoln's Inn Fields,"
a performance of Elkanah Settle's *Empress of Morocco* in the
reign of Charles II, engraving by Richard Sawyer — 27. "Mrs.
Pinchwife in Wycherley's *Country Wife*," illustration from
Bell's *British Theatre*, 1780 — 28. "Cleopatra in Dryden's
All for Love," illustration from Bell's *British Theatre*, 1780
— 29. "An Eighteenth-Century Performance of *Hamlet*," oil
painting by F. Hayman, 1708-1776 — 31. "The 'Screen Scene'
From *A School for Scandal*," a performance at Drury Lane
Theatre, May 8th, 1777 — 34. "Theatre in Tankard Street,
Ipswich," engraving c. 1800, from Wilkinson's *Theatrum
Illustrata* — 35. "Scene From *Twelfth Night*," painted by
William Hamilton for Boydell's 'Shakespeare Gallery' — 37.
"David Garrick in the Green Room," oil painting by William
Hogarth, 1697-1764 — 38. "Interior of the Regency Theatre,
Tottenham Court Road, 1817," a performance of *Othello*, en-
graving from Wilkinson's *Theatrum Illustrata* — 39. "Arthur
Cecil as Mr. Poskett in Pinero's *The Magistrate*," water
colour by Graham Robertson — 43. "J. M. Barrie," drawing by
W.T. Monnington, 1932 — 44. "J. M. Synge," wash drawing by
J.B. Yeats — 47. "Design for *The Winter's Tale*," drawing by
Albert Rutherston, 1928 — 48. [Tailpieces] "Theatre Checks
and Tickets," engravings from Wilkinson's *Theatrum Illustrata*,
1825.

Notes: The copy examined is in the collection of the compiler.
       Greene's contribution to the well known "Britain in
Pictures" series under the editorship of W.J. Turner came
early in the war and was later reprinted with Sir Herbert
Grierson's *The English Bible*, Lord David Cecil's *The English
Poets*, E.L. Woodward's *British Historians*, Kate O'Brien's
English Diaries and Journals, Elizabeth Bowen's *English
Novelists* and Kenneth Matthews' *British Philosophers*, as *The
Romance of English Literature*. It is Greene's only attempt,
with the possible exception of his biography of Lord Roches-
ter, at an extended critical essay.

Greene wrote most of *British Dramatists* while journeying to his Foreign Office post in West Africa aboard a small cargo vessel, part of a convoy. The trip was made between December 1941 and early January 1942, and the weather most of the way was cold and rough. Greene attributes his harsh appraisal of an "amateur author," Congreve, to the rough seas and having to stand cold watches (see *In Search of a Character*).

A18   THE MINISTRY OF FEAR   1943

a. *First Edition*

THE / MINISTRY OF FEAR / *An Entertainment* / BY GRAHAM GREENE
/ [publisher's device] / [rule] / WILLIAM HEINEMANN LTD /
LONDON :: TORONTO

Collation: [A]^8 B-O^8 P/P*$^{2/8}$, 122 leaves.

Pagination: p. [i] half-title; p. [ii] author's advertisement;
p. [iii] title-page; p. [iv] publication and printing notices;
p [v] CONTENTS; p. [vi] blank; p. 1 BOOK ONE: THE UNHAPPY
MAN / CHAPTER ONE: THE FREE MOTHERS / 1; pp. 1-108 text of
book one; p. 1 CHAPTER ONE: THE FREE MOTHERS; p. 23 CHAPTER
TWO: PRIVATE INQUIRIES; p. 36 CHAPTER THREE: FRONTAL
ASSAULT [see notes]; p. 46 CHAPTER THREE: AN EVENING WITH
MRS. BELLAIRS; p. 60 CHAPTER FOUR: BETWEEN SLEEPING AND
WAKING; p. 66 CHAPTER FIVE: OUT OF TOUCH; p. 87 CHAPTER SIX:
A LOAD OF BOOKS, with numbered division headings on pp. 1, 12,
14, 23, 29, 32, 35, 46, 66, 71, 81, 87, 91; p. 110 BOOK TWO:
THE HAPPY MAN / CHAPTER ONE: CONVERSATIONS IN ARCADY / 1;
pp. 110-156 text of book two; p. 110 CHAPTER ONE: CONVERSA-
TIONS IN ARCADY; p. 140 CHAPTER TWO: THE SICK BAY, with num-
bered division headings on pp. 110, 115, 116, 122, 126, 132,
136, 140, 143, 149; p. 157 BOOK THREE: BITS AND PIECES /
CHAPTER ONE: THE ROMAN DEATH / 1; pp. 157-204 text of book
three; p. 157 CHAPTER ONE: THE ROMAN DEATH; p. 181 CHAPTER
TWO: MOPPING UP; p. 199 CHAPTER THREE: WRONG NUMBERS, with
numbered division headings on pp. 157, 164, 173, 181, 186,
191, 199; p. 205 BOOK FOUR: THE WHOLE MAN / CHAPTER ONE:
JOURNEY'S END / 1; pp. 205-236 text of book four; p. 205
CHAPTER ONE: JOURNEY'S END, with numbered division headings
on pp. 205, 209, 220, 234; pp. [237-238] blank.

Printing: Imprint, 11 pt., printed in Great Britain at the
Windmill Press, Kingswood, Surrey.

12 x 18.5 cm., white paper, all edges trimmed; bound in yellow cloth over boards with the title, author and publisher
stamped in black on the spine and a windmill device stamped
in black at the right tail of the back cover.

Price: 8s. 6d. Published in May 1943.

Contents: Book One: The Unhappy Man. Chapter One: The Free
Mothers -- 1. Chapter Two: Private Inquiries -- 23.

Chapter Three: An Evening with Mrs. Bellairs -- 46. Chapter
Four: Between Sleeping and Waking -- 60. Chapter Five: Out
of Touch -- 66. Chapter Six: A Load of Books -- 87. Book
Two: The Happy Man. Chapter One: Conversations in Arcady --
110. Chapter Two: The Sick Bay -- 140. Book Three: Bits
and Pieces. Chapter One: The Roman Death -- 157. Chapter
Two: Mopping Up -- 187. Chapter Three: Wrong Numbers --
199. Book Four: The Whole Man. Chapter One: Journey's
End -- 205.

Notes: The copy examined is in the collection of the compiler.
     This is the first of Greene's novels to be printed in
conformity with the wartime economy standards. A comparison
with any of the earlier novels shows that Heinemann (as well
as other wartime publishers) was reduced to a format reserved
earlier for cheap reprint editions. Besides the lower quality
binding and paper, the tight leading between lines and the
overall reduction of the book's size, there are other signs
of wartime strain as well. For example, Book One has two
Chapter Threes, the first of which, entitled "Frontal Assault,"
is not listed in the contents page. Another example is the
misnumbering of the third section in the only chapter of
Book Four.
     From April 1940 until October, Greene worked in the
Literary Section of the Ministry of Information. Then he
joined the Foreign Office and in December 1941 was sent to
West Africa where he stayed until February 1943, when he re-
turned to England for the duration of the war. Greene has
mentioned little of this time other than to describe the
shadow world of his friend Philby. The nature of his work
and his wartime experience certainly provided base material
for *The Ministry of Fear*, *The Heart of the Matter*, *Our Man
In Havana* and *The Human Factor*.
     Critics suggest that *The Ministry of Fear* was an exercise
in preparation for the longer, more "serious" *The Heart of
the Matter*. Yet the manic, almost dreamlike quality of *The
Ministry of Fear* is not translated into the later novel. And
it is precisely this quality which makes the book one of the
few accurate representations of the psychology associated
with wartime city life.
     The manuscript at the Humanities Research Center is in-
scribed for Dorothy Craigie, the illustrator for Greene's
children's books and a collaborator on *Victorian Detective
Fiction*.

b. *First American Edition* (1943)

The *MINISTRY* / *OF FEAR* / *An Entertainment by* / *Graham Greene* / THE VIKING PRESS • NEW YORK • 1943

Collation: [1]-[14]^8 [15]^4 [16]^8, 124 leaves.

Pagination: p. [i] author's advertisement; p. [ii] blank; p. [iii] title-page; p. [iv] copyright, publishing and printing notices; p. [v] CONTENTS; p. [vi] blank; p. [1] BOOK ONE / THE UNHAPPY MAN; p. [2] blank; pp. 3-108 text of book one; p. 3 CHAPTER ONE / THE FREE MOTHERS; p. 25 CHAPTER TWO / PRIVATE INQUIRIES; p. 34 CHAPTER THREE / FRONTAL ASSAULT; p. 48 CHAPTER FOUR / AN EVENING WITH MRS. BELLAIRS; p. 61 CHAPTER FIVE / BETWEEN SLEEPING AND WAKING; p. 67 CHAPTER SIX / OUT OF TOUCH; p. 88 CHAPTER SEVEN / A LOAD OF BOOKS, with numbered division headings on pp. 3, 14, 16, 25, 31, 34, 37, 67, 72, 81, 88, 91; p. [109] BOOK TWO / THE HAPPY MAN; p. [110] blank; pp. 111-156 text of book two; p. 111 CHAPTER ONE / CONVERSATIONS IN ARCADY; p. 141 CHAPTER TWO / THE SICK BAY, with numbered division headings on pp. 111, 115, 117, 122, 127, 132, 135, 141, 143, 149; p. [157] BOOK THREE / BITS AND PIECES; p. [158] blank; pp. 159-205 text of book three; p. 159 CHAPTER ONE / THE ROMAN DEATH; p. 183 CHAPTER TWO / MOPPING UP; p. 200 CHAPTER THREE / WRONG NUMBERS, with numbered division headings on pp. 159, 166, 174, 183, 187, 192; p. [206] blank; p. [207] BOOK FOUR / THE WHOLE MAN; pp. 209-239 text of book four; p. 209 CHAPTER ONE / JOURNEY'S END, with numbered division headings on pp. 209, 213, 224, 237; pp. [240-242] blank.

Printing: Baskerville, 11 pt., printed in the U.S.A.

13.5 x 20.1 cm., white paper, all edges trimmed, top edges colored blue; bound in black cloth over boards with the title stamped in silver on the cover and the author, title and publisher stamped in silver on the spine.

Price: $2.50. Published in May 1943.

Contents: Book One: The Unhappy Man. Chapter One: The Free Mothers -- 3. Chapter Two: Private Inquiries -- 25. Chapter Three: Frontal Assault -- 34. Chapter Four: An Evening with Mrs. Bellairs -- 48. Chapter Five: Between Sleeping and Waking -- 61. Chapter Six: Out of Touch -- 67. Chapter Seven: A Load of Books -- 88. Book Two: The Happy Man. Chapter One: Conversations in Arcady -- 111. Chapter

Two: The Sick Bay -- 141.   Book Three: Bits and Pieces.
Chapter One: The Roman Death -- 159.   Chapter Two: Mopping
Up -- 183.   Chapter Three: Wrong Numbers -- 200.   Book Four:
The Whole Man.   Chapter One: Journey's End -- 209.

Notes: The copy examined is in the Library of Congress
(PZ3/.G8319/Mi/3).
    A note on the verso of the title-page indicates that as
in the case of the English edition, this book is also published "in full compliance with all war production board con-
servation orders."

A19 THE LITTLE TRAIN [1946]

a. *First Edition*

THE LITTLE TRAIN / DOROTHY CRAIGIE / [illustration of train
on tracks facing reader]

Collation: [1]-[3]^8, 24 leaves.

Pagination: p. [i] title-page and illustration; p. [ii] dedication, publishing notice and illustration; p. [iii] illustration; pp. 1-[3] text and illustrations; p. 4 text; pp. [5-6]
illustrations; p. 7 text and illustration; p. 8 text; pp. [9-15]
text and illustrations; p. 16 text; pp. [17]-19 text and illustrations; p. 20 text; pp. [21-23] illustrations; p. 24 text;
p. 25 illustration; p. 26 text; p. [27] illustration; p. 28
text; pp. [29-30] text and illustrations; pp. [31-32] illustrations; p. 33 text; p. [34] text and illustration; pp. 35-
37 text; p. [38] illustration; p. 39 text; pp. [40]-42 text
and illustrations; p. [43] illustration; p. 44 text and illustration; p. [45] illustration.

Printing: an old style (similar to Perpetua), 24 pt., printed
in Great Britain by Jarrold and Sons, Ltd. at the Empire
Press, Norwich.

24 x 17.5 cm., white paper, all edges trimmed; bound in yellow cloth over boards with the title, author (Dorothy Craigie)
and small engines printed on the cover, and a signal light in
the center of the back cover; illustrated.

Price: 8s. 6d. Published in June 1946.

Dedication: To the guard of the twelve o'clock to Brighton

Illustrations: [endpapers] [title-page - train on tracks
facing reader]. [title-page verso - platform clock] --
[ii]. [portrait of Little Train] -- [iii]. [station, telegraph lines and signal] -- 1-2. [Mrs. Trolley setting her
clock] -- [3]. [Little Snoreing] -- [5-6]. [Little Train at
a crossing] -- 7. [the porter] -- [9]. [Little Train leaving town] -- [10]. [cat-tails, tortoise and horse] -- [11].
[train on tracks (facing reader) identical to title-page
illustration] -- [12]. [telegraph wires] -- [13]. [signal
light] -- [14]. [train junctions] -- [15]. [The Express] --
[17]. [bridge and steamer] -- 18. [castle on hill] -- 19.

[Little Train in valley with eagle soaring above] -- [21-22].
[cattle in valley] -- [23]. [bull looking at Little Train] --
[25]. [industrial chimneys and smoke] -- [27]. [noises -
white on black] -- [29-30]. [large express] -- [31-32].
[Little Train running in reverse] -- [34]. [front of large
engine] -- [38]. [train cars as border to page] -- [40].
[tracks, Little Train and large train across top of both
pages] -- 41-42. [the celebration] -- [43]-44. [smoke puffs]
-- [45].

Notes: The copy examined is in the British Library (12828 a
70).
       Though there is no recorded publishing date, the year
given in the British Library catalogue (1961, p. 520) is
1946.
       This is the first of Greene's children's books done in
collaboration with illustrator Dorothy Craigie and reprinted
with new illustrations by Edward Ardizzone.
       The book was published by Eyre and Spottiswoode Ltd.,
14, 15 & 16 Bedford Street, London W.C. 2.
       The endpapers are decorated with a map of the fictitious
area in which the story takes place.
       Greene's name does not appear on the title-page of this
edition, though it does on later editions.

b. *First American Edition* (1958)

The Little Train [in red script] / GRAHAM GREENE /
ILLUSTRATED BY DOROTHY CRAIGIE / [illustration of train on
winding track] / LOTHROP, LEE & SHEPARD CO., INC. / 419
FOURTH AVENUE, NEW YORK 16, N.Y.
[facing page:] © GRAHAM GREENE 1958 / PRINTED IN GREAT
BRITAIN BY / WOOD, ROZELAAR AND WILKES LTD / LONDON

Collation: [1]-[3]^6, 18 leaves.

Pagination: p. [1] half-title; p. [2] copyright, printing
notices and illustration; p. [3] title-page and illustration;
pp. 4-5 text and illustration; pp. 6-[7] text and illustration; pp. 8-9 text and illustrations; p. [10] illustration;
p. [11] text and illustration; p. 12 text and illustration;
p. 13 text and illustration; pp. 14-15 text and illustration;
pp. [16-17] illustration; pp. [18]-19 text and illustration;
pp. 20-21 text and illustration; pp. [22-23] text and illustration; p. [24] illustration; p. 25 text and illustration;

pp. 26-27 text and illustration; pp. 28-[29] text and illustration; pp. [30-31] text and illustration; pp. 32-[33] text and illustration; pp. 34-[35] text and illustration; p. 36 illustration.

Printing: Baskerville, 18 pt., printed in Great Britain by Wood, Rozelaar and Wilkes Ltd.

18 x 21.2 cm., white paper, all edges trimmed; bound in gray cloth over boards with the title and a train on tracks facing the reader stamped in red on the front cover; the title, author and publisher are stamped in red on the spine.

Price: $2.00. Published in 1958.

Illustrations: [facing title-page and title-page - station, tracks and Little Train]. [platform and tracks passing under viaduct] -- 4-5. [Mrs. Trolley setting her clock] -- 6. [Little Snoreing] -- [7]. [Little Train at a crossing] -- 8. [the porter] -- 9. [Little Train leaving town] -- [10-11]. [foal, hedgehog and tortoise] -- 12. [train on tracks facing reader] -- 13. [telegraph wires] -- 14. [signal light] -- 15. [train junctions] -- [16-17]. [The Express] -- [18]-19. [Little Train in valley surrounded by mountains, with eagle soaring above] -- 20-21. [industrial chimneys and smoke] -- [22-23]. [noises - white on blue] -- [24]-25. [assorted items and Little Train running in reverse] -- 26-27. [junction] -- 28. [stars - white on blue] -- [29]. [Little Train] -- [30]. [front of large engine] -- [31]. [Scotch express facing Little Train on tracks, engines only] -- 32. [Little Train facing Scotch express on tracks] -- [33]. [the celebration] -- 34-[35]. [smoke puffs] -- 36.

Notes: The copy examined is in the library of Miami University (Oxford, Ohio, E/G8221i).

a. *First Edition*

NINETEEN STORIES / BY / GRAHAM GREENE / [publisher's device] / [rule] / WILLIAM HEINEMANN LTD / LONDON :: TORONTO

Collation: [A]/A*$^{8/8}$ B/B*–G/G*$^{8/8}$ H^8, 120 leaves.

Pagination: pp. [i-ii] blank; p. [iii] half-title; p. [iv] author's advertisement; p. [v] title-page; p. [vi] publishing and printing notices; p. [vii] CONTENTS; p. [viii] AUTHOR'S NOTE; pp. 1-32 text of THE BASEMENT ROOM, with numbered divisions on pp. 1, 7, 14, 20, 25; pp. 33-44 text of THE END OF THE PARTY; pp. 45-48 text of I SPY; pp. 49-54 text of THE INNOCENT; pp. 55-71 text of A DRIVE IN THE COUNTRY; pp. 72-83 text of ACROSS THE BRIDGE; pp. 84-91 text of JUBILEE; pp. 92-100 text of BROTHER; pp. 101-105 text of PROOF POSITIVE; pp. 106-124 text of A CHANCE FOR MR. LEVER; pp. 125-139 text of THE LOTTERY TICKET; pp. 140-146 text of THE SECOND DEATH; pp. 147-152 text of A DAY SAVED; pp. 153-160 text of A LITTLE PLACE OFF THE EDGWARE ROAD; pp. 161-165 text of THE CASE FOR THE DEFENCE; pp. 166-183 text of WHEN GREEK MEETS GREEK, with numbered divisions on pp. 166, 170, 173, 176, 179; pp. 184-191 text of MEN AT WORK; pp. 192-195 text of ALAS, POOR MALING; pp. 196-231 text of THE OTHER SIDE OF THE BORDER; pp. 196-197 NOTE; pp. 197-220 PART ONE / THE MAP, with numbered division headings on pp. 200, 207, 211, 217, 220; pp. 221-231 PART TWO / THE EXPEDITION; p. [232] blank.

Printing: Imprint, 12 pt., printed in Great Britain at the Windmill Press, Kingswood, Surrey.

12 x 18.5 cm., white paper, all edges trimmed; bound in black cloth over boards with the title, author and publisher stamped in silver on the spine; a windmill device is blind stamped at the right tail of the back cover.

Price: 8s. 6d. Published in July 1947.

Contents: The Basement Room -- 1. The End of the Party -- 33. I Spy -- 45. The Innocent -- 49. A Drive in the Country -- 55. Across the Bridge -- 72. Jubilee -- 84. Brother -- 92. Proof Positive -- 101. A Chance for Mr. Lever -- 106. The Lottery Ticket -- 125. The Second Death -- 140. A Day Saved -- 147. A Little Place Off the Edgware

Road -- 153. The Case for the Defence -- 161. When Greek
Meets Greek -- 166. Men At Work -- 184. Alas, Poor Maling --
192. The Other Side of the Border -- 196.

Notes: The copy examined is in the British Library (N.N.
37379).

In an "Author's Note" on page [viii] of the preliminaries Greene comments that eight of the stories in this collection appeared in an earlier volume called *The Basement Room*,
published in 1936 by Cresset Press (though he is actually
mistaken about the date, which is 1935).

The stories new to the collection are: "The Innocent,"
"A Drive in the Country," "Across the Bridge," "The Lottery
Ticket" (which does not survive in *Twenty-One Stories*), "The
Second Death," "A Little Place Off the Edgware Road," "The
Case for the Defence," "When Greek Meets Greek," "Men At
Work," "Alas, Poor Maling," and "The Other Side of the Border"
(which also was excised from the later collections).

The stories in this collection are dated and, as Greene
notes, they were written at intervals between 1929 and 1941.
At the time of publication Greene still considered the stories
"by-products" of his career as a novelist.

b. *First American Edition* (1949)

Nineteen Stories / by Graham Greene / New York · THE VIKING
PRESS · Mcmxlix / [title and author's name surrounded in oval
border]

Collation: [1]^8 [2]-[8]^{16} [9]^8, 128 leaves.

Pagination: p. [i] half-title; p. [ii] author's advertisement; p. [iii] title-page; p. [iv] copyright, publishing,
acknowledgments and printing notices; pp. v-[vi] CONTENTS;
p. vii AUTHOR'S NOTE; p. [viii] blank; p. [1] fly-title;
p. [2] blank; pp. 1-36 text of THE BASEMENT ROOM, with numbered divisions on pp. 3, 10, 17, 23, 29; pp. 37-48 text of
THE END OF THE PARTY; pp. 49-52 text of I SPY; pp. 53-59 text
of THE INNOCENT; pp. 60-77 text of A DRIVE IN THE COUNTRY;
pp. 78-90 text of ACROSS THE BRIDGE; pp. 91-98 text of
JUBILEE; pp. 99-108 text of BROTHER; pp. 109-114 text of
PROOF POSITIVE; pp. 115-134 text of A CHANCE FOR MR. LEVER;
pp. 135-150 text of THE HINT OF AN EXPLANATION; pp. 151-158
text of THE SECOND DEATH; pp. 195-164 text of A DAY SAVED;
pp. 165-172 text of A LITTLE PLACE OFF THE EDGWARE ROAD;
pp. 173-177 text of THE CASE FOR THE DEFENCE; pp. 178-196

text of WHEN GREEK MEETS GREEK, with numbered divisions on
pp. 178, 182, 185, 189, 192; pp. 197-204 text of MEN AT WORK;
pp. 205-209 text of ALAS, POOR MALING; pp. 210-247 text of
THE OTHER SIDE OF THE BORDER; pp. 210-211 NOTE; pp. 211-236
PART ONE / THE MAP, with numbered division headings on pp.
215, 221, 226, 232, 236; pp. 237-247 PART TWO / THE EXPEDI-
TION; p. [248] blank.

Printing: Baskerville, 11 pt., printed in the U.S.A. by The
Vail-Ballou Press, Inc.

13.5 x 19.2 cm., white paper, all edges trimmed, top edges
colored blue; bound in blue cloth over boards with the title
and author surrounded by an oval border printed in darker
blue on the cover and on the spine; the publisher is also
printed on the spine in darker blue.

Price: $2.75. Published in February 1949.

Contents: The Basement Room -- 3. The End of the Party --
37. I Spy -- 49. The Innocent -- 53. A Drive in the
Country -- 60. Across the Bridge -- 78. Jubilee -- 91.
Brother -- 99. Proof Positive -- 109. A Chance for Mr.
Lever -- 115. The Hint of an Explanation -- 135. The Second
Death -- 151. A Day Saved -- 159. A Little Place Off the
Edgware Road -- 165. The Case for the Defence -- 173. When
Greek Meets Greek -- 178. Men At Work -- 197. Alas, Poor
Maling -- 205. The Other Side of the Border -- 210.

Notes: The copy examined is in the Library of Congress
(PZ3/.G8319/Ni/2).

A21   THE HEART OF THE MATTER   1948

a. *First Edition*

THE HEART / OF THE MATTER / BY / GRAHAM GREENE / [publisher's
device] / [rule] / WILLIAM HEINEMANN LTD / MELBOURNE ::
LONDON :: TORONTO

Collation: [A]/A*$^{8/8}$ B/B*-I/I*$^{8/8}$ K^8, 152 leaves.

Pagination: p. [i] half-title; p. [ii] author's advertisement;
p. [iii] title-page; p. [iv] publication and printing notices;
p. [v] dedication, disclaimer and acknowledgment; p. [vi]
quotation; p. 1 BOOK ONE / PART ONE / CHAPTER I / 1; pp. 1-
109 text of book one, with part headings on pp. 1, 61, 81,
chapter headings on pp. 1, 40, 61, 76, 81, and numbered division headings on pp. 1, 5, 12, 18, 27, 31, 34, 37, 40, 43,
50, 55, 61, 67, 72, 81, 94, 98, 104; p. 110 BOOK TWO / PART
ONE / CHAPTER I / 1; pp. 110-217 text of book two, with part
headings on pp. 110, 172, 187, chapter headings on pp. 110,
137, 162, 187, 203, and numbered division headings on pp. 110,
116, 122, 127, 134, 137, 145, 151, 154, 160, 162, 169, 172,
177, 178, 183, 187, 193, 196, 203, 216; p. 218 BOOK THREE /
PART ONE / CHAPTER I / 1; pp. 218-297 text of book three, with
part headings on pp. 218, 270, 291, chapter headings on pp.
218, 228, 243, 257, 270, 277, 283, 291, and numbered division
headings on pp. 218, 225, 228, 234, 243, 253, 257, 270, 274,
277, 283, 284, 291, 293; p. [298] blank.

Printing: Imprint, 11 pt., printed in Great Britain at the
Windmill Press, Kingswood, Surrey.

12 x 18.5 cm., white paper, all edges trimmed; bound in blue
cloth over boards with the title, author and publisher
stamped in silver on the spine and a windmill design blind
stamped at the right tail of the back cover.

Price: 9s. 6d. Published in May 1948 in a dust jacket
printed in red with the title, "a novel by," the author and
publisher in white on the cover and advertisements on the
back cover.

Dedication: To V.G., L.C.G., and F.C.G.

Notes: The copy examined is in the British Library (N.N.
38354). Another copy, identical to the British Library copy
except for having the dust jacket described above, was seen

at Bertram Rota, Booksellers, 30 and 31 Long Acre, London,
WC2E 9LT.

On page [v] of the preliminaries following the dedication Greene makes it clear that he wants his disclaimer about
living persons to be taken very seriously. The geographical
location of the story, however, is drawn from his personal
experiences in West Africa. The poem he has quoted on page
288 is from *Selected Poems of Rainer Maria Rilke*, translated
by J.D. Leishman (Hogarth Press, 1941).

Page [vi] carries the following quotation from Péguy:
"Le pécheur est au coeur même de chrétienté ... Nul n'est
aussi compétent que le pécheur en matière de chrétienté.
Nul, si ce n'est le saint."

In his "Introduction" to *The Heart of the Matter*, first
printed in *Introductions to Three Novels* (Stockholm, Norstedt,
1962), Greene reminds the reader that after the war his
novelist's tools were "sadly rusted." It was a popular book
with the readers, but Greene finds several things not so well
done as he would like. In particular he regrets the stilted
view of Louise Scobie caused by only seeing her from the
point of view of either Scobie or Wilson, and Greene offers
the reader a scene played by Mrs. Scobie and Wilson at the
end of Part II, Chapter I, before Chapter 2. The scene, cut
from the original draft of the novel, is offered not so much
as a revision but as an alternative.

Greene's background finds its way into his novels in odd
ways. An example can be seen in Book II, Part II, Chapter I,
when Harris borrows Wilson's old school magazine, the *Down-
hamian*. There must be an element of self-parody here. The
magazine is exactly the same as the magazine of Greene's own
school, *The Berkhamstedian*. In fact, Harris begins to read
in it a story entitled "The Tick of the Clock," a story which
Greene himself wrote and which was published, unsigned, in
The Berkhamstedian.

b. *First American Edition* (1948)

GRAHAM GREENE / The / Heart / of the / Matter / New York ·
The Viking Press · 1948

Collation: [1]-[10]^{16}, 160 leaves.

Pagination: pp. [i-ii] blank; p. [iii] half-title; p. [iv]
author's advertisement; p. [v] title-page; p. [vi] copyright,
publication and printing notices; p. [vii] dedication;

p. [viii] blank; p. [ix] quotation; p. [x] blank; p. [xi]
author's note and disclaimer; p. [xii] blank; p. [1] BOOK 1;
p. [2] blank; p. 3 PART ONE / I; pp. 3-110 text of book one,
with part headings on pp. 3, 62, 82, and chapter headings on
pp. 3, 42, 62, 78, and numbered division headings on pp. 7,
14, 20, 29, 33, 39, 44, 51, 57, 68, 73, 95, 99, 105; p. [111]
BOOK 2; p. [112] blank; p. 113 PART ONE / I; pp. 113-222 text
of book two, with part headings on pp. 113, 176, 191, and
chapter headings on pp. 113, 141, 166, 191, 208, and numbered
division headings on pp. 119, 125, 131, 137, 148, 155, 158,
163, 173, 181, 182, 187, 197, 200, 220, p. [223] BOOK 3;
p. [224] blank; p. 225 PART ONE / I; pp. 225-306 text of book
three, with part headings on pp. 225, 278, 300, and chapter
headings on pp. 225, 236, 251, 266, 278, 286, 292, and numbered division headings on pp. 232, 241, 261, 282, 293, 302,
305; pp. [307-308] blank.

Printing: Caslon and Baskerville, 11 pt., printed in the
U.S.A. by The Colonial Press, Inc.

13 x 20.2 cm., white paper, all edges trimmed; bound in
boards covered in maroon embossed paper with the spine in
ivory cloth; the author, title and publisher are stamped in
maroon on a central panel of the spine with horizontal ruled
lines at the head and tail; the front cover carries the
author's initials with ruled lines above and below and all
printing in gray.

Price: $3.00. Published in July 1948.

Dedication: as first English edition.

Notes: The copy described is in the compiler's collection.
Another copy from the library of Bluefield State College in
West Virginia lists four printings in July 1948, implying a
very large first edition. The binding of this copy differs
from the first printing in that the boards are gray with blue
printing and the spine is red with blue printing. The top
edges are also colored blue.
    Another copy has been seen at the University of Louis-
ville which is one of 750 copies specially bound for distribution to friends of the Viking Press. This copy is bound in
gray buckram cloth over boards with the front cover carrying
the author's interlocked initials in red and gold bordered at
the top, right side and bottom by a triple three-sided rectangle of which the lines on the open side continue onto the
spine; the outer and inner rectangles are in red while the
middle rectangle is in gold; the spine carries the author,
title and publisher stamped in gold.

A22   WHY DO I WRITE?   1948

First Edition

Why Do I Write? / AN EXCHANGE OF VIEWS / BETWEEN / *Elizabeth Bowen* / *Graham Greene* / & / *V. S. Pritchett* / [device] / LONDON / *Percival Marshall*

Collation: [1]-[3]^8 [4]^6, 30 leaves.

Pagination: p. [1] half-title; p. [2] blank; p. [3] title-page; p. [4] publication and publishing notices; p. [5] CONTENTS; p. [6] blank; pp. 7-10 PREFACE / BY V. S. PRITCHETT; pp. 11-15 THE CORRESPONDENCE BEGINS WITH A LETTER WRITTEN BY V. S. PRITCHETT TO ELIZABETH BOWEN; pp. 16-19 A SECOND LETTER FOLLOWS: V. S. PRITCHETT TO ELIZABETH BOWEN; pp. 20-26 THE FOLLOWING REPLY CAME FROM GRAHAM GREENE TO V. S. PRITCHETT; pp. 27-33 THE THREE LETTERS WERE SENT TO GRAHAM GREENE WHO REPLIED TO ELIZABETH BOWEN; pp. 34-45 THE CORRESPONDENCE NOW CAME BACK TO V. S. PRITCHETT / V. S. PRITCHETT TO GRAHAM GREENE; pp. 46-52 GRAHAM GREENE REPLIED TO V. S. PRITCHETT; pp. 53-[58] THE INTERCHANGE BETWEEN GRAHAM GREENE AND V. S. PRITCHETT WAS SENT TO ELIZABETH BOWEN WHO REPLIED TO GRAHAM GREENE; pp. [59-60] blank.

Printing: Baskerville, 11 pt., printed in Great Britain by Electrical Press Ltd., Cordwallis Works, Maidenhead, Berks.

12.5 x 21.5 cm., white paper, top and bottom edges trimmed; bound in boards in decorated paper of vertical rules alternating with twisting vines printed red on white with the title, authors and publisher in red along the spine.

Price: 6s. Published in November 1948.

Contents: Preface -- 7. V. S. Pritchett to Elizabeth Bowen -- 11. V. S. Pritchett to Elizabeth Bowen -- 16. Elizabeth Bowen to V. S. Pritchett -- 20. Graham Greene to Elizabeth Bowen -- 27. V. S. Pritchett to Graham Greene -- 34. Graham Greene to V. S. Pritchett -- 46. Elizabeth Bowen to Graham Greene -- 53.

Notes: The copy examined is in the British Library (11867/cc37).

In the exchange of views which makes up this volume Greene writes twice, the first time to Elizabeth Bowen and the second to V.S. Pritchett. An overall subject is the

artist's relation to society, and Greene discusses what he
feels is the writer's duty: "to tell the truth as he sees it
and to accept no special privileges from the state." His
other comments are an expansion upon and extension of this
statement.

The correspondence, which began in 1947, was broadcast
by the BBC on a Third Programme called "The Artist in Society"
on October 7, 1948, with all participants reading their letters. Besides this volume, the correspondence was printed
later in *From the Third Programme, a Ten Years Anthology:
Imagination, Argument, Experience, Exposition*, edited by John
Morris and published in London by the Nonesuch Press in 1956.
The edition was limited to 1,300 copies.

A23   THE THIRD MAN and THE FALLEN IDOL   1950

a. *First Edition*

THE THIRD MAN / *and* / THE FALLEN IDOL / *by* / GRAHAM GREENE /
[publisher's device] / WILLIAM HEINEMANN LTD / MELBOURNE ::
LONDON :: TORONTO

Collation: $[A]^8$ $B-L^8$ M^{10}, 98 leaves.

Pagination: p. [i] half-title; p. [ii] author's advertisement;
p. [iii] title-page; p. [iv] publication and printing notices;
p. [v] dedication; p. [vi] blank; p. [1] THE THIRD MAN; p. [2]
blank; pp. 3-6 PREFACE; pp. 7-142 text, with chapter headings
on pp. 7, 10, 28, 35, 41, 47, 51, 60, 65, 86, 96, 103, 112,
117, 127, 130, 140; p. [143] THE FALLEN IDOL; p. [144] blank;
pp. 145-146 PREFACE; pp. 147-188 text, with numbered divisions on pp. 147, 155, 164, 171, 179; pp. [189-190] blank.

Printing: typeface similar to Imprint, 11 pt., printed in
Great Britain at the Windmill Press, Kingswood, Surrey.

12 x 18 cm., white paper, all edges trimmed; bound in black
cloth over boards with titles, author and publisher stamped
silver on the spine, and a windmill design blind stamped at
the right tail of the back cover.

Price: 6s. Published in July 1950 in a black and white dust
jacket consisting of a photo design with Trevor Howard,
Alida Valli and Orson Welles on the cover with titles printed
over in red and white, and on the back cover a scene from
The Fallen Idol.

Dedication: To Carol Reed in admiration and affection and in
memory of so many early morning Vienna hours at Maxim's, the
Casanova, the Oriental

Notes: The copy examined is in the collection of the compiler.
      The author's advertisement neglects to mention *The Con-
fidential Agent.*
      This edition carries a preface for each title. The pre-
face to *The Third Man* relates that the story was first written
as a kind of screen treatment, "raw material," for the film
and not for publication. Greene comments that the film is
better because it is the "finished state of the story." He
also discusses differences between the story, the script and
the film.

The preface to *The Fallen Idol* indicates that this story is actually "The Basement Room" and that unlike *The Third Man* it was not written with the film in mind but rather as a diversion from the boredom of the return trip from Liberia, the trip described in *Journey Without Maps*. Greene discusses the changes made for the sake of the film and also his collaboration with Carol Reed.

The idea for *The Third Man* seems to have come as the result of several factors. Greene remarks that Alexander Korda had sent him to Vienna for three weeks. There, during the last two days of his trip, Greene heard of the diluted penicillin racket and he was given a tour of the sewers. He says the two ideas came together and he had *The Third Man*. Another factor Greene may have missed is the similarity of the plot of the story to that of Eric Ambler's *The Mask of Dimitrios*, a favorite of Greene's that accompanied him on his second trip to Africa.

The Third Man is the first of Greene's longer creations to use the first-person narrative technique. Just as *The Ministry of Fear* seemed to serve as an experimental ground for the later *The Heart of the Matter*, there are similar parallels between *The Third Man* and *The End of the Affair*.

b. *First American Edition* (1950)

GRAHAM / GREENE / [Harry Lime silhouette device] / THE / THIRD MAN / NEW YORK • THE VIKING PRESS • 1950

Collation: [1]-[5]^{16}, 80 leaves.

Pagination: p. [1] half-title; p. [2] author's advertisement; p. [3] title-page; p. [4] copyright, publishing, acknowledgment and printing notices; p. [5] dedication; p. [6] blank; pp. 7-10 PREFACE; p. [11] fly-title; p. [12] blank; pp. 13-157 text, with chapter headings on pp. 13, 16, 35, 44, 50, 57, 62, 72, 78, 100, 111, 118, 125, 130, 141, 145, 156; pp. [158-160] blank.

Printing: Caledonia, 11 pt., printed in the U.S.A. by The Colonial Press, Inc.

12.3 x 18.7 cm., white paper, all edges trimmed, top edges colored blue; bound in boards covered with paper embossed to look like dark gray cloth; the spine in red cloth carries the author, title and publisher stamped in black.

Price: $2.00.   Published in March 1950.

Dedication: as first English edition.

Notes: The copy examined is in the library of Oberlin College (823.91/G832T).

A24   THE LITTLE FIRE ENGINE   1950

a. *First Edition*

The Little Fire Engine [in script] / *BY THE AUTHOR OF* THE
LITTLE TRAIN / GRAHAM GREENE / *ILLUSTRATED BY* / DOROTHY
CRAIGIE

Collation: [1]-[3]^8, 24 leaves.

Pagination: p. [i] title-page and illustration; p. [ii]
printing and publishing notices; pp. 1-2 text; p. 3 illustration; p. 4 text; p. 5 illustration; p. 6 text; p. 7 illustration; pp. [8-9] text and illustrations; pp. 10-11 text and
illustrations; p. [12] text and illustration; pp. 13-14 text
and illustrations; p. 15 text; pp. [16-17] illustration;
p. 18 text; pp. 19-20 text and illustrations; p. 21 illustration; p. 22 text; p. 23-27 text and illustrations; p. 28
text; p. [29] illustration; p. 30 text; p. [31] illustration;
p. 32 text and illustration; p. [33] text incorporated into
illustration; p. 34 text; p. [35] text and illustration;
p. 36 text; p. [37] text and illustration; p. 38 text; p. 39
text and illustration; p. 40 text; pp. [41-42] text and illustration; p. 43 text and illustration; p. 44 text; p. [45]
illustration; p. [46] blank.

Printing: Perpetua, 21 pt., printed in Great Britain by
Jarrold and Sons Ltd., The Empire Press, Norwich.

17.5 x 28 cm., white paper, all edges trimmed; bound in
decorated paper-covered boards with the title, author and
illustrator on the cover which carries an illustration representing a fireman taking a hose from a hydrant (all in red);
the back cover bears an illustration of a small horse-drawn
fire engine on a blue field; the title, author and publisher
are along the spine.

Price: 7s. 6d. Published in October 1950.

Illustrations: [title-page - fire hat and hatchet motif] --
1. [firemen on couch] -- 3. [old fire engine] -- 5.
[horse drinking from fire bucket] -- 7. [mayor of Much
Snoreing] -- [8]. [a letter with a seal] -- [9]. [calendar
showing May 30] -- 10. [letter typewritten from the mayor to
Mr. Trolley] -- 11. [old fire engine] -- [12]. [new fire
engine] -- 13. [folded newspaper] -- 14. [games and amuse-
ments] -- [16-17]. [fireman's uniform on hanger and fireman

sitting on fire bucket] -- 19. [a higgler's cart and horse]
-- 20. [old fire engine and horse] --21. [falling leaves]
-- 23. [rain, boot, umbrella] -- 24. [fireman with feet on
tub] -- 25. [old engine rusting away] -- 26. [horse stable
and cobwebs] -- 27. [snow falling on house tops] -- [29].
[firemen throwing snowballs at house] -- [31]. [old engine,
firemen, horse and Christmas decorations] -- 32. [white
across blue "That night when everyone was asleep ..."] --
[33]. [Cootes farmyard] -- [35]. [firemen drinking and
dancing] -- [37]. [two firemen and a young woman] -- 39.
[old fire engine, horse and fireman going to a fire] -- [41].
[firemen, horse and old engine] -- [42]. [hat, medal and box
of sugar] -- 43. [fire house] -- [45].

Notes: The copy examined is in the British Library (cup
1253 de 75).

   Though this book is the first of the children's books to
bear his name, Greene had written *The Little Train* (1946)
reprinted by the publishers of this book, Max Parrish and Co.,
Ltd., Adprint House, Rathbone Place, London, W1.

b. *First American Edition* (1953)

The Little Red Fire Engine [in script] / GRAHAM GREENE /
ILLUSTRATED BY / DOROTHY CRAIGIE / LOTHROP, LEE & SHEPARD CO.,
INC. NEW YORK [page decorated with helmets in yellow and
axes in blue, letters are in blue]

Collation: as first English edition.

Pagination: as first English edition.

Printing: as first English edition, printed in Great Britain
by Jarrold & Sons Limited, Norwich.

17.3 x 27 cm., white paper, all edges trimmed; bound in
decorated paper-covered boards illustrated and marked just as
the English edition.

Price: $2.00 cloth ($1.75 paper). Published in April 1953.

Illustrations: as first English edition.

Notes: The copy examined is in the Library of Congress
(PZ7/.G8295/Li/2).

A25 THE BEST OF SAKI 1950

a. *First Edition*

Guild Books No 423 / [rule] / The Best of / SAKI / (H. H.
MUNRO) / with an introduction by / GRAHAM / GREENE / [publi-
sher's device] / Published for / The British Publisher's
Guild Limited / by John Lane   The Bodley Head Ltd.

Collation: 96 leaves.

Pagination: p. [i] half-title; p. [ii] blank; p. [iii] title-
page; p. [iv] publication, reprinting and publishing notices;
pp. v-vi CONTENTS; pp. vii-xi INTRODUCTION; p. [xii] blank;
pp. 1-179 text; p. [180] blank.

Printing: Times Roman, 11 pt. (Introduction) and 10 pt.
(text), printed in Great Britain.

10.5 x 18 cm., white paper, all edges trimmed; perfect binding and printed wrappers with the following printed in red
and yellow on the cover: The Best of Saki / Selected and /
introduced by / Graham Greene / Guild Books / one shilling
and six pence net / [publishing device], and a man and woman
in Edwardian dress in the background. The back cover carries
a description of the collection (black on white) and a small
numeral 423 in the lower right corner. The title and author
are on the spine.

Price: 1s. 6d. First published in Guild Book in December
1950.

Contents: Introduction -- vii. Reginald (1904). Reginald at
the Theatre -- 1. Reginald on House-Parties -- 3. Reginald's
Drama -- 5. Reginald in Russia (1910). The Reticence of
Lady Anne -- 8. Gabriel-Ernest -- 11. Cross-Currents --
17. The Mouse -- 23. The Chronicles of Clovis (1911).
Esmé -- 27. The Match-Maker -- 32. Tobermory -- 34. The
Background -- 42. The Unrest-Cure -- 45. The Jesting of
Arlington Stringham -- 51. Sredni Vashtar -- 54. The Quest
-- 59. The Easter Egg -- 64. The Peace of Mowsle Barton --
68. The Talking-Out of Tarrington -- 75. The Secret Sin of
Septimus Brope -- 77. Beasts and Super-Beasts (1914). The
She-Wolf -- 86. The Boar-Pig -- 92. The Brogue -- 97. The
Open Window -- 102. The Schartz-Metter-Klume Method -- 105.
The Seventh Pullet -- 110. Clovis on Parental Responsibili-
ties -- 116. A Holiday Task -- 119. The Stalled Ox -- 124.

The Story-Teller -- 129.   A Defensive Diamond -- 134.   The
Elk -- 138.   The Lumber Room -- 143.   The Toys of Peace
(1923).   Louise -- 149.   The Couests -- 153.   The Penance --
157.   Quail Seed -- 162.   The Seven Cream Jugs -- 168.
Hyacinth -- 174.

Notes: The copy examined is in the British Library
(W.P. 10101/62).
    The printing and publishing notices on the verso of the
title-page indicate that the date of the first edition is
1930, that it was reprinted ten times and that the last reprint was in 1943.   The first Guild Book printing is noted as
1950.   This would imply that the 1950 edition is simply another reprint; however, a note on the back cover says that
Greene has chosen these stories and that his introduction is
an "accompaniment to his selection."   Greene's introduction
is reprinted in *The Lost Childhood* and *Collected Essays* as
"The Burden of Childhood."   Greene has dated the essay 1950
in the reprinting.

b. *First American Edition* (1961)

THE BEST OF / SAKI / (H. H. MUNRO) / *Selected and with an
Introduction by* / GRAHAM GREENE / New York: THE VIKING
PRESS: Publishers

Collation: perfect bound, 96 leaves.

Pagination: as first English edition, except p. [ii] carries
author's advertisement.

Printing: typeface as in English edition, printed in the
U.S.A. by the Murray Printing Company.

12 x 19 cm., white paper, all edges trimmed; bound in card
wrappers printed blue, magenta and black on white on the
front cover with the title and author included in the cover
design signed "Woods" at the right tail.   The back cover carries advertisements.

Price: $1.25.   Published in 1961.

Notes: The copy examined is in the compiler's collection.
Another copy has been seen in the Library of Congress
(PZ3/.M9274/Bg).

A26   THE LOST CHILDHOOD   1951

a. *First Edition*

THE / LOST CHILDHOOD / and other essays / by / GRAHAM GREENE /
1951 / EYRE & SPOTTISWOODE / London

Collation: [A]^8 B-M^8, 96 leaves.

Pagination: p. [1] half-title; p. [2] author's advertisement;
p. [3] title-page; p. [4] printing and publishing notices;
p. [5] acknowledgments; p. [6] blank; pp. 7-[8] CONTENTS;
p. [9] fly-title; p. [10] blank; p. [11] PART ONE / PERSONAL
PROLOGUE; p. [12] blank; pp. 13-17 text of part one; pp. 13-
17 THE LOST CHILDHOOD; p. [18] blank; p. [19] PART TWO /
NOVELS AND NOVELISTS; p. [20] blank; pp. 21-117 text of part
two; pp. 21-30 HENRY JAMES: THE PRIVATE UNIVERSE; pp. 31-39
HENRY JAMES: THE RELIGIOUS ASPECT; pp. 40-44 THE PORTRAIT OF
A LADY; pp. 45-48 THE PLAYS OF HENRY JAMES; pp. 49-50 THE
LESSON OF THE MASTER; pp. 51-57 THE YOUNG DICKENS; pp. 58-65
FIELDING AND STERNE; pp. 66-68 FROM FEATHERS TO IRON; pp. 69-
73 FRANÇOIS MAURIAC; pp. 74-76 THE BURDEN OF CHILDHOOD;
pp. 77-78 MAN MADE ANGRY; pp. 79-83 WALTER DE LA MARE'S SHORT
STORIES; pp. 84-86 THE SARATOGA TRUNK; pp. 87-88 THE POKER-
FACE; pp. 89-91 FORD MADOX FORD; pp. 92-94 FREDERICK ROLFE /
EDWARDIAN INFERNO; pp. 94-96 FROM THE DEVIL'S SIDE; pp. 96-97
A SPOILED PRIEST; pp. 98-99 REMEMBERING MR. JONES; pp. 100-
101 THE DOMESTIC BACKGROUND; pp. 102-103 ISIS IDOL; pp. 104-
105 THE LAST BUCHAN; pp. 106-111 BEATRIX POTTER; pp. 112-114
HARKAWAY'S OXFORD; pp. 115-117 THE UNKNOWN WAR; p. [118]
blank; p. [119] PART THREE / SOME CHARACTERS; p. [120] blank;
pp. 121-170 text of part three; pp. 121-125 FRANCIS PARKMAN;
pp. 126-128 SAMUEL BUTLER; pp. 129-131 THE UGLY ACT; pp. 132-
134 ERIC GILL; pp. 135-136 INVINCIBLE IGNORANCE; pp. 137-142
HERBERT READ; pp. 143-152 GEORGE DARLEY; pp. 153-155 AN UN-
HEROIC DRAMATIST; pp. 156-157 DR. OATES OF SALAMANCA; pp. 158-
160 A HOAX ON MR. HULTON; pp. 161-162 DON IN MEXICO; pp. 163-
164 PORTRAIT OF A MAIDEN LADY; pp. 165-167 MR. COOK'S CENTURY;
pp. 168-170 GREAT DOG OF WEIMAR; p. [171] PART FOUR / PER-
SONAL POSTSCRIPT; p. [172] blank; pp. 173-191 text of part
four; pp. 173-176 THE REVOLVER IN THE CORNER CUPBOARD;
pp. 177-179 VIVE LE ROI; pp. 180-182 FILM LUNCH; pp. 183-185
BOOK MARKET; pp. 186-188 BOMBING MANOEUVRE; pp. 189-191 AT
HOME; p. [192] blank.

Printing: an old face type, similar to Poliphilus, 11 pt.,
printed in Great Britain by Butler and Tanner Ltd., Frome and
London.

13.5 x 21.5 cm., white paper, all edges trimmed; bound in
gray cloth over boards with the title, author and publisher
stamped in black on the spine.

Price: 12s. 6d. Published in March 1951.

Contents: Part One: Personal Prologue. The Lost Childhood --
13. Part Two: Novels and Novelists. Henry James: The Pri-
vate Universe -- 21. Henry James: The Religious Aspect -- 31.
The Portrait of a Lady -- 40. The Plays of Henry James -- 45.
The Lesson of the Master -- 49. The Young Dickens -- 51.
Fielding and Sterne -- 58. From Feathers to Iron -- 66.
François Mauriac -- 69. The Burden of Childhood -- 74. Man
Made Angry -- 77. Walter de la Mare's Short Stories -- 79.
The Saratoga Trunk -- 84. The Poker-Face -- 87. Ford Madox
Ford -- 89. Frederick Rolfe: Edwardian Inferno -- 92.
Frederick Rolfe: From the Devil's Side -- 94. Frederick
Rolfe: A Spoiled Priest -- 96. Remembering Mr. Jones -- 98.
The Domestic Background -- 100. Isis Idol -- 102. The Last
Buchan -- 104. Beatrix Potter -- 106. Harkaway's Oxford --
112. The Unknown War -- 115. Part Three: Some Characters.
Francis Parkman -- 121. Samuel Butler -- 126. The Ugly
Act -- 129. Eric Gill -- 132. Invincible Ignorance -- 135.
Herbert Read -- 137. George Darley -- 143. An Unheroic
Dramatist -- 153. Dr. Oates of Salamanca -- 156. A Hoax on
Mr. Hulton -- 158. Don in Mexico -- 161. Portrait of a
Maiden Lady -- 163. Mr. Cook's Century -- 165. Great Dog of
Weimar -- 168. Part Four: Personal Postscript. The Revolver
in the Corner Cupboard -- 173. Vive Le Roi -- 177. Film
Lunch -- 180. Book Market -- 183. Bombing Monoeuvre -- 186.
At Home -- 189.

Notes: The copy examined is in the British Library
(12360/ff 35).
       "Henry James: The Private Universe" first appeared in
The English Novelists, edited by Derek Verschoyle. "Henry
James: The Religious Aspect" first appeared in *Contemporary
Essays 1933,* edited by Sylva Norman. The introduction to
The Portrait of a Lady was first published in the Oxford Uni-
versity Press "World's Classics" edition of the novel. "The
Young Dickens" appeared earlier as an introduction in the
Hamish Hamilton edition of *Oliver Twist.* "Fielding and
Sterne" first appeared in *From Anne to Victoria,* edited by
Bonamy Dobrée. "The Burden of Childhood" appeared in

John Lane's *The Best of Saki* as an introduction. The essay
on "Walter de la Mare's Short Stories" was first published in
Faber and Faber's *Tribute to Walter de la Mare*. "The Revolver
in the Corner Cupboard" appeared first in *The Saturday Book*.
Other essays appeared first in the following periodicals: *The
New Statesman*, *The Spectator*, *Time and Tide*, *The London Mer-
cury*, *Night and Day*, *France Libre*, *Horizon*, *The Month*, *The
Tablet* and *The Listener*.

b. *First American Edition* (1952)

THE / LOST CHILDHOOD / and other essays / by / GRAHAM GREENE /
1952 / THE VIKING PRESS / New York

Collation: as first English edition, 96 leaves.

Pagination: as first English edition.

Printing: similar to Poliphilus, 11 pt., printed in the
U.S.A.

13.8 x 21.5 cm., white paper, all edges trimmed, top edges
colored yellow; bound in brown cloth over boards with the
author, title and publisher separated by curved line devices
and stamped in gold on the spine.

Price: $3.50. Published in February 1952.

Notes: The copy examined is in the Library of Congress
(PR99/.GG843/1952).
    Aside from slight changes in the author's advertisement,
the title-page, and the title-page verso, this edition seems
to be an exact reprint of the English edition, utilizing,
perhaps, the identical plates.

A27   THE END OF THE AFFAIR   1951

a. *First Edition*

THE END OF THE / AFFAIR / *by* / Graham Greene / [publisher's device] / [rule] / WILLIAM HEINEMANN LTD / MELBOURNE :: LONDON :: TORONTO

Collation: $[A]^8$ $B-O^8$ $P/P*^{2/8}$, 244 leaves.

Pagination: p. [i] half-title; p. [ii] author's advertisement; p. [iii] title-page; p. [iv] publication and printing notices; p. [v] dedication; p. [vi] quotation; p. 1 BOOK ONE / I; pp. 1-51 text of book one, with divisional numerals on pp. 1, 17, 24, 28, 31, 36, 46; p. 52 BOOK TWO / I; pp. 52-104 text of book two, with divisional numerals on pp. 52, 58, 69, 75, 79, 86, 91, 100; p. 105 BOOK THREE / I; pp. 105-149 text of book three, with divisional numerals on pp. 105, 107, 114, 121, 124, 135, 136; p. 150 BOOK FOUR / I; pp. 150-162 text of book four, with divisional numerals on pp. 150 and 159; p. 163 BOOK FIVE / I; pp. 163-237 text of book five, with divisional numerals on pp. 163, 180, 186, 191, 204, 210, 214, 227; p. [238] blank

Printing: Goudy Old Style, 11 pt., printed in Great Britain at the Windmill Press, Kingswood, Surrey.

12 x 18 cm., white paper, all edges trimmed; bound in gray cloth over boards with the title, author and publisher stamped in gold on the spine; a windmill device is blind stamped at the right tail of the back cover.

Price: 10s. 6d. Published in September 1951 in a dust jacket with the top half printed gray (the title in white) and the bottom half white (the author in gray) on the front cover.

Dedication: To C.

Notes: The copies examined were in the British Library (NNN 1900) and at Bertram Rota, Booksellers, 30-31 Long Acre, London, WC2 E9LT.

     In this edition the divisional numeral for [chapter] VIII of Book Two seems to be missing. This oversight is corrected in later editions.

     Greene prefaces the novel with a quotation from Leon Bloy: "Man has places in his heart which do not yet exist,

and into them enters suffering in order that they may have
existence."

In the "Introduction" to the novel first published in
Introductions to Three Novels (Stockholm, Norstedt, 1962)
Greene reminds the reader that along with *The Third Man* -- a
novel developed out of a screenplay -- *The End of the Affair*
was one of his first attempts to use the first person and
that it was practice for the more successful (in his estimation) novel about Vietnam, *The Quiet American*. Though Wayne
Booth mentions Fowler in his "Gallery of Unreliable Narrators"
(*The Rhetoric of Fiction*, Chicago, 1963), he misses Bendrix,
who deserves the honor at least as much.

Greene also remarks that the book began to take shape in
December 1948 in Capri and that *Great Expectations* and Ford
Madox Ford's *The Good Soldier* were very influential on *The
End of the Affair*. He judges *The Quiet American*, though, to
be more successful.

The American edition is dedicated "To Catherine with
Love" rather than "To C." When Greene mentions that the
Baron von Hügel study of St. Catherine of Genoa also had an
influence on the book, one sees that the name was on the
author's mind.

b. *First American Edition* (1951)

Graham Greene / THE / *End of the Affair* [rectangular device
surrounding title] / *New York* / THE VIKING PRESS / MCMLI

Collation: [1]-[3]^{16} [4]-[5]^{14} [6]-[8]^{16}, 124 leaves.

Pagination: p. [i] half-title; p. [ii] author's advertisement; p. [iii] title-page; p. [iv] copyright, publishing,
publication, type and printing notices; p. [v] dedication;
p. [vi] blank; p. [1] fly-title and quotation; p. [2] blank;
p. 3 BOOK ONE / I; pp. 3-53 text of book one, with divisional
numerals on pp. 3, 19, 26, 30, 33, 38, 48; p. [54] blank;
p. 55 BOOK TWO / I; pp. 55-107 text of book two, with divisional numerals on pp. 55, 61, 72, 78, 82, 89, 94, 103;
p. [108] blank; p. 109 BOOK THREE / I; pp. 109-152 text of
book three, with divisional numerals on pp. 109, 111, 118,
125, 127, 138, 139; p. 153 BOOK FOUR / I; pp. 153-165 text of
book four, with divisional numerals on pp. 153 and 162;
p. [166] blank; p. 167 BOOK FIVE / I; pp. 167-240 text of
book five, with divisional numerals on pp. 167, 184, 190,
195, 208, 214, 218, 230; pp. [241-242] blank.

Printing: Granjon and Deepdene, 12 pt., printed in the U.S.A.
by The Colonial Press, Inc.

13.5 x 20 cm., white paper, top edge colored green, all edges
trimmed; the spine is in black cloth with the author, title
and publisher stamped in gold and separated by green vertical
rule devices stamped in green; the front cover is in brown
cloth with the title surrounded by a rectangular rule device
stamped in green, with the back cover in the same black cloth
as the spine.

Price: $3.00. Published in October 1951 in a dust jacket
which has a green-over-gold background on the front cover and
spine; the front cover carries the title in white above the
author in gold and "Author of *The Heart of the Matter*" in
white; the spine also carries the title in white, the author
in gold and the publisher in white; the back cover carries a
comment by Evelyn Waugh on Greene.

Dedication: To Catherine with love

Notes: The copies examined are in the Library of Congress
(PZ3/.G8319/E1) and in the libraries of the University of
Louisville (this copy having the dust jacket described) and
West Virginia State College.

    The novel carries the same epigraph as does the English
edition.

    For a note on the dedication, see the English edition.

A28   THE LITTLE HORSE BUS   1952

a. *First Edition*

The Little Horse Bus [in script] / GRAHAM GREENE /
ILLUSTRATED BY / DOROTHY CRAIGIE / COPYRIGHT 1952 • PRINTED
IN GREAT BRITAIN BY JARROLD & SONS LIMITED NORWICH / MAX
PARRISH • LONDON

Collation: [1]-4^4, 16 leaves.

Pagination: p. [1] recto of free endpaper and half of illustration; pp. [2-3] title-page and illustration; pp. 4-5 text
and illustration; pp. 6-7 text and illustration; p. 8 text and
illustration; p. [9] illustration; pp. 10-[11] text and illustration; p. 12 text and illustration; p. [13] illustration;
p. [14] text and illustration; p. [15] text and illustration;
pp. [16-17] text and illustration; pp. 18-19 text and illustrations; p. [20] text and illustration; p. [21] illustration; pp. 22-[23] text and illustration; pp. [24-25] text and
illustration; p. [26] text and illustration; p. 27 illustration; p. [28] text and illustration; p. [29] illustration;
p. 30 text and illustration; p. [31] text and illustration;
pp. [32-33] illustration; p. [34] text and illustration;
p. 35 recto of back free endpaper and text and illustration.

Printing: Baskerville, 18 pt., printed in Great Britain by
Jarrold & Sons Limited, Norwich.

17.5 x 21.5 cm., white paper, all edges trimmed; bound in red
cloth over boards with title, author and publisher stamped in
gold along the spine; a design representing the horse bus is
stamped in gold on the cover; illustrated endpapers form part
of the book (see *Notes*).

Price: 8s. 6d. Published in November 1952.

Illustrations: [the Little Horse Bus and the hansom cab meeting head-on] — [front endpaper and page 1]. [Little Horse
Bus chasing thieves in hansom cab] — [2-3]. [street and Mr.
Potter's shop] — 4-5. [Hygienic Emporium] — 6. [the cats
have to go] — 7. [the hansom cab, driver and Beauty, the
horse] — 8-[9]. [Tim making deliveries on his bicycle] —
10. [Mr. Potter "dreaming"] — [11]. [Mr. Potter finds the
neglected horse bus in the garage] — 12-[13]. [delivery
notice and picture of Brandy, the horse] — [14]. [old lady
returning to Mr. Potter's shop] — [15]. [hansom cab making

deposit to bank, thieves lurking behind pillar box] -- [16-
17]. [puzzle -- find the thieves] -- 18. [wanted poster
showing the two thieves] -- 19. [Little Horse Bus in pursuit
of the thieves in the Hansom Cab] -- [20-21]. [policeman
phoning Scotland Yard] -- 22-[23]. [Brandy chasing the Hansom Cab] -- [24-25]. [Hangman's Wharf] -- [26]-27. [the
Little Horse Bus still looking for the hansom cab] -- [28-
29]. [fingerprints] -- 30. ["to Hangman's Wharf"] -- [31].
[the Little Horse Bus discovers the hansom cab] -- [32-33].
[the reward ceremony] -- [34]. [Hygienic Emporium, To Let]
-- 35. [Mr. Potter's shop crowded with people] -- [back
endpaper].

Notes: The copy examined is in the British Library (12834
b.b. 46).
    Concerning the pagination of this volume, page [1] be-
gins with the recto of the front free endpaper. This page
also serves as the second half of an illustration. Page 35
is the recto of the back free endpaper.
    The Little Horse Bus is the third of Greene's children's
books.

b. *First American Edition* (1954)

The Little Horse Bus [in script] / GRAHAM GREENE /
ILLUSTRATED BY / DOROTHY CRAIGIE / COPYRIGHT 1952 · LOTHROP,
LEE & SHEPARD CO., INC. / 419 FOURTH AVENUE, NEW YORK 16,
N.Y.

Collation: as first English edition, 16 leaves.

Pagination: as first English edition.

Printing: as first English edition.

18 x 21.5 cm., white paper, all edges trimmed; bound in gray
embossed paper over boards with title, author and publisher
stamped in black on the spine and a design representing the
horse bus stamped in black on the cover; illustrated endpapers form part of the book (see *Notes*).

Price: $2.00. Published in March 1954.

Illustrations: as first English edition.

Notes: The copy examined is in the Miami University Library
(E/G8221).

   As in the first English edition, page [1] begins with
the recto of the front free endpaper. This page also serves
as the second half of an illustration. Page 35 is the recto
of the back free endpaper.

A29   THE LIVING ROOM   1953

a. *First Edition*

THE LIVING ROOM / *A Play in Two Acts* / BY / GRAHAM GREENE /
[small star device] / [publisher's device] / [rule] /
WILLIAM HEINEMANN LTD / MELBOURNE :: LONDON :: TORONTO

Collation: [A]^8 B-E^8, 40 leaves.

Pagination: p. [i-ii] blank; p. [iii] half-title; p. [iv]
author's advertisement; p. [v] title-page; p. [vi] performing
rights, copyright, acknowledgments, publishing, publication
and printing notices; p. [vii] dedication; p. [viii] CHARAC-
TERS; p. [ix] SCENES; p. [x] notes on the first production;
p. 1 ACT I / SCENE I; pp. 1-37 text of act one, with scenes
beginning on pp. 1 and 18; p. 38 ACT II / SCENE I; pp. 38-67
text of act two, with scenes beginning on pp. 38 and 61;
pp. [68-70] blank.

Printing: Garamond, 11 pt., printed in Great Britain at the
Windmill Press, Kingswood, Surrey.

12 x 18.5 cm., white paper, all edges trimmed; bound in red
cloth over boards with author, title and publisher stamped
in gold along the spine; a windmill device is blind stamped
at the right tail of the back cover.

Price: 7s. 6d. Published on May 18, 1953.

Dedication: To Catherine with love

Notes: The copy examined is in the British Library
(11784/aa 66).
    On page [vi] Greene thanks Roy Campbell for permission
to use a passage from his translation of "The Poems of St.
John of the Cross" (The Harvil Press) at the beginning of
Act II.
    The play produced by Peter Glenville with scenery by
Leslie Hurry was first presented on Thursday, April 16, 1953,
at Wyndham's Theatre, London. The cast is listed below.

Mary (the daily woman)	Dorothy Dewhurst
Michael Dennis	John Robinson
Rose Pemberton	Dorothy Tutin
Miss Teressa Browne	Mary Jerrold
Miss Helen Browne	Violet Farebrother

Father James Browne   Eric Portman
Mrs. Dennis   Valerie Taylor

In *Three Plays* (an omnibus reprint of *The Living Room*, *The Potting Shed* and *The Complaisant Lover* [Mercury Books - 1961]) Greene says that his turn to the drama was a welcome change of pace from writing novels and films. This break required a shift in technique immediately evident when one considers his first play, *The Living Room*, and the fact that all the play's action is restricted to the one room of the title. Of interest also is Greene's attraction toward melodrama. One aspect linking Greene's favorite plays in his essay *British Dramatists* is that they are usually melodramatic or farcical. Generally Greene prefers social comedy full of satire while his tastes in tragedy, perhaps predictably, run toward the Jacobean.

The first appearance of *The Living Room* was in a Swedish translation published by P.A. Norstedt & Söners, Stockholm, 1952.

The play seems to have begun to take shape with some sketched lines on the back endpapers of Greene's copy of *Devotional Poets of the XVIIth Century*. A mimeograph script of *The Living Room* bears a typing service stamp: "1952 June 19." This was not the final version.

b. *First American Edition* (1954)

THE / LIVING ROOM / A Play in Two Acts by / GRAHAM GREENE / New York • The Viking Press • 1954

Collation: [1]-[4]^{16}, 64 leaves.

Pagination: p. [1] half-title; p. [2] author's advertisement; p. [3] title-page; p. [4] copyright, publishing, caution, acknowledgments, Library of Congress number and printing notices; p. [5] dedication; p. [6] blank; p. [7] notes on the first production; p. [8] SCENES; p. [9] fly-title; p. [10] blank; p. 11 ACT ONE / SCENE I; pp. 11-75 text of act one, with scenes beginning on pp. 11 and 42; p. 76 ACT TWO / SCENE I; pp. 76-126 text of act two, with scenes beginning on pp. 76 and 115; pp. [127-128] blank.

Printing: Baskerville, 11 pt., printed in the U.S.A. by The Colonial Press, Inc.

12 x 18.5 cm., white paper, all edges trimmed; front and back
covers bound in maroon decorated paper over boards, with the
spine in gray cloth and the author, title and publisher
stamped in red.

Price: $2.50. Published in June 1954.

Dedication: To Catherine with love

Notes: The copy examined is in the library of West Virginia
State College (PR 6013/R44 L5).

A30   THE LITTLE STEAMROLLER   1953

a. *First Edition*

The Little Steamroller [in script] / A STORY OF ADVENTURE,
MYSTERY AND DETECTION / GRAHAM GREENE / ILLUSTRATED BY
DOROTHY CRAIGIE / MAX PARRISH · LONDON

Collation: [1]-[3]^6, 18 leaves.

Pagination: p. [1] half-title; p. [2] copyright and printing
notices and illustration; p. [3] title-page and illustration;
pp. [4-5] text and illustration; p. [6] illustration; p. [7]
text and illustration; p. 8 text and illustration; p. [9] text
and illustration; pp. 10-13 text and illustrations; p. [14]
text and illustration; p. 15 illustration; p. 16 text and
illustration; p. 17 illustration; pp. 18-19 text and illus-
tration; pp. [20-21] text and illustrations; p. [22] illus-
tration; p. [23] text and illustration; p. 24 text and illus-
tration; p. 25 illustration; p. [26] illustration; p. [27]
text and illustration; p. [28] text and illustration; p. 29
illustration; p. [30] text and illustration; p. [31] illustration; pp. 32-33 text and illustration; pp. [34-35] illustration; p. [36] text and illustration.

Printing: Baskerville, 16 pt., printed in Great Britain by
Graphic Reproductions Ltd., London.

18.5 x 21.5 cm., white paper, all edges trimmed; bound in
illustrated paper over boards with the title, author and
publisher printed in red and brown on a yellow spine; the
title, author, illustrator and illustrations are on the
front cover; illustrations on the back cover and the covers
are predominantly blue.

Price: 8s. 6d. Published on October 5, 1953.

Illustrations: [terminal, Mr. King with baggage cart and
Bill Driver looking at paper pinned under Little Steamroller]
-- [2-3]. [aerial view of London airport] -- [4-5]. [Bill
Driver, Little Steamroller and policeman at the gate] --
[6-7]. [secret mark of the Black Hand gang] -- 8. [Custom's
Officer and smugglers] -- [9]. [illustration of code] --
10-11. [Little Steamroller and dark cloud] -- 12-13. [Mr.
King and Mr. Scott plotting in Africa] -- [14]-15. [plane
flying through clouds -- 16-17. [snow falling on runway and
terminal] -- 18-19. [announcement speaker box] -- 20.

[Little Steamroller (front view)] -- [21]. [Mr. King leaving plane] -- [22-23]. [Bill Driver awakened by the puffing from the Little Steamroller's stack] -- 24-25. [Mr. King passing through H.M. Customs] -- [26-27]. [Mr. King leaving customs and Mr. King's paper under Little Steamroller's wheels] -- [28]. [Police! Smugglers! Help!] -- 29. [Little Steamroller "charging" Mr. King] -- [30-31]. [Mr. King, stunned, sitting on ground and surrounded by policemen; Bill Driver approaching] -- 32-33. [Little Steamroller, Bill Driver and policemen outside Scotland Yard] -- [34-35]. [Little Steamroller wearing the Queen's Police Medal (front view)] -- 35.

Notes: The copy examined is in the British Library (12836 d.d. 11).
      This volume is the fourth and last of Greene's children's books.

b. *First American Edition* (1955)

The Little Steamroller [in script] / A STORY OF ADVENTURE, MYSTERY AND DETECTION / GRAHAM GREENE / ILLUSTRATED BY DOROTHY CRAIGIE / LOTHROP, LEE & SHEPARD CO., INC. / 419 FOURTH AVENUE, NEW YORK 16, N.Y. / [facing title page:] FIRST PUBLISHED 1955. PRINTED IN GREAT BRITAIN / BY GRAPHIC REPRODUCTIONS LTD LONDON

Collation: as first English edition.

Pagination: as first English edition.

Printing: as first English edition.

Price: $2.00. Published in March 1955.

Notes: The copy examined is in the Library of Congress (PZ7/.G8295/Lj). The library has stamped September 12, 1955, on the title-page verso.

A31   NINO CAFFÈ   1953

First Edition

[facsimile of a painting entitled "Red Ladder"] / NINO CAFFÈ /
KNOEDLER / *14 East 57th Street* / NEW YORK

Collation: [1]^2, 2 leaves.

Pagination: p. [1] cover and title-page; pp. [2-3] text;
p. [4] printing notice.

Printing: Bodoni, 11 pt., printed in Italy by Instituto
Grafico Tiberino, Via Graeta 14, Rome.

16 x 23.3 cm., two conjugate leaves -- one sheet horizontal
format pamphlet with a full-color reproduction of a painting
entitled "Red Ladder" by Nino Caffè on the cover; the signed
text of Greene's remarks covers the two inside pages; the
back cover is blank except for the printer's name and address
at the tail.

Price: distributed free during the exhibition in December
1953.

Notes: The copy examined is in the library of M. Knoedler &
Company, Inc., 19 East 170th Street, New York, New York 10021
(Bne/1).
       The number printed is unknown.
       It is evident that Greene's reason for discussing in
this pamphlet the work of the painter Nino Caffè is his attraction toward the painter's subject matter: priests or
nuns caught in amusing but revealing moments when the empiri-
cal world impinges on their lives. Greene comments on the
interesting combinations of observable qualities in these
figures, a touch of vanity, bewilderment and "childlike en-
joyment." Where the artist is most accurate, though, according to Greene, is in his remembering that these people, for
all the amusement they cause, are people with vocations.

A32   ESSAIS CATHOLIQUES   1953

First Edition

GRAHAM GREENE / ESSAIS / CATHOLIQUES / TRADUCTION DE /
MARCELLE SIBON / *ÉDITIONS DU SEUIL* / *27, rue Jacob, Paris VI*^{c}

Collation: [1]-[8]^8, 64 leaves.

Pagination: pp. [1-2] blank; p. [3] half-title; p. [4]
author's advertisement; p. [5] title-page; p. [6] blank;
p. [7] MESSAGE AUX CATHOLIQUES FRANÇAIS; p. [8] blank;
pp. 9-[14] text; p. 15 LA CIVILIZATION CHRÉTIENNE / EST-ELLE
EN PÉRIL?; p. [16] blank; pp. 17-[35] text; p. [36] blank;
p. [37] LES PARADOXES / DU CHRISTIANISME; p. [38] blank;
pp. 39-[49] text; p. [50] blank; p. [51] LE PARADOXE DU PAPE;
p. [52] blank; pp. 53-[78] text; p. [79] NOTRE DAME / ET SON
ASSOMPTION; p. [80] blank; pp. 81-[98] text; p. [99] L'ASPECT
RELIGIEUX / DE HENRY JAMES; p. [100] blank; pp. 101-[121]
text; p. [122] blank; p. [123] TABLE; p. [124] blank; p. [125]
CONTENTS; p. [126] colophon; pp. [127-128] blank.

Printing: Garamond, 14 pt., printed in France by André
Tournon and Company.

13.5 x 18.5 cm., white paper, all edges trimmed; printed
wrappers with the author, title, translator and publisher on
the cover and advertisements for other works on the back
cover; printing on the cover in black and green; colophon.

Price: 300 francs. Published in 1953.

Contents: Message Aux Catholiques Français -- 9. La Civilization Chrétienne Est-Elle En Péril? -- 17. Les Paradoxes Du
Christianisme -- 39. Le Paradoxe Du Pape -- 53. Notre Dame
Et Son Assomption -- 81. L'Aspect Religieux De Henry James
-- 101.

Notes: The copy examined is in the British Library
(x.108/10864).
      The colophon on page [126] is as follows: Acheve D'
Imprimar / Sur Alfa cellunof / en 1953 Par / André Tournon et
c^{ie} / D. L. 1er tr 1953 - N° 533 / (N° 630).
      Of the six essays in this collection translated from the
English by Marcelle Sibon, the first three have never appeared in English, though they did appear earlier in French

("Message Aux Catholiques Français" in *Dieu Vivant*, No. 14 (1949), pp. 31-35;"La Civilisation Chrétienne Est-Elle En Péril?" in *La Table Ronde*, No. 2 (1948), pp. 211-223; "Les Paradoxes Du Christianisme" in *Dieu Vivant*, No. 18 (1951), pp. 35-42).

A33   TWENTY-ONE STORIES   1954

a. *First Edition*

[rule] / TWENTY-ONE STORIES / GRAHAM GREENE / [publisher's
device] / [rule] / WILLIAM HEINEMANN LTD · LONDON / MELBOURNE
··· TORONTO

Collation: [A]^8 B-O^8 P^4 Q^8, 124 leaves.

Pagination: pp. [i-ii] blank; p. [iii] half-title; p. iv
author's advertisement; p. [v] title-page; p. [vi] publication and printing notices; p. [vii] CONTENTS; p. [viii] note
of additional stories not published in the first collection;
pp. 1-34 THE BASEMENT ROOM, with numbered division headings
on pp. 1, 8, 14, 20, 27; pp. 35-46 THE END OF THE PARTY;
pp. 47-50 I SPY; pp. 51-56 THE INNOCENT; pp. 57-74 A DRIVE IN
THE COUNTRY; pp. [75]-87 ACROSS THE BRIDGE; pp. 88-95
JUBILEE; pp. 96-105 BROTHER; pp. 106-111 PROOF POSITIVE;
pp. 112-131 A CHANCE FOR MR. LEVER; pp. 132-146 THE HINT OF
AN EXPLANATION; pp. 147-154 THE SECOND DEATH; pp. 155-160 A
DAY SAVED; pp. 161-168 A LITTLE PLACE OFF THE EDGWARE ROAD;
pp. 169-173 THE CASE FOR THE DEFENCE; pp. 174-191 WHEN GREEK
MEETS GREEK, with numbered division headings on pp. 174, 178,
181, 184, 187; pp. 192-199 MEN AT WORK; pp. 200-204 ALAS,
POOR MALING; pp. [205]-210 THE BLUE FILM; pp. [211]-218
SPECIAL DUTIES; pp. 219-239 THE DESTRUCTORS, with numbered
division headings on pp. 219, 227, 230, 237; p. [240] blank.

Printing: Bembo, 11 pt., printed in Great Britain at the
Windmill Press, Kingswood, Surrey.

11 x 17 cm., white paper, all edges trimmed; bound in black
cloth over boards with author and title stamped in gold over
a red rectangle at the top of the spine, with the publisher
stamped in gold at the bottom of the spine; a windmill device
is blind stamped at the right tail of the back cover.

Price: 8s. 6d. Published November 8, 1954.

Contents: The Basement Room -- 1. The End of the Party --
35. I Spy -- 47. The Innocent -- 51. A Drive in the
Country -- 57. Across the Bridge -- 75. Jubilee -- 88.
Brother -- 96. Proof Positive -- 106. A Chance for Mr.
Lever -- 112. The Hint of an Explanation -- 132. The Second
Death -- 147. A Day Saved -- 155. A Little Place Off the
Edgware Road -- 161. A Case for the Defence -- 169. When

Greek Meets Greek -- 174.   Men At Work -- 192.   Alas, Poor
Maling -- 200.   The Blue Film -- 205.   Special Duties -- 211.
The Destructors -- 219.

Notes: The copies examined are in the British Library
(12653 bb 37) and the Library of Congress (PZ3/.G8319/Tw/2).
    As usual with library copies, the dust jackets have not
survived, but the "Uniform Edition" of Greene's works (of
which this item is volume 12 in the series) was issued with
a uniform dust jacket which may be described as follows: the
spine and front cover are divided horizontally into thirds,
the top and bottom thirds being maroon and the middle third
being gray.   On the cover on the top third the author is
printed in white, on the middle third the title is printed in
maroon, and on the bottom third is printed in white the edition with the Heinemann windmill device.   The spine carries
author and title on the top third, volume number on the middle third and publisher at the tail.
    This collection includes four stories that did not appear
in *Nineteen Stories*.   They are: "The Hint of an Explanation,"
"The Blue Film," "Special Duties," and "The Destructors."
Greene has withdrawn two stories which appeared in *Nineteen
Stories*.   These are: "The Lottery Ticket" and his unfinished
novel, "The Other Side of the Border."

b. *First American Edition* (1962)

21 Stories / by Graham Greene / [publisher's device] / *The
Viking Press* / *New York*

Collation: [1]-[8]^{16}, 128 leaves.

Pagination: p. [i] half-title; p. [ii] author's advertisement; p. [iii] title-page; p. [iv] copyright, printing, publishing, acknowledgment and Library of Congress card number;
pp. v-[vi] CONTENTS; p. [vii] note of additional stories not
published in first collection; p. [viii] blank; p. [1] fly-
title; p. [2] blank; pp. 3-36 text of THE BASEMENT ROOM, with
numbered division headings on pp. 3, 10, 17, 23, 29; pp. 37-
48 text of THE END OF THE PARTY; pp. 49-52 text of I SPY;
pp. 53-59 text of THE INNOCENT; pp. 60-77 text of A DRIVE IN
THE COUNTRY; pp. 78-90 text of ACROSS THE BRIDGE; pp. 91-98
text of JUBILEE; pp. 99-108 text of BROTHER; pp. 109-114 text
of PROOF POSITIVE; pp. 115-134 text of A CHANCE FOR MR.
LEVER; pp. 135-150 text of THE HINT OF AN EXPLANATION;

pp. 151–158 text of THE SECOND DEATH; pp. 159–164 text of A
DAY SAVED; pp. 165–172 text of A LITTLE PLACE OFF THE EDGWARE
ROAD; pp. 173–177 text of THE CASE FOR THE DEFENCE; pp. 178–
196 text of WHEN GREEK MEETS GREEK, with numbered division
headings on pp. 178, 182, 185, 189, 192; pp. 197–204 text of
MEN AT WORK; pp. 205–209 text of ALAS, POOR MALING; pp. 210–
216 text of THE BLUE FILM; pp. 217–224 text of SPECIAL DUTIES;
pp. 225–245 text of THE DESTRUCTORS, with numbered division
headings on pp. 225, 233, 236, 243; pp. [246–248] blank.

Printing: Baskerville, 11 pt., printed in the U.S.A.

13.4 x 20.3 cm., white paper, all edges trimmed, top edges
colored orange; bound in orange cloth over boards with the
publisher's viking ship device blind stamped at the bottom
right tail of the front cover and the title, author and publisher stamped in black on the spine.

Price: $3.95. Published in April 1962 in a dust jacket hav-
ing a front cover in stylized black, green and orange checker-
board pattern with the title and author over in white; the
spine carries the title, author and publisher in white on
black; the back cover carries a photo of the author.

Contents: The Basement Room –– 3. The End of the Party ––
37. I Spy –– 49. The Innocent –– 53. A Drive in the
Country –– 60. Across the Bridge –– 78. Jubilee –– 91.
Brother –– 99. Proof Positive –– 109. A Chance for Mr.
Lever –– 115. The Hint of an Explanation –– 135. The Second
Death –– 151. A Day Saved –– 159. A Little Place Off the
Edgware Road –– 165. The Case for the Defence –– 173. When
Greek Meets Greek –– 178. Men At Work –– 197. Alas, Poor
Maling –– 205. The Blue Film –– 210. Special Duties –– 217.
The Destructors –– 225.

Notes: The copies examined are at the libraries of the University of Florida (823.91G799n/1962) and the University of
Louisville. The copy with the dust jacket described was seen
at the University of Louisville.

A34   LOSER TAKES ALL   1955

a. *First Edition*

LOSER TAKES ALL / *by* / GRAHAM GREENE / [publisher's device] /
[rule] / WILLIAM HEINEMANN LTD / MELBOURNE :: LONDON ::
TORONTO

Collation: [A]^8 B-H^8 I/I*$^{2/8}$, 74 leaves.

Pagination: pp. [i-ii] blank; p. [iii] half-title; p. [iv]
author's advertisement; p. [v] title-page; p. [vi] publishing
and printing notices; p. [vii] dedication; p. [viii] blank;
p. [1] PART ONE; p. [2] blank; pp. 3-72 text of part one,
with chapter headings on pp. 3, 4, 9, 12, 22, 28, 37, 48, 60;
p. [73] PART TWO; p. [74] blank; pp. 75-125 text of part two,
with chapter headings on pp. 75, 90, 99, 115, 119; p. [126]
blank; p. [127] PART THREE; p. [128] blank; pp. 129-140 text
of part three, with chapter headings on pp. 129 and 136.

Printing: Baskerville, 12 pt., printed in Great Britain at
the Windmill Press, Kingswood, Surrey.

12 x 18.5 cm., white paper, all edges trimmed; bound in blue
cloth over boards with the title surrounded by a border
stamped in gold on the cover, and with ruling, title, author,
ruling and publisher stamped in gold on the spine; a windmill
device is blind stamped on the right tail of the back cover.

Price: 7s. 6d. Published on January 31, 1955.

Dedication: Dear Frere, ...

Notes: The copy examined is in the British Library (N.N.N.
5828). A later impression with the same binding was issued
in a dust jacket printed in blue and yellow on white. The
cover carried the author's name in white block letters across
the top and the title in italic black and blue across the
bottom. A stylized café table in blue and white on the left
side of the front cover turns into a stylized roulette wheel
in yellow and white; the author and publisher are printed
head and tail in black on yellow with the title between in
blue.
    In Greene's dedication to A. S. Frere of Heinemann's, he
makes it clear that he is not to be mistaken for the "I"
narrator. But, of course, once the idea is placed before the
reader, the comparison is tempting. Bertram is an accountant

who becomes obsessed with the challenge of gambling. Greene,
who was introduced to gambling at the tables by Alexander
Korda, likes not only the game but gambling on the stock market as well. His fascination with numbers has led him, according to Kenneth Tynan (*Persona Grata*, London, Wingate,
1953, p. 55) to collect auto registration numbers as does
Bendrix in *The End of the Affair*. In fact, one sees in Bertram the Greene that Greene thinks the critics see, the hell-
haunted Catholic involved with moral dilemmas and theological
paradoxes.

But what is more important is that *Loser Takes All* is
Greene's first published experiment with extended comedy.
And the novel is an attempt to link comedy (especially satire,
parody and burlesque) to the religious thriller.

b. *First American Edition* (1957)

LOSER / TAKES / ALL / [device] / *Graham Greene* / 1957 / *New
York* : *The Viking Press* [all surrounded by a square decorative border]

Collation: (perfect binding), 64 leaves.

Pagination: p. [1] half-title; p. [2] author's advertisement;
p. [3] title-page; p. [4] copyright, publishing, acknowledgment, Library of Congress card number and printing notices;
p. [5] dedication; p. [6] blank; p. [7] PART ONE; p. [8]
blank; pp. 9-68 text of part one, with chapter headings on
pp. 9, 10, 14, 17, 26, 31, 38, 47, 57; p. [69] PART TWO;
p. [70] blank; pp. 71-113 text of part two, with chapter
headings on pp. 71, 83, 91, 104, 108; p. [114] blank; p. [115]
PART THREE; p. [116] blank; pp. 117-126 text of part three,
with chapter headings on pp. 117 and 122; pp. [127-128] blank.

Printing: Imprint, 11 pt., printed in the U.S.A. by The
Colonial Press, Inc.

11.6 x 19.6 cm., white paper, all edges trimmed; bound in
card wrappers printed with a partial roulette wheel motif in
red, gold and black on the front cover, with the title, author
and "First U.S. book publication," "Compass Books," and "95
cents" also on the front cover; the back cover carries an
advertisement for the book; the author and title are printed
on the spine.

Price: $ .95. Published in September 1957.

Dedication: as first English edition.

Notes: The copy examined is in the Library of Congress (PZ3/.G8319/Lo/2). The library has stamped two dates, September 6, 1957, and September 11, 1957, on the title-page verso.

The cover design is by Bill English.

The first appearance of *Loser Takes All* in the U.S. was in a serialized version in *Harper's Magazine* for October, November and December 1955 and January 1956.

A35   THE QUIET AMERICAN   1955

a. *First Edition*

THE / QUIET AMERICAN / *by* / GRAHAM GREENE / [publisher's de-
vice] / [rule] / WILLIAM HEINEMANN LTD / MELBOURNE :: LONDON
:: TORONTO

Collation: [A]^{16} B–H^{16}, 128 leaves.

Pagination: p. [i] half-title; p. [ii] author's advertisement;
p. [iii] title-page; p. [iv] publication and printing notices;
p. [v] dedication and disclaimer; p. [vi] blank; p. [vii]
quotations; p. [viii] blank; p. [1] PART ONE; p. [2] blank;
pp. 3–83 text of part one, with chapter headings on pp. 3,
20, 34, 52, 74, and numbered division headings on pp. 20, 25,
34, 43, 52, 66, 74; p. [84] blank; p. [85] PART TWO; p. [86]
blank; pp. 87–174 text of part two, with chapter headings on
pp. 87, 103, 147, and numbered division headings on pp. 103,
112, 115, 137, 147, 156, 168; p. [175] PART THREE; p. [176]
blank; pp. 177–214 text of part three, with chapter headings
on pp. 177 and 201, and numbered division headings on pp.
177, 181, 189, 192, 196, 201, 206; p. [215] PART FOUR;
p. [216] blank; pp. 217–247 text of part four, with chapter
headings on pp. 217, 224, 244, and numbered division headings
on pp. 224, 228, 236; p. [248] blank.

Printing: Baskerville, 11 pt., printed in Great Britain at
the Windmill Press, Kingswood, Surrey.

12.5 x 19.5 cm., white paper, all edges trimmed; bound in
dark blue cloth over boards with the title, author and publisher stamped in gold on the spine and a windmill device
blind stamped at the right tail of the back cover.

Price: 13s. 6d. Published on December 5, 1955 ("overseas"
edition distributed November 28, 1955), having a dust jacket
with the author in red and title in black on a gray and white
background representing a woven wall; the title, author and
publisher are on the spine with advertisements for *Loser
Takes All* on the back.

Dedication: Dear Réné and Phuong, ...

Notes: The copies examined are in the British Library (N.N.N
7379) and the Library of Congress (PZ3/.G8319/Qui). Another
copy, identical to the above except for its having the dust

jacket described, was seen at Bell, Book and Radmall, 80 Long
Acre, London, WC2E 9N6.

The dedication is in the form of a letter and it is also
a disclaimer to the effect that Pyle, Granger, Fowler, Vigot
and Joe had no originals in Saigon or Hanoi. Greene also admits to having rearranged events. "This is a story and not
a piece of history...."

Greene has prefaced the text with the following quotations: "I do not like being moved: for the will is excited;
/ and action / Is a most dangerous thing; I tremble for something / factitious, / Some malpractice of heart and illegiti-
mate process; / We're so prone to these things, with our
terrible / notions of duty." -- A. H. CLOUGH. And "This is
the patent age of new inventions / For killing bodies, and
for saving souls / All propagated with the best intentions."
-- BYRON.

The text of the novel is dated "March 1952-June 1955."
These dates generally agree with Greene's trips to Indo-China
first for *Paris-Match*, then for *The Sunday Times* and *Le
Figaro*.

In the first part of his "Introduction" in the Collected
Edition, Greene describes his relationship with the French
commander in Hanoi, the rather comic-heroic and later pathe-
tic General de Lattre, and the general's suspicions that
Greene was a British agent.

He goes on to discuss the originals for some of the
characters, especially Pyle and Granger. He discusses the
"direct *rapportage*" of this novel and how his determination
to use what he had learned of first-person narrative and
time-shift technique in *The End of the Affair* was the de-
ciding factor in the choice of the journalist, Fowler, as
narrator.

b. *First American Edition* (1956)

GRAHAM GREENE / [decorative rule] / *The Quiet American* /
NEW YORK · THE VIKING PRESS · 1956

Collation: [1]-[8]^{16}, 128 leaves.

Pagination: p. [i] half-title; p. [ii] author's advertisement; p. [iii] title-page; p. [iv] copyright, publishing,
Library of Congress card number and printing notices; p. [v]
dedication and disclaimer; p. [vi] quotations; p. [1] PART
ONE; p. [2] blank; pp. 3-83 text of part one, with chapter

headings on pp. 3, 20, 34, 52, 74, and numbered division
headings on pp. 20, 25, 34, 43, 52, 67, 74; p. [84] blank;
p. [85] PART TWO; p. [86] blank; pp. 87-175 text of part two,
with chapter headings on pp. 87, 103, 148, and numbered division headings on pp. 103, 112, 115, 137, 148, 157, 169;
p. [176] blank; p. [177] PART THREE; p. [178] blank; pp. 179-
216 text of part three, with chapter headings on pp. 179 and
203, and numbered division headings on pp. 179, 183, 191, 194,
198, 203, 208; p. [217] PART FOUR; p. [218] blank; pp. 219-
249 text of part four, with chapter headings on pp. 219, 226,
246, and numbered division headings on pp. 226, 230, 238;
p. [250] blank.

Printing: Baskerville, 11 pt., printed in the U.S.A. by The
Colonial Press, Inc.

13.5 x 20.3 cm., white paper, all edges trimmed, top edges
colored red; bound in brown paper-covered boards with a black
cloth spine carrying the author, title and publisher stamped
in gold.

Price: $3.50.   Published in March 1956.

Dedication: as first English edition.

Notes: The copy examined is in the library of the University
of Virginia (PR/6013/.R44/Q5/1956/copy 2).

A36   THE SPY'S BEDSIDE BOOK   1957

First Edition

THE SPY'S BEDSIDE BOOK / an anthology edited by / Graham
Greene / and / Hugh Greene / *That night I slept but little* /
William Le Queux / [publisher's device] / RUPERT HART-DAVIS /
SOHO SQUARE LONDON / 1957

Collation: [A] -Q^8, 128 leaves.

Pagination: p. [1] half-title; p. [2] frontispiece; p. [3]
title-page; p. [4] copyright and printing notices; p. [5]
dedication; p. [6] quotation; pp. 7-10 CONTENTS; p. 10 acknowledgments; pp. 11-13 INTRODUCTION; p. [14] blank; pp. 17-
249 text, with divisional title pages on pp. [15, 37, 77, 91,
121, 129, 165, 179, 191, 197, 213], and with pp. [16, 36, 38,
76, 78, 122, 128, 166, 180, 190, 192, 196, 198, 214, 248,
252] blank and unnumbered; illustrations on pp. 92, 167, 220-
222, 227; pp. 253-256 BIBLIOGRAPHY.

Printing: a modern serif face similar to Walbaum, 11 pt.,
printed in Great Britain by Western Printing Services Ltd.,
Bristol.

12 x 18.5 cm., white paper, all edges trimmed; bound in dark
green cloth over boards with the title and the publisher's
initials stamped in silver on the spine.

Price: 15s. Published on November 15, 1957, in a red, white
and blue dust jacket with Graham Greene's name above the
title on the cover and Hugh Greene's name beneath printed
over a design representing game pieces -- each a military
figure or a spy; the back cover carries facsimile advertisements for nineteenth-century yellowbacks.

Dedication: To the immortal memory of William Le Queux and
John Buchan

Contents: Introduction, Graham Greene -- 11. For Beginners.
A Mission is Proposed, John Buchan -- 17. Directive to
Colonel Zabotin -- 27. A Damned Good Story, W. Somerset
Maugham -- 28. A Late Call at the German Embassy, L. C.
Moyzisch -- 30. The Value of Hide-and-Seek, Sir Robert Baden-
Powell -- 33. Take a Hard-Boiled Egg, Bernard Newman -- 34.
Examples of Invisible Writing -- 35. Hazards of the Profes-
sion. Tricked, William Le Queux -- 39. A Whip of the

Circassian Sort, T. E. Lawrence -- 39. A Nasty Scratch,
William Le Queux -- 40. A Spy Advertises, Herbert Greene --
41. A Bathroom at the Paris Ritz, Denis Wheatley -- 42. A
Trussed Fowl, William Le Queux -- 43. In the Back of the
Head, Vladimir Petrov -- 44. A Little Black Beret, Peter
Fleming -- 46. At the Social Club, George Griffith -- 47.
"That indeed is to die," Fenimore Cooper -- 52. Seduced with
the Old Tricks, W. H. Auden -- 53. An Excellent Babadagly,
William Le Queux -- 54. I Spy, Graham Greene -- 55. A Seg-
ment of German Sausage, Peter Fleming -- 59. The Sad Fate
of Major André, Richard Garnett and Anna Seward -- 61. The
Police Spy, Joseph Conrad -- 65. Seven Miles from Calais,
Max Pemberton -- 69. A Twinge, William Le Queux -- 75.
Delights of the Profession. A Narrow Squeak, Sir Paul Dukes
-- 79. A Cross-Country Run, Belle Boyd -- 82. Good Hunting,
Maurice Paléologue -- 86. Foreign Travel, Ian Fleming and
Walter Schellenberg -- 87. Seex Fat English Pigs, Lechmere
Worrall and J. E. Harold Terry -- 88. Room at the Bottom.
The Case of the Dixon Torpedo, Arthur Morrison -- 93. The
Adventures of Bonaparte, Compton Mackenzie -- 115. Unexpec-
ted Encounters. Colette and Mata Hari, Colette -- 123. The
Man in the Soft Cap, Edmund Blunden -- 125. A Meet in the
Shires, William Le Queux -- 126. Not Known to the Secret
Services. The Spies' March, 1913, Rudyard Kipling -- 131.
A Royal Spy, Alan H. Burgoyne -- 134. Schnitzel Alias Jones,
Richard Harding Davis -- 139. How It Strikes a Contemporary,
Robert Browning -- 161. Some Simple Disguises. Could Not
Believe His Eyes, Sir Robert Baden-Powell -- 167. None Other
Than ..., William Le Queux -- 168. The Waiters' Union, E.
Phillips Oppenheim -- 168. Professional Perquisites. Royal
Gifts, William Le Queux -- 181. A Well-Appointed Office, Wal-
ter Schellenberg -- 181. Blanc de Blanc Brut, 1943, Ian
Fleming -- 182. A Certificate from General Washington,
Fenimore Cooper -- 184. Spare Time Activities. Prison
Reading, R. H. Bruce Lockhart -- 193. Planning a Novel, Eric
Ambler -- 193. Love, Major André -- 195. A Gaggle of Sus-
pects. Queer People, Sir Basil Thomson -- 199. The Lauren-
ces, Hugh Kingsmill -- 203. Operation Goethe, Thomas Mann
-- 205. What the Soldier Said, William Blake -- 205.
Coleridge and Wordsworth, Suspects, S. T. Coleridge -- 206.
A Lawyer from Kent, Walter Schellenberg -- 210. The Amorous
Duchess, Maurice Paléologue -- 210. Postscript to Dreyfus,
Guy Chapman -- 212. Tricks of the Trade. Beneath the Open
Windows, Thomas Hardy -- 215. The Ordinary Route, Maurice
Paléologue -- 217. Equipment for Tibet, Lieutenant-Colonel
F. M. Bailey -- 218. Vodka with Pepper, Ian Fleming -- 219.
Dichlorethyl Sulphide, R. L. Green -- 219. Butterfly-Hunting
in Dalmatia, Sir Robert Baden-Powell -- 220. Carrier Pigeons,

H. R. Berndorff -- 223. A Visit to the Lavatory, R. H. Bruce
Lockhart -- 224. Top People Read "The Times," William Le
Queux -- 225. The Ambassador's Valet, Maurice Paléologue --
226. Russian Methods, H. R. Berndorff -- 228. The Explosive
Cigar, William Le Queux -- 229. A Plant, Admiral Sir William
James -- 230. The German Governess, The Simplest Thing in
the World. An Early Microphone, Lechmere Worrall and J. E.
Harold Terry -- 235. The Hansom Cab Approach, George Grif-
fith -- 238. Calloway's Code, O. Henry -- 238. Epilogue,
Hugh Greene -- 249. Bibliography -- 253.

Notes: The copy examined is in the British Library (1230 ff
12). Another copy, identical to that in the British Library
except for having the dust jacket described, was seen at Bertram Rota, Booksellers, 30 and 31 Long Acre, London, WC2E 9LT.
   Page [6] of the preliminaries carries a quotation from
Balzac which is as follows: "The trade of a spy is a very
fine one, when the spy is working on his own account. Is it
not in fact enjoying the excitements of a thief, while still
retaining the character of an honest citizen? But a man who
undertakes this trade must make up his mind to simmer with
wrath, to fret with impatience, to stand about in the mud
with his feet freezing, to be chilled or to be scorched, and
to be deceived by false hopes. He must be ready, on the faith
of a mere indication, to work up to an unknown goal; he must
bear the disappointment of failing in his aim; he must be
prepared to run, to be motionless, to remain for hours watch-
ing a window; to invent a thousand theories of action....
The only excitement which can compare with it is that of the
life of a gambler." -- HONORÉ DE BALZAC.
   This collection was the first published indication of
the interest of the brothers Greene in antique thrillers.
Hugh went on to his collection *Rivals of Sherlock Holmes* and
its sequel, and Graham and Dorothy Craigie published a catalogue of their collection of *Victorian Détective Fiction* in
1966. The only blatant use of this material for creative
purposes has been Graham Greene's drama *The Return of A. J.
Raffles* (1975).

a. *First Edition*

THE / POTTING SHED / *A Play in Three Acts* / *by* / GRAHAM
GREENE / [publisher's device] / HEINEMANN / LONDON   MELBOURNE
TORONTO

Collation: [A]^8 B–D^8 E/E*$^{2/8}$, 42 leaves.

Pagination: p. [i] half-title; p. [ii] author's advertisement; p. [iii] title-page; p. [iv] publishing, copyright,
performing rights, publication and printing notices; p. [v]
CHARACTERS / (IN ORDER OF APPEARANCE); p. [vi] notes on the
first London production and AUTHOR'S NOTE; p. [vii] SCENES;
p. [viii] blank; p. 1 ACT I / SCENE I; pp. 1–30 text of act
one, with scenes beginning on pp. 1 and 17; p. 31 ACT II /
SCENE I; pp. 31–61 text of act two, with scenes beginning on
pp. 31 and 50; p. 62 ACT THREE; pp. 62–76 text of act three.

Printing: Garamond, 11 pt., printed in Great Britain at the
Windmill Press, Kingswood, Surrey.

12 x 18.5 cm., white paper, all edges trimmed; bound in blue
cloth over boards with the title, author and publisher
separated by stars and bordered by a rectangle stamped in
gold along the spine; a windmill device is blind stamped at
the right tail of the back cover.

Price: 8s. 6d.   Published on February 3, 1958, in a dust
jacket printed in green with the title in orange on the cover
and spine and the author in white on the cover and spine with
the publisher in white on the spine.

Notes: The copy examined is in the British Library (11785
c. 83).   Another copy, identical to that in the British
Library except that it has the dust jacket described, is in
the compiler's collection.
    An "Author's Note" on page [vi] of the preliminaries in-
dicates that the version of the play produced in New York in
1957 and also published in the United States that year had a
third act different from that of the first English production.
Greene mentions that this later production uses the third act
as he originally wrote it and that it is the only authorized
version for Great Britain.
    The play was first produced in London on February 5,
1958, at the Globe Theatre by H. M. Tennent Ltd. and Donmar

Productions Ltd. with the following in the cast:

Dr. Frederick Baston	Walter Hudd
Anne Callifer	Sarah Long
Sara Callifer	Irene Worth
Mrs. Callifer	Gwen Ffrangçon-Davies
John Callifer	Lockwood West
James Callifer	John Gielgud
Dr. Kreuzer	Peter Illing
Corner	William Peacock
Mrs. Potter	Dorothy Dewhurst
Miss Connolly	Aithna Gover
Father William Callifer	Redmond Phillips

The play was directed by Michael Macowan with sets by Paul Mayo.

In 1945 Greene began a novel set in Nottingham. The writing of *The Heart of the Matter* interrupted and he never finished the earlier novel. Later he adapted the idea into *The Potting Shed*, which he refers to in *A Sort of Life* as "an unsatisfactory play," a play in which he gave an off-stage part to his "unsatisfactory dog."

In *In Search of a Character: Two African Journals* he relates an incident in a Catholic Presbytery in Belfast that became part of Scene II, Act II of *The Potting Shed*.

Another interesting clue to the working of the artist's mind is the probable origin of the surname, "Callifer," of the family in *The Potting Shed*. In *The Lawless Roads* Greene remembers with horror a student at Berkhamsted named "Collifax who practised torments with dividers." The associations are not difficult to disentangle. Collifax tormented with dividers. The technical term for divider is *calliper*. The head of the Callifer family, a family divided by a miraculous event in the past, is one H. C. Callifer, a logical hair splitter, "high minded rather pedantic ... a little outmoded."

b. *First American Edition* (1957)

[rule device] / The / Potting Shed / A PLAY IN THREE ACTS BY / Graham Greene / New York • THE VIKING PRESS • 1957

Collation: [1]-[4]^{16}, 64 leaves.

Pagination: p. [1] half-title; p. [2] blank; p. [3] author's advertisement; p. [4] blank; frontispiece tipped in, with blank back; p. [5] title-page; p. [6] copyright, publication, publishing, performing rights, Library of Congress card number and printing notices; p. 7 notes on the first production; p. [8] blank; p. 9 SCENES; p. [10] blank; p. [11] ACT ONE; p. [12] blank; p. 13 ACT ONE / SCENE ONE; pp. 13-51 text of act one, with scenes beginning on pp. 13 and 35; p. [52] blank; p. [53] ACT TWO; p. [54] blank; p. 55 ACT TWO / SCENE ONE; pp. 55-95 text of act two, with scenes beginning on pp. 55 and 81; p. [96] blank; p. [97] ACT THREE; p. [98] blank; p. 99 ACT THREE; pp. 99-123 text of act three; pp. [124-128] blank.

Printing: Baskerville, 11 pt., printed in the U.S.A.

13.5 x 20.5 cm., white paper, all edges trimmed; bound in tan cloth over boards with the author, title and publisher separated by rules stamped in green on the spine; title and "a play by / Graham Greene" with a horizontal rule above and below stamped in green on the cover.

Price: $3.00. Published in February 1957.

Notes: The copy examined is in the library of West Virginia State College (PR/60B/R44 P58).
     Though this edition was published one year earlier than the English edition, it has a third act different from the later edition. The later version is as Greene originally wrote it.
     The play was first produced on Tuesday, January 29, 1957, by Carmen Capalbo and Stanley Chase, with scenery by Chester Rakeman Scenic Studios, designed by William Pitkin, lighting by Peggy Clark, and costumes by Patricia Zipprodt in New York at the Bijou Theater with the following cast:

Dr. Frederick Baston	Lewis Casson
Anne Callifer	Carol Lynley
Sara Callifer	Leueen MacGrath
Mrs. Callifer	Sybil Thorndike
John Callifer	Stanley Lemin
James Callifer	Robert Flemyng
Dr. Kreuzer	Rudolf Weiss
Corner	Richard Longman
Mrs. Potter	Eda Heinemann
Miss Connolly	Joan Croydon
Father William Callifer	Frank Conroy

A38   OUR MAN IN HAVANA   1958

a. *First Edition*

GRAHAM GREENE / [double rule] / Our Man in Havana / AN
ENTERTAINMENT / [publisher's device] / HEINEMANN / LONDON
MELBOURNE   TORONTO

Collation: $[A]^{16}$ $B-H^{16}$ $[I]/I*^{2/10}$, 140 leaves.

Pagination: p. [i] half-title; p. [ii] author's advertisement;
p. [iii] title-page; p. [iv] publishing, publication, copyright and printing notices; p. [v] disclaimer; p. [vi] quotation; p. [1] PART I; p. [2] blank; pp. 3-49 text of part one,
with chapter headings on pp. 3, 12, 22, 36, and numbered division headings on pp. 3, 7, 22, 24, 31, 36, 47; p. [50]
blank; p. [51] INTERLUDE IN LONDON; p. [52] blank; pp. 53-60
text of Interlude in London; p. [61] PART II; p. [62] blank;
pp. 63-92 text of part two, with chapter headings on pp. 63,
74, 83, and numbered division headings on pp. 63, 68, 70, 74,
76; p. [93] INTERLUDE IN LONDON; p. [94] blank; pp. 95-100
text of Interlude in London; p. [101] PART III; p. [102]
blank; pp. 103-140 text of part three, with chapter headings
on pp. 103, 113, 125, and numbered division headings on
pp. 113, 117, 125, 132; p. [141] PART IV; p. [142] blank;
pp. 143-177 text of part four, with chapter headings on
pp. 143 and 171, and numbered division headings on pp. 143,
149, 157, 164; p. [178] blank; p. [179] INTERLUDE IN LONDON;
p. [180] blank; pp. 181-183 text of Interlude in London;
p. [184] blank; p. [185] PART V; p. [186] blank; pp. 187-262
text of part five, with chapter headings on pp. 187, 196, 207,
223, 237, 253, and numbered division headings on pp. 196, 197,
207, 209, 211, 222, 223, 229, 237, 243, 253, 255, 258, 260;
p. [263] EPILOGUE IN LONDON; p. [264] blank; pp. 265-273 text
of Epilogue in London, with numbered division headings on
pp. 265 and 268; p. [274] blank.

Printing: Baskerville, 11 pt., printed in Great Britain at
the Windmill Press, Kingswood, Surrey.

12.5 x 19.5 cm., white paper, all edges trimmed; bound in
blue cloth over boards with the title, a small double rule,
the author and publisher stamped in gold on the spine and a
windmill device blind stamped at the right tail of the back
cover.

Price: 15s. Published on October 6, 1958, in a dust jacket
printed in purple, blue and green representing decorative
iron-work with the author in white and the title printed over
in yellow; the back cover carries advertisements for *The
Quiet American.*

Notes: The copies examined are in the British Library
(N.N.N. 12422) and the Library of Congress (PZ3/.G8319/Ou2).
Another copy, identical to those above except that it has
the dust jacket described, was seen at Bell, Book and Radmall,
80 Long Acre, London, WC2E 9N6.

On page [v] of the preliminaries Greene makes the usual
disclaimer about the similarity of his characters to living
people, but he prefaces his disclaimer with the remark that
"a fairy story like this" should hardly require it.

Page [vi] carries a quotation from George Herbert: "And
the sad man is cock of all his jests."

In his "Introduction" in the Collected Edition Greene
discusses how the novel came to be written, the origins of
some of the ideas and characters, particularly the engaging
Dr. Hasselbacher, who, it appears, was modeled on a Baron
Schacht, a friend of Norman Douglas on Capri. As to its beginnings, the novel started as an outline for a film treatment, written at the request of Greene's friend Alberto
Cavalcanti, the film-maker. The setting in this version was
Estonia in 1938, changed later to Batista's Cuba, but the
original plot survived more or less intact.

But Greene does not mention that the world of *Our Man
in Havana* can be traced directly back to his earliest novels
of espionage. *Stamboul Train* already shows touches of the
same black comedy which appear even more clearly in *The
Ministry of Fear.* There is also a suggestion that Greene is
paying homage to Conrad's *Nostromo* and Conrad's own quite
considerable satiric talents.

b. *First American Edition* (1958)

[double rule] / GRAHAM GREENE / *Our Man* / *in Havana* [title in
script] / AN ENTERTAINMENT / "*And the sad man is cock of all
his jests.*" / --GEORGE HERBERT / *1958* / THE VIKING PRESS •
NEW YORK / [double rule]

Collation: [1]-[8]^{16}, 178 leaves.

Pagination: p. [i] half-title; p. [ii] author's advertisement; p. [iii] title-page; p. [iv] copyright, publishing and printing notices; p. [v] disclaimer; p. [vi] blank; p. [1] PART ONE; p. [2] blank; pp. 3-47 text of part one, with chapter headings on pp. 3, 12, 22, 35, and numbered division headings on pp. 3, 7, 12, 22, 24, 30, 35, 45; p. 48 INTERLUDE IN LONDON; pp. 48-54 text of Interlude in London; p. [55] PART TWO; p. [56] blank; pp. 57-84 text of part two, with chapter headings on pp. 57, 67, 76, and numbered division headings on pp. 57, 62, 64, 67, 69; p. 85 INTERLUDE IN LONDON; pp. 85-89 text of Interlude in London; p. [90] blank; p. [91] PART THREE; p. [92] blank; pp. 93-127 text of part three, with chapter headings on pp. 93, 102, 113, with numbered division headings on pp. 102, 105, 113, 119; p. [128] blank; p. [129] PART FOUR; p. [130] blank; pp. 131-162 text of part four, with chapter headings on pp. 131 and 156, and numbered division headings on pp. 131, 136, 143, 151, 156; p. 163 INTERLUDE IN LONDON; pp. 163-165 text of Interlude in London; p. [166] blank; p. [167] PART FIVE; p. [168] blank; pp. 169-238 text of part five, with chapter headings on pp. 169, 177, 187, 202, 215, 230, and numbered division headings on pp. 177, 178, 183, 187, 189, 191, 201, 202, 207, 215, 221, 230, 234, 236; p. 239 EPILOGUE IN LONDON; pp. 239-247 text of Epilogue in London, with numbered division headings on pp. 239 and 241; pp. [243-250] blank.

Printing: Bulmer, 11 pt., printed in the U.S.A. by American Book-Stratford Press.

13.5 x 20 cm., white paper, all edges trimmed; bound in salmon-colored cloth over boards, with an image representing Mr. Wormold and his vacuum cleaner stamped in black at the lower right of the front cover and the author, title and publisher between double lines stamped in black on the spine.

Price: $3.50. Published in October 1958 in a dust jacket which carries the title in yellow and the author in white on the front cover. A representation of a schematic drawing on folded paper occupies the lower half of the cover beneath the author, and a line drawing of a man and vacuum cleaner (identical to that stamped on the cover of the binding) is at the right head of the front cover. Coloring shades from black on the spine to salmon on the front cover. The spine carries the author, title, line drawing and publisher in white. The back cover carries quotations from the novel in black on white.

Notes: The copy examined is in the collection of the compiler. Another copy seen is in the library of the University of Illinois (823/G83ou/cop. 2).

A39   THE COMPLAISANT LOVER   1959

a. *First Edition*

THE / COMPLAISANT / LOVER / *A Comedy* / GRAHAM GREENE /
[publisher's device] / HEINEMANN / LONDON MELBOURNE TORONTO

Collation: [A]^8 B-D^8 E^4 F^8, 44 leaves.

Pagination: pp. [i-ii] blank; p. [iii] half-title; p. [iv]
author's advertisement; p. [v] title-page; p. [vi] publishing,
copyright, performing rights, publication and printing notices; p. [vii] CHARACTERS / (IN ORDER OF APPEARANCE);
p. [viii] notes on the first production; p. [ix] SYNOPSIS OF
SCENES; p. [x] blank; p. 1 ACT I / SCENE I; pp. 1-48 text of
act one, with scenes beginning on pp. 1 and 31; p. 49 ACT II /
SCENE I; pp. 49-77 text of act two, with scenes beginning on
pp. 49 and 60; p. 77 POSTSCRIPT ON CENSORSHIP; p. [78] blank.

Printing: Garamond, 11 pt., printed in Great Britain by the
Windmill Press Ltd., Kingswood, Surrey.

12 x 18.5 cm., white paper, all edges trimmed; bound in dark
blue ribbed cloth over boards with the title, author and publisher stamped along the spine in gold surrounded by a border
in gold; a windmill device is blind stamped at the right tail
of the back cover.

Price: 8s. 6d. Published on June 29, 1959.

Notes: The copy examined is in the British Library (11785 ccc
37). The compiler has seen a 1966 reprint (which seems to be
the second impression) in a pale green dust jacket with the
author and title on the cover and spine in blue and red and
reviews of *The Living Room*, *The Potting Shed* and *The Complaisant Lover* on the back cover.
    On page 77 Greene has added a "Postscript on Censorship"
in which he satirically remarks that the Lord Chamberlain is
to be praised for admitting homosexuality as a theme to the
English stage. He adds that he has hopes for heterosexuality
as a theme for the future and this book's readers might enjoy
trying to guess which adjective and passage of three lines
"the Lord Chamberlain and his officers have found too indecent
for the theatre."
    The play was produced by Sir John Gielgud, with sets by
Care Toms, at the Globe Theatre, London, on June 18, 1959.
The cast was as follows:

Victor Rhodes	Ralph Richardson
William Howard	Lockwood West
Clive Root	Paul Scofield
Ann Howard	Polly Adams
Margaret Howard	Madge Compton
Mary Rhodes	Phyllis Calvert
Robin Rhodes	Hugh James
A Hotel Valet	Gerald Flood
Dr. Van Droog	Oliver Burt

Greene's third play is more of an experiment than his first two. Though it covers much the same ground as the others, though his characters are placed in equally melodramatic situations, there is an obvious change in his approach to melodrama, that is, his change to the comic form. His black comedy seems to be a way of keeping the melodrama which dissolves into sentimentality approaching self-parody in his earlier plays from becoming just that in *The Complaisant Lover*.

The play was adapted for the French stage by playwright Jean Anouilh.

b. *First American Edition* (1961)

THE / COMPLAISANT / LOVER / A *Comedy* / GRAHAM GREENE / [publisher's device] / NEW YORK : THE VIKING PRESS

Collation: [1]-[6]^8, 48 leaves.

Pagination: p. [i] half-title; p. [ii] author's advertisement; p. [iii] title-page; p. [iv] copyright, publishing, performing rights, Library of Congress card number and printing notices; p. [v] notes on the first production; p. [vi] blank; p. [1] fly-title; p. [2] CHARACTERS / (IN ORDER OF APPEARANCE) / synopsis of SCENES; p. 3 ACT / ONE / SCENE I; pp. 3-56 text of act one, with scenes beginning on pp. 3 and 37; p. 57 ACT / TWO / SCENE I; pp. 57-87 text of act two, with scenes beginning on pp. 57 and 69; pp. [88-90] blank.

Printing: Garamond, 11 pt., printed in the U.S.A. by Vail-Ballou Press.

13.5 x 20.3 cm., white paper, all edges trimmed; bound in red paper over boards, decorated in small repeating design alternating in gold and black; the spine is in ivory cloth with the author, title and publisher stamped in red.

Price: $3.00. Published in 1961.

Notes: The copy examined is in the Library of Congress (PR/6013/.R44C55/1961).
   The first performance of *The Complaisant Lover* on the New York stage was November 1, 1961, at the Ethel Barrymore Theater. It was directed by Glen Byam Shaw with sets and costumes by Motley. The play was produced by Irene Mayer Selznik with the following cast:

Victor Rhodes	Sir Michael Redgrave
William Howard	George Turner
Clive Root	Richard Johnson
Ann Howard	Sandy Dennis
Margaret Howard	Christine Thomas
Mary Rhodes	Googie Withers
Robin Rhodes	Nicholas Hammond
Hotel Valet	Gene Wilder
Dr. Van Droog	Bert Nelson

   Walter Kerr began his "First Night Report," "One must be deeply grateful to Graham Greene for having such a hopelessly unconventional mind.... he is stating a brand new truth for the theater ... that adultery is a great deal funnier if you will only take it seriously."

A40   A VISIT TO MORIN   1960

First Edition

GRAHAM GREENE / A Visit to Morin / HEINEMANN / LONDON MEL-
BOURNE TORONTO [page bordered by a rectangle of three ruled
lines in green]

Collation: [A]^4 B-E^4, 16 leaves.

Pagination: pp. [i-ii] blank; p. [1] half-title; p. [2] blank;
p. [3] title-page; p. [4] publication, copyright and printing
notices; p. [5] notice of prior publication and limitation of
this edition; p. [6] blank; pp. [7]-26 text; pp. [27-30] blank.

Printing: Plantin, 11 pt., printed in Great Britain by the
Windmill Press Ltd., Kingswood, Surrey.

13 x 21 cm., white paper, all edges trimmed; bound in green
cloth over boards with the author, title and publisher
stamped in gold on the spine; a green rayon ribbon marker,
attached to the head of the spine, is 28.5 cm. long.

Price: distributed as gifts, Christmas 1960. In an off-white
dust jacket having the author, title and publisher in black
surrounded by a rectangle of three ruled lines in green on
the front cover; the spine carries the author in black, the
title in green and the publisher in black; the back cover is
blank.

Notes: The copy examined is in the collection of Hofstra University (PR6013/R44V5/959).
     On the Hofstra copy, p. [i] carries the following: "For
John with love from Graham Christmas 1960." Page [5] carries
the notice, "A Visit to Morin was first published in the
London Magazine. 250 copies only have been printed and the
type has been distributed."

A41   A BURNT-OUT CASE   1961

a. *First Edition*

GRAHAM GREENE / [double rule] / A Burnt-Out Case / [publisher's device] / HEINEMANN / LONDON MELBOURNE TORONTO

Collation: $[A]^{16}$ $B-G^{16}$ H^4 I^{16}, 132 leaves.

Pagination: p. [i] half-title; p. [ii] author's advertisement; p. [iii] title-page; p. [iv] publishing, copyright and printing notices; p. [v] quotations; p. [vi] blank; pp. [vii-viii] dedication and disclaimer; p. [1] PART I; p. [2] blank; pp. 3-21 text of part one, with chapter headings on pp. 3 and 13, and numbered division headings on pp. 3, 8, 13, 17; p. [22] blank; p. [23] PART II; p. [24] blank; pp. 25-69 text of part two, with chapter headings on pp. 25, 38, 48, 61, and numbered division headings on pp. 25, 31, 34, 38, 48, 57, 61, 67; p. [70] blank; p. [71] PART III; p. [72] blank; pp. 73-95 text of part three, with chapter headings on pp. 73 and 85, and numbered division headings on pp. 73, 79, 85; p. [96] blank; p. [97] PART IV; p. [98] blank; pp. 99-149 text of part four, with chapter headings on pp. 99, 118, 128, and numbered division headings on pp. 99, 104, 110, 118, 119, 128, 137; p. [150] blank; p. [151] PART V; p. [152] blank; pp. 153-174 text of part five, with chapter headings on pp. 153 and 162, and numbered division headings on pp. 153 and 162; p. [175] PART VI; p. [176] blank; pp. 177-256 text of part six, with chapter headings on pp. 177, 206, 223, and numbered division headings on pp. 177, 192, 206, 213, 223, 228, 233, 240, 246, 252.

Printing: Baskerville, 11 pt., printed in Great Britain by the Windmill Press Ltd., Kingswood, Surrey.

12.5 x 19.5 cm., white paper, all edges trimmed; bound in black cloth over boards with the title, author and publisher stamped in silver on the spine and a windmill device blind stamped at the right tail of the back cover.

Price: 16s. Published on January 16, 1961, in a dust jacket having a green cover with a flower design in blue-red-brown with title and author in white; also having an advertisement for *Our Man in Havana* on the back cover.

Dedication: To Docteur Michel Lechat
            Dear Michel, ...

Notes: The copy examined is in the British Library (N.N.N.
15961). Another copy, identical to that above except for
having the described dust jacket, was seen at Bell, Book and
Radmall, 80 Long Acre, London, WC2E 9NG.

Page [v] of the preliminaries carries two quotations
which follow: "Io non mori', e non rimasi vivo." (I did not
die, yet nothing of life remained). -- DANTE, and "Within
limits of normality, every individual loves himself. In cases
where he has a deformity or abnormality or develops it later,
his own aesthetic sense revolts and he develops a sort of dis-
gust towards himself. Though with time, he becomes recon-
ciled to his deformities, it is only at the conscious level.
His sub-conscious mind, which continues to bear the mark of
injury, brings about certain changes in his whole personality,
making him suspicious of society." -- R.V. WARDECKER in a pamphlet on leprosy.

The dedicatory letter on pages [vii] and [viii] seems to
serve partly as a disclaimer. Greene says that to try to
identify Querry, the Ryckers, Parkinson or Father Thomas would
be "a waste of time." This novel is not a *"Roman a clef*, but
an attempt to give dramatic expression to various types of belief, half-belief and non-belief in the kind of setting ...
where such differences are felt acutely and find expression.
This Congo is a region of the mind...."

The book *In Search of a Character: Two African Journals*
(1961) documents part of Greene's research for this novel.
His "Introduction" in the Collected Edition suggests that the
novel at least partly resulted from his reputation, following
the success of *The Heart of the Matter*, as a Catholic writer,
the pleas to him for help from suffering Catholics, and his
own feelings of impotence in these cases. Querry perhaps is
an outgrowth of the French Catholic writer in "A Visit to
Morin." Greene quotes long passages of a correspondence he
carried on with Evelyn Waugh about this matter, a discussion
of atheism and the confusion of some Catholic critics.
Greene also speculates on the possibility that his reading
Unamuno's *Life and Death of Don Quixote* thirty years before
writing *A Burnt-Out Case* may have struck a spark which smol-
dered over the years.

The earliest edition of the novel is the Swedish translation by Torsten Blomkvist, *Utbrand*, published by P.A. Norstedt & Söners, Stockholm, 1960. This company has published
nearly all of Greene's books in both trade and cheaper editions, and plans to continue making available in Swedish a
wide range of Greene's work.

b. *First American Edition* (1961)

A / *BURNT-OUT* / *CASE* / [rule] / *The Viking Press* • *New York* •
1961 / [rule] / *GRAHAM* / *GREENE*

Collation: [1]-[8]^{16}, 128 leaves.

Pagination: p. [i] half-title; p. [ii] author's advertisement;
p. [iii] title-page; p. [iv] copyright, publishing, Library of
Congress card number and printing notices; p. [v] quotations;
p. [vi] blank; pp. vii-viii dedication and disclaimer; p. [1]
PART ONE; p. [2] blank; pp. 3-21 text of part one, with chapter headings on pp. 3 and 13, and numbered division headings
on pp. 3, 7, 13, 17; p. [22] blank; p. [23] PART TWO; p. [24]
blank; pp. 25-68 text of part two, with chapter headings on
pp. 25, 38, 48, 61, and numbered division headings on pp. 25,
31, 34, 38, 48, 57, 61, 66; p. [69] PART THREE; p. [70] blank;
pp. 71-91 text of part three, with chapter headings on pp. 71
and 82, and numbered division headings on pp. 71, 76, 82;
p. [92] blank; p. [93] PART FOUR; p. [94] blank; pp. 95-143
text of part four, with chapter headings on pp. 95, 113, 123,
and numbered division headings on pp. 95, 99, 106, 113, 114,
123, 131; p. [144] blank; p. [145] PART FIVE; p. [146] blank;
pp. 147-168 text of part five, with chapter headings on pp.
147 and 156, and numbered division headings on pp. 147 and
156; p. [169] PART SIX; p. [170] blank; pp. 171-248 text of
part six, with chapter headings on pp. 171, 199, 216, and numbered division headings on pp. 171, 186, 199, 206, 216, 221,
226, 233, 238, 244.

Printing: Caslon, 12 pt., printed in the U.S.A. by H. Wolff,
New York.

13.5 x 20 cm., white paper, all edges trimmed; bound in green
cloth over boards with spine in black cloth, title and publisher stamped in red-gold, author stamped in green.

Price: $3.95. Published in February 1961 in a dust jacket
in red, green and black with white horizontal bands on both
covers; bands on the front cover contain the title and author
in black, and bands on the back cover contain reviews in
black; the author is in green, the title in pink, and the
publisher in white on a black spine.

Dedication: as first English edition.

Notes: The copies examined are in the compiler's collection
and the Library of Congress (PZ3/.G8319/Bu).

A note on the inside front of the dust jacket indicates
that the novel is a Book-of-the-Month Club selection which
would almost certainly have guaranteed sales of between
30,000 and 40,000 copies.

A42   IN SEARCH OF A CHARACTER   1961

a. *First Edition*

Graham Greene / IN SEARCH OF A / CHARACTER / Two African /
Journals / [publisher's device] / THE BODLEY HEAD / LONDON

Collation: [1]-[6]^8 [7]^6 [8]^8, 62 leaves.

Pagination: p. [1] half-title; p. [2] author's advertisement;
p. [3] title-page; p. [4] acknowledgment, copyright, printing,
publishing, type and publication notices; p. [5] CONTENTS;
p. [6] blank; pp. 7-9 INTRODUCTION; p. [10] blank; p. [11] I /
CONGO JOURNAL; p. [12] blank; pp. 13-93 text of part one, with
divisions on pp. 13, 16, 18, 20, 26, 30, 31, 36, 39, 41, 44,
46, 52, 54, 62, 64, 66, 67, 68, 70, 71, 72, 75, 76, 77, 78, 82,
83, 88, 89, 90, 91; p. [94] blank; p. [95] II / CONVOY TO WEST
AFRICA; p. [96] blank; pp. 97-123 text of part two, with divisions on pp. 97, 99, 101, 103, 106, 108, 109, 110, 112, 113,
114, 115, 117, 118, 119, 120, 121, 122; p. [124] blank.

Printing: Monotype Erhardt, 11 pt., printed and bound in
Great Britain by William Clowes & Sons Ltd., London and
Beccles.

11 x 18.5 cm., white paper, all edges trimmed, top edges
colored green; bound in olive elephant-hide paper over boards,
with the author, title and publisher stamped in gold on an
orange cloth spine; the endpapers are printed white on green
and are a facsimile of the author's manuscript, the facsimile
corresponding to most of page 39 and half of page 40 in the
text.

Price: 10s. 6d. Published on October 26, 1961, in a yellow
dust jacket having title and subtitle in red, author in black
on the cover, author and title in black along the spine; the
back cover is blank.

Contents: Introduction -- 7. I. Congo Journal -- 11.
II. Convoy to West Africa -- 95.

Notes: The copy examined is in the compiler's collection.
       This is the first of Greene's books to contain in any way
a facsimile of his manuscript hand. A comparison with the
pages of the text indicates that some editing has taken place.
In his "Introduction" Greene discusses correcting his notes
at a later time with the aid of his friend Dr. Michel Lechat

to whom he dedicated *A Burnt-Out Case.*

Both of these journals should be of interest to the reader who is curious to follow the intricate paths of lite-rary creation.

The earlier of the two journals, "Convoy to West Africa," first published in *The Mint: A Miscellany of Literature, Art and Criticism*, Volume I, edited by Geoffrey Grigson (London, Routledge, 1946, pp. 40-55) is the journal Greene kept on his way to an intelligence post at Freetown in 1941, from which *The Heart of the Matter* would emerge some years later. The "Congo Journal" documents Greene's research for *A Burnt-Out Case.*

b. *First American Edition* (1962)

IN / Search / OF A / Character / TWO AFRICAN JOURNALS / BY / Graham Greene / THE VIKING PRESS • NEW YORK

Collation: [1]-[3]^{16} [4]^{8}, 56 leaves.

Pagination: p. [i] publisher's device; p. [ii] blank; p. [iii] half-title; p. [iv] blank; p. [v] author's advertisement; p. [vi] blank; p. [vii] title-page; p. [viii] copyright, pub-lishing, Library of Congress card number and printing notices; p. [ix] CONTENTS; p. [x] blank; p. [xi] INTRODUCTION; p. [xii] blank; pp. xiii-xv text of introduction; p. [xvi] blank; p. [1] I / CONGO JOURNAL; p. [2] blank; pp. 3-67 text of part one, with divisions on pp. 3, 5, 7, 9, 14, 17, 18, 22, 24, 26, 28, 30, 34, 36, 39, 41, 43, 45, 46, 47, 49, 50, 52, 53, 54, 55, 58, 59, 63, 64, 65, 66; p. [68] blank; p. [69] II / CONVOY TO WEST AFRICA; p. [70] blank; pp. 71-93 text of part two, with divisions on pp. 71, 73, 74, 76, 79, 81, 82, 84, 85, 86, 88, 89, 90, 91, 92, 93; pp. [94-96] blank.

Printing: Deepdene, 12 pt., printed in the U.S.A. by The Colonial Press, Inc.

13.5 x 22.8 cm., white paper, all edges trimmed; bound in brown cloth over boards with title, author and publisher stamped in gold on the spine.

Price: $3.50. Published in January 1962.

Contents: Introduction -- xi. Part I. Congo Journal -- 1. Part II. Convoy to West Africa -- 69.

Notes: The copy examined is in the library of West Virginia State College (916.6/G799).

The endpapers, reproducing a page from the original journal, are identical to those in the first English edition.

c. *Limited American Edition* (1961)

Title-page: as the ordinary American edition.

Collation: as the ordinary American edition.

Pagination: as the ordinary American edition except for p. [i] which carries notice of limitation, publisher's device and "Christmas 1961."

Printing: as the ordinary American edition.

13.5 x 22.8 cm., white paper, all edges trimmed; bound in green Cockerell's marble paper over boards with a green buckram spine and the author, title and publisher stamped in gold on the spine.

Price: undisclosed (but may have been distributed free). Published in December 1961.

Contents: as the ordinary American edition.

Notes: The copy examined is in the Rare Book Department of the Library of Congress (PR/6013/R4425/1962).

A note on the first page notifies the reader that: "This is one of 600 advance copies of *In Search of a Character* specially designed for friends of the author and the publishers." It is dated Christmas, 1961. The manuscript facsimile is reproduced on the endpapers as in the ordinary edition.

A43   THE BODLEY HEAD FORD MADOX FORD   1962

First Edition

THE BODLEY HEAD / FORD / MADOX FORD / VOLUME I / THE GOOD
SOLDIER / SELECTED MEMORIES / POEMS / [publisher's device] /
THE BODLEY HEAD / LONDON

Collation: [1]/[1*]$^{8/8}$ 2/2*-11/11*$^{8/8}$ 12 ^{14}, 190 leaves.

Pagination: p. [1] half-title; p. [2] blank; p. [3] title-
page; p. [4] printing, publishing, type and publication
notices; pp. 5-6 CONTENTS; pp. 7-12 INTRODUCTION; p. [13] THE
GOOD SOLDIER / A TALE OF PASSION; p. [14] blank; pp. 15-220
text; p. [221] SELECTED MEMORIES / DRAWN FROM *RETURN TO
YESTERDAY*, / *ANCIENT LIGHTS*, *MIGHTIER THAN THE SWORD*, AND
THE HEART OF THE COUNTRY; p. [222] blank; pp. 223-356 text;
p. [357] POEMS; p. [358] blank; pp. 359-380 text.

Printing: Plantin, 10 pt., printed and bound in Great Britain
by William Clowes and Sons Ltd., Beccles.

11.5 x 19 cm., white paper, all edges trimmed; bound in blue
paper (embossed to look like cloth) over boards; the title,
surrounded with a rectangular border, is stamped in gold at
the head of the spine, a single star in gold beneath (to denote Volume I) and the publisher at the tail.

Price: 25s. Published June 14, 1962.

Contents: The Good Soldier -- 13. Selected Memories -- 221.
The Early Years -- 223. My Grandfather's House -- 223. My
Nurse, Mrs. Atterbury -- 236. My Cousins, the Rossettis --
238. Poetesses in Four-Wheelers -- 240. The Abbé Liszt --
242. A Pre-Raphaelite Poetess -- 245. My Unhappiest Night --
247. The Music Critic of *The Times* -- 249. A German Master
-- 253. The Pines, Putney -- 254. A Mr. Hardy -- 257. Some
Writers and Artists -- 261. Ford Madox Brown -- 261. Mr.
Howell and Mr. Rossetti -- 264. A Settlement of Aliens --
266. The Old Man -- 278. Mr. James and Mr. Kipling -- 288.
Collaborating with Conrad -- 291. W. H. Hudson -- 295. A
Kind of Criticism -- 299. The Apotheosis of John Galsworthy
-- 302. Before the Wars -- 305. Portrait of the Artist as
a Dandy -- 305. A Literary Party -- 307. Starting a Review
-- 309. Enter Ezra Pound -- 318. ... and D. H. Lawrence --
320. The Marconi Commission -- 327. A Shameful Episode --
333. Alas! -- 336. The Heart of the Country -- 337.

'Meary' -- 337. Carew and Other Tramps -- 343. Table Talk --
349. Myself -- 349. Good Friday -- 349. Rossetti's Inver-
ness Cape -- 349. A Fabian Debate -- 350. The Music Stopped
-- 351. Strawberry Jam and Oysters -- 351. Pre-Raphaelite
Love -- 352. On Obsolete Words -- 353. Mr. Ruskin's Epithet
-- 353. Mixing Up Names -- 354. Walter Crane's Gloves --
354. The City of Dreadful Night -- 355. Maupassant and the
Naked Lady -- 356. A Novelist's Credo -- 356. Poems -- 357.
On Heaven -- 359. Antwerp -- 373. Views -- 378. 'When the
World Was in Building ...' -- 380.

THE BODLEY HEAD / FORD / MADOX FORD / VOLUME II / THE FIFTH
QUEEN / PRIVY SEAL / THE FIFTH QUEEN CROWNED / [publisher's
device] / THE BODLEY HEAD / LONDON

Collation: [1]/[1*]$^{8/8}$ 2/2*-17/17*$^{8/8}$ 18^8 19/19*$^{8/8}$, 296
leaves.

Pagination: p. [1] half-title; p. [2] blank; p. [3] title-
page; p. [4] printing, publishing, type and publication notices; p. [5] CONTENTS; p. [6] blank; p. [7] THE FIFTH QUEEN
AND HOW SHE CAME TO COURT; p. [8] dedication; p. [9] contents
of The Fifth Queen; p. [10] blank; pp. 11-232 text; p. [223]
PRIVY SEAL / HIS LAST VENTURE / and quotation; p. [234] dedication; p. [235] contents of Privy Seal; p. [236] blank;
pp. 237-413 text; p. [414] blank; p. [415] THE FIFTH QUEEN
CROWNED / A ROMANCE / and quotation; p. [416] dedication;
p. [417] contents of The Fifth Queen Crowned; p. [418] blank;
pp. 419-592 text.

Printing: Plantin, 10 pt., printed and bound in Great Britain
by William Clowes and Sons Ltd., Beccles.

11.5 x 19 cm., white paper, all edges trimmed; bound in blue
paper (embossed to look like cloth) over boards; the title,
surrounded with a rectangular border, is stamped in gold at
the head of the spine; two stars in gold beneath (to denote
Volume II) and the publisher at the tail.

Price: 25s. Published June 14, 1962.

Dedications: p. [8] To Joseph Conrad; p. [234] To Frau Laura
Schmedding who has so often combated my prejudices and cor-
rected my assertions this with affection; p. [416] To Arthur
Marwood.

Contents: The Fifth Queen. Part One: The Coming -- 11. Part
Two: The House of Eyes -- 71. Part Three: The King Moves --
179. Privy Seal. Part One: The Rising Sun -- 237. Part
Two: The Distant Cloud -- 311. Part Three: The Sunburst --
389. The Fifth Queen Crowned. Part One: The Major Cord --
419. Part Two: The Threatened Rift -- 493. Part Three: The
Dwindling Melody -- 541. Part Four: The End of the Song --
559.

(1963)

THE BODLEY HEAD / FORD / MADOX FORD / VOLUME III / PARADE'S
END: PART ONE / SOME DO NOT ... / *WITH AN INTRODUCTION BY* /
GRAHAM GREENE / [publisher's device] / THE BODLEY HEAD /
LONDON

Collation: [1]/[1*]$^{8/8}$ 2/2*-10/10*$^{8/8}$ 11^{18}, 178 leaves.

Pagination: p. [1] half-title; p. [2] blank; p. [3] title-
page; p. [4] printing, publishing, type and publication
notices; pp. 5-8 INTRODUCTION; p. [9] SOME DO NOT ...; p. [10]
blank; pp. 11-356 text.

Printing: Plantin, 10 pt., printed and bound in Great Britain
by William Clowes and Sons Ltd., Beccles.

11.5 x 19 cm., white paper, all edges trimmed; bound in blue
paper (embossed to look like cloth) over boards; the title,
surrounded with a rectangular border, is stamped in gold at
the head of the spine, three stars in gold beneath (to denote
Volume III) and the publisher at the tail.

Price: 25s.   Published May 13, 1963.

THE BODLEY HEAD / FORD MADOX FORD / VOLUME IV / PARADE'S END /
PART TWO: NO MORE PARADES / PART THREE: A MAN COULD STAND UP /
[publisher's device] / THE BODLEY HEAD / LONDON

Collation: [1]/[1*]$^{8/8}$ 2/2*-13/13*$^{8/8}$ 14^{12} 15/15*$^{8/8}$, 236
leaves.

Pagination: p. [1] half-title; p. [2] blank; p. [3] title-page;
p. [4] printing, publishing, type and publication notices;

p. 5 CONTENTS; p. [6] blank; p. [7] NO MORE PARADES; p. [8]
blank; pp. 9-260 text; p. [261] A MAN COULD STAND UP; p. [262]
blank; pp. 263-470 text; pp. [471-472] blank.

Printing: Plantin, 10 pt., printed and bound in Great Britain
by William Clowes and Sons Ltd., Beccles.

11.5 x 19 cm., white paper, all edges trimmed; bound in blue
paper (embossed to look like cloth) over boards; the title,
surrounded with a rectangular border, is stamped in gold at
the head of the spine, four stars in gold beneath (to denote
Volume IV) and the publisher at the tail.

Price: 25s. Published May 13, 1963.

Contents: No More Parades -- 9. A Man Could Stand Up -- 263.

Notes: The copies examined are in the British Library
(11567.g.3).
    The Bodley Head Ford Madox Ford was originally contained
in the four volumes edited by Graham Greene. A fifth volume,
Memories and Impressions, selected by Michael Killigrew, was
added in 1971. This volume has been published in the United
States by Holt, Rinehart and Winston Inc. with the title:
*Your Mirror to My Times, The Selected Autobiographies and
Impressions of Ford Madox Ford.*
    For the four volumes which he has edited Greene has
written an introduction which starts in Volume I and is continued in Volume III. Immediately evident is the high esteem
in which Greene holds the old novelist. Greene's often-
reprinted essays have made one aware that he takes James as
his master (while at the time owning the influence of Joseph
Conrad and lesser writers of romantic novels). However, in
Greene's estimation, Ford is on the pinnacle: "No one in our
century except James has been more attentive to the craft of
letters." It is "craft" above all that draws Greene's attention to Ford, and Greene's remarks on Ford's techniques tell
one of Greene's interest in his own work.
    Ford's *Fifth Queen*, for instance, is praised for the ex-
periment with the impressionist method which Ford would later
use with such success in *A Man Could Stand Up*. Greene comments particularly on the use of light and compares the novel
with a stage production. A reader more familiar with Greene's
work would perhaps draw the parallel further toward motion
picture production and the mixing of light with point of view.
    For Ford, the technician, Greene finds that *The Good
Soldier* is his "masterpiece." It is the fruit born of his

apprenticeship with Conrad. But it is Ford's involvement in
the novel that Greene wonders most at, and he asks what in
Ford's life gave rise to *The Saddest Story*, the novel's alternate title.

In the second part of his "Introduction" Greene points
out that the printing of *Some Do Not* ..., *No More Parades*, and
A Man Could Stand Up in this edition as a trilogy is for the
first time the version of *Parade's End* that Ford preferred but
never had the fortune to see.

A44   INTRODUCTIONS TO THREE NOVELS   1962

First Edition

Graham Greene / Introductions / to Three Novels / P. A. NOR-
STEDT & SÖNERS FÖRLAG / STOCKHOLM

Collation: [1]/[1*]$^{2/4}$ 2-6^4, 26 leaves.

Pagination: pp. [1-2] blank; p. [3] title-page; p. [4] copyright and publishing notices; pp. 5-8 introduction signed
Ragnar Svanström (in Swedish); p. [9] THE POWER AND THE GLORY;
p. [10] blank; pp. 11-19 text; p. [20] blank; p. [21] THE
HEART OF THE MATTER; p. [22] blank; pp. 23-39 text; p. [40]
blank; p. [41] THE END OF THE AFFAIR; p. [42] blank; pp. 43-
[48] text; p. [49] colophon; pp. [50-52] blank.

Printing: Berling Antique, 11 pt., printed in Sweden by Karl-
Erik Forsberg.

11.5 x 19.5 cm., hand laid cream paper, edges untrimmed and
uncut; bound in tan wrappers with the author in dark gray on
the spine and cover and the title in red on the spine and
cover; the publisher is in gray on the cover.

Price: Undetermined. Published in 1962.

Notes: The copies examined are in the compiler's collection.
     The colophon found on page [49] is as follows: Denna
skrift utgör Norstedts julbok 1962. Den är tryckt hos Kungl.
Boktryckeriet P. A. Norstedt & Söner, Stockholm, samma år.
Texten är satt med Berling antikva och tryckt på 130 grams
festskriftpapper. Typografi Karl-Erik Forsberg. Norstedts'
Christmas Gift Book 1962.
     This beautifully printed little edition carries the
first appearance of several introductory essays to the novels.
They have all been reprinted in the Collected Edition. In-
cluded are the introductions to *The Power and the Glory*, *The
Heart of the Matter* and *The End of the Affair.*

A45   A SENSE OF REALITY   1963

a. *First Edition*

Graham Greene / A SENSE OF REALITY / [publisher's device] /
THE BODLEY HEAD / LONDON

Collation: [1]-[3]^{16} [4]^{8} [5]^{16}, 72 leaves.

Pagination: p. [1] half-title; p. [2] author's advertisement;
p. [3] title-page; p. [4] dedication, copyright, printing,
publishing and type notices; p. [5] CONTENTS; p. [6] blank;
p. [7] UNDER THE GARDEN; p. [8] blank; pp. 9-75 text, with
numbered part headings on pp. 9, 29, 69, and numbered division
headings on pp. 9, 11, 14, 16, 25, 29, 33, 36, 50, 55, 60,
65, 69, 72, 75; p. [76] blank; p. [77] A VISIT TO MORIN;
p. [78] blank; pp. 79-96 text, with numbered division headings
on pp. 79, 82, 88; p. [97] DREAM OF A STRANGE LAND; p. [98]
blank; pp. 99-114 text, with numbered division headings on
pp. 99, 103, 107, 109, 113; p. [115] A DISCOVERY IN THE
WOODS; p. [116] blank; pp. 117-140 text, with numbered division headings on pp. 117, 124, 127, 128, 130, 134; pp. [141-
144] blank.

Printing: Ehrhardt, 11 pt., printed in Great Britain by
William Clowes & Sons Ltd., Beccles.

13 x 19.5 cm., white paper, all edges trimmed, top edges
colored blue-green; bound in green cloth over boards with
the author and title stamped in gold along the spine.

Price: 15s. Published June 20, 1963.

Dedication: To John and Gillian Sutro

Contents: Under the Garden -- 7. A Visit to Morin -- 77.
Dream of a Strange Land -- 97. A Discovery in the Woods --
115.

Notes: The copies examined are in the British Library
(11567 i 40) and the Library of Congress (PZ3/.G8319/Se/2).
     The reader familiar with most of Greene's work may al-
ready be aware of the writer's interest in mythology approached
by means of the dream. Two of the stories in this collection
take their "reality" from the dream state, "Under the Garden"
and "Dream of a Strange Land." The first of these Greene
places among his best work and the tone of this long story,

along with the subject matter, suggests that symbolic elements
are perhaps derived from personal memories. The story "A
Visit to Morin," about an aging French writer who has lost his
faith, has been interpreted as autobiographical, but the wary
reader knows that Greene enjoys a good game and that the game
sometimes can be self-parody. The final story in the collection, "A Discovery in the Woods," is Greene's only attempt at
science fiction.

b. *First American Edition* (1963)

a / *SENSE* / *of* / *REALITY* / GRAHAM / GREENE / [publisher's de-
vice] / THE VIKING PRESS   NEW YORK

Collation: [1]-[4]^{16}, 64 leaves.

Pagination: p. [i] half-title; p. [ii] author's advertisement;
p. [iii] title-page; p. [iv] copyright, printing, publishing
notices and Library of Congress card number; p. [v] dedication;
p. [vi] blank; p. [vii] CONTENTS; p. [viii] blank; p. [1]
UNDER THE GARDEN; p. [2] blank; pp. 3-61 text, with numbered
part headings on pp. 3, 21, 56, and numbered division headings
on pp. 3, 5, 7, 9, 17, 21, 24, 27, 39, 44, 49, 53, 56, 59, 61;
p. [62] blank; p. [63] A VISIT TO MORIN; p. [64] blank; pp.
65-80 text, with numbered division headings on pp. 65, 68, 73;
p. [81] DREAM OF A STRANGE LAND; p. [82] blank; pp. 83-96 text,
with numbered division headings on pp. 83, 86, 90, 92, 96;
p. [97] A DISCOVERY IN THE WOODS; p. [98] blank; pp. 99-119
text, with numbered division headings on pp. 99, 105, 108,
109, 110, 114; p. [120] blank.

Printing: an old style, 11 pt., printed in the U.S.A. by Vail-
Ballou Press, Inc.

13 x 20.5 cm., white paper, all edges trimmed, top edges
colored green; the covers are in half blue cloth over boards,
with the spine and half covers in tan cloth, and titles of
four stories stamped in black on the front cover; the title,
author and publisher are stamped white on black on the spine.

Price: $3.50. Published in July 1963 in a green, coral and
black dust jacket with the title and author in white on black
surrounded by the titles of the stories on the front cover;
the title, author and publisher are on the spine, and descriptions of the stories on the back cover.

Dedication: as first English edition.

Notes: The copies examined are in the compiler's collection
and the Library of Congress (PZ3/.G8319/Se/copy 2).

A46   THE REVENGE   1963

First Edition

THE / REVENGE / *An autobiographical fragment by* / Graham /
GREENE / PRIVATELY PRINTED / 1963

Collation: [1]^8, 8 leaves.

Pagination: pp. [1-2] blank; p. [3] half-title; p. [4] blank;
p. [5] title-page; p. [6] blank; pp. 7-11 text; p. [12] blank;
p. [13] colophon (or notice of the edition); pp. [14-16]
blank.

Printing: Ehrhardt, 11 pt., printed in Great Gritain at the
Stellar Press in Barnet, Herts.

11 x 18.5 cm., hand laid cream paper, edges untrimmed; bound
in a green wrapper over white card with title, subtitle and
author printed in black on the cover.

Price: distributed free during December 1963.

Notes: The copy examined is in the British Library (CUP 510
aa 7).
    "The Revenge" was printed in an edition of 300 copies for
distribution by the author and the publisher.
    The British Library copy is contained in a hard case
covered in green cloth. The author's autograph on the first
page of this copy reads, "For John for his collection. / A
Happy Christmas & love from Graham." The catalogue reports
that the copy had belonged to John Hayward, the biographer,
bookman and Greene's friend.
    Most of "The Revenge" has been printed elsewhere and at
an earlier date. The latest reprinting is in *A Sort of Life*
(Bodley Head, pp. 79-82).

First Edition

Graham Greene / CARVING A / STATUE / A Play / [publisher's
device] / THE BODLEY HEAD / LONDON

Collation: [1]^8 2-4^8 5^4 6^8, 44 leaves.

Pagination: pp. [i-ii] blank; p. [1] half-title; p. [2]
author's advertisement; p. [3] title-page; p. [4] performing
rights, printing, publishing, type and publication notices;
p. [5] CHARACTERS; p. [6] notes on the first production;
pp. 7-8 EPITAPH FOR A PLAY; p. 9 ACT I; pp. 9-30 text of act
one; p. 31 ACT II; pp. 31-56 text of act two; p. 57 ACT III;
pp. 57-82 text of act three; pp. [83-86] blank.

Printing: Monotype Ehrhardt, 11 pt., printed in Great Britain
by William Clowes and Sons Ltd., Beccles.

11 x 18.5 cm., white paper, all edges trimmed, top edges
colored red; bound in dark green cloth over boards with author
and title stamped in gold along the spine; red endpapers.

Price: 12s. 6d. Published on November 11, 1964, in a red
dust jacket with black printing, and a front cover with the
feet of a statue surrounded by scaffolding, the author's name
beneath and the title in white at the tail of the cover; reviews of *In Search of a Character* are on the back cover.

Notes: The copy examined is in the compiler's collection.
    The first production of *Carving a Statue* was by Peter
Wood with sets by Desmond Heeley at the Haymarket Theatre,
London, on September 17, 1964, with the following cast:

The Father	Ralph Richardson
His Son	Dennis Waterman
The First Girl	Barbara Ferris
The Second Girl	Jane Birkin
Dr. Parker	Roland Culver

    This was Ralph Richardson's second Greene play. *The
Complaisant Lover* had been his first. Of course, he had also
played in *The Fallen Idol*, the film of "The Basement Room" by
Greene and Carol Reed.
    Carving a Statue is even more of a departure for Greene
from his traditional methods than was *The Complaisant Lover*.

The play combines elements of fantasy, surrealism and the theatre of the absurd by means of associations that Greene's readers will recognize. The major character is a return to the theme of the obsessed artist haunted by a sense of failure. But the form and language of the play are the real experiments. One hears some dialogue that could be Pinter, some that could be Beckett, and the form is related more to fairy tale, to the imaginative flight of "Under the Garden," than it is to Greene's religious thrillers.

A48   THE COMEDIANS   1966

a. *First Edition*

THE / COMEDIANS / Graham Greene / '... Aspects are within
us, / and who seems / Most kingly is the King.' / *Thomas
Hardy* / [publisher's device] / THE BODLEY HEAD / LONDON

Collation: B/B*-L/L*$^{8/8}$, 160 leaves.

Pagination: p. [1] half-title; p. [2] author's advertisement;
p. [3] title-page; p. [4] copyright, printing, publishing,
type and publication notices; pp. 5-6 dedication; p. [7] PART
I; p. [8] blank; pp. 9-164 text of part one, with chapter
headings on pp. 9, 46, 64, 102, 124, and numbered division
headings on pp. 9, 14, 18, 25, 32, 34, 42, 64, 68, 72, 91,
102, 106, 114, 120, 124, 140, 153, 162; p. [165] PART II;
p. [166] blank; pp. 167-221 text of part two, with chapter
headings on pp. 167, 194, 210, and numbered division headings
on pp. 167, 173, 178, 183, 190, 194, 199, 204, 210, 217;
p. [222] blank; p. [223] PART III; p. [224] blank; pp. 225-
313 text of part three, with chapter headings on pp. 225, 244,
272, 294, and numbered division headings on pp. 225, 241, 244,
250, 260, 264, 267, 272, 276, 279, 294, 297, 302, 308;
pp. [314-320] blank.

Printing: Monotype Ehrhardt, 11 pt., printed and bound in
Great Britain by William Clowes & Sons Ltd., Beccles.

13 x 19.5 cm., white paper, all edges trimmed, top edges
colored blue-gray; bound in green cloth over boards with the
author, title and publisher stamped in gold along the spine.

Price: 25s. Published in January 1966 in a green on green
dust jacket with a tropical plant motif decorating both
covers; author and title are at the top of the spine, publisher at the bottom; author and title are at the top of the
front cover.

Dedication: "To A. S. Frere." is followed by a dedicatory
letter to Frere in which Greene mentions that this is the
first novel that he has written since A. S. Frere ceased to
be associated with W. H. Heinemann Ltd. and that Greene, "like
many other authors on your list, felt that it was time to
find another home."

Notes: The copies examined are in the compiler's collection and the Library of Congress (PZ3/.G8319/Cm/2). Another copy, identical to those above except for the dust jacket described, was seen at Bertram Rota, Booksellers, 30 and 31 Long Acre, London, WC2E 9LT.

According to an interview V.S. Naipaul had with Greene, published in *The Daily Telegraph Magazine* (#179, March 8, 1968), *The Comedians* sold 60,000 copies.

In his dedicatory letter to A.S. Frere, formerly of Heinemann, Greene recalls his thirty-year association with that firm before his move to The Bodley Head. He then develops a lengthy disclaimer to the effect that Brown, the hotel-keeper and narrator, is not Greene, but that outside of the principal characters who are all creations from the novelist's stockpile of observations, "poor Haiti itself" is accurately represented.

By the time of the writing of *The Comedians* the first-person narrative technique was no longer an experiment for Greene. This time the endeavor was in a different direction. Some reviewers missed the spiritual intensity of his earlier work perhaps because they were looking for a different sort of book. But Greene was now working out a new method, a melodramatic hybrid incorporating both the tragic and the farcical. Brown concludes that there are only two possible attitudes in the comedy of which Port-au-Prince, Papa Doc and he, himself, are a part: "the rational and the irrational, misery or gaiety...." Eventually, the saving sense of the irrational and gaiety is modulated by Dr. Magiot's committed humanism.

b. *First American Edition*   (1966)

THE / COMEDIANS / *Graham Greene* / THE VIKING PRESS · NEW YORK

Collation: [1]-[10]^{16}, 160 leaves.

Pagination: p. [i] publisher's device; p. [ii] author's advertisement; p. [iii] half-title; p. [iv] blank; p. [v] title-page; p. [vi] copyright, publishing, Library of Congress card number and printing notices; p. [vii] quotation; p. [viii] blank; pp. [ix-x] dedication; p. [1] PART ONE; p. [2] blank; pp. 3-159 text of part one, with chapter headings on pp. 3, 40, 58, 96, 119, and numbered division headings on pp. 3, 8,

12, 19, 26, 28, 36, 58, 62, 66, 85, 96, 100, 109, 114, 119,
135, 148, 157; p. [160] blank; p. [161] PART TWO; p. [162]
blank; pp. 163-218 text of part two, with chapter headings on
pp. 163, 190, 206, and numbered division headings on pp. 163,
169, 174, 179, 186, 190, 195, 200, 206, 213; p. [219] PART
THREE; p. [220] blank; pp. 221-309 text of part three, with
chapter headings on pp. 221, 240, 268, 290, and numbered division headings on pp. 221, 237, 240, 247, 256, 261, 264,
268, 272, 275, 290, 293, 299, 304; p. [310] blank.

Printing: an old face, 11 pt., printed in the U.S.A. by H.
Wolff Book Mfg. Co.

13.7 x 21.2 cm., white paper, all edges trimmed, top edges
colored dark blue; bound in green paper (slightly marbled in
black) over boards with the spine in black cloth and the
author, title (each surrounded by rectangular borders) and
the publisher stamped in gold.

Price: $5.75. Published in January 1966 in a dust jacket
having a front cover with stylized players' masks in colors
over green, with the author in white, the title in yellow and
the words "a novel" in white; the spine also carries the author in white, the title in yellow and the publisher in white;
the back cover carries advertisements for *The Comedians* in
black over green.

Notes: The copy examined is in the library of West Virginia
State College (PZ/3/G8319/Cm). Another copy seen at the University of Louisville has the dust jacket described.
    The endpapers are in pale green and the typeface is the
same as that on the Viking *A Sense of Reality.*
    Another copy in the West Virginia State College library
with an identical title-page and title-page verso, except
that it is missing the Library of Congress card number and
only says Printed in the U.S.A., is obviously a cheap reprint
-- though the type (same face) has been reset, it has pp. [i]-
x as preliminaries and pp. [1]-275 as text with p. [276]
blank. The binding is a light blue simulated hide (plastic)
over boards with the same spine design as the first edition
except that it is printed in black.
    A specially bound copy, one of 500 "specially bound for
presentation to friends of the author and the publisher in
advance of publication. Christmas 1965," was also seen at the
University of Louisville. This copy is the same as the trade
edition except for the binding of green buckram cloth over
boards with the author and title stamped in gold in black
panels on the spine and the notice of special binding tipped
in before the title-page.

A49 VICTORIAN DETECTIVE FICTION 1966

First Edition

VICTORIAN / DETECTIVE FICTION / [rule device] / A CATALOGUE
OF THE COLLECTION MADE BY / DOROTHY GLOVER & GRAHAM GREENE /
BIBLIOGRAPHICALLY ARRANGED / BY ERIC OSBORNE AND / INTRODUCED
BY JOHN CARTER / [publisher's device in green] / WITH A PRE-
FACE BY / GRAHAM GREENE / THE BODLEY HEAD · LONDON / SYDNEY &
TORONTO

Collation: $[A]^8$ $B-H^8$ I^4 K^8 $L/L2^{2/8}$, 78 leaves.

Pagination: p. [i] half-title; p. [ii] blank; p. [iii] title-
page; p. [iv] printing, publishing and copyright notices;
p. [v] CONTENTS; p. [vi] blank; pp. vii-viii preface by Graham
Greene; pp. ix-xv introduction by John Carter; p. [xvi] blank;
pp. xvii-xviii compiler's note by Eric Osborne; p. [xix] THE
CATALOGUE; p. [xx] blank; pp. 1-121 text of the catalogue;
p. [122] blank; pp. 123-126 APPENDIX; p. [127] note on endpapers; p. [128] blank; p. [129] INDEX OF DETECTIVES; p. [130]
blank; pp. 131-136 text of index of detectives; p. [137] INDEX
OF ILLUSTRATORS; p. [138] blank; pp. 139-140 text of index of
illustrators; p. [141] INDEX OF TITLES; p. [142] blank;
pp. 143-149 text of index of titles; p. [150] blank; p. [151]
colophon, notice of editions and signatures; p. [152] blank.

Printing: Ehrhardt, 11 pt., printed in Great Britain at The
Stellar Press in Barnet, Herts., by Bill Hummerstone on
Strathmore mould-made paper and bound by William Clowes at
Beccles.

16 x 24.8 cm., cream laid paper, all edges trimmed; bound in
green cloth over boards with the title stamped in gold along
the spine and the endpapers decorated in gray on white after
two drawings by Millais; colophon.

Price: 5 guineas. Published in October 1966.

Notes: The copies examined are in the British Library
(2785 CSA.5) and the University of Kentucky Library
(016.823/C844).
    The edition was limited to 500 copies (of which twenty-
five copies were not for sale) and was signed by Dorothy
Glover, John Carter and Graham Greene. The British Library
copy was not numbered in series nor had it been signed by
Greene, though the two other signatures were present. The

British Library copy also had its top edges colored green.
The Kentucky copy was numbered 346 and all three of the signatures were present.

The collection has been assembled by Dorothy Glover and
Graham Greene, arranged by Eric Osborne and introduced by
John Carter. The inclusion of Greene's name on the title-
page of this book comes as no surprise to those who know that
Graham and his brother Hugh are very well versed in this particular form of the thriller. Other related books are their
collection *The Spy's Bedside Book*, and Hugh's *Rivals of
Sherlock Holmes* and its sequel. Besides being a boon to col-
lectors, the indexes for this volume should prove useful
tools for the researcher.

Greene and Dorothy Glover (formerly Dorothy Craigie, the
illustrator of the first editions of Greene's children's
books) began the collection after the war when there were
fewer competitors for many of the included items.

John Carter's introduction puts this collection into its
proper bibliographical context and Eric Osborne's notes indicate that Frank Ochs also worked on the collection. Dorothy
Glover has annotated the catalogue.

A50   MAY WE BORROW YOUR HUSBAND?   1967
                  AND OTHER COMEDIES OF THE SEXUAL LIFE

a. *First Edition*

Graham Greene / May We Borrow / Your Husband? / *And Other
Comedies of* / *the Sexual Life* / *Cling to the virtues normally* /
manifested by all Lebanese. / Prime Minister Sami-as-Sulh /
[publisher's device] / THE BODLEY HEAD / LONDON SYDNEY /
TORONTO

Collation: [1]/1*$^{8/8}$ 2/2*-6/6*$^{8/8}$, 96 leaves.

Pagination: p. [1] half-title; p. [2] author's advertisement;
p. [3] title-page; p. [4] copyright, publishing, printing,
type and publication notices; p. [5] CONTENTS; p. [6] blank;
p. [7] MAY WE BORROW YOUR HUSBAND?; p. [8] blank; pp. 9-46
text, with numbered divisions on pp. 9, 15, 18, 23, 29, 31,
38, 43; p. [47] BEAUTY; p. [48] blank; pp. 49-53 text, with an
unnumbered division on p. 51; p. [54] blank; p. [55] CHAGRIN
IN THREE PARTS; p. [56] blank; pp. 57-65 text, with numbered
divisions on pp. 62 and 64; p. [66] blank; p. [67] THE OVER-
NIGHT BAG; p. [68] blank; pp. 69-76 text; p. [77] MORTMAIN;
p. [78] blank; pp. 79-91 text, with an unnumbered division on
p. 82; p. [92] blank; p. [93] CHEAP IN AUGUST; p. [94] blank;
pp. 95-123 text, with numbered divisions on pp. 95, 102, 110,
117; p. [124] blank; p. [125] A SHOCKING ACCIDENT; p. [126]
blank; pp. 127-134 text, with numbered divisions on pp. 127
and 129; p. [135] THE INVISIBLE JAPANESE GENTLEMEN; p. [136]
blank; pp. 137-141 text; p. [142] blank; p. [143] AWFUL WHEN
YOU THINK OF IT; p. [144] blank; pp. 145-148 text; p. [149]
DOCTOR CROMBIE; p. [150] blank; pp. 151-158 text; p. [159]
THE ROOT OF ALL EVIL; p. [160] blank; pp. 161-175 text;
p. [176] blank; p. [177] TWO GENTLE PEOPLE; p. [178] blank;
pp. 179-188 text; pp. [189-192] blank.

Printing: Ehrhardt, 11 pt., printed and bound in Great Britain
by William Clowes and Sons Ltd., Beccles.

13 x 19.5 cm., white paper, all edges trimmed, top edges
colored blue-gray; bound in green cloth over boards with
author, title and publisher stamped in gold along the spine.

Price: This edition sold for 21s. A signed edition, limited
to 500 copies, was also sold at 5 guineas (see *Notes*).
Published in March 1967 in a dust jacket having the author and
title printed over a design of chairs and table under a palm

tree in pink, red, yellow and black on white, back cover
having reviews of *The Comedians*.

Contents: May We Borrow Your Husband? -- 7. Beauty -- 47.
Chagrin in Three Parts -- 55. The Over-Night Bag -- 67.
Mortmain -- 77. Cheap in August -- 93. A Shocking Accident
-- 125. The Invisible Japanese Gentlemen -- 135. Awful When
You Think of It -- 143. Doctor Crombie -- 149. The Root of
All Evil -- 159. Two Gentle People -- 177.

Notes: The copy examined is in the compiler's collection. The
limited edition has been seen at the University of Louisville
and is identical to the public edition save for the fact that
it has a notice of limitation which is signed, numbered (113)
and tipped in between the title-page verso and the contents
page, and it has a slightly different binding consisting of
decorated paper (alternating green and brown decorative vertical lines) over boards with a green cloth spine and gold
stamping; the binding is protected by a clear plastic wrapper.
    In an interview with V.S. Naipaul, Greene placed sales
for this collection of stories at 25,000 copies.
    In his "Introduction" to the Collected Edition of his
short stories, Greene relates that the stories in this collection were written while he was setting up his apartment in
Antibes and that they were written in a mood of "sad hilarity."
The title story, rather reminiscent of Mann's *Death In Venice*,
in that it depends upon a similar irony for its effect but in
a comic vein, is based upon an incident Greene saw at St.
Jean-Cap Ferrat while working upon *A Burnt-Out Case*. Greene
says the stories in this collection were an "escape in humour
from the thought of death." One story in particular, which he
identifies with his best work, "Cheap in August," takes this
idea partly as its theme. It was elegantly dramatized by
Philip Mackie for the television series "Shades of Greene,"
with Virginia McKenna and Leo McKern in the roles and with
direction by Alvin Rakoff.

b. *First American Edition* (1967)

May We Borrow / *Your Husband?* / [rule] / AND OTHER COMEDIES /
OF THE SEXUAL LIFE / NEW YORK [short diagonal line] THE VIKING
PRESS
[facing page:] *Graham Greene* / Cling to the virtues normally
manifested by all Lebanese. / --Prime Minister Sami-as-Sulh

Collation: [1]-[6]^{16}, 96 leaves.

Pagination: p. [i] half-title; p. [ii] blank; p. [iii] author's advertisement; p. [iv] facing title-page; p. [v] title-page; p. [vi] copyright, publishing, Library of Congress card number, printing notices and acknowledgments; p. [vii] CONTENTS; p. [viii] blank; p. [1] MAY WE BORROW YOUR HUSBAND?; p. [2] blank; pp. 3-46 text, with numbered divisions on pp. 3, 11, 14, 20, 26, 30, 37, 43; pp. 47-52 text of BEAUTY; pp. 53-62 text of CHAGRIN IN THREE PARTS, with numbered divisions on pp. 53, 60, 61; pp. 63-71 text of THE OVER-NIGHT BAG; p. [72] blank; pp. 73-87 text of MORTMAIN; p. [88] blank; pp. 89-122 text of CHEAP IN AUGUST, with numbered divisions on pp. 89, 97, 107, 116; pp. 123-131 text of A SHOCKING ACCIDENT, with numbered divisions on pp. 123 and 125; p. [132] blank; pp. 133-138 text of THE INVISIBLE JAPANESE GENTLEMEN; pp. 139-143 text of AWFUL WHEN YOU THINK OF IT; p. [144] blank; pp. 145-153 text of DOCTOR CROMBIE; p. [154] blank; pp. 155-172 text of THE ROOT OF ALL EVIL; pp. 173-183 text of TWO GENTLE PEOPLE; p. [184] blank.

Printing: an old face, 12 pt., printed in the U.S.A. by H. Wolff Book Mfg. Co.

13.5 x 21.2 cm., white paper, top and fore edges trimmed, top edges colored green; bound in green paper over boards with the author's initials in script stamped in gold on the front cover, with the spine in black cloth and the author, publisher and title stamped in gold.

Price: $4.50. Published in April 1967.

Contents: May We Borrow Your Husband? -- 3. Beauty -- 47. Chagrin in Three Parts -- 53. The Over-Night Bag -- 63. Mortmain -- 73. Cheap in August -- 89. A Shocking Accident -- 123. The Invisible Japanese Gentlemen -- 133. Awful When You Think of It -- 139. Doctor Crombie -- 145. The Root of All Evil -- 155. Two Gentle People -- 173.

Notes: The copy examined is in the collection of the library of West Virginia State College (PZ/3/G8319/May).

    The acknowledgments on p. [vi] indicate that "Mortmain" first appeared in *Playboy* and "Two Gentle People" in *Vogue* (as "The Secret"). Other stories in this collection were first published in *Esquire*, *Rogue*, *Saturday Evening Post*, *Show* and *Status*.

A51   MODERN FILM SCRIPTS   1968
                                    THE THIRD MAN

a. *First Edition*

MODERN / FILM / SCRIPTS / THE THIRD MAN / a film by / Graham
Greene / and Carol Reed / Lorrimer, London

Collation: [1]–[6]$^{8/12}$ [7]^{8}, 68 leaves.

Pagination: p. [1] title-page; p. [2] copyright, publishing,
publication, sales limitation and printing notices; p. [3]
CONTENTS; p. [4] ACKNOWLEDGMENTS; pp. 5–6 INTRODUCTION;
pp. 7–9 MAIN CHARACTERS; p. 10 CREDITS; p. 11 CAST; pp. 12–13
NOTE; p. [14] blank; pp. 15–134 text, with pp. [17–20, 37–40,
57–60, 77–80, 97–100, 117–120] being black and white photographs; p. [135] blank; p. [136] errata slip tipped in.

Printing: Baskerville, 11 pt., manufactured in Great Britain
by Villiers Publications Ltd., London NW5.

13.5 x 20 cm., white paper, all edges trimmed; bound in
printed wrappers with title and authors in white over a still
of Orson Welles on the front cover; the title, authors, the
number in series and the publisher are in black on white
along the spine; the back cover has a still of Trevor Howard
and Joseph Cotten and advertisements for other scripts in
the series, printed black on green.

Price: 12s. 6d. Published in December 1968.

Notes: The copy examined is in the compiler's collection.
    The acknowledgments indicate that the edited text has
been derived from Carol Reed's personal copy of the script
which was vetted by Graham Greene before publication. The
editors, who remain anonymous, thank Martin Hayden for his
assistance, Joel Finler, the British Film Institute and the
Museum of Modern Art (N.Y.) for the use of their stills.
    The book is number 13 in the series "Modern Film Scripts,"
by Lorrimer Publishing Limited, 47 Dean Street, London W1.
    According to Andrew Sinclair's "Introduction," notes and
brackets in the text show the changes made by Carol Reed and
Orson Welles in the film's final version. Sinclair also indicates that Greene has retained all literary rights in the
property, a rarity in the film business.
    This is the only one of Greene's scripts to be
published.

b. *First American Edition* (1969)

Title-Page: as first English edition with the exception that Simon and Schuster, New York, replaces Lorrimer, London.

Collation: as first English edition.

Pagination: as first English edition.

Printing: as first English edition.

Description: as first English edition.

Price: $1.95. Published in 1969.

A52   COLLECTED ESSAYS   1969

a. *First Edition*

Graham Greene / Collected Essays / [publisher's device] /
THE BODLEY HEAD / LONDON   SYDNEY / TORONTO

Collation: [1]^8 2-29^8, 232 leaves.

Pagination: p. [1] half-title; p. [2] author's advertisement;
p. [3] title-page; p. [4] copyright, printing, publishing,
type and publication notices; pp. 5-8 CONTENTS; p. 9 AUTHOR'S
NOTE; p. 10 ACKNOWLEDGMENTS; p. [11] PART I / PERSONAL PRO-
LOGUE; p. [12] blank; pp. 13-19 text of part one; pp. 13-19
THE LOST CHILDHOOD; p. [20] blank; p. [21] PART II / NOVELS
AND NOVELISTS; p. [22] blank; pp. 23-82 text of part two,
division one; pp. 23-40 HENRY JAMES: THE PRIVATE UNIVERSE;
pp. 41-53 HENRY JAMES: THE RELIGIOUS ASPECT; pp. 54-61 THE
PORTRAIT OF A LADY; pp. 62-68 THE PLAYS OF HENRY JAMES;
pp. 69-74 THE DARK BACKWARD: A FOOTNOTE; pp. 75-78 TWO
FRIENDS; pp. 79-82 FROM FEATHERS TO IRON; pp. 83-114 text of
part two, division two; pp. 83-94 FIELDING AND STERNE; pp. 95-
97 SERVANTS OF THE NOVEL; pp. 98-100 ROMANCE IN PIMLICO;
pp. 101-110 THE YOUNG DICKENS; pp. 111-114 Hans Andersen;
pp. 115-245 text of part two, division three; pp. 115-121
FRANÇOIS MAURIAC; pp. 122-126 BERNANOS, THE BEGINNER; pp. 127-
131 THE BURDEN OF CHILDHOOD; pp. 132-134 MAN MADE ANGRY;
pp. 135-140 G. K. CHESTERTON, with numbered divisions on
pp. 135 and 137; pp. 141-148 WALTER DE LA MARE'S SHORT STORIES;
pp. 149-152 THE SARATOGA TRUNK; pp. 153-155 ARABIA DESERTA;
pp. 156-158 THE POKER-FACE; pp. 159-171 FORD MADOX FORD, with
numbered divisions on pp. 159, 162, 167; pp. 172-175 FREDERICK
ROLFE: EDWARDIAN INFERNO; pp. 176-178 FREDERICK ROLFE: FROM
THE DEVIL'S SIDE; pp. 179-181 FREDERICK ROLFE: A SPOILED
PRIEST; pp. 182-184 REMEMBERING MR. JONES; pp. 185-187 THE
DOMESTIC BACKGROUND; pp. 188-190 THE PUBLIC LIFE; pp. 191-196
GOATS AND INCENSE; pp. 197-205 SOME NOTES ON SOMERSET MAUGHAM,
with numbered divisions on pp. 197, 199, 202; pp. 206-208 THE
TOWN OF MALGUDI; pp. 209-214 RIDER HAGGARD'S SECRET; pp. 215-
219 JOURNEY INTO SUCCESS; pp. 220-222 ISIS IDOL; pp. 223-225
THE LAST BUCHAN; pp. 226-231 EDGAR WALLACE; pp. 232-240 BEATRIX
POTTER; pp. 241-245 HARKAWAY'S OXFORD; p. [246] blank; p. [247]
PART III / SOME CHARACTERS; p. [248] blank; pp. 249-291 text
of part three, division one; pp. 249-252 POETRY FROM LIMBO;
pp. 253-256 AN UNHEROIC DRAMATIST; pp. 257-259 DR. OATES OF
SALAMANCA; pp. 260-262 ANTHONY A WOOD; pp. 263-267 JOHN

EVELYN; pp. 268-270 BACKGROUND FOR HEROES; pp. 271-275 A HOAX
ON MR. HULTON; pp. 276-279 A JACOBITE POET; pp. 280-283
CHARLES CHURCHILL; pp. 284-288 THE LOVER OF LEEDS; pp. 289-291
INSIDE OXFORD; pp. 292-339 text of part three, division two;
pp. 292-306 GEORGE DARLEY; pp. 307-311 THE APOSTLES INTERVENE;
pp. 312-315 MR. COOK'S CENTURY; pp. 316-321 THE EXPLORERS;
pp. 322-328 'SORE BONES; MUCH HEADACHE'; pp. 329-336 FRANCIS
PARKMAN; pp. 337-339 DON IN MEXICO; pp. 340-419 text of part
three, division three; pp. 340-342 SAMUEL BUTLER; pp. 343-346
THE UGLY ACT; pp. 347-350 ERIC GILL; pp. 351-358 HERBERT READ;
pp. 359-361 THE CONSERVATIVE; pp. 362-365 NORMAN DOUGLAS;
pp. 366-368 INVINCIBLE IGNORANCE; pp. 369-371 THE VICTOR AND
THE VICTIM; pp. 372-375 SIMONE WEIL; pp. 376-401 THREE
PRIESTS (pp. 376-379, 1. THE OXFORD CHAPLAIN; pp. 380-396, 2.
THE PARADOX OF A POPE; pp. 397-401, 3. EIGHTY YEARS ON THE
BARRACK SQUARE); pp. 402-419 THREE REVOLUTIONARIES (pp. 402-
404, 1. THE MAN AS PURE AS LUCIFER; pp. 405-413, 2. THE
MARXIST HERETIC; pp. 414-419, 3. I SPY); pp. 420-451 text of
part three, division four; pp. 420-422 PORTRAIT OF A MAIDEN
LADY; pp. 423-426 FILM LUNCH; pp. 427-431 THE UNKNOWN WAR;
pp. 432-436 GREAT DOG OF WEIMAR; pp. 437-441 THE BRITISH PIG;
pp. 442-446 GEORGE MOORE AND OTHERS; pp. 447-451 AT HOME;
p. [452] blank; p. [453] PART IV / PERSONAL POSTSCRIPT;
p. [454] blank; pp. 455-463 text of part four; pp. 455-463
THE SOUPSWEET LAND; p. [464] blank.

Printing: Monotype Plantin Light, 10 pt., printed and bound in
Great Britain by William Clowes & Sons Ltd., Beccles.

12.5 x 19.5 cm., white paper, all edges trimmed, top edges
colored blue-gray; bound in green cloth over boards with the
author and title in a double ruled rectangle and the publisher
stamped in gold on the spine.

Price: 42s. Published in March 1969 in a gray dust jacket
with the author in white and the title in black separated by a
blue horizontal line on the front cover; on the white spine
the author is in black while the title and publisher are in
blue; the back cover carries reviews of *The Lost Childhood*.

Notes: The copy examined is in the compiler's collection.
    In an "Author's Note" on p. 9 Greene discusses his prin-
ciple of selection of the essays reprinted in this volume. He
says he has not included any work which if it were written
at the time of writing the note, he would have written in "a
different sense." He goes on that this principle is inclusive
of his likes as well as his dislikes. He feels that a writer
"should be judged by his enmities as well as by his
friendships."

It is interesting that, noting the fact that Greene's reputation as a critic rests largely on the essays he has collected for this volume, he has done a considerable amount of culling over the years. The essays in *Collected Essays* represent a small percentage of his total critical output. *The Spectator* magazine alone printed over 400 reviews and articles during the nine years he was with that journal. A reader who wishes a complete view of Greene as a critic must consult those periodicals in which most of the reviews first appeared or wait for the appearance, one hopes, of a truly comprehensive collection.

b. *First American Edition* (1969)

Graham Greene / COLLECTED ESSAYS / [device] / New York [short diagonal line]   The Viking Press

Collation: [1]-[7]^{16} [8]^{8} [9]-[15]^{16}, 232 leaves.

Pagination: as first English edition.

Printing: Monotype Plantin Light, 10 pt., printed in the U.S.A. by The Colonial Press, Inc.

12.5 x 19.5 cm., white wove paper, all edges trimmed, top edges colored orange; bound in cloth over boards with the spine and a third of the covers in orange, and the remaining cover in tan with the author, title and publisher stamped in black on the spine and a device stamped in gold between author and title.

Price: $7.95.   Published in June 1969.

Notes: The copy examined is in the library at West Virginia State College (PR6013/R44 A16).
     Though the English and American editions collate differently, there are only slight differences between the two editions.   On the American edition:
a.   the half-title page carries only the title;
b.   the author's advertisement lists the American titles with English titles in parentheses;
c.   the subtitle of *May We Borrow Your Husband?* is missing in the author's advertisement;
d.   the play *Carving a Statue* is not listed in the author's advertisement.

A53   TRAVELS WITH MY AUNT   1969

a. *First Edition*

TRAVELS / WITH MY AUNT / *A NOVEL* / Graham Greene / [publisher's device] / THE BODLEY HEAD / LONDON   SYDNEY   TORONTO

Collation: $[1]^{16}$ 2-10^{16}, 160 leaves.

Pagination: p. [1] half-title; p. [2] author's advertisement, p. [3] title-page; p. [4] copyright, publishing, printing and type notices; p. [5] dedication; p. [6] blank; p. [7] PART I; p. [8] blank; pp. 9-219 text of part one, with chapter headings on pp. 9, 15, 19, 30, 41, 51, 59, 75, 85, 95, 104, 113, 123, 133, 148, 166, 174, 181, 193, 212; p. [220] blank; p. [221] PART II; p. [222] blank; pp. 223-319 text of part two, with chapter headings on pp. 223, 236, 242, 256, 272, 284, 296, 309; p. [320] blank.

Printing: Ehrhardt, 11 pt., printed and bound in Great Britain by William Clowes & Sons Ltd., Beccles.

13 x 19.5 cm., white paper, all edges trimmed, top edges colored blue-gray; bound in green cloth over boards with the author, title and publisher stamped in gold on the spine.

Price: 30s. Published in November 1969 in a white dust jacket with author's name in capitals at the head of the cover with the title below in script; also on the cover is an illustration beneath of blue-red birds under a glass dust cover and red dahlias in a black urn, all on a black and white marble tabletop with Italian designs in yellow, red, blue and green; the author and title in black are separated by a red ruled line on the spine with the publisher at the tail; the back cover carries five reviews of *The Collected Essays*.

Dedication: To H.H.K. who helped me more than I can tell

Notes: The copy examined is in the compiler's collection.
    This novel seems, by comparison, to be the most unusual of Greene's later novels. Appearing at first glance formless, it has, in fact, a very specific form designed for a purpose. The first two-thirds are part picaresque, with Aunt Augusta as picaroon, and part apprenticeship novel, with her middle-aged "nephew" Henry as the innocent abroad. The final third is a river voyage for the "nephew" into darkest South America and, by way of Henry's examination of his background, along

with his travels, one is provided a literary pilgrimage to all
the "dog eared pages" in Greene's books. This novel quite
literally maps out practically every conscious influence on
Greene's work and no doubt a few unconscious ones too. *Travels
with My Aunt* is a fictional autobiography not so much of
events but of the ideas and impressions that have dominated
Greene's life as an artist. An enumeration here of the material included would not be helpful. The reader is advised to
reread as much of Greene's work as possible before attempting
a serious study of this book.

b. *First American Edition* (1970)

TRAVELS / WITH MY AUNT / New York [short diagonal line]
The Viking Press
[facing page:] A NOVEL BY / [device] / GRAHAM GREENE

Collation: [1]-[8]^{16}, 128 leaves.

Pagination: p. [1] half-title; p. [ii] blank; p. [iii] author's
advertisement; p. [iv] facing title-page; p. [v] title-page;
p. [vi] copyright, publishing, Library of Congress card number
and printing notices; p. [vii] dedication; p. [viii] blank;
p. [1] PART I; p. [2] blank; pp. 3-165 text of part one, with
chapter headings on pp. 3, 7, 10, 18, 27, 35, 41, 54, 61, 68,
75, 83, 91, 98, 109, 123, 129, 135, 144, 159; p. [166] blank;
p. [167] PART II; p. [168] blank; pp. 169-244 text of part
two, with chapter headings on pp. 169, 179, 184, 194, 207,
216, 226, 236; pp. [245-248] blank.

Printing: Times Roman, 10 pt., printed in the U.S.A. by Vail-
Ballou Press, Inc.

14.5 x 21.5 cm., white paper, top edges colored violet and
trimmed, all others untrimmed; bound in boards with the spine
in ivory cloth, the covers and endpapers in violet paper, the
author, title and publisher on the spine in violet with a
device, "GG," stamped in gold on the cover.

Price: $5.95. Published in January 1970.

Dedication: as first English edition.

Notes: The copy examined is in the library of West Virginia
State College (Pr 6013/R44).

A54   MR. VISCONTI ... AN EXTRACT FROM   1969
                    TRAVELS WITH MY AUNT

First Edition

300 copies published in London, privately printed and bound
in wrappers.
     Probably one of the Christmas books, but the compiler
can provide no further information, having not seen a copy.

A55   A SORT OF LIFE   1971

a. *First Edition*

A / SORT / OF / LIFE / [rule] / Graham Greene / [rule] /
[publisher's device] / THE BODLEY HEAD / LONDON SYDNEY /
TORONTO

Collation: [1]/1*$^{8/8}$ 2/2*-7/7*$^{8/8}$, 112 leaves.

Pagination: pp. [i-ii] blank; p. [1] half-title; p. [2]
author's advertisement; p. [3] title-page; p. [4] copyright,
printing, publishing, type and publication notices; p. [5]
dedication; p. [6] blank; p. [7] quotation; p. [8] blank;
pp. 9-10 foreword; pp. 11-[216] text, with chapter headings
on pp. 11, 42, 71, 92, 104, 121, 132, 144, 158, 168, 196, and
numbered division headings on pp. 11, 14, 31, 42, 60, 71, 79,
83, 86, 92, 96, 104, 111, 119, 121, 126, 132, 134, 136, 144,
156, 158, 161, 168, 170, 176, 180, 182, 190, 193, 196, 200,
202, 207, 212; pp. [217-222] blank.

Printing: Ehrhardt, 11 pt., printed and bound in Great Britain
by William Clowes & Sons Ltd., Beccles.

13 x 19.5 cm., white paper, all edges trimmed, top edges
colored green-gray; bound in green cloth over boards with
the title, author and publisher stamped in gold on the spine.

Price: £1.80. Published in September 1971 in a dust jacket
printed in blue-gray with author in white, a magenta horizontal line and title in yellow on the cover with author in yellow, title in white and publisher in magenta along the spine.

Dedication: For the survivors, Raymond Greene, Hugh Greene
and Elisabeth Dennys

Notes: The copy examined is in the compiler's collection.
      Page [7] carries the following quotation from Kierke-
gaard: "Only robbers and gypsies say that one must never
return where one has once been."
      The autobiographical fragments Greene had already pub-
lished in various places and formats along with personal
pronouncements and memories that are often found in his critical writing -- and this is to disregard the autobiographical
element in his fiction -- had already covered some of what is
presented in this volume. The very fact that this is the
first attempt on Greene's part at extensive autobiography

makes it valuable. The moment one turns the pages it is obvious that the book will provide some insight into the writer's mind and imagination. However, if the reader intends
to use *A Sort of Life* as a tool of literary research, he
would be advised to become familiar first with those texts of
Greene's fiction and drama which draw much of their material
from aspects covered in this autobiography. A list of these
works would include: *The Man Within*, *The Name of Action*,
Rumour at Nightfall, *The Basement Room and Other Stories*,
"Under the Garden," *The Potting Shed*, *Carving a Statue* and
Travels with My Aunt.

b. *First American Edition* (1971)

A / SORT / OF LIFE / [rule] / GRAHAM GREENE / SIMON AND
SCHUSTER / NEW YORK

Collation: [1]-[7]^{16}, 112 leaves.

Pagination: p. [1] publisher's device; pp. [2-3] author's
advertisement; p. [4] blank; p. [5] title-page; p. [6] reproduction rights, copyright, publishing, Library of Congress
card number, design and manufacturing notices; p. [7] dedication; p. [8] blank; p. [9] quotation; p. [10] blank;
pp. 11-12 foreword; pp. 13-220 text, with chapter headings
on pp. 13, 44, 73, 94, 106, 123, 134, 147, 161, 171, 200, and
numbered division headings on pp. 13, 17, 33, 44, 63, 73, 81,
85, 88, 94, 98, 106, 113, 121, 123, 128, 134, 137, 138, 147,
159, 161, 164, 171, 174, 180, 184, 186, 194, 197, 200, 204,
207, 211, 216; pp. [221-224] blank.

Printing: Baskerville, 12 pt., printed in the U.S.A.

13.7 x 20.9 cm., white paper, all edges trimmed; bound in
black cloth over boards with the author, title and publisher
stamped in silver on the spine.

Price: $6.95. Published in September 1971 in a white plastic-
coated dust jacket with the author and title in black on the
front cover, the author in black, title in red and publisher
in purple on the spine, and a portrait of the author by Karsh
on the back cover.

Dedication: as first English edition.

Notes: The copy examined is in the Rare Book Department of
the Library of Congress (PR6013/.R44252/copy 2).

The quotation on p. [9] is identical to that on p. [7]
of the first English edition.

A56 COLLECTED STORIES 1972

a. *First Edition*

Graham Greene / COLLECTED / STORIES / INCLUDING / May We
Borrow Your Husband? / A Sense of Reality / Twenty-One
Stories / [monogram-device] / THE BODLEY HEAD / & / WILLIAM
HEINEMANN / LONDON

Collation: [1]-[18]^{16}, 288 leaves.

Pagination: p. [i] half-title and volume number; p. [ii]
author's advertisement; p. [iii] title-page; p. [iv] copy-
right, printing, type and publication notices; pp. v-vi
CONTENTS; pp. vii-xii INTRODUCTION; p. [1] MAY WE BORROW YOUR
HUSBAND? AND OTHER COMEDIES OF THE SEXUAL LIFE and quotation;
p. [2] blank; pp. 3-161 text; pp. 3-42 MAY WE BORROW YOUR
HUSBAND?, with numbered divisions on pp. 3, 10, 13, 18, 24,
27, 34, 39; pp. 43-47 BEAUTY; pp. 48-56 CHAGRIN IN THREE
PARTS, with numbered divisions on pp. 48, 54, 55; pp. 57-64
THE OVER-NIGHT BAG; pp. 65-78 MORTMAIN; pp. 79-109 CHEAP IN
AUGUST, with numbered divisions on pp. 79, 86, 95, 103;
pp. 110-117 A SHOCKING ACCIDENT, with numbered divisions on
pp. 110 and 112; pp. 118-123 THE INVISIBLE JAPANESE GENTLE-
MEN; pp. 124-127 AWFUL WHEN YOU THINK OF IT; pp. 128-135
DOCTOR CROMBIE; pp. 136-151 THE ROOT OF ALL EVIL; pp. 152-161
TWO GENTLE PEOPLE; p. [162] blank; p. [163] A SENSE OF REALITY;
p. [164] blank; pp. 165-323 text; pp. 165-237 UNDER THE GAR-
DEN, with part headings on pp. 165, 187, 230, and numbered
divisions on pp. 165, 167, 170, 173, 182, 187, 191, 194, 209,
214, 221, 226, 230, 233, 236; pp. 238-256 A VISIT TO MORIN,
with numbered divisions on pp. 238, 242, 247; pp. 257-264
THE BLESSING; pp. 265-272 CHURCH MILITANT; pp. 273-280 DEAR
DR. FALKENHEIM; pp. 281-297 DREAM OF A STRANGE LAND, with
numbered divisions on pp. 281, 285, 289, 292, 296; pp. 298-
323 A DISCOVERY IN THE WOODS, with numbered divisions on
pp. 298, 305, 309, 310, 312, 316; p. [324] blank; p. [325]
TWENTY-ONE STORIES; p. [326] blank; pp. 327-[562] text;
pp. 327-346 THE DESTRUCTORS, with numbered divisions on pp.
327, 334, 338, 344; pp. 347-354 SPECIAL DUTIES; pp. 355-360
THE BLUE FILM; pp. 361-375 THE HINT OF AN EXPLANATION; pp.
376-393 WHEN GREEK MEETS GREEK, with numbered divisions on
pp. 376, 380, 383, 386, 389; pp. 394-401 MEN AT WORK; pp.
402-406 ALAS, POOR MALING; pp. 407-411 THE CASE FOR THE
DEFENCE; pp. 412-419 A LITTLE PLACE OFF THE EDGWARE ROAD;
pp. 420-432 ACROSS THE BRIDGE; pp. 433-450 A DRIVE IN THE

COUNTRY; pp. 451–456 THE INNOCENT; pp. 457–489 THE BASEMENT
ROOM, with numbered divisions on pp. 457, 464, 470, 476, 482;
pp. 490–509 A CHANCE FOR MR. LEVER; pp. 510–519 BROTHER;
pp. 520–527 JUBILEE; pp. 528–533 A DAY SAVED; pp. 534–537 I
SPY; pp. 538–543 PROOF POSITIVE; pp. 544–550 THE SECOND DEATH;
pp. 551–[562] THE END OF THE PARTY; pp. [563–564] blank.

Printing: Plantin Light, 10 pt., printed and bound in Great
Britain by William Clowes & Sons Ltd., Beccles.

11.5 x 19 cm., white paper, all edges trimmed, top edges
colored blue-gray; bound in green cloth over boards with the
title, bordered by double ruled lines, and the publishers
stamped in gold on the spine.

Price: £3.25.   Published in September 1972.

Contents: Introduction -- vii-xii. May We Borrow Your Husband:
May We Borrow Your Husband? -- 3. Beauty -- 43. Chagrin in
Three Parts -- 48. The Over-Night Bag -- 57. Mortmain -- 65.
Cheap in August -- 79. A Shocking Accident -- 110. The Invisible Japanese Gentlemen -- 118. Awful When You Think Of
It -- 124. Doctor Crombie -- 128. The Root of All Evil --
136. Two Gentle People -- 152. A Sense of Reality: Under
the Garden -- 165. A Visit to Morin -- 238. The Blessing --
257. Church Militant -- 265. Dear Dr. Falkenheim -- 273.
Dream of a Strange Land -- 281. A Discovery in the Woods --
298. Twenty-One Stories: The Destructors -- 327. Special
Duties -- 347. The Blue Film -- 355. The Hint of an Explanation -- 361. When Greek Meets Greek -- 376. Men At Work --
394. Alas, Poor Maling -- 402. The Case for the Defence --
407. A Little Place Off the Edgware Road -- 412. Across
the Bridge -- 420. A Drive in the Country -- 433. The Innocent -- 451. The Basement Room -- 457. A Chance for Mr.
Lever -- 490. Brother -- 510. Jubilee -- 520. A Day Saved
-- 528. I Spy -- 534. Proof Positive -- 538. The Second
Death -- 544. The End of the Party -- 551.

Notes: The copy examined is in the library of the University
of North Carolina (PR 6013/R44/A6/1972). The book is volume 8
of the Collected Edition.
    Though the collection appears to be only a reprint of the
three previous collections, close scrutiny indicates that
Greene has made a significant change in the *A Sense of Reality*
section for this volume, a change which might be easily over-
looked (it is alluded to only very briefly in the publication
notices on the title-page verso). Greene has added three
previously uncollected stories to *A Sense of Reality*. These

stories are "Church Militant" (first published in *New States-man* and *Commonweal* in 1956), "Dear Dr. Falkenheim" (first published in *Vogue* in 1963) and "The Blessing" (first published in *New Statesman* in 1966). There are no other changes in the collections.

Greene has written a six-page "Introduction" to the volume which informs the reader about the author's attitude toward the short story form and gives some information about the origins of certain stories.

Stories in the *Twenty-One Stories* section are dated as are those added to *A Sense of Reality* ("Church Militant," "Dear Dr. Falkenheim," and "The Blessing"), but the other stories in *A Sense of Reality* and in *May We Borrow Your Husband?* are not dated.

b. *First American Edition* (1973)

GRAHAM / GREENE / Collected / Stories / [monogram device] / INCLUDING / May We Borrow Your Husband? / A Sense of Reality / Twenty-One Stories / THE VIKING PRESS NEW YORK

Collation: 288 leaves (perfect binding).

Pagination: as first English edition.

Printing: Plantin Light, 10 pt., printed in the U.S.A.

13 x 20.3 cm., white paper, all edges trimmed, top edges colored green; bound in black cloth over boards with the author and publisher stamped in silver, the title stamped in green and a circled lower case monogram "g" blind stamped on the spine.

Price: $10.00. Published in September 1973.

Notes: The copy examined is in the library of West Virginia State College (PZ/3/G8319/CK3).

A57   THE PLEASURE-DOME   1972

a. *First Edition*

THE / PLEASURE -/ DOME / Graham Greene / The Collected Film
Criticism 1935-40 / Edited by John Russell Taylor / *'It was
a miracle of rare device, / A sunny pleasure-dome with caves
of ice.'* / Secker & Warburg / London

Collation: [1]-[18]^8, 144 leaves.

Pagination: p. [i] back of frontispiece; p. [ii] frontispiece; p. [iii] title-page; p. [iv] copyright, publishing,
printing notices and Library of Congress number; pp. 1-4
INTRODUCTION; pp. 5-275 text, with black and white stills on
pp. 5, 9, 12, 13, 15, 17, 21, 23, 27, 30, 31, 33, 38, 43, 44,
46, 48, 49, 52, 55, 59, 60, 63, 68, 69, [70], 71, 77, 79, 83,
85, 88, 93, 99, 102, 105, 107, 110, 112, 114, 116, [118]-119,
125, [128]-129, 135, 136, 138, 142, [146]-147, 152-153, 158-
159, 164, 168-169, 170, 176, 177, 182-183, 185, 188-189, 193,
196, 202, 207, 208-209, 212, 214, [216]-217, 219, 226, 232-
233, 244, 251, 253, 256, 260, 263, 266, 267, 269, 271, 272,
274; pp. 276-277 APPENDIX; pp. 278-284 INDEX.

Printing: Times Roman, 12 pt., printed in Great Britain by
Jarrold & Sons Ltd., Norwich.

17 x 24.5 cm., white paper, all edges trimmed; bound in black
cloth over boards with a double rule, author and title, another double rule and the publisher stamped in silver on the
spine; the printed endpapers have a photographic reproduction
in black and magenta of the inside of a large movie house.

Price: £3.50. Printed in October 1972.

Contents: The Bride of Frankenstein; The Glass Key; No More
Ladies; Abyssinia -- 5-6. St. Petersburg; Paris Love Song;
The Phantom Light -- 6-7. Becky Sharp; Public Hero No. 1;
Barcarole -- 8, 10. The Voice of Britain; Mimi -- 10-11.
The Trunk Mystery; Hands of Orlac; Look Up and Laugh; The
Memory Expert -- 11-12. Der Schimmelreiter; Star of Midnight
-- 14. Where's George; The Great God Gold; Boys Will be Boys;
The Murder Man -- 15-16. The Crusades -- 16-18. Dood Wasser;
Me and Marlborough -- 18-19. On Wings of Song; Peg of Old
Drury; Break of Hearts -- 20-22. The Black Room -- 22-23.
Jazz Comedy; Two for Tonight -- 23-24. Song of Ceylon -- 25.
Anna Karenina; The Informer -- 25-26. A Midsummer Night's

Dream -- 28-29. Joan of Arc; Turn of the Tide; Top Hat; She
-- 29-30, 32. Barbary Coast; Episode; The Passing of the
Third Floor Back -- 32-34. Last Love; Moscow Nights; Oil for
the Lamps of China -- 35-36. Arms and the Girl; Accent on
Youth -- 36-37. The Last Outpost -- 37-38. La Bandéra; Come
Out of the Pantry -- 38-39. Riders to the Sea -- 39-40. The
Ghost Goes West -- 40-41. The Guv'nor; Midshipman Easy;
Treasure Island -- 42, 44. Reifende Jugend; The Bride Comes
Home -- 45-46. Second Bureau; Sans Famille -- 46-47. The
Case of the Lucky Legs; Charlie Chan in Shanghai -- 48-50.
Dr. Socrates; The Man Who Broke the Bank at Monte Carlo; The
Imperfect Lady -- 50-51. Modern Times -- 51-53. I Dream Too
Much; Anything Goes; Faust; Hohe Schule; Captain Blood --
53-54. Things to Come; Bonne Chance -- 54-56; Rose of the
Rancho; Jack of All Trades -- 56-57. Crime et Châtiment;
Veille d'Armes -- 57-58. The Milky Way; Strike Me Pink; Night
Mail; Crime and Punishment -- 58-61. Rhodes of Africa;
October -- 61-62. Merlusse; The Day of the Great Adventure;
Desire -- 62, 64; Liebesmelodie; Pot Luck; If Only You Could
Cook; One Way Ticket -- 64-65. Kliou the Tiger -- 65-66. Fol-
low the Fleet; The Peace Film -- 67, 69. These Three; The
Student of Prague -- 69, 72. Anne-Marie; Tudor Rose -- 73-74.
The Trail of the Lonesome Pine; Secret Agent -- 74-75. Klondyke Annie; Professional Soldier -- 75-76. The Robber Symphony; The Littlest Rebel; The Emperor's Candlesticks -- 76,
78. The Marriage of Corbal -- 78-80. The Country Doctor --
80-81. Dangerous; Big Brown Eyes -- 81-82. Show Boat; The
Moon's Our Home -- 82-84. Fury; The Story of Louis Pasteur --
84-86. One Rainy Afternoon; Janosik; The Phantom Gondola --
86-87. Poppy; Living Dangerously; Charlie Chan at the Circus
-- 87-89. The Petrified Forest -- 89-90. Laburnum Grove; Ourselves Alone -- 90-91. Under Two Flags; Captain January --
91-92. Rhythm on the Range -- 93-94. Everything Is Thunder;
Die Kribbebijter -- 94-95. Mr. Deeds Goes to Town -- 96-97.
The Man Who Could Work Miracles -- 97-98. As You Like It;
Cover to Cover -- 98, 100. The Great Ziegfeld; It's Love
Again; Marchand D'Amour; East Meets West -- 100-101. The Song
of Freedom; Anthony Adverse -- 103-104. Maria Bashkirtseff;
My Man Godfrey -- 104, 106. The Texas Rangers; Savoy Hotel
217; The King Steps Out -- 106-108. Nutrition -- 108-109.
Romeo and Juliet -- 109-111. La Kermesse Héroïque; The
General Died at Dawn -- 111-113. Dodsworth; Mayerling; Fox
Hunt -- 113, 115. Fredlös; The Gay Desperado -- 115-117.
Rembrandt -- 117, 120. The New Gulliver; Bullets or Ballots;
The White Angel -- 120-121. The Green Pastures -- 121-122.
Sabotage; The Tenth Man -- 122-123. Girl's Dormitory; Go
West, Young Man; Hortobagy -- 124-125. The Garden of Allah
-- 125-126. The Jungle Princess; Windbag the Sailor -- 126-

127. Sensation; Mazurka -- 130-131. The Plainsman; The
Great Barrier -- 131-132. The Deserter; Dreaming Lips --
132-133. We From Kronstadt -- 133-134. Fire Over England;
Maid of Salem; Theodora Goes Wild -- 135-137. Pluck of the
Irish; Sequel to Second Bureau; Thunder in the City; Head
Over Heels -- 137-139. Three Smart Girls; For Valour -- 139-
140. The Good Earth; Dark Journey -- 140-141. Winterset --
141-143. Elephant Boy -- 143-144. Pépé le Moko; The Golem
-- 144-145. Lost Horizon -- 145, 148. Generation of Con-
querors; Lloyds of London; The Gap; Glamorous Night -- 149-
150. We From Kronstadt; The Frog; Make Way for Tomorrow;
Der Herrscher -- 150-151. Black Legion; Night Must Fall;
Top of the Town; The Last Train from Madrid -- 151, 154.
God's Country and the Woman; Michael Strogoff -- 154-155.
Parnell; Call It a Day -- 155-156. The High Command; On the
Avenue; Yiddle with His Fiddle -- 156-157, 160. A Day at the
Races; King Solomon's Mines -- 160-161. Slave Ship; Stradi-
varius; Woman Chases Man -- 162-163. Saratoga; High, Wide
and Handsome; His Affair -- 163-164. A Castle in Flanders;
For You Alone -- 165-166. Marked Woman -- 166. Action for
Slander; Brief Ecstacy -- 167. Knight Without Armour; Café
Metropole -- 170-172. The Road Back; Gangway -- 172-173.
Big City; Tales from the Vienna Woods; Children at School --
173-174. Les Perles de la Couronne; Exclusive -- 175-176.
Wee Willie Winkie; The Life of Emile Zola -- 176-177. They
Won't Forget -- 178-179. Land Without Bread; Personality
Parade -- 179-180. Dead End -- 180-181. Lo Squadrone Bianco
-- 181, 184. Un Carnet de Bal; Underworld -- 184. Monica
and Martin; Mademoiselle Docteur; Eastern Valley -- 186-187.
Marie Walewska; True Confession -- 187, 190. Orage -- 190-
192. L'Alibi; A Slight Case of Murder -- 192-193. From the
Manger to the Cross; Swing, Sister, Swing; Sally, Irene and
Mary; Sinners in Paradise; The Devil's Party -- 194-195.
L'Homme du Jour; You and Me -- 195-197. Kidnapped; I Cover
the Waterfront -- 197-198. Little Tough Guy -- 198-199.
Son of Mongolia -- 199-200. Fools for Scandal; Booloo;
Five Faces -- 200-201. Katia; Sixty Glorious Years -- 201,
203. You Can't Take It with You -- 203-204. Alerte en
Méditerranée; Men with Wings -- 204-205. Lenin in October --
206-207. The Dawn Patrol; Persons in Hiding; Kentucky;
Never Say Die -- 207, 210. Three Smart Girls Grow Up; Black
Eyes; Inspector Hornleigh -- 211-212. Hotel Imperial --
213-214. Idiot's Delight; Beach Picnic; They Drive by Night
-- 214-215. The Four Feathers; The Sisters; Thanks for
Everything -- 218-219. Wuthering Heights; La Bête Humaine --
219-220. The Oklahoma Kid; The Lone Ranger -- 221-222.
Jamaica Inn -- 222-223. Men in Danger; Spare Time; Health of
a Nation; An Elephant Never Forgets -- 223-224. Union

Pacific; The Lone Ranger -- 224-225. The Story of Vernon and Irene Castle; La Femme du Boulanger -- 225, 227. Goodbye Mr. Chips; Louise -- 227-228. Confessions of a Nazi Spy; Hôtel du Nord -- 229-230. Beethoven; Peter the Great; This Man in Paris -- 230-231. The Hound of the Baskervilles -- 231, 234. Hostages -- 224-225. Le Drame de Shanghai; The Rebel Son -- 235-236. The Rich Bride -- 236-237. Beau Geste; Un de la Légion -- 237-238. Shipyard Sally; Blind Alley -- 239. Les Disparus de St. Agil -- 239-240. Professor Mamlock -- 240-241. Young Mr. Lincoln -- 241-242. [on newsreels] -- 242-243. An Englishman's Home; The Face at the Window -- 243-245. Ignace -- 245-246. Stanley and Livingstone; Only Angels Have Wings -- 246-247. Nurse Edith Cavell; French Without Tears; 'Arf a Mo' Hitler -- 247-248. The Lion Has Wings -- 249. Daughters Courageous; Poison Pen -- 250, 252. The Frozen Limits -- 252-254. Juarez -- 254-255. Golden Boy; On the Night of the Fire -- 255-256. The Marx Brothers at the Circus; Disputed Passage -- 257-258. First Love; Our Neighbors -- the Carters -- 258-259. Remontons les Champs-Elysées -- 259. Mr. Smith Goes to Washington -- 260-261. The Real Glory; Twenty-one Days -- 261-262. The Light That Failed; The Old Maid -- 262, 264. The Stars Look Down; Escape to Happiness -- 265-266. The Arsenal Stadium Mystery; Pièges -- 266-268. The Wizard of Oz; Africa's Skyways -- 268-269. Dark Rapture; Destry Rides Again; The Hunchback of Notre-Dame -- 270-271. Ninotchka; On Your Toes; A Chump at Oxford; These Children A·e Safe -- 271-273. Sherlock Holmes -- 273-274. The Proud Valley -- 275.

Notes: The copy examined is in the British Library (X.981/3664).

This volume contains an index, but no contents page is provided. Accordingly, the contents of this edition listed above have been assembled by the compiler. It should be pointed out that an examination of the list of contents indicates that the book is not a comprehensive collection of Greene's film reviews but rather a selection.

The volume contains an "Introduction" by Graham Greene in which he discusses his meeting with and subsequent employment by Alexander Korda, who eventually produced *The Third Man*. Greene also describes working with Carol Reed and meeting David O. Selznick.

This edition also contains an appendix describing the "Shirley Temple Libel Action" and an account of the settlement of the action before the Lord Chief Justice.

b. *First American Edition* (1972)

GRAHAM GREENE / ON FILM / Collected Film Criticism 1935–1940
/ Edited by John Russell Taylor / SIMON AND SCHUSTER / New
York

Collation: as first English edition.

Pagination: as first English edition.

Printing: as first English edition.

Description: as first English edition.

Price: $12.50. Published in December 1972 in a dust jacket
which is printed white on black with the author and title on
the front cover, and the author, title and publisher on the
spine; a photo of the author by Karsh of Ottawa is on the
back cover, all on a very glossy stock.

Notes: The copy examined is in the compiler's collection.
    This edition is identical to the English edition except
for the title-page and the title-page verso which words the
copyright notice differently, lists Simon and Schuster rather
than Secker and Warburg as publisher, lists the SBN number
(671-21412-8) and Library of Congress card number (72-83894)
and notes that the book was manufactured in Great Britain.

A58   THE VIRTUE OF DISLOYALTY   1972

First Edition

300 copies published in London, privately printed and bound
in wrappers.

Probably one of the Christmas books, the text is of an
address given by Greene on the occasion of the University
of Hamburg honoring him with the Shakespeare Prize, June 6,
1969. This is reprinted in *The Portable Graham Greene*,
edited by Philip Stratford (New York, The Viking Press,
1973), pp. 606-610.

The compiler has not seen a copy.

a. *First Edition*

THE HONORARY / CONSUL / [rule device] / Graham Greene / 'All
things merge in one another-- / good into evil, generosity
into / justice, religion into politics...' / *Thomas Hardy* /
[publisher's device] / THE BODLEY HEAD / LONDON   SYDNEY /
TORONTO

Collation: [1]-[9]^{16} [10]^8 [11]^{16}, 168 leaves.

Pagination: p. [1] half-title; p. [2] author's advertisement;
p. [3] title-page; p. [4] disclaimer, copyright, printing,
publishing, type and publication notices; p. [5] dedication;
p. [6] blank; p. [7] PART ONE; p. [8] blank; pp. 9-44 text
of part one, with chapter headings on pp. 9 and 28; p. [45]
PART TWO; p. [46] blank; pp. 47-102 text of part two, with
chapter headings on pp. 47, 63, 73; p. [103] PART THREE;
p. [104] blank; pp. 105-159 text of part three, with chapter
headings on pp. 105, 123, 131; p. [160] blank; p. [161] PART
FOUR; pp. 163-223 text of part four, with chapter headings on
pp. 163 and 187; p. [224] blank; p. [225] PART FIVE; p. [226]
blank; pp. 227-[335] text of part five, with chapter headings
on pp. 227, 248, 268, 299, 317; p. [336] blank.

Printing: Monotype Ehrhardt, 11 pt., printed and bound in
Great Britain by William Clowes and Sons Ltd., Beccles.

12.5 x 19.5 cm., white paper, all edges trimmed, top edges
colored blue-gray; bound in green cloth over boards with the
author, title and publisher stamped in gold on the spine.

Price: £2.00. Published in September 1973 in a dust jacket
with both covers having the author in blue over the title in
green and both on a dark blue background; on the spine the
author is in blue, the title in dark blue, the publisher in
green and all are on a white background.

Dedication: For Victoria Ocampo with love, and in memory of
the many happy weeks I have passed at San Isidro and Mar del
Plata

Notes: The copy examined is in the Rare Book Department of the
Library of Congress (PR6013/.R44/H6).
    Page [4] of the preliminaries carries the usual disclaim-
er, although Greene admits that the location, with some

changes, may bear some resemblance to a real place which he would rather not name because of the liberties he has taken with street plans and so on.

The Honorary Consul returns to that third world the critics call "Greeneland," where the writer's characters live on the ragged edge. The novel seems to focus on variations on the theme of the father. Though other Greene stories have covered this material, none has gone at the male parent symbol with such intensity. The result is a novel that becomes a companion piece to the earlier *Travels with My Aunt*.

b. *First American Edition* (1973)

THE / HONORARY / CONSUL / [rule] / GRAHAM GREENE / [rule] / SIMON AND SCHUSTER / NEW YORK

Collation: [1]–[10]^{16}, 160 leaves.

Pagination: p. [1] publisher's device; pp. [2–3] author's advertisement; p. [4] blank; p. [5] title-page; p. [6] copyright, publishing, Library of Congress card number, design and manufacturing notices; p. [7] disclaimer; p. [8] blank; p. [9] dedication; p. [10] blank; p. [11] quotation; p. [12] blank; p. [13] PART ONE; p. [14] blank; pp. 15–47 text of part one, with chapter headings on pp. 15 and 32; p. [48] blank; p. [49] PART TWO; p. [50] blank; pp. 51–101 text of part two, with chapter headings on pp. 51, 66, 75; p. [102] blank; p. [103] PART THREE; p. [104] blank; pp. 105–155 text of part three, with chapter headings on pp. 105, 121, 129; p. [156] blank; p. [157] PART FOUR; p. [158] blank; pp. 159–214 text of part four, with chapter headings on pp. 159 and 181; p. [215] PART FIVE; p. [216] blank; pp. 217–315 text of part five, with chapter headings on pp. 217, 236, 254, 282, 299; pp. [316–320] blank.

Printing: an old face, 12 pt., printed in the U.S.A.

15.5 x 23.2 cm., white paper, all edges trimmed; bound in dark blue cloth over boards with the title, author and publisher stamped in gold along the spine.

Price: $7.95. Published in September 1973.

Dedication: as first English edition.

Notes: The copies examined are in the library of West Virginia State College (PZ/3/G8319/Ho) and the Library of Congress (PZ3/.G8319/Ho).

The disclaimer is the same as that in the first English edition.

The Thomas Hardy epigraph is on page [11] instead of the title-page, as in the first English edition.

A60   LORD ROCHESTER'S MONKEY   1974

a. *First Edition*

Graham Greene / *Lord Rochester's Monkey* [type having decora-
tive ascenders and descenders] / *being the Life of John
Wilmot,* / *Second Earl of Rochester* / *Bodley Head* / *London* •
Sydney • *Toronto*

Collation: $[1]^{10}$ $[2]-[3]^{8}$ $[4]-[7]^{10/8}$ $[8]-[9]^{10}$ $[10]^{8}$ $[11]^{10}$
$[12]-[13]^{8}$, 116 leaves.

Pagination: p. [1] illustrated back of frontispiece; p. [2]
frontispiece; p. [3] title-page; p. [4] copyright, design,
publishing and printing notices; p. [5] quotations; p. [6]
blank; p. [7] CONTENTS; p. [8] COLOUR PLATES; pp. 9-11 PREF-
ACE; p. [12] illustration; pp. 13-221 text, with chapter
headings on pp. 13, 35, 47, 69, 85, 105, 119, 143, 159, 173,
197, and colour plates on pp. [19, 20, 61, 62-63, 64, 97, 98-
99, 100, 133, 134-135, 136, 153, 154, 155, 156, 181, 182, 199,
200]; pp. 222-223 BIBLIOGRAPHY; pp. 224-226 ILLUSTRATIONS AND
ACKNOWLEDGMENTS; pp. 226-231 INDEX; p. [232] blank.

Printing: Garamond, 12 pt., printed and bound in Great Britain by Jarrold & Sons Limited, Norwich; color plates printed
by Westerham Press Limited, Westerham.

18.5 x 25 cm., white paper and glossy enamel stock, all edges
trimmed, top edges colored yellow; bound in brown cloth over
boards with the author, title and publisher along the spine;
the endpapers photographically reproduce in black and white
a decorated ceiling.

Price: £5.00. Published in September 1974. The dust jacket
of the English edition has not been seen but it is reasonable
to surmise that it is identical in description to the jacket
for the American edition which follows.

Contents: List of Colour Plates -- 8. Preface -- 9.
I. Landscape -- 13. II. The Heiress of the West -- 35.
III. Seascape -- 47. IV. The Age of Spleen -- 69. V. The
Poet and the King -- 85. VI. The Affray at Epsom -- 105.
VII. Elizabeth Barry -- 119. VIII. Still-life -- 143.
IX. 'What Evil Angel Enemy ...?' -- 159. X. The Literary
Jungle -- 173. XI. The Death of Dorimat -- 197. Biblio-
graphy -- 222. Index -- 227.

Color Plates: Allegory of the Restoration by John Michael
Wright [reverse of frontispiece]. John Wilmot, Second Earl
of Rochester, attributed to Jacob Huysmans [frontispiece].
A row of almshouses in the village of Spelsbury, Oxfordshire,
built by John Cary -- 19. One of the four silver pint pots
which Rochester presented to Wadham College, Oxford -- 20.
Elizabeth Mallet, Countess of Rochester, by Sir Peter Lely
-- 61. Raid on the Dutch at Bergen, by William Van de
Velde II -- 62-63. The Palace of Whitehall seen across St.
James's Park, by Hendrick Danckerts -- 64. Louis XIV and his
Court attending a performance of the ballet *Psyche* at the
Louvre, by Charles le Brun -- 64. Charles II, by Sir Godfrey
Kneller -- 97. Mr. Rose, the royal gardener, presenting
Charles II with the first pineapple successfully raised in
England, by Thomas Danckerts -- 98-99. Louise de Kéroualle,
Duchess of Portsmith, by Philippe Mignard -- 100. Elizabeth
Barry after Sir Godfrey Kneller -- 133. Nell Gwyn, by Sir
Peter Lely -- 134-135. Woodstock Park, Oxfordshire -- 136.
Lady Anne Wilmot, by Sir Godfrey Kneller -- 153. Lord
Charles Wilmot, by William Wissing -- 154. Lady Elizabeth
and Lady Mallet Wilmot, by Sir Peter Lely -- 155. Adderbury
House, Oxfordshire -- 156. John Dryden, by Jacques Maubert
-- 181. John Wilmot, Second Earl of Rochester, by Sir Peter
Lely -- 182. The church vaults at Spelsbury -- 199. Spels-
bury Church, Oxfordshire -- 200.

Notes: The copy examined is in the British Library (x.981/
9189).
        Concerning the collation: those gatherings which have
10 leaves are actually octavo sections with an added conjugate pair of double-faced color plates inserted either behind the first and last leaf of the gathering or between the
fourth and fifth leaves.
        The book was designed and produced by George Rainbird
Limited, Marble Arch House, 44 Edgware Road, London W2 for
the Bodley Head Ltd., 9 Bow Street, London WC2E 7AL. The
house editor was Erica Hunningher, the associate house editor, Felicity Luard, the designer, Judith Allan, and the
indexer, Myra Clark.
        Page [5] of the preliminaries carries the following quo-
tations from Rochester: "Most human affairs are carried on
at the same nonsensical rate, which makes me (who am now
grown superstitious) think it a fault to laugh at the monkey
we have here, when I compare his condition with mankind." --
Lord Rochester in a letter to Henry Savile, and "Were I, who
to my cost, already am / One of those strange, prodigious
creatures, Man, / A spirit free, to choose for my own share /
What sort of flesh and blood I pleas'd to wear, / I'd be a

dog, a monkey or a bear, / Or any thing but that vain animal, / Who is so proud of being rational." --Rochester, "In Imitation of the Eighth Satire of Boileau."

The history of this book, perhaps physically the most attractive of Greene's books to appear, is nearly as intriguing as the life it illustrates. Though Greene wrote the biography in the early thirties (between 1931 and 1934), it was to be forty years before it would appear. One immediate irony is that, appearing at this point in Greene's career, it is certainly a much more lavishly produced book than it would have been, had it been printed when Greene originally submitted it to W. H. Heinemann.

Another factor to which Greene calls the reader's attention in his "Preface" is the "almost Victorian atmosphere of the time when the book was written, of the censorship and suppression of Rochester's poetry and his reputation as a pornographic poet."

Greene acknowledges particularly his friend the late John Hayward, editor of the Nonesuch edition of Rochester's poetry. Greene also makes it clear that he had had no intention of publishing this biography. The original typescript, part of the Greene manuscript collection at the Humanities Research Center of the University of Texas, in fact, had to be copied for Greene so that he could make revisions. He indicates that his revisions have been no more extensive than they would have been had the book been published when it was written.

An autograph manuscript of "Rochester" in the Humanities Research Center is dated: "1931 June 10--."

b. *First American Edition* (1974)

Graham Greene / *Lord Rochester's Monkey* [type having decorative ascenders and descenders] / *being the Life of John Wilmot,* / *Second Earl of Rochester* / *A Studio Book* / *The Viking Press* • *New York*

Collation: as first English edition.

Pagination: as first English edition.

Printing: as first English edition, as are the descriptions of the measurements, paper and binding.

Price: $15.95. Published in September 1974. The dust jacket reproduces on the front cover a portrait of John Wilmot by Jacob Huysmans with the author printed at the head in white and the title printed at the tail in white; the author, title and publisher are in white on brown on the spine, and the back cover reproduces a facsimile of Wilmot's Ms. "To a Lady: in a Letter" in white on brown.

Notes: The copy examined is in the collection of the compiler.
      Aside from the title-page the only other differences between the American and English editions occur on the title-page verso and are comprised of the substitution of The Viking Press and its address for the English publisher and the substitution of the SBN number (670-44055-8) and the Library of Congress number (73-17955) for the ISBN number. The "all rights reserved ..." notice has also been removed from the American edition.

A61   AN IMPOSSIBLE WOMAN   1975

a. *First Edition*

AN IMPOSSIBLE WOMAN / The Memories of / Dottoressa Moor of
Capri / [double rule] / Edited and with an Epilogue by /
Graham Greene / [publisher's device] / THE BODLEY HEAD /
LONDON SYDNEY TORONTO

Collation: [1]-[13]^8, 104 leaves.

Pagination: p. [1] half-title; p. [2] blank; p. [3] title-
page; p. [4] copyright, printing, publishing and type notices; p. [5] quotation; p. [6] blank; p. [7] EDITOR'S NOTE;
p. [8] blank; pp. [9-10] CONTENTS; pp. 11-[14] PREFACE;
pp. 17-190 text, with divisional title-pages on pp. [15, 89,
113, 171, 191]; pp. [49, 54, 58, 88, 111, 120, 127, 138, 145,
147, 156, 164, 169, 190] being unnumbered; pp. [16, 90,
112, 114, 170, 172, 192] being blank and unnumbered; pp. 193-
[205] epilogue; pp. [206-208] blank.

Printing: Imprint, 12 pt., printed and bound in Great Britain
by William Clowes and Sons Ltd., Beccles.

13.5 x 21.5 cm., white paper, all edges trimmed; bound in
blue embossed (to look like cloth) paper over boards with the
title, editor and publisher stamped in gold on the spine.

Price: £3.00. Published in September 1975.

Contents: Editor's Note -- 7. Preface -- 11. Part I: The
Hairdressers' Child -- 17. Always Alone -- 18. A Holy Bitch
-- 23. A Beating in Anacapri -- 26. The Archduke -- 28.
With the Nuns -- 30. First Love -- 33. A Sort of Hotel --
35. The Big Time -- 37. Studying Medicine -- 38. Another
Affair -- 40. A Certain Alfons -- 43. Meeting Gigi Moor --
45. In Tunisia with Baudisch -- 50. Steerage with the Cows
-- 55. Happiness in Vienna -- 59. Shirts for Gigi -- 61.
War Declared -- 65. Marrying Gigi -- 68. Because of a Simple
Foetus ... -- 72. The Russian Lover -- 79. Don Domenico and
the Devil -- 81. Gigi and Maja -- 86. Part 2: Typhoid in
Capri -- 91. Naval Officer Called Tutino -- 93. A Daughter
of the Devil -- 96. An Agreement with Gigi -- 98. The Torments of Jealousy -- 100. So Strange is Life -- 104. The
Birth of Andrea -- 105. A Divorce -- 108. Part 3: To Anacapri -- 115. The Cerios -- 118. A Vile Coward, a Creep --
121. Grand Patients and Poor People -- 124. A Handful of

Men -- 128. Seeing Gigi Again -- 131. In East Prussia --
133. An Urgent Call from Basel -- 135. The Black Princess
-- 137. The Compton Mackenzies -- 139. Axel Munthe -- 140.
Count Fersen -- 144. Fear in Capri -- 146. An Island of
Much Pain -- 148. The Co-respondent -- 154. The Anacapri
Murderer -- 155. Baron von Schacht -- 157. An Exile from
Capri -- 158. A Secret Return -- 165. Part 4: Anacapri
Again -- 173. The Death of Andrea -- 177. Epilogue by
Graham Greene.

Notes: The copy examined is in the British Library
(X.809/40316).
   The book seems to have been planned by Kenneth Macpherson, along with Graham Greene, with Macpherson the intended
editor. While the book was in preparation Macpherson died
and Greene continued the task. The book is a translated and
edited transcription of a tape-recorded interview of Dottoressa Moor conducted for the editors by someone who had not
known her. Every attempt has been made by both Macpherson
and Greene to give the translation the flavor of her "vivid
and incorrect English." Greene has also inserted memories
which did not appear on the tapes because the interviewer
had failed to ask the right question.
   In his Epilogue Greene confesses that it was Dottoressa
Moor's special style and fervor for life which gave him the
character of Augusta in *Travels with My Aunt.*

b. *First American Edition* (1976)

AN IMPOSSIBLE WOMAN / The Memories of / Dottoressa Moor of
Capri / [double rule] / Edited and with an Epilogue by /
Graham Greene / [publisher's device] / THE VIKING PRESS NEW
YORK

Collation: $[1]-[3]^{16}$ $[4]^{8}$ $[5]-[7]^{16}$, 104 leaves.

Pagination: Pagination and contents are the same as the first
English edition with the exception that the unnumbered pages
of the text in the English edition are numbered here and the
"Editor's Note" has been deleted from the contents page.

Printing: Imprint, 12 pt., printed in the U.S.A.

14 x 21.5 cm., white paper, top edges trimmed; bound in
blue embossed (to look like cloth) paper over boards; the
spine is in black cloth with the title and publisher stamped
in silver and the author and editor stamped in blue.

Price: $7.95. Published in April 1976.

Contents: as first English edition.

Notes: The copy examined is in the library of the University of Iowa (R 520/M66A34).

This edition is, no doubt, simply a reprinting of the first English edition with small changes on the preliminaries.

A62   THE RETURN OF A. J. RAFFLES   1975

a. *First Edition*

Graham Greene / [device] / THE RETURN OF / A. J. RAFFLES /
An Edwardian Comedy / in Three Acts based somewhat loosely /
on E. W. Hornung's characters in / *The Amateur Cracksman* /
[publisher's device] / THE BODLEY HEAD / LONDON   SYDNEY /
TORONTO

Collation: $[1]-[5]^8$, 40 leaves.

Pagination: p. [1] half-title; p. [2] author's advertisement;
p. [3] title-page; p. [4] copyright, printing, publication,
type, publishing and performing rights notices; p. [5]
AUTHOR'S NOTE; p. [6] blank; p. [7] CHARACTERS and scenes;
p. [8] blank; p. 9 ACT I; pp. 9-31 text of act one; p. 32
ACT II; pp. 32-55 text of act two; p. 56 ACT III; pp. 56-[80]
text of act three.

Printing: Ehrhardt, 11 pt., printed and bound in Great Britain by William Clowes and Sons Ltd., Beccles.

11.5 x 19 cm., cream laid paper, all edges trimmed; bound in
stiff, glossy finished, printed wrappers with author and title
printed in red and brown along the spine; the front cover has
the title in red above a rule in yellow and the author in
brown below the rule; advertisements for *The Collected Edition*
are on the back cover; the wrapper is tan overall.

Price: £1.95. Published in December 1975.

Notes: The copies examined are in the British Library
(X.908/40244) and the Library of Congress (PR 6013/.R44 R4/
1975/copy 2).
    The Return of A. J. Raffles opened at the Aldwych
Theatre, London, on December 4, 1975. The production was
directed by David Jones, designed by Alan Tagg, with music by
Guy Woolfden and lighting by Stewart Leviton.
    The cast was as follows:

A. J. Raffles	Denholm Elliott
Bunny	Clive Francis
Lord Alfred Douglas	Peter Blythe
"Mr. Portland"	Paul Rogers
Inspector Mackenzie	Raymond Westwell
A Lady called Alice	Jane How

A Lady's Maid called Mary	Jane Cussons
Mr. Smith, head porter	
of Albany	Gordon Gostelow
Captain von Blixen	Michael Bryant

A. J. Raffles, the amateur cracksman, was the creation of E.W. Hornung, brother-in-law to Arthur Conan Doyle. Raffles was meant to be a counterpart to Doyle's Sherlock Holmes and, in fact, in Edwardian England he became almost as popular as the cerebral detective. The idea for the play occurred to Greene after seeing the Royal Shakespeare Company production of *Sherlock Holmes* in 1974. Raffles survives the death Hornung planned for him. Greene also has Bunny in Reading Gaol where he meets Oscar Wilde.

For Greene, who is at least as much an expert on Victorian and Edwardian crime fiction as he is on the outsider or criminal of conscience, Raffles seems almost natural subject matter.

b. *First American Edition* (1976)

The Return of / *A. J. Raffles* / An Edwardian Comedy in Three Acts / based somewhat loosely on / E. W. Hornung's characters in / *The Amateur Cracksman* / *Graham Greene* / SIMON AND SCHUSTER / NEW YORK [all surrounded by a rule border]

Collation: perfect binding, 48 leaves.

Pagination: p. [1] publisher's device; pp. [2-3] author's advertisement; p. [4] blank; p. [5] title-page; p. [6] copyright, publishing, design, Library of Congress card number and performing rights notices; p. [7] AUTHOR'S NOTE; p. [8] blank; p. [9] CHARACTERS and scenes; p. [10] blank; p. 11 ACT I; pp. 11-35 text of act one; p. 36 ACT II; pp. 36-63 text of act two; p. 64 ACT III; pp. 64-92 text of act three; pp. [93-96] blank.

Printing: Bulmer, 11 pt., printed in the U.S.A.

13.3 x 20.9 cm., white paper, all edges trimmed; bound in black cloth over boards with the author, title and publisher stamped in silver on the spine and a small rule stamped in silver between the author and the title.

Price: $5.95. Published in 1976.

Notes: The copy examined is in the Library of Congress
(PR6013/.R44R4/1975b).

A63 THE HUMAN FACTOR 1978

a. *First Edition*

THE HUMAN / FACTOR / [small device] / Graham Greene / 'I only know that he who forms a tie is lost. The / germ of corruption has entered into his soul.' / *Joseph Conrad* / [publisher's device] / THE BODLEY HEAD / LONDON   SYDNEY / TORONTO

Collation: $[1]-[9]^{16} [10]^{8+2} [11]^{16}$, 170 leaves.

Pagination: p. [1] half-title; p. [2] author's advertisement; p. [3] title-page; p. [4] disclaimer, copyright, printing, publishing, type and publication notices; p. [5] dedication; p. [6] blank; p. [7] PART ONE; p. [8] blank; pp. 9-[46] text of part one, with chapter headings on pp. 9, 19, 30, and numbered division headings on pp. 30, 35, 44; p. [47] PART TWO; p. [48] blank; pp. 49-[93] text of part two, with chapter headings on pp. 49, 67, 74, 86, and numbered division headings on pp. 49, 52, 60, 74, 76, 86, 90; p. [94] blank; p. [95] PART THREE; p. [96] blank; pp. 97-[187] text of part three, with chapter headings on pp. 97, 111, 119, 136, 144, 157, 167, 181, and numbered division headings on pp. 97, 104, 111, 115, 117, 119, 133, 136, 141, 144, 154, 157, 161, 167, 174, 181, 185; p. [188] blank; p. [189] PART FOUR; p. [190] blank; pp. 191-[224] text of part four, with chapter headings on pp. 191 and 203, and numbered division headings on pp. 191, 194, 203, 205, 208, 217, 222; p. [225] PART FIVE; p. [226] blank; pp. 227-[290] text of part five, with chapter headings on pp. 227, 240, 250, and numbered division headings on pp. 227, 234, 250, 254, 256, 269, 274, 279, 284; p. [291] PART SIX; p. [292] blank; pp. 293-[339] text of part six, with chapter headings on pp. 293, 314, 333, and numbered division headings on pp. 293, 303, 307, 314, 319, 323, 326, 328, 333, 337; p. [340] blank.

Printing: Monophoto Ehrhardt, 11 pt., printed and bound in Great Britain by William Clowes and Sons Ltd., Beccles.

12.7 x 19.8 cm., white paper, all edges trimmed, top edges colored green; bound in green cloth over boards with the author, title and publisher stamped in gold on the spine.

Price: 4.50. Published in March 1978 in a white dust jacket with the front cover having the author in red printed over the title which is oblique and in gold outline and the title

repeated at the tail in solid gold; the back cover is the
same except that the author is in blue; the spine carries the
title in gold, author in red and publisher in blue.

Dedication: To my sister Elisabeth Dennys, who cannot deny
some responsibility

Notes: The copy examined is in the compiler's collection.

b. *First American Edition* (1978)

Graham Greene / [rule] / THE / HUMAN / FACTOR / [publisher's
device] / Simon and Schuster • New York

Collation: [1]-[11]^{16}, 176 leaves.

Pagination: p. [1] publisher's device; pp. [2-3] author's
advertisement; p. [4] blank; p. [5] title-page; p. [6] copyright, publishing, manufacturing and Library of Congress
notices; p. [7] disclaimer; p. [8] blank; p. [9] dedication;
p. [10] blank; p. [11] quotation; p. [12] blank; p. [13] PART
ONE; p. [14] blank; pp. 15-52 text of part one, with chapter
headings on pp. 15, 25, 36, and numbered division headings on
pp. 36, 42, 50; p. [53] PART TWO; p. [54] blank; pp. 55-99
text of part two, with chapter headings on pp. 55, 73, 80,
92, and numbered division headings on pp. 55, 59, 66, 80, 82,
92, 97; p. [100] blank; p. [101] PART THREE; p. [102] blank;
pp. 103-195 text of part three, with chapter headings on
pp. 103, 117, 125, 142, 151, 164, 174, 188, and numbered division headings on pp. 103, 110, 117, 122, 125, 139, 142,
147, 151, 161, 164, 168, 174, 181, 188, 192; p. [196] blank;
p. [197] PART FOUR; p. [198] blank; pp. 199-232 text of part
four, with chapter headings on pp. 199 and 211, and numbered
division headings on pp. 199, 202, 211, 213, 217, 225, 230;
p. [233] PART FIVE; p. [234] blank; pp. 235-297 text of part
five, with chapter headings on pp. 235, 248, 258, and numbered
division headings on pp. 235, 242, 248, 258, 262, 265, 277,
282, 286, 291; p. [298] blank; p. [299] PART SIX; p. [300]
blank; pp. 301-347 text of part six, with chapter headings on
pp. 301, 322, 341, and numbered division headings on pp. 301,
311, 315, 322, 327, 331, 334, 336, 341, 345; pp. [348-352]
blank.

Printing: Bulmer, 11 pt., printed in the U.S.A.

15.5 x 23.3 cm., white paper, all edges trimmed; bound in black cloth over boards with the title, author and publisher stamped in silver on the spine.

Price: $9.95. Published in March 1978 in a dust jacket having on the cover the author in red and the title in black with a small autumn scene insert between the author and title. The back cover carries a photo of the author by Karsh of Ottawa.

Dedication: as first English edition.

Notes: The copies examined are in the Library of Congress (PZ3/.G8319/Hu/1978) and the West Virginia Library Commission (NFG 803868, this copy having the dust jacket).

c. *Limited Edition* (1978)

THE FIRST EDITION SOCIETY / *Graham Greene* / THE / HUMAN / FACTOR / [device] / Illustrated by Bernard Fuchs / THE FRANKLIN LIBRARY / *Franklin Center*, Pennsylvania / 1978

Collation: [1]-[20]^8, 160 leaves.

Pagination: pp. [i-ii] blank; p. [iii] first limited edition notice; p. [iv] blank; p. [v] author's advertisement; p. [vi] blank; p. [vii] half-title; p. [viii] blank; p. [ix] author's SPECIAL MESSAGE TO THE MEMBERS OF THE FIRST EDITION SOCIETY; p. [x] quotation; p. [xi] title-page; p. [xii] disclaimer, publishing, copyright and printing notices; p. [xiii] dedication; pp. [xiv-1] illustration; p. [xiv] PART ONE; p. [2] blank; pp. [3]-37 text of part one, with chapter headings on pp. [3, 12, 22], and numbered division headings on pp. [22], 27, 34; pp. [38-39] illustration; p. [38] PART TWO; p. [40] blank; pp. [41]-80 text of part two, with chapter headings on pp. [40, 57, 63, 74], and numbered division headings on pp. [41], 44, 51, [63], 65, [74], 78; p. [81] blank; pp. [82-83] illustration; p. [82] PART THREE; p. [84] blank; pp. [85]-167 text of part three, with chapter headings on pp. [85, 97, 104, 120, 127, 139, 148, 161], and numbered division headings on pp. [85], 91, [97], 101, 103, [104], 116, [120], [124], [127], 136, [139], 143, [148], 154, [161], 164; pp. [168-169] illustration; p. [168] PART FOUR; p. [170] blank; pp. [171]-200 text of part four, with chapter headings on pp. [171 and 182], and numbered division headings on pp. [171], 174, [182], 184, 187, 194, 199; p. [201] blank; pp. [202-203] illustration;

p. [202] PART FIVE; p. [204] blank; pp. [205]-261 text of
part five, with chapter headings on pp. [205, 217, 226], and
numbered division headings on pp. [205], 212, [226], 230,
232, 243, 251, 255; pp. [262-263] illustration; p. [262] PART
SIX; p. [264] blank; pp. [265]-306 text of part six, with
chapter headings on pp. [265, 284, 301], and numbered division headings on pp. [265], 274, 277, [284], 288, 292, 295,
296, [301], 305.

Printing: Caslon, 12 pt., printed in the U.S.A.

14.7 x 22.8 cm., white paper, all edges trimmed, all edges
have been covered with gold; bound in green morocco leather
over boards with the front and back covers decorated with a
design of rectangular stamping in gold and the author, title,
"First Edition" and publisher stamped in gold in individual
panels between raised bands; a green ribbon marker is sewn
in at the head of the spine.

Price: unknown. Published early 1978.

Notes: The copy examined is in the Library of Congress
(PZ3/.G8319/Hu/1978b/2). The verso of the title-page carries
the date of receipt of copyright copies as April 14, 1978.

LATER EDITIONS

A2 THE MAN WITHIN

Leipzig: Bernard Tauchnitz, 1930 (No. 4917).
London: Heinemann, 1952 (Uniform Edition).
London: Heinemann, 1959 (Library Edition).
Harmondsworth, Middlesex: Penguin Books, 1971.
London: Heinemann and Bodley Head, 1976 (Collected
   Edition).

New York: Viking, 1947.
New York: Bantam Books, 1948.
New York: Berkley Books, 1958.

A3 THE NAME OF ACTION

London: Heinemann, 1931 (Cheap Edition).

A4 RUMOUR AT NIGHTFALL

London: Heinemann, 1933 (Cheap Edition).

A5 STAMBOUL TRAIN (ORIENT EXPRESS)

London: Heinemann, 1934.
London: Heinemann, 1947 (Uniform Edition).
London: Heinemann, 1959 (Library Edition).
Harmondsworth, Middlesex: Penguin Books, 1963.
London: Heinemann and Bodley Head, 1974 (Collected
   Edition).

ORIENT EXPRESS

New York: Grosset & Dunlap, 1934.
New York: Sun Dial Press, 1942.
New York: Bantam Books, 1956.
New York: Bantam Books, 1970 (New Bantam Edition).
New York: Pocket Books, 1975.

A6   IT'S A BATTLEFIELD

    London: Heinemann, 1935 (Cheap Edition).
    Harmondsworth, Middlesex: Penguin Books, 1940.
    London: Heinemann, 1948 (Uniform Edition).
    London: Heinemann, 1959 (Library Edition).
    London: Heinemann and Bodley Head, 1970 (Collected
      Edition).
    Harmondsworth, Middlesex: Penguin Books, 1971.

    New York: Viking, 1962.

A7   THE OLD SCHOOL

    London: Jonathan Cape, 1937 (Cheap Edition).

A8   ENGLAND MADE ME (sometimes *The Shipwrecked* in the U.S.A.)

    London: Heinemann, 1937 (Cheap Edition).
    Harmondsworth, Middlesex: Penguin Books, 1943.
    London: Heinemann, 1947 (Uniform Edition).
    London: Pan Books, 1954.
    London: Heinemann, 1960 (Library Edition).
    London: Heinemann and Bodley Head, 1970 (Collected
      Edition).
    Harmondsworth, Middlesex: Penguin Books, 1970 (new
      edition).

    Toronto: Doubleday, 1935 (Sun Dial Book).

    as *The Shipwrecked*, New York: Viking, 1953.
    as *The Shipwrecked*, New York: Bantam Books, 1956.
    New York: Pocket Books, 1974.

A9   THE BEAR FELL FREE

    Folcroft, Pa.: Folcroft Library Editions, 1977.

A10 THE BASEMENT ROOM AND OTHER STORIES

    in *24 Short Stories* by Graham Greene, James Laver and
    Sylvia Townsend Warner. London: Cresset Press, n.d.
    [1939] (seems to be an exact reprint of *The Basement
    Room and Other Stories*).

A11   JOURNEY WITHOUT MAPS

London/Paris: Pan Books, 1948.
London: Heinemann, 1950 (Uniform Edition).
in *The Travel Books,* London: Heinemann, 1963.
Harmondsworth, Middlesex: Penguin Books, 1971.

New York: Viking, 1961 (Compass Books).

A12   A GUN FOR SALE (as *This Gun for Hire* in the U.S.A.)

London: Heinemann, 1938 (Cheap Edition).
London: Heinemann, 1940 (Evergreen Books).
London: Heinemann, 1947 (Uniform Edition).
Stockholm/London: The Continental Book Company, 1947
    (Zephyr Books).
London: Heinemann, 1959 (Library Edition).
Harmondsworth, Middlesex: Penguin Books, 1963.
London: Heinemann and Bodley Head, 1973 (Collected
    Edition).

This Gun for Hire, Toronto: Blue Ribbon Books, 1942.
This Gun for Hire, Harrisburg, Penn.: Superior Reprints,
    1945.
in *3 by Graham Greene,* New York: Viking, 1952.
This Gun for Hire, New York: Bantam Books, 1955.
in *3 by Graham Greene,* New York: Viking, 1968 (Compass
    Books).
in *Triple Pursuit: a Graham Greene Omnibus,* New York:
    Viking, 1971.
This Gun for Hire, New York: Pocket Books, 1975.

A13   BRIGHTON ROCK

London: Heinemann, 1939 (Cheap Edition).
Harmondsworth, Middlesex: Penguin Books, 1943.
London: Heinemann, 1947 (Uniform Edition).
London: Heinemann, 1959 (Library Edition).
London: Heinemann, 1968 (Modern Novel Series).
London: Heinemann and Bodley Head, 1970 (Collected
    Edition).

New York: Viking, 1948.
New York: Bantam Books, 1949.
New York: Viking, 1956 (Compass Books).

A14   THE LAWLESS ROADS (as *Another Mexico* in the U.S.A.)

      London: Eyre & Spottiswoode, 1947 (2nd Edition).
      Harmondsworth, Middlesex: Penguin Books, 1947.
      London: Eyre & Spottiswoode, 1950 (3rd Edition).
      London: Heinemann, 1955 (Uniform Edition).
      London: Heinemann, 1960 (Library Edition).
      in *The Travel Books*, London: Heinemann, 1963.

      as *Another Mexico*, New York: Viking, 1964 (Compass
      Books).

A15   THE CONFIDENTIAL AGENT

      London: Heinemann, 1952 (Uniform Edition).
      London: Heinemann (in association with Chatto & Windus),
      1954 (Vanguard Library Series, No. 23).
      London: Heinemann, 1960 (Library Edition).
      Harmondsworth, Middlesex: Penguin Books, 1963.
      London: Heinemann and Bodley Head, 1971 (Collected
      Edition).

      in *Three Famous Spy Novels*. Edited by Bennett Cerf.
      New York: Random House, 1942.
      New York: New American Library, 1943 (Signet).
      New York: Sun Dial Press, 1945.
      in *3 by Graham Greene*, New York: Viking, 1952.
      New York: Bantam Books, 1952.
      New York: Bantam Books, 1958.
      New York: Viking, 1967.
      in *3 by Graham Greene*, New York: Viking, 1968
      (Compass Books).

A16   THE POWER AND THE GLORY (sometimes as *The Labyrinthine
      Ways* in the U.S.A.)

      London: Readers Union and Heinemann, 1941.
      London: Heinemann, 1945 (Heinemann Pocket Edition).
      London: Heinemann, 1946 (2nd Edition).
      London: Heinemann, 1949 (Uniform Edition).
      London: Heinemann (in association with Chatto & Windus),
      1952 (Vanguard Library, No. 3).
      London: Heinemann, 1959 (Library Edition).
      Harmondsworth, Middlesex: Penguin Books, 1962.
      London: Heinemann, 1963 (Modern Novel Series).
      London: Heinemann and Bodley Head, 1971 (Collected
      Edition).
      Bath: Lythway Press, 1975 (Large Print Edition).

New York: Viking, 1946.
New York: Bantam Books, 1954.
New York: Viking, 1958 (Compass Books).
New York: Time Inc., 1962 (Time Reading Program).
New York: Viking, 1963 (Compass Edition with
Greene's "Introduction").
New York: Viking Press, 1970 (Viking Critical
Library).
Toronto: Bantam Books, 1972 (Bantam Pathfinder
Edition).

A17   BRITISH DRAMATISTS

in *Romance of English Literature*. Edited by W.J.
Turner. London: Collins, 1944.
in *Romance of English Literature*. Edited by W.J.
Turner. New York: Hastings, 1944.

A18   MINISTRY OF FEAR

London: Heinemann, 1950 (Uniform Edition).
London: Heinemann, 1960 (Library Edition).
Harmondsworth, Middlesex: Penguin Books, 1963.
London: Heinemann and Bodley Head, 1973 (Collected
Edition).

New York: Sun Dial Press, 1944.
New York: New American Library, 1944 (Signet).
Toronto: Blue Ribbon Books, 1944.
in *3 by Graham Greene*, New York: Viking, 1952.
New York: Bantam Books, 1963.
in *3 by Graham Greene*, New York: Viking, 1968
(Compass Books).

A19   THE LITTLE TRAIN

London: Parrish, 1957.
London: Bodley Head, 1973 (with Edward Ardizzone).

Garden City, New York: Doubleday, 1974 (with
Edward Ardizzone).

A20   NINETEEN STORIES

      New York: Lion Books, 1955.
      New York: Bantam Books, 1960.

A21   THE HEART OF THE MATTER

      London: Heinemann, 1951 (Uniform Edition).
      London: Heinemann, 1959 (Library Edition).
      Harmondsworth, Middlesex: Penguin Books, 1962.
      London: Heinemann, 1968 (Modern English Language
         Texts).
      London: Heinemann, 1969 (Modern Novel Series).
      London: Heinemann and Bodley Head, 1971 (Collected
         Edition).

      Garden City, New York: Garden City Books, 1951.
      New York: Bantam Books, 1956.
      New York: Viking, 1957.
      New York: Viking, 1960 (Compass Books).

A22   WHY DO I WRITE?

      Folcroft, Pa.: Folcroft Library Editions, 1969.
      New York: Haskell House Publishers, 1975.

A23   THE THIRD MAN AND THE FALLEN IDOL

      London: Heinemann, 1958.
      Harmondsworth, Middlesex: Penguin Books, 1971.
      London: Heinemann, 1971 (New Windmill).
      in *The Third Man* and *Loser Takes All*, London:
         Heinemann and Bodley Head, 1976 (Collected Edition).
      Bath: Lythway Press, 1977 (Large Print Edition).

      New York: Bantam Books, 1950.
      The Third Man, New York: Bantam Books, 1962 (New
         Bantam Edition).
      The Third Man in *Triple Pursuit: a Graham Greene
         Omnibus*, New York: Viking, 1971.

A24   LITTLE FIRE ENGINE

      London: Parrish, 1961.
      London: Bodley Head, 1973 (with Edward Ardizzone).

Garden City, New York: Doubleday, 1973 (with Edward Ardizzone).

A25 THE BEST OF SAKI

Harmondsworth, Middlesex: Penguin Books, 1977.

A26 THE LOST CHILDHOOD AND OTHER ESSAYS

Harmondsworth, Middlesex: Penguin Books, 1962.

New York: Viking, 1962 (Compass Books).

A27 THE END OF THE AFFAIR

London: Heinemann, 1955 (Uniform Edition).
London: Heinemann, 1959 (Library Edition).
Harmondsworth, Middlesex: Penguin Books, 1962.
London: Heinemann and Bodley Head, 1974 (Collected Edition).

New York: Bantam, 1955.
New York: Viking, 1961 (Compass Books).

A28 THE LITTLE HORSEBUS

London: Bodley Head, 1974 (with Edward Ardizzone).

Garden City, New York: Doubleday, 1975 (with Edward Ardizzone).

A29 THE LIVING ROOM

London: Heinemann, 1955 (Drama Library).
in *Three Plays*, London: Mercury Books, 1961.
Harmondsworth, Middlesex: Penguin Books, 1970.

New York: Samuel French, 1955 (French's Acting Edition).

A30 THE LITTLE STEAMROLLER

London: Bodley Head, 1974 (with Edward Ardizzone).

Garden City, New York: Doubleday, 1975 (with
   Edward Ardizzone).

A33 TWENTY-ONE STORIES

Harmondsworth, Middlesex: Penguin Books, 1970.

New York: Viking, 1962 (Compass Books).
New York: Bantam Books, 1966.
New York: Pocket Books, 1976.

A34 LOSER TAKES ALL

Harmondsworth, Middlesex: Penguin Books, 1971.
in *The Third Man* and *Loser Takes All*, London:
   Heinemann and Bodley Head, 1976 (Collected Edition).

A35 THE QUIET AMERICAN

London: Reprint Society, 1957.
London: Heinemann, 1960 (Uniform Edition).
London: Heinemann, 1961 (Library Edition).
Harmondsworth, Middlesex: Penguin Books, 1962.
London: Heinemann and Bodley Head, 1973 (Collected
   Edition).

New York: Viking, 1957 (Compass Books).
New York: Bantam Books, 1957.
New York: Modern Library, 1967.

A36 THE SPY'S BEDSIDE BOOK

London: New English Library, 1962 (Four Square Books).
London: Rupert Hart-Davis and Penguin, 1971.

A37 THE POTTING SHED

London: Samuel French, [1959] (French's Acting Edition).
in *Three Plays*, London: Mercury Books, 1961.

Harmondsworth, Middlesex: Penguin, 1971.

New York: Samuel French, [1957] (French's Acting
   Edition).
New York: Viking, 1961 (Compass Books).

A38   OUR MAN IN HAVANA

Harmondsworth, Middlesex: Penguin, 1962.
London: Heinemann, 1966 (Modern Novel Series, Heinemann
   Educational Books).
London: Heinemann and Bodley Head, 1970 (Collected
   Edition).

in *Triple Pursuit: a Graham Greene Omnibus*, New York:
   Viking, 1971.
New York: Pocket Books, 1974.

A39   THE COMPLAISANT LOVER

London: Samuel French, 1959 (French's Acting Edition).
in *Three Plays*, London: Mercury Books, 1961.
Harmondsworth, Middlesex: Penguin Books, 1971.

A41   A BURNT-OUT CASE

Harmondsworth, Middlesex: Penguin, 1963.
London: Heinemann and Bodley Head, 1974 (Collected
   Edition).

New York: Bantam Books, 1962.
New York: Viking, 1967 (Compass Books).

A42   IN SEARCH OF A CHARACTER

Harmondsworth, Middlesex: Penguin, 1968.

A45   A SENSE OF REALITY

Harmondsworth, Middlesex: Penguin Books, 1968.

A47 CARVING A STATUE

Harmondsworth, Middlesex: Penguin Books, 1972.

A48 THE COMEDIANS

Harmondsworth, Middlesex: Penguin, 1967.
London: Heinemann and Bodley Head, 1976 (Collected
    Edition).

New York: Bantam Books, 1967.
New York: Viking, 1970 (Compass Books).

A50 MAY WE BORROW YOUR HUSBAND?

Harmondsworth, Middlesex: Penguin Books, 1969.

A52 COLLECTED ESSAYS

Harmondsworth, Middlesex: Penguin Books, 1970.

A53 TRAVELS WITH MY AUNT

Harmondsworth, Middlesex: Penguin Books, 1972.

A55 A SORT OF LIFE

Harmondsworth, Middlesex: Penguin Books, 1974.

New York: Pocket Books, 1973.
New York: Simon and Schuster, 1978 (Touchstone Book).

A56 COLLECTED STORIES

in *Shades of Greene*, London: Heinemann and Bodley
    Head, 1975 (a partial reprint; containing those
    stories dramatized in the Thames Television series).

in *Shades of Greene*, New York: Penguin, 1977.

A59 THE HONORARY CONSUL

Harmondsworth, Middlesex: Penguin Books, 1975.

Boston: G. K. Hall, 1974 (Large Print Edition).

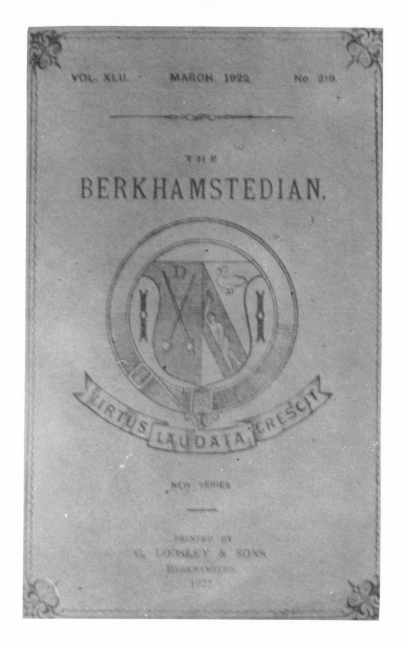

1. *The Berkhamstedian*, March 1922
   contains Greene's fable "The Tyranny of Realism" (C2)

No. 24, Vol. V.   NOVEMBER, 1923.   1/- NET.

THE
Oxford Outlook

A Literary Review Edited by Undergraduates.

Published monthly during Term.

Editor:
C. H. O. SCAIFE.

Sub-Editor:
GRAHAM GREENE.

CONTENTS.

BABBLING APRIL
BY GRAHAM GREENE

OXFORD: BASIL BLACKWELL
1925

3. *Babbling April*, Blackwell, 1925 (A1)

THE MAN WITHIN

BY

GRAHAM GREENE

◆

"There's another man within me
that's angry with me."

SIR THOMAS BROWNE.

LONDON : WILLIAM HEINEMANN LTD.

4. *The Man Within*, Heinemann, 1929 (A2a)

THE
MAN
WITHIN

BY GRAHAM GREENE

*"There's another man within me
that's angry with me."*

Sir Thomas Browne.

DOUBLEDAY, DORAN & COMPANY, INC.

GARDEN CITY, NEW YORK

MCMXXIX

5. *The Man Within*, Doubleday, 1929 (A2b)

THE
NAME
OF ACTION

by

Graham Greene

"   .   *and lose the name of action.*"
Hamlet

LONDON
WILLIAM HEINEMANN LTD

6. *The Name of Action*, Heinemann, 1930 (A3a)

Rumour at Nightfall

by

Graham Greene

London
William Heinemann Ltd

7. *Rumour at Nightfall*, Heinemann, 1931 (A4a)

8. Bindings for 1st English Editions of
   The Name of Action, 1930 (A3a)
   Rumour at Nightfall, 1931 (A4a)

9. Dust jackets for
   British Dramatists, 1942 (A17)
   The Name of Action, 1930 (A3a)
   Rumour at Nightfall, 1931 (A4a)

The
OLD SCHOOL

Essays
by Divers Hands

Edited by
GRAHAM GREENE

Jonathan Cape
Thirty Bedford Square
London

10. *The Old School*, Cape, 1934 (A7)

ENGLAND MADE ME

A NOVEL

BY

GRAHAM GREENE

WILLIAM HEINEMANN LTD
LONDON   ::   TORONTO

11. *England Made Me*, Heinemann, 1935 (A8a)

GRAHAM GREENE

England Made Me

A Novel

Garden City   *New York*

Doubleday, Doran & Company, Inc.

1935

12. *England Made Me*, Doubleday, 1935 (A8b)

THE GRAYSON BOOKS
Edited by *JOHN HACKNEY*

The Bear Fell Free

·

Graham Greene

GRAYSON & GRAYSON
LONDON: MDCCCCXXXV

13. *The Bear Fell Free*, Grayson & Grayson, 1935 (A9)

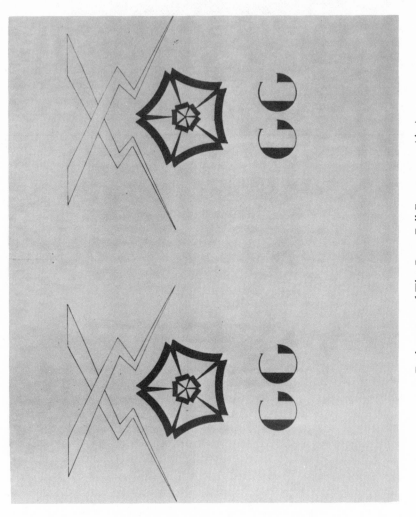

14. Endpapers of *The Bear Fell Free*, 1935 (A9)

Graham Greene

THE BASEMENT ROOM

and other stories

THE CRESSET PRESS LIMITED
11 FITZROY SQUARE
LONDON

15. *The Basement Room*, Cresset Press, 1935 (A10)

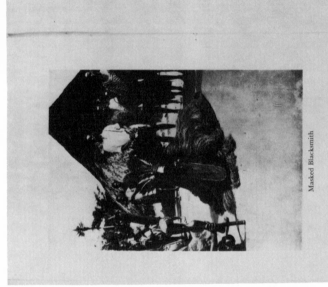

JOURNEY
WITHOUT MAPS

BY
GRAHAM GREENE

WILLIAM HEINEMANN LTD.
LONDON :: TORONTO

Masked Blacksmith

16. *Journey Without Maps*, Heinemann, 1936 (A11a)
Frontispiece and title-page

17. *The Lawless Roads*, Longmans, Green and Co., 1939 (A14a)
Frontispiece and title-page

GRAHAM GREENE

THE

LABYRINTHINE

WAYS

NEW YORK

1940 · THE VIKING PRESS

18. *The Labyrinthine Ways*, Viking, 1940 (A16b)

Why Do I Write?

AN EXCHANGE OF VIEWS

BETWEEN

Elizabeth Bowen

Graham Greene

&

V. S. Pritchett

WITH A PREFACE BY

V. S. PRITCHETT

LONDON

Percival Marshall

19. *Why Do I Write?* Percival Marshall, 1948 (A22)

THE
LOST CHILDHOOD
and other essays

by

GRAHAM GREENE

1951
EYRE & SPOTTISWOODE
London

20. *The Lost Childhood*, Eyre & Spottiswoode, 1951 (A26)

Graham Greene

Introductions to Three Novels

Norstedts

21. *Introductions to Three Novels*, Norstedts, 1962 (A44)
Front cover of wrapper

VICTORIAN
DETECTIVE FICTION

A CATALOGUE OF THE COLLECTION MADE BY
DOROTHY GLOVER & GRAHAM GREENE
BIBLIOGRAPHICALLY ARRANGED
BY ERIC OSBORNE AND
INTRODUCED BY JOHN CARTER

WITH A PREFACE BY
GRAHAM GREENE

THE BODLEY HEAD · LONDON
SYDNEY & TORONTO

22. *Victorian Detective Fiction*, Bodley Head, 1966 (A49)

B

BOOKS WITH CONTRIBUTIONS BY GRAHAM GREENE

This list indicates only first publications. The many an-
thologies which contain Greene's stories are not listed. An
item preceded by one asterisk is fiction. An item preceded
by two asterisks is poetry. The list is arranged
chronologically.

B1 **"Apologia." *Oxford Poetry, 1923.* Edited by David
    Cleghorn Thompson and F.W. Bateson. Oxford: Basil
    Blackwell, 1923, p. 28.

B2 **"Stepping Stones." *Oxford Poetry, 1923.* Edited by
    David Cleghorn Thompson and F.W. Bateson. Oxford:
    Basil Blackwell, 1923, p. 27.

B3 **"The Gamesters." *Public School Verse: An Anthology,
    III, 1921-1922.* Edited by Martin Gilkes, Richard
    Hughes and P.H.B. Lyon. London: Heinemann, 1923, p. 15.

B4 **"Childishness." *Oxford Poetry, 1924.* Edited by Harold
    Acton and Peter Quennell. Oxford: Basil Blackwell,
    1924, p. 17.

B5 **"Paint and Wood." *Oxford Poetry, 1924.* Edited by
    Harold Acton and Peter Quennell. Oxford: Basil Black-
    well, 1924, p. 16.

B6 **"A Tramp Finds Himself Inspected by an Owl." *The Best
    Poems of 1925.* Edited by L.A.G. Strong. Boston:
    Small, Maynard and Company, 1925, p. 112.

B7 **"I Shall Be Happy." *Oxford Poetry, 1925.* Edited by
    Patrick Monkhouse and Charles Plumb. Oxford: Basil
    Blackwell, 1925, p. 19.

B8 **"Sonnet--All These Belong ..." *Oxford Poetry, 1925.*
    Edited by Patrick Monkhouse and Charles Plumb. Oxford:
    Basil Blackwell, 1925, p. 20.

B9 "Anthony à Wood." *Spectator's Gallery: Essays,
    Sketches, Short Stories and Poems from The Spectator,
    1932.* Edited by Peter Fleming and Derek Verschoyle.
    London: Cape, 1933.

B10 "Henry James: The Religious Aspect." *Contemporary Essays,
    1933.* Edited by Sylva Norman. London: Mathews &
    Marriot, 1933, pp. 65-75.

B11 *"A Day Saved." *Nine O'Clock Stories by Fourteen
    Authors.* London: G. Bell and Sons, 1934, pp. 69-79.

B12 "The Travellers' Library." *Then and Now: A Selection of
    Articles, Stories and Poems, Taken from the First Fifty
    Numbers of Now and Then, Together with Some Illustrations,*

and *Certain Other Work Now Printed for the First Time*.
London: Cape, 1935, pp. 153-155.

B13   "Henry James: The Private Universe." *English Novel-
        ists: A Survey of the Novel by Twenty Contemporary
        Novelists*. Edited by Derek Verschoyle. London:
        Chatto & Windus, 1936, pp. 231-246.

B14   "Fielding and Sterne." *From Anne to Victoria*. Edited
        by Bonamy Dobrée. London: Cassell, 1937, pp. 279-289.

B15   "Introduction." *The Bachelor of Arts* by R.K. Narayan.
        London: Nelson, 1937, pp. v-x.

B16   "Selection of Film Criticism." *Garbo and the Night
        Watchman: A Selection from the Writings of British and
        American Film Critics*. Assembled and edited by Ali-
        stair Cooke. London: Cape, 1937, pp. 207-239, 344-
        346.

B17   "Subjects and Stories." *Footnotes to the Film*. Edi-
        ted by Charles Davy. London: Lovat Dickson, 1937,
        pp. 57-70; New York: Oxford University Press, 1937.

B18   "Convoy to West Africa." *The Mint: A Miscellany of
        Literature, Art and Criticism, Volume I*. Edited by
        Geoffrey Grigson. London: Routledge and Kegan Paul,
        1946, pp. 40-55.

B19   "The Revolver in the Corner Cupboard." *The Saturday
        Book, Sixth Year*. Edited by Leonard Russell. London:
        Hutchinson, 1946, pp. 135-138.

B20   "Introduction." *The Green Child* by Herbert Read.
        London: Eyre and Spottiswoode, 1947, pp. v-viii.

B21   "The Portrait of a Lady." Introduction to *The Portrait
        of a Lady* by Henry James. World's Classics, No. 509.
        London: Oxford University Press, 1947, pp. v-xi.

B22   "The Short Stories." *Tribute to Walter De La Mare on
        His Seventy-Fifth Birthday*. London: Faber & Faber,
        1948, pp. 71-77.

B23   "Prefatory Letter." *Graham Greene, Temoin Des Temps
        Tragiques* by Paul Rostenne. Paris: Julliard, 1949,
        pp. 11-12.

B24 "Speech" to the Centre Catholique des Intellectuels Français ('Le Crétien est-il de la Terre?') printed in *Foi en Jésus Christ et Monde d'Aujourd'hui*. Paris: Editions de Flore, 1949.

B25 "Introduction." *The Living God* by Armand Pierhal. Translated from the French by Wilhemina Guérard. New York: Harper & Bros., 1950, pp. 7-9.

B26 "The Young Dickens." Introduction to *Oliver Twist* by Charles Dickens. The Novel Library Edition. London: Hamish Hamilton, 1950, pp. vii-xiv.

B27 "Introduction." *The Autobiography of an Elizabethan* by John Gerard. Translated from the Latin by Philip Caraman. London: Longmans, Green, 1951, pp. vii-xi.

B28 "Introduction." *The Financial Expert* by R.K. Narayan. London: Methuen, 1952, pp. v-vi.

B29 "Introduction." *Venus in the Kitchen: or Love's Cookery Book* by "Pilaff Bey." Edited by Norman Douglas. London: Heinemann, 1952, pp. vii-x.

B30 "Introduction." *Eight European Artists*. Photographed and edited by Felix H. Man. London: Heinemann, 1954, p. vii.

B31 "Introduction." *Father Six: Parish Priest and Viceroy* by Mgr. Armand Olichon. Translated from the French by Barbara Wall. London: Burns and Oates, 1954, pp. v-vi.

B32 "Don Fernando." *The Maugham Enigma*. Edited by Klaus W. Jones. London: Peter Owen, 1954, pp. 194-196. Review of *Spanish Gold*.

B33 "Preface." *Un Homme Dans La Riziére* by Colonel Jean Leroy. Translated into French by Marcelle Sibon. Paris: Editions de Paris, 1955.

B34 "Prefatory Letter." *Men: A Dialogue Between Women* by Allegra Sanders. Translated from the French by Vyvyan Holland. London: Cresset Press, 1955, pp. 5-8.

B35 "The Novelist and the Cinema--A Personal Experience." *International Film Annual Number 2*. Edited by William Whitebait. London: Calder, 1958, pp. 54-61.

B36   "Introductory Note." *The Viper of Milan: A Romance
        of Lombardy* by Marjorie Bowen. London: Bodley Head,
        1960, pp. 9-10.

B37   "Preface." *African Sketchbook*. Text and drawings by
        Frederick Franck. London: Peter Davies, 1961; New
        York: Holt, Rinehart and Winston, 1962, pp. vii-viii.

B38   "Introduction." *Edgar Wallace: The Biography of a
        Phenomenon* by Margaret Lane. London: Hamish Hamilton,
        1964, pp. xi-xiv.

B39   "Ghosts of Possible Adventure." *Parnassus Near Pica-
        dilly, an Anthology*. The Cafe Royal Centenary Book.
        Edited by Leslie Frewin. London: Leslie Frewin, 1965,
        pp. 9-11.

B40   "Introduction." *The Good Soldier* by Ford Madox Ford.
        London: Mayflower-Dell, 1965.

B41   *Authors Take Sides on Vietnam*. Edited by Cecil Woolf
        and John Bagguley. New York: Simon and Schuster,
        1967, p. 37.

B42   "Introduction." *My Silent War* by Kim Philby. London:
        MacGibbon and Kee, 1968.

B43   *¡Viva Che!: Contributions in Tribute to Ernesto 'Che'
        Guevara*. Edited by Marianne Alexandre. London:
        Lorrimer, 1968, p. 71.

B44   "Foreword." *Papa Doc: The Truth about Haiti Today* by
        Bernard Diederich and Al Burt. New York: McGraw-Hill,
        1969, pp. vii-x.

B45   "Foreword." *Eleven* by Patricia Highsmith. London:
        Heinemann, 1970, pp. ix-xi.

B46   "Foreword." *Diplomat: Memoirs of a Swedish Envoy in
        London. Paris. Berlin. Moscow. Washington* by Gunnar
        Haggloff. London: Bodley Head, 1972, pp. 7-9.

B47   "Introduction." *With All Faults* by Sir David Low.
        Tehran: Amate Press, 1973, pp. xiii-xvii.

B48   "A Personal Foreword." *The Contrary Experience* by
        Herbert Read. London: Secker and Warburg; New York:
        Horizon Press, 1973, pp. 7-10.

B49 "The Virtue of Disloyalty." *The Portable Graham Greene*. Edited by Philip Stratford. New York: The Viking Press, 1973, pp. 606-610.

B50 "Preface." *Miss Silver's Past* by Josef Skvorecky. New York: Grove Press, 1974, pp. ix-xi.

B51 "Introduction." *The Sign of Four* by Sir Arthur Conan Doyle. London: John Murray and Jonathan Cape, 1974, pp. 7-10; New York: Doubleday, 1974.

C

CONTRIBUTIONS TO NEWSPAPERS AND PERIODICALS
BY GRAHAM GREENE

When an item has been reprinted in *The Lost Childhood* or
Collected Essays and its title has been changed, the later
title is noted. An item preceded by one asterisk is fiction.
An item preceded by two asterisks is poetry.

Film Criticism: Because *The Pleasure-Dome* (*Graham Greene on
Film* in the U.S.A.) is subtitled "Collected Film Criticism,"
many readers may have been led to believe that this collection is comprehensive, which it is not. Unfortunately this
problem comes at a time when there is not only a rapidly ex-
panding interest in film studies but also a growing body of
readers who have a special interest in Greene's involvement
with the cinema. As a partial remedy to the problem, Greene's
film criticism and commentary are not listed with his other
periodical contributions but rather in a separate subsection
following the main section.

Competitions: There is some evidence in the Greene manuscript
Collection at the Humanities Research Center (see DI) that
Graham Greene has entered at least five *New Statesman* "Week-
end Competitions," several of which have been competitions to
parody Greene. A letter to the editor (April 14, 1961, p.
585) signed with Greene's name claims that a prize winner
named H.A. Baxter in Competition #1621 is actually Greene.
There have undoubtedly been other entries by Greene, but the
editors themselves seem unable to identify these items. Con-
sidering the atmosphere of frivolity and double-think
associated with the competitions, little solid evidence is
available to identify further items.

1920

C1   *"The Tick of the Clock," *The Berkhamstedian*, XL
       (December), pp. 118-119.

       Not signed; acknowledged; reprinted in *The Star*, a
       London evening newspaper, in 1921.

1922

C2   *"The Tyranny of Realism," *The Berkhamstedian*, XLII
       (March), pp. 2-3.

       Initialed.

C3   *"Magic," *The Weekly Westminster Gazette*, I (May 6),
       p. 16.

C4   *"An Epic Fragment from 'The Dish Pioneers' Attributed
       to A__F__D N__Y__S," *The Berkhamstedian*, XLII (July),
       pp. 46-47.

       Initialed.

C5   **"My New Books," *The Weekly Westminster Gazette*, I
       (September 30), p. 13.

1923

C6   **"Stepping Stones," *The Weekly Westminster Gazette*, I
       (February 10), p. 5.

C7   *"The Trial of Pan," *The Oxford Outlook*, V (February),
       pp. 47-50.

C8   **"Old Age of a Georgian," *The Weekly Westminster
       Gazette*, II (May 12), p. 8.

C9   **"Atmosphere," *The Oxford Chronicle* (June 15), p. 15.

C10   **"Selfdom," *The Oxford Outlook*, V (June), p. 79.

C11 **"Paint and Wood," *The Weekly Westminster Gazette*, II
     (August 4), p. 15.

C12 **"A Pauper's Wealth," *The Oxford Chronicle* (October 26),
     p. 15.

C13 **"Old Love," *The Oxford Chronicle* (November 9), p. 16.

C14 *"The New House," *The Oxford Outlook*, V (November),
     pp. 112-115.

C15 **"At the Theatre," *The Oxford Outlook*, V (November),
     p. 150.

C16 **"The Coming," *The Oxford Outlook*, V (November), p. 150.

                              1924

C17 **"Apologia," *The Weekly Westminster Gazette*, I (January
     26), p. 407.

C18 **"Fears," *The Oxford Outlook*, VI (January), p. 24.

C19 **"Paradisal Tea," *The Oxford Outlook*, VI (January),
     p. 24.

C20 Untitled, *The Oxford Outlook*, VI (January), p. 58.

     Initialed; review of *The Education Outlook* for
     January.

C21 "Eight More Harvard Poets: Bretano's," *The Oxford
     Outlook*, VI (February), pp. 124-128.

     Initialed; review of *Eight More Harvard Poets* edited
     by Samuel F. Damon and Robert S. Hillyer.

C22 "John Drinkwater," *The Oxford Outlook*, VI (February),
     pp. 120-123.

     Review of *Collected Poems* (2 vols.) by John Drinkwater.

C23 **"The Coming--To J.G.W.," *The Golden Hind*, II (April),
     p. 31.

C24 "In the Occupied Area. An Oxford Undergraduate's Impressions," *The Oxford Chronicle* (May 9), p. 16.

C25 **"The Judgement," *The Oxford Chronicle* (May 30), p. 15.

C26 "The French Peace," *The Oxford Outlook*, VI (June), pp. 212-216.

C27 Untitled, *The Oxford Outlook*, VI (June), pp. 243-244.

Review of *The Ding Dong Bell* by Walter de la Mare.

C28 Untitled, *The Oxford Outlook*, VI (June), pp. 238-239.

Review of *Kensington Gardens* by Humbert Wolfe.

C29 Untitled, *The Oxford Outlook*, VI (June), pp. 239-240.

Review of *Little Mexican* by Aldous Huxley.

C30 **"The History Schools," *The Oxford Chronicle* (October 17), p. 15.

C31 **"The Secret Room," *The Oxford Chronicle* (October 31), p. 15.

C32 **"I.M." *The Oxford Chronicle* (November 14), p. 15.

C33 "The Improbable Tale of the Archbishop of Canter-bridge," *The Cherwell*, n.s. XII (November 15), pp. 187, 189, 191.

Initialed.

C34 "The Mitre," *The Cherwell*, n.s. XII (November 15), pp. 212-213.

Review of *Round About "The Mitre" at Oxford: Episodes of the University City and Hotel*; *Crossings: A Fairy Play* by Walter de la Mare; and *The Rivet in Grandfather's Neck: A Comedy of Limitations* by James Branch Cabell.

C35 **"Apres Vous," *The Cherwell*, n.s. XII (November 22), p. 252.

C36 **"Childishness," *The Oxford Outlook*, VI (November), p. 272.

C37   **"Small Talk," *The Decachord*, I (Christmas, November),
      p. 17.

C38   **"The Adventurer," *The Decachord*, I (November-December),
      p. 144.

C39   **"The Heritage," *The Decachord*, I (November-December),
      p. 144.

C40   Untitled, *The Isis*, No. 668 (December 3), p. 16.

      Review of *Parent or Pedagogue* by Esmi Wingfield.

C41   **"1930," *The Oxford Outlook*, VI (December), p. 318.

C42   **"Sonnet," *The Oxford Outlook*, VI (December), p. 318.

C43   Untitled, *The Oxford Outlook*, VI (December), pp. 359-
      360.

      Review of *No. 2 Joy Street*, a children's annual.

C44   Untitled, *The Oxford Outlook*, VI (December), pp. 357-
      358.

      Review of *Sard Harker* by John Masefield.

                              1925

C45   **"Childishness," *Literary Digest*, XXCIV (January 3),
      p. 31.

C46   **"The Godly Distance," *The Weekly Westminster*, III
      (January 24), p. 379.

C47   "Poetry by Wireless," *The Oxford Chronicle* (January 30),
      p. 15.

C48   **"Death and Cosmetics," *The Oxford Outlook*, VII
      (January), p. 11.

C49   **"If You Were Dead," *The Oxford Outlook*, VII (January),
      p. 7.

      Signed "Hilary Trench" (Greene pseudonym).

C50 **"Paradisal Tea," *The Decachord*, II (January-February), p. 14.

C51 **"On a Walking Tour," *The Oxford Chronicle* (February 6), p. 15.

C52 Untitled, *The Isis*, No. 672 (February 12), p. 16.

Review of a production of Farquhar's *Beaux Strategem* by St. Hugh's Dramatic Society.

C53 **"Sonnet," *The Oxford Chronicle* (February 27), p. 15.

C54 **"The Back Porch," *The Oxford Outlook*, VII (February), pp. 73-74.

C55 Untitled, *The Oxford Outlook*, VII (February), pp. 104-105.

Review of *An Indian Ass* by Harold Acton.

C56 Untitled, *The Oxford Outlook*, VII (February), pp. 106-107.

Signed "Hilary Trench" (Greene pseudonym); review of *Verse in Bloom* by Norman Gale.

C57 **"Before Breakfast," *The Oxford Chronicle* (March 13), p. 65.

C58 **"Lippens," *The Oxford Chronicle* (May 8), p. 15.

C59 "The Poets Fight," *The Cherwell*, n.s. XIV (May 16), p. 59.

Letter to the editor *re* Harold Acton's review of *Babbling April*.

C60 **"Casual Myrrh," *The Oxford Outlook*, VII (May), p. 114.

C61 **"Fragment from 'Angina Pectoris': A Long Poem," *The Isis*, No. 682 (June 3), p. 2.

Entire poem published as "Sad Cure" in *The Cherwell* in February and March 1926.

C62 *"The Lord Knows," *The Oxford Chronicle* (June 5), p. 16.

C63 **"Cowardice," *The Oxford Outlook*, VII (June), p. 186.

C64   "Mr. Priestley in Search of the Comic," *The Weekly
       Westminster Gazette*, n.s. IV (October 17), p. 648.

       Review of *Fools and Philosophers*, an anthology com-
       piled by J.B. Priestley.

C65 **"The Unconquered," *The Weekly Westminster Gazette*, n.s.
       IV (October 24), p. 665.

C66   "Stendhal," *The Weekly Westminster Gazette*, n.s. V
       (November 7), p. 18.

       Review of *The Life of Henri Brulard* by Henry Beyle-
       Stendhal.

                              1926

C67 **"Spawn," *The Cherwell*, n.s. XVI (January 23), p. 17.

C68 **"Sad Cure. The Life and Death of John Perry-Perkins,"
       The Cherwell, n.s. XVI, No. 5 (February 20), pp. 139-
       140; No. 6 (February 27), pp. 172-174; No. 7 (March 6),
       pp. 209-211.

       Unsigned; first thirty lines published as "Fragment
       from 'Angina Pectoris': A Long Poem," in *The Isis*,
       June 3, 1925, p. 2, signed.

C69 **"The Secret Room," *The Decachord*, II (May-June),
       p. 121.

C70 **"Sonnet," *The Decachord*, II (May-June), p. 121.

                              1927

C71 **"Caesar's Ghost," *London Mercury*, XVI (July), p. 236.

                              1929

C72   "George Darley," *London Mercury*, XIX (March),
       pp. 498-506.

Review of *The Life and Letters of George Darley, Poet and Critic* by Claude Colleer Abbott.

C73   *"Murder for the Wrong Reason," *The Graphic*, CXXVI, No. 3121 (October 5), pp. 16-17; No. 3122 (October 12), pp. 82-83; No. 3123 (October 19), p. 132.

1930

C74   "Oberammergau," *The Graphic* CXXVII (May 17), p. 345.

Review of the passion play at Oberammergau.

1931

C75   Letter, *Times Literary Supplement* (September 24), p. 730.

Re the Earl of Rochester.

1932

C76   "The Facts of Fiction," *The Spectator*, CXLVIII (January 23), p. 117.

Review of *The Facts of Fiction* by Norman Collins.

C77   "Daniel Defoe," *The Spectator*, CXLVIII (January 30), p. 152.

Review of *The Life of Daniel Defoe* by Thomas Wright.

C78   *"The End of the Party," *London Mercury*, XXV (January), pp. 238-244.

C79   "Escape," *The Spectator*, CXLVIII (February 20), p. 259.

Review of *A World Can End* by Irina Skariätina and *One Lives to Tell the Tale* by Edmund Gilligan.

C80   "Strange Prisons," *The Spectator*, CXLVIII (March 5), pp. 339-340.

Review of *The Road to Oblivion* by Vladimir Zenzinov;
The Escapes of Captain O'Brien, R.N. 1804-1808; and
Harpoon by Henry Ferguson.

C81   "Taking Stock," *The Spectator*, CXLVIII (April 2),
       pp. 485-486.

       Review of *But for the Grace of God* by J.W.N. Sullivan;
       Chances and Mischances by Charles Gibson; and *The
       Rest is Lies* by Martin Carey.

C82   "The Newgate Calendar," *The Spectator*, CXLVIII
       (April 16), p. 563.

       Review of *The Newgate Calendar or Malefactors' Bloody
       Register*, compiled by Andrew Baldwin and Werner Laurie.

C83   "Strange Worlds," *The Spectator*, CXLVIII (May 14),
       p. 705.

       Review of *I Lost My Memory. The Case as the Patient
       Saw It*; *Wild Oats* by Eric Muspratt; and *In the Line.
       1914-1918* by Georg Bucher.

C84   "The Irrational Age," *The Spectator*, CXLVIII (May 21),
       pp. 734-735.

       Review of *Under the Fifth Rib. A Belligerent Auto-
       biography* by C.E.M. Joad; *Thirteen Such Years* by Alec
       Waugh; and *My Flesh and Blood, A Lyric Autobiography*
       by G.S. Viereck.

C85   "Inflation," *The Spectator*, CXLVIII (June 4), p. 807.

       Review of *Blockade. The Diary of an Austrian Middle-
       Class Woman, 1914-24* by Anna Eisenmenger and *Peace
       Broke Out* by Heinz Liepmann.

C86   "The Unsentimental Journey," *The Spectator*, CLXVIII
       (June 11), pp. 837-838.

       Review of *A Tower of Skulls* by Gerald Reitlinger;
       Across Lapland by Olive Murray Chapman; *The Wake of
       the Southern Cross* by Cecil Wilson, D.D.; and *Adven-
       tures of an Alpine Guide* by Christian Klucker.

C87   "Casanova and Others," *The Spectator*, CXLIX (July 9).
       pp. 54-55.

       Review of *My Life and Adventures* by Casanova; *The
       Chevalier D'Eon* by M. Coryn; *The Dandy Hun* by Konstantin
       Maglic; and *The Maniac*.

C88   "Victoriana," *The Spectator*, CXLIX (July 16), p. 88.

Review of *Songs of the Affections* by Thomas Haynes
Bayly, edited by W.L. Hanchant; *Mirth and Mocking of
Sinner Stocking* by Malthys Merryfellow, edited by W.L.
Hanchant; and *The Newgate Garland*, edited by W.L.
Hanchant.

C89   "Adventures in Four Continents," *The Spectator*, CXLIX
(July 30), pp. 160-161.

Review of *Regiment Reichstag* by Kurt Lamprecht;
Angels on Horseback by Brigadier-General F.P. Crozier;
Men on the Horizon by Guy Murchie; and *Klengenberg of
the Arctic. An Autobiography*, edited by Tom Macinnes.

C90   "Servants of the Novel," *The Spectator*, CXLIX
August 20), pp. 238-239.

Review of *The Popular Novel in England, 1770-1800* by
J.M.S. Tompkins.

C91   "A Prisoner of the Forsytes," *The Spectator*, CXLIX
(October 8), p. 454.

Review of *Candelabra: Selected Essays and Addresses* by
John Galsworthy.

C92   "Anthony à Wood," *The Spectator*, CXLIX (November 4),
pp. 636, 638.

Review of *The Life and Times of Anthony à Wood*,
edited by Llewelyn Powys.

C93   "Three Poets," *Oxford Magazine*, LI (November 10),
pp. 158-159.

Review of *The Collected Poems of D. H. Lawrence*; *Halfway House* by Edmund Blunden; *The Orators* by W.H. Auden;
Collected Poems by Edwin Arlington Robinson; *Farewell,
My Muse* by Clifford Bax; and *Known Signatures*, edited
by John Gawsworth.

C94   "Bow Street Nights," *The Spectator*, CXLIX (December 16),
pp. 872-873.

Review of *The History of the Bow Street Runners, 1729-
1829* by Gilbert Armitage.

C95   "The Horoscopic Approach," *The Spectator*, CXLIX
(December 23), pp. 897-898.

Review of *Pretty Witty Nell* by Clifford Bax.

1933

C96   "Beatrix Potter: A Critical Estimate," *London Mercury*,
        n.s. XXVII (January), pp. 241-245.

C97   "Fiction," *The Spectator*, CL (February 10), pp. 194,
        196.

        Review of *Mandoa, Mandoa!* by Winifred Holtby; *Shadows
        of Ecstasy* by Charles Williams; *The Strange River* by
        Julian Green; *Tiger Juan* by Ramon Pérez de Ayala; and
        Revolt by A.P. Roley.

C98   "Death in the Cotswolds," *The Spectator*, CL
        (February 24), p. 247.

C99   "Gold Bricks," *The Spectator*, CL (March 3), p. 308.

        Review of *Ivar Kreuger* by George Soloveytchik.

C100   "Casanova," *The Spectator*, CL (March 17), p. 392.

        Review of *Casanova* by Bonamy Dobrée.

C101   "Charles II," *The Spectator*, CL (March 31), pp. 469-
        470.

        Review of *Charles II* by John Hayward.

C102   "Fiction," *The Spectator*, CL (April 7), p. 508.

        Review of *Company K* by William Marsh; *The Progress of
        Julius* by Daphne du Maurier; *The World His Pillow* by
        James Barke; *Manassas* by Upton Sinclair; and *Angel-
        Face* by Archibald Marshall.

C103   "A Jacobite Poet," *The Spectator*, CL (April 14),
        pp. 540-541.

        Review of *Granville the Polite: The Life of George
        Granville Lord Lansdowne* by Elizabeth Handasyde.

C104   "Fiction," *The Spectator*, CL (April 21), p. 579.

        Review of *Doctor Gion* by Hans Carossa; *Little Man What
        Now* by Hans Fallada; *The Wheel of Life* by Hermynia Zur
        Mühlen; *Julian Grant Loses His Way* by Claude Houghton;
        Laughter in Heaven by C. Lloyd-Jones; and *Moods and
        Tenses* by W.F. Harvey.

C105   "Seventeenth-Century Verse," *The Spectator*, CL
         (April 28), pp. 613-614.

         Review of *Aspects of Seventeenth-Century Verse*,
         selected and prefaced by Peter Quennell.

C106   "Fiction," *The Spectator*, CL (May 5), p. 654.

         Review of *Human Nature* by Edith Wharton; *The Kaiser
         Goes: the Generals Remain* by Theodor Pliver; *After
         the Party* by R.D. Dorthy; *Hindu Heaven* by Max Wylie;
         Flo by F.C. Boden; and *Mutiny!* by Charles Nordhoff and
         James Norman Hall.

C107   "Fiction," *The Spectator*, CL (May 19), p. 728.

         Review of *Grand Canary* by A.J. Cronin; *Durbar* by Denis
         Kincaid; *Mrs. Van Kleek* by Elinor Mordaunt; *The Enemy
         at the Gate* by A. t'Serstevens; and *An Oxford Tragedy*
         by J.C. Masterman.

C108   "Fiction," *The Spectator*, CL (June 2), p. 812.

         Review of *Original Design* by Eardley Beswick; *The
         Plebeian's Progress* by Frank Tilsley; *The Balcony* by
         R.G. Coulson; *Hardy Perennial* by Helen Hull; and *The
         Lord of Life* by Neil Bell.

C109   "Fiction," *The Spectator*, CL (June 16), p. 880.

         Review of *Short Stories* by Per Hallstrom; *Rubber* by
         Madelon H. Lulofs; *Panorama with Music* by Grace E.
         Thompson; *Tandem* by Violet Trefusis; *Singing Out of
         Tune* by Bryan Guinness; and *Knight Without Armour* by
         James Hilton.

C110   "Fiction," *The Spectator*, CL (June 30), p. 956.

         Review of *Little Friend* by Ernest Lothar; *Love on the
         Dole* by Walter Greenwood; *Yet in My Flesh* by M.E.
         Mitchell; *Gentlemen--The Regiment* by Hugh Talbot; and
         The Story of a Country Town by E.W. Howe.

C111   "Fiction," *The Spectator*, CLI (July 14), p. 58.

         Review of *Mrs. Ritchie* by Willa Muir; *Daughter to
         Phillip* by Beatrice Kean Seymour; *Discovery by Torch-
         light* by P. Whitehouse; *Sun Circle* by Neil M. Gunn;
         and *The Old Man Dies* by Elizabeth Sprigge.

C112   "Fiction," *The Spectator*, CLI (July 28), p. 138.

Review of *The Cage Bird* by Francis Brett Young; *Salah and His American* by Leland Hall; *The Black Mountain* by Alan Hillgarth; *Name of Gentlemen* by Barbara Willard; and *Tops and Bottoms* by Noel Streatfield.

C113   "Fiction," *The Spectator*, CLI (August 11), p. 198.

Review of *Hag's Harvest* by J.B. Morton; *Water on the Brain* by Compton Mackenzie; *The Flowering Thorn* by Margery Sharp; *Hot-House* by G.E. Trevelyan; *Two Loves I Have* by Owen Pitman; and *Mr. J. Jay* by Frank Aldworth.

C114   "The Rash Act," *Now and Then*, No. 45 (Summer), pp. 19-20.

Review of *The Rash Act* by Ford Madox Ford.

C115   "Fiction," *The Spectator*, CLI (September 22), p. 380.

Review of *Traveller's Pack* by Elinor Mordaunt; *The First Wife* by Pearl S. Buck; *Shake Hands with the Devil* by Rearden Conner; *No Second Spring* by Janet Beith; and *Two Black Sheep* by Warwick Deeping.

C116   "Fiction Chronicle," *The Spectator*, CLI (October 6), p. 455.

Review of *A Nest of Simple Folk* by Seán O'Faoláin; *The Valiant Wife* by Margaret Wilson; *Tobacco Road* by Erskine Caldwell; and *Tinkers' Wind* by G. Scott Moncrieff.

C117   "Fiction," *The Spectator*, CLI (October 20), p. 538.

Review of *Great Circle* by Conrad Aiken; *The Cuban Farm* by Wilson Wright; *The Artificial Silk Girl* by Irmgard Keun; and *No Castle in Spain* by William McFee.

C118   "Two Capitals," *The Spectator*, CLI (October 20), pp. 520-521.

C119   "Fiction," *The Spectator*, CLI (November 3), p. 638.

Review of *Miracle on Sinai* by Osbert Sitwell; *Youth Can't Be Served* by Norah Hoult; *The Curse of the Wise Woman* by Lord Dunsany; *Escape to Life* by Ferene Körmendi; and *Yonder Lies Jericho* by Samuel B. Harrison.

C120   "Fiction," *The Spectator,* CLI (November 17), pp. 728, 730.

Review of *Mediterranean Blues* by Yvonne Cloud; *The Camberwell Miracle* by J.D. Beresford; *Bonfire* by Dorothy Canfield; and *The Ladies* by Stanley Hopkins.

C121   "The Final Pepys," *The Spectator*, CLI (November 24), pp. 777-778.

Review of *Samuel Pepys: The Man in the Making* by Arthur Bryant.

C122   "Fiction," *The Spectator*, CLI (December 1), p. 820.

Review of *Lost Paradise* by Francesca Claremont; *The Journey of 'The Flame'* by A. de Fierro Blanco; *The Cross of Peace* by Philip Gibbs; and *Alanna Autumnal* by George Barker.

C123   "A Note on Hans Andersen," *The Spectator*, CLI (December 8), p. 854.

Review of *Hans Christian Andersen* by Signe Toksvig; in *Collected Essays* as "Hans Andersen."

C124   "Fiction," *The Spectator*, CLI (December 15), p. 910.

Review of *The Gates of Hell* by Erik R. von Kuhnelt-Leddihn; *Dawn of Darkness* by Balder Olden; and *Rabble in Arms* by Kenneth Roberts.

C125   "Rochester's Poems," *The Spectator*, CLI (December 22), p. 941.

Review of *The Poetical Works of John Wilmot Earl of Rochester*, edited by Quilter Johns.

C126   "Fiction," *The Spectator*, CLI (December 29), p. 973.

Review of *About Levy* by Arthur Calder-Marshall; *The Golden Net* by Sarah Barlow; *Christmas Tree* by Lady Eleanor Smith; and *Albert Goes Through* by J.B. Priestley.

1934

C127   "Rebel Manqué," *The Spectator*, CLII (January 12),
        p. 56.

        Review of *The Smith of Smiths* by Hesketh Pearson.

C128   "John Evelyn," *The Spectator*, CLII (January 19),
        p. 90.

        Review of *John Evelyn* by Arthur Ponsonby.

C129   "Oslo and Stockholm," *The Living Age*, CCCXLV
        (January), pp. 424-426.

C130   "Samuel Butler," *The Spectator*, CLII (February 9),
        p. 205.

        Review of *Further Extracts from the Note-Books of
        Samuel Butler*, edited by A.T. Bartholomew.

C131   "Strike in Paris," *The Spectator*, CLII (February 16),
        pp. 229-230.

C132   "Edwardian Inferno," *The Spectator*, CLII (February 16),
        p. 240.

        Review of *The Quest for Corvo* by A.J.A. Symons; in
        Lost Childhood and *Collected Essays* as "Frederick
        Rolfe: Edwardian Inferno."

C133   "Short Stories," *The Spectator*, CLII (March 16),
        p. 424.

        Review of *The Woman Who Had Imagination* by H.E. Bates;
        General Buntop's Miracle by Martin Armstrong; *Children
        with Fire* by Ashley Smith; and *After Such Pleasures*
        by Dorothy Parker.

C134   "Lamb's Testimonials," *The Spectator*, CLII (March 30),
        pp. 512-513.

        Review of *Charles Lamb. His Life Recorded by his
        Contemporaries*, compiled by Edmund Blunden; and *At the
        Shrine of St. Charles* by E.V. Lucas.

C135   "Fiction," *The Spectator*, CLII (April 6), p. 551.

        Review of *Semi-Precious Stones* by A.I. Voinova; *And
        Quiet Flows the Don* by Michael Sholokhov; and *Five
        Silver Daughters* by Louis Golding.

C136   "Fiction," *The Spectator*, CLII (April 20), p. 634.

Review of *Company Parade* by Storm Jameson; *That Was the End* by Bruno Brehm; and *Entertaining the Islanders* by Struthers Burt.

C137   "After Strange Gods," *Life and Letters*, X (April), pp. 111-113.

Review of *After Strange Gods* by T.S. Eliot.

C138   "Fiction," *The Spectator*, CLII (May 4), p. 714.

Review of *I Claudius* by Robert Graves; *Swallows* by Elizabeth Montgomery; and *Single Combat* by Agnes Mure Mackenzie.

C139   "Fiction," *The Spectator*, CLII (May 18), p. 786.

Review of *News from Havre* by Georges Duhamel; *Family Parade* by Laurence Oliver; *Picaro* by Rupert Croft-Cooke; and *Black Exchange* by Patrick Kirwan.

C140   "The Traveller's Library," *Now and Then*, No. 47 (Spring), pp. 25-26.

C141   "Fiction," *The Spectator*, CLII (June 1), p. 864.

Review of *Cactus Land* by Dennis Kincaid; *London Bridge is Falling* by Philip Lindsay; *Here To-day and Gone Tomorrow* by Louis Bromfield; and *Falling Star* by Vicki Baum.

C142   "The Norwegian Way," *The Spectator*, CLII (June 8), pp. 895-896.

Review of *Saga of Saints* by Sigrid Undset.

C143   "Fiction," *The Spectator*, CLII (June 15), p. 938.

Review of *The Ginger Griffin* by Ann Bridge; *The Balliols* by Alec Waugh; *Rhondda Roundabout* by Jack Jones; and *The Children Triumphant* by Phillis Paul.

C144   "Fiction," *The Spectator*, CLII (June 29), pp. 1010-1011.

Review of *The Last Cargo* by Andrew Andrews; *Gay Pagan* by Hugh Talbot; *Andrew's Harvest* by John Evans; *Concert Pitch* by Theodora Benson; and *Wild Strawberries* by Angela Thirkell.

C145   "Fiction," *The Spectator*, CLIII (July 13), p. 64.

Review of *Kaleidoscope* by Stefan Zweig; *Crack of Whips* by H.A. Manhood; *Legion of the Rearguard* by Francis Carty; and *Ann and Aurelia* by Adrian Alington.

C146   "Fiction," *The Spectator*, CLIII (July 27), p. 144.

Review of *Lamb in His Bosom* by Caroline Miller; *Hordubal* by Karel Capek; *The World Went Mad* by John Brophy; and *India's Coral Strand* by Richard Oke.

C147   "The Theatre," *The Spectator*, CLIII (July 27), p. 129.

Review of "A Man's House" by John Drinkwater.

C148   "All the Facts of Fiction," *The Spectator*, CLIII (August 3), p. 170.

Review of *The History of the English Novel. The Novel of Sentiment and the Gothic Romance* by Ernest A. Baker.

C149   "The Theatre," *The Spectator*, CLIII (August 3), p. 161.

Review of "The Moon in the Yellow River" by Denis Johnston and "Mutiny" by David Stewart.

C150   "Fiction," *The Spectator*, CLIII (August 10), p. 201.

Review of *The Goose-Man* by Jacob Wassermann; *Unfinished Cathedral* by T.S. Stribling; and *Dew on the Grass* by Eiluned Lewis.

C151   "Fiction," *The Spectator*, CLIII (August 24), p. 264.

Review of *Come in at the Door* by William March; *Blind Men Crossing a Bridge* by Susan Miles; and *Deep Streets* by Benedict Thielen.

C152   "Mr. Maugham's Short Stories," *The Spectator*, CLIII (August 31), p. 297.

Review of *Altogether. The Collected Short Stories of W. Somerset Maugham*; in *Collected Essays* as "Some Notes on Somerset Maugham - 2."

C153   "The Seed Cake and the Lovely Lady," *Life and Letters*, X (August), pp. 517-523.

A reply to Charles Morgan's "Defense of Story Telling," *Life and Letters*, X (August), pp. 517-524.

C154 "Fiction," *The Spectator*, CLIII (September 7), p. 336.

Review of *At Sea* by Arthur Calder-Marshall; *The Curate's Wife* by E.H. Young; *Barnham Rectory* by Doreen Wallace; and *Dark Windows* by Velia Ercole.

C155 "Fiction," *The Spectator*, CLIII (September 21), p. 412.

Review of *Captain Nicholas* by Hugh Walpole; *His Worship the Mayor* by Walter Greenwood; *Dew in April* by John Clayton; and *Seven Stars and Orion* by Stephen Hockaby.

C156 "Background to Henry James," *The Spectator* , CLIII (September 28), pp. 446, 448.

Review of *Alice James. Her Brothers -- Her Journal*, edited by Anna Robeson Burr.

C157 "Fiction," *The Spectator*, CLIII (October 5), p. 498.

Review of *Resurrection* by William Gerhardi; *Women Must Work* by Richard Aldington; *Three Men Die* by Sarah Gertrude Millin; and *Angel Making Music* by Ferenc Molnar.

C158 "Fiction," *The Spectator*, CLIII (October 19), p. 578.

Review of *Dead Woman's Shoes* by Charles Briabant; *Good Merchant* by John L. Graham; *The Endless Furrow* by A.G. Street; and *Seven Gothic Tales* by Isak Dinesen.

C159 "Airport," *Time and Tide*, XV (October 20), pp. 1317-1318.

C160 "Fiction," *The Spectator*, CLIII (November 2), pp. 690-691.

Review of *The Sun in Capricorn* by Edward Sackville West; *Fontamara* by Ignazio Silone; *The Progress to the Lake* by Richard Heron Ward; and *Earth Stopped* by T.H. White.

C161 *"Brother," *Time and Tide*, XV (November 17), pp. 1470-1472.

C162 "Short Stories," *The Spectator*, CLIII (November 23), pp. 28, 30 in "Literary Supplement."

Review of *Honeymoon* by Malachi Whitaker; *Mr. Jorkens Remembers Africa* by Lord Dunsany; *Ricochets* by André Maurois; *Silver Collar Boy* by Constance Wright; *Sophy Cassmajor* by Margery Sharp; *A Froward Child* by Walter de la Mare; and *Cathedral Carol Service* by Hugh Walpole.

C163   "From the Devil's Side," *The Spectator*, CLIII (December 7), p. 890.

Review of *The Desire and Pursuit of the Whole* by Frederick Rolfe; in *Lost Childhood* and *Collected Essays* as "Frederick Rolfe: From the Devil's Side."

1935

C164   "Creative Reading," *The Spectator*, CLIV (February 15), pp. 256-257.

Review of *The Art of the Novel from 1700 to the Present Time* by Pelham Edgar.

C165   "West Coast," *The Spectator*, CLIV (April 12), pp. 620, 622.

Review of *Africa Dances* by Geoffrey Gorer.

C166   "Myers and Myers," *The Spectator*, CLIV (April 19), pp. 664, 666.

Review of *The Root and the Flower* by L.H. Myers.

C167   "The Lesson of the Master," *The Spectator*, CLIV (April 26), p. 698.

Review of *The Art of the Novel* by Henry James.

C168   "The Waste Land," *The Spectator*, CLIV (June 7), p. 986.

Review of *Zulu Paraclete* by Leonard Barnes.

C169   "Short Stories," *The Spectator*, CLIV (June 14), p. 1034.

Review of *Half Way East* by David Footman; *O. Henry Memorial Award Prize Stories*, selected by Harry Hansen; *What the Sweet Hell?* by Peter Chamberlain; and *Selected Short Stories* by Hjalmar Söderberg.

C170   "Spanish Gold," *The Spectator*, CLIV (June 21), p. 1076.

Review of *Don Fernando* by W. Somerset Maugham; in *Collected Essays* as "Some Notes on Somerset Maugham - 1."

C171   "The Domestic Background," *The Spectator*, CLIV (July 26), p. 164.

Review of *Joseph Conrad and his Circle* by Jessie Conrad.

C172   "The Man of Mode," *The Spectator*, CLV (August 9), p. 232.

Review of *Rochester: Portrait of a Restoration Poet* by Professor V. De Sola Pinto.

C173   "A Restoration Fantasia," *The Spectator*, CLV (September 13), pp. 400-401.

Review of *Rochester* by Charles Williams.

C174   "Isis Idol," *The Spectator*, CLV (September 20), pp. 439-440.

Review of *Anthony Hope and His Books* by Sir Charles Mallet.

C175   "Analysis of a Journey," *The Spectator*, CLV (September 27), pp. 459-460.

C176   "The Camera Eye," *The Spectator*, CLV (September 27), p. 472.

Review of *A Grammar of the Film* by Raymond Spottis-woode.

C177   "Manoeuvres in Kent," *The Spectator*, CLV (October 11), pp. 570, 572.

Review of *Beany-Eye* by David Garnett.

C178   "Jubilee," *Time and Tide*, XVI (October 26), pp. 1522-1523.

C179   "The Dark Backward: A Footnote," *London Mercury*, XXXII (October), pp. 562-565.

C180   "Graduates of Douai," *The Spectator*, CLV (November 1), pp. 734, 736.

Review of *Edmund Campion* by Evelyn Waugh; and *Robert Southwell the Writer* by Pierre Janelle.

C181   Letter, *Times Literary Supplement* (November 2),
        p. 697.

        Re Rochester and Lee.

C182   "Arabia Deserta," *The Spectator*, CLV (November 8),
        p. 788.

        Review of *King Coffin* by Conrad Aiken.

C183   "Short Stories," *The Spectator*, CLV (November 22),
        pp. 36, 38 in "Literary Supplement."

        Review of *Cut and Come Again* by H.E. Bates; *Fierce and Gentle* by H.A. Manhood; *To Blush Unseen* by Valentine Dobrée; *New Joy in Heaven* by Sylvia Townsend Warner; *The Beginning* by Mervyne Lagden; *And Lastly the Fireworks* by John Pudney; and *The Laburnum Tree* by James Laver.

C184   "A Boat-Load of Politicians," *The Spectator*, CLV
        (December 6), pp. 938-939.

C185   "A Spoiled Priest," *The Spectator*, CLV (December 6),
        p. 956.

        Review of *Hubert's Arthur* by Frederick Rolfe; in *Lost Childhood* and *Collected Essays* as "Frederick Rolfe: A Spoiled Priest."

                              1936

C186   "The Dictator of Grand Bassa," *The Spectator*, CLVI
        (January 17), pp. 89-90.

C187   "Wings Over Wardour Street," *The Spectator*, CLVI
        (January 24), p. 137.

        Review of *Documentary Film* by Paul Rotha and *Plan for Cinema* by Dallas Bower.

C188   *"A Chance for Mr. Lever," *Story*, VIII (January),
        pp. 9-22.

C189   "The Public Life," *The Spectator*, CLVI (February 28),
        p. 362.

        Review of *Arnold Bennett's Letters to His Nephew* by
        Richard Bennett.

C190   "Devil-Blacksmith," *The Spectator*, CLVI (March 6),
        pp. 393-394.

C191   "Short Stories," *The Spectator*, CLVI (April 17),
        pp. 718, 720.

        Review of *From Death to Morning* by Thomas Wolfe;
        The Marchesa by K. Swinstead-Smith; *The Cosy Room* by
        Arthur Machen; and *Cosmopolitans* by W. Somerset
        Maugham.

C192   "Legend," *The Spectator*, CLVI (April 24), p. 766.

        Review of *The Burning Cactus* by Stephen Spender;
        Flowering Judas by Katherine Anne Porter; and *Tea on
        Sunday* by Leslie Halward.

C193   "Short Stories," *The Spectator*, CLVI (May 22), p. 950.

        Review of *You Must Break Out Sometimes* by T.O. Beach-
        croft; *Kneel to the Rising Sun* by Erskine Caldwell;
        The Trouble I've Seen by Martha Gelhorn; *The World
        Over* by Edith Wharton; and the *O. Henry Memorial
        Award Prize Stories of 1935*.

C194   Letter, *Times Literary Supplement* (May 30), p. 460.

        Re Journey Without Maps.

C195   "The Fortnightly Library," *The Fortnightly* [Review],
        CXLV (May), pp. 633-634.

        Review of *Green Hills of Africa* by Ernest Hemingway.

C196   "Portrait of a Lady," *The Spectator*, CLVII
        (August 28), pp. 351-352.

        Review of *No Place Like Home* by Beverley Nichols; in
        Lost Childhood and *Collected Essays* as "Portrait of a
        Maiden Lady."

C197   "A Medium of Exchange," *London Mercury*, XXXIV (August),
        pp. 370-371.

        Review of *Gold Fever* by L.M. Nesbitt.

C198   "Bird Alone," *Now and Then*, No. 54 (Summer), pp. 14–15.

         Review of *Bird Alone* by Seán O'Faoláin.

C199   "Two Tall Travellers," *The Spectator*, CLVII
         (September 11), p. 428.

         Review of *Unknown Liberia* by Harry J. Greenwall and
         Roland Wild.

C200   "The Dark Enemy," *The Spectator*, CLVII (October 2),
         pp. 556, 558.

         Review of *The Wind Blows Over* by Walter de la Mare.

C201   "Fiction Chronicle," *The Tablet*, CLXVIII (October 3),
         pp. 461–462.

         Review of *Stories of Three Decades* by Thomas Mann and
         Steam Packet by David Mathew.

C202   "Short Stories," *The Spectator*, CLVII (October 9),
         pp. 604, 606.

         Review of *Steam Packet* by David Mathew; *The Things
         Men Do* by Rhys Davies; *A Chaste Polygamy* by Edward
         Mather; *Fellow Mortals* by Winifred Williams; and *365
         Days*, edited by Kay Boyle, Laurence Vail and Nina
         Conarain.

C203   "Fiction Chronicle," *The Tablet*, CLXVIII (October 24),
         p. 575.

         Review of *Midnight* by Julian Green; *Novel on Yellow
         Paper* by Stevie Smith; *And Then You Wish* by John Van
         Druten; and *The Splendour Falls* by Romilly Caven.

C204   "Fiction Chronicle," *The Tablet*, CLXVIII (November 14),
         pp. 678–679.

         Review of *Nightwood* by Djuna Barnes; *Of Mortal Love*
         by William Gerhardi; *Antigua, Penny, Puce* by Robert
         Graves; *The Missing Miniature* by Erich Kastner; and
         Parody Party, edited by Leonard Russell.

C205   "Short Stories," *The Spectator*, CLVII (November 20),
         pp. 32, 34 in "Literary Supplement."

         Review of *The Best Short Stories of 1936. English and
         American*, edited by E.J. O'Brien; *The Tramp* by Dal
         Stivens; *Collected Short Stories* by Stella Benson;

Hungaria by various authors; and *The Song in the House* by Anne Bridge.

C206   "Gladstone Bags and Marmalade," *London Mercury*, XXXV (November), p. 85.

Review of *Henry Airbubble in Search of a Circumference to His Breath* by W.J. Turner.

C207   "Movie Memories," *The Spectator*, CLVII (December 11), p. 1056.

Review of *Movie Parade* by Paul Rotha.

C208   "A Grand Little Horse," *London Mercury*, XXXV (December), pp. 203-204.

Review of *EGO 2: Being a Second Installment of a Contemporary Diary* by James Agate.

1937

C209   "Fiction Chronicle," *The Tablet*, CXLIX (January 9), pp. 58-59.

Review of *Salvin* by Georges Duhamel; *The Big Money* by John Dos Passos; *The Law and the McLaughlins* by Margaret Wilson; and *Ilonka Speaks of Hungary* by John Brophy.

C210   "Background for Heroes," *The Spectator*, CLVIII (January 29), pp. 178, 180.

Review of *Life in a Nobel Household. 1641-1700* by Gladys Scott Thomson.

C211   "Fiction Chronicle," *The Tablet*, CLXIX (January 30), pp. 162-163.

Review of *Bread and Wine* by Ignazio Silone; *Pie in the Sky* by Arthur Calder-Marshall; and *Eggs and Baker* by John Masefield.

C212   "Short Stories," *The Spectator*, CLVIII (February 12), p. 280.

Review of *People Are Fascinating* by Sally Benson; *The Blue Bed* by Glyn Jones; *A Case of Conscience and Other*

Tales by Martin Armstrong; and *Mr. White, The Red
Barn, Hell and Bridewater* by Booth Tarkington.

C213   "Fiction Chronicle," *The Tablet*, CLXIX (February 20),
pp. 274-276.

Review of *The Porch* by Richard Church; *Delicate
Monster* by Storm Jameson; *War with the Newts* by Karel
Capek; and *By-Road* by Adrian Bell.

C214   "The Landowner in Revolt," *London Mercury*, XXXV
(February), pp. 424-425.

Review of *Great Trade Route. A Sentimental Journey*
by Ford Madox Ford.

C215   "Tread Softly," *The Spectator*, CLVIII (March 12),
p. 482.

Review of *The Shadow Across the Page* by G.W. Stonier.

C216   "Fiction Chronicle," *The Tablet*, CLXIX (March 27),
pp. 449-450.

Review of *Theatre* by W. Somerset Maugham; *The Fleshy
Screen* by Edward Dodge; *The Bachelor of Arts* by R.K.
Narayan; *Dinosaur Tracks and Other Stories* by Benedict
Thielen; and *Juan in China* by Eric Linklater.

C217   "The Furries in Mississippi," *London Mercury*, XXXV
(March), pp. 517-518.

Review of *Absalom, Absalom!* by William Faulkner.

C218   "R.L.S. for Adults," *The Spectator*, CLVIII (April 2),
p. 630.

Review of *R. L. Stevenson* by Janet Adam Smith.

C219   "Elephant Boy," *The Spectator*, CLVIII (April 30),
p. 811.

Letter to the editor.

C220   "A Typewriter in the Desert," *London Mercury*, XXXV
(April), p. 635.

Review of *Midnight on the Desert* by J.B. Priestley.

C221   "The Thatched Cottagers," *The Spectator*, CLVIII
(June 25), pp. 1200, 1202.

Review of *The Cotswolds* by John Moore and *A Cotswold Year* by C. Henry Warren.

C222   "The Byronic East," *London Mercury*, XXXVI (June), pp. 195-196.

Review of *The Road to Oxiana* by Robert Byron.

C223   "Thunder in the Air," *The Spectator*, CLIX (August 6), p. 252.

Review of *Something Short and Sweet* by H.E. Bates.

C224   "An Unheroic Dramatist," *The Spectator*, CLIX (August 27), p. 356.

Review of *The Dramatic Works of Roger Boyle, Earl of Orrery* edited by William Smith Clark.

C225   "A Veteran at Play," *London Mercury*, XXXVI (August), pp. 389-390.

Review of *Vive Le Roy* by Ford Madox Ford.

C226   "Remembering Mr. Jones," *The Spectator*, CLIX (September 17), pp. 469-470.

Review of *Conrad's Prefaces to His Works* with an essay by Edward Garnett.

C227   "The Theatre," *The Spectator*, CLIX (September 24), p. 499.

Review of "Sir Martin Marr-All" by John Dryden.

C228   "A Vestryman for St. Pancras," *London Mercury*, XXXVI (September), p. 482.

Review of *Shaw: George Versus Bernard* by J.P. Hackett.

C229   "A Novelist's Notebook," *The Spectator*, CLIX (October 1), p. 557.

Review of *A Date with a Duchess and Other Stories* by Arthur Calder-Marshall.

C230   "The Nudest Book of the Week," *Night and Day*, I (October 7), p. 33.

Review of *Eve in the Sunlight* by Bertram Park and Yvonne Gregory.

C231   "Chilean Adventure," *The Spectator*, CLIX (October 8),
        p. 602.

        Review of *Revolt on the Pampas* by Theodore Plivier.

C232   "Comments on Auden," *New Verse*, Nos. 26-27 (November),
        pp. 29-30.

        By Greene and others.

C233   "Matured in Bottle," *London Mercury*, XXXVII (November),
        pp. 77-78.

        Review of *Daylight and Champaign* by G.M. Young.

C234   "Irish Short Stories," *The Spectator*, CLIX
        (December 3), p. 1014.

        Review of *A Purse of Coppers* by Seán O'Faoláin and
        The Short Stories of Liam O'Flaherty.

C235   Letter, *Times Literary Supplement* (December 4), p. 928.

        Re H. Plunket Greene.

C236   "Alfred Tennyson Intervenes," *The Spectator*, CLIX
        (December 10), p. 1058.

        In *Collected Essays* as "The Apostles Intervene."

C237   "Short Stories," *The Spectator*, CLIX (December 24),
        pp. 1155-1156.

        Review of *The Faber Book of Modern Stories*, edited by
        Elizabeth Bowen; *Little Children* by William Saroyan;
        Ghosts by Edith Wharton; *Kissing the Rod* by Viola
        Meynell; *Fellow Countrymen* by James T. Farrell; *Best
        Short Stories of 1937*, edited by E.J. O'Brien; *The
        Pieces of a Fan* by Vincent Sheean; and *Pavements
        at Anderby* by Winifred Holtby.

C238   "Homage to the Bombardier," *London Mercury*, XXXVII
        (December), pp. 219-220.

        Review of *Blasting and Bombardiering* by Wyndham Lewis.

C239   "Portrait by G. Wylde," *London Mercury*, XXXVII
        (December), p. 140a.

1938

C240 "Mr. Maugham's Pattern," *The Spectator*, CLX
(January 14), p. 59.

Review of *The Summing Up* by W. Somerset Maugham; in
Collected Essays as "Some Notes on Somerset Maugham -
3."

C241 "Harkaway's Oxford," *The Spectator*, CLX (January 21),
pp. 85-86.

C242 "A Day at the General's," *The Spectator*, CLX
(April 15), p. 670.

Reprinted as "A Day with Cedillo" in *The Living Age*,
CCCLIV (June 1938), pp. 330-332.

C243 "Mexican Sunday," *The Tablet*, CLXXI (May 14),
pp. 626-627.

C244 Letter, *The Times* (June 3), p. 10.

Re churches in Tabasco.

C245 "From the Mantlepiece," *The Spectator*, CLX (June 17),
pp. 1110, 1112.

Review of *Three Guineas* by Virginia Woolf.

C246 "Inside Oxford," *The Spectator*, CLX (June 24),
pp. 1154, 1156.

Review of *Anatomy of Oxford. An Anthology*, compiled
by C. Day Lewis and Charles Fenby.

C247 "A Day with Cedillo," *The Living Age*, CCCLIV (June),
pp. 330-332.

Also published as "A Day at the General's," *The
Spectator*, CLX (April 15, 1938), p. 670.

C248 "The Blind Eye," *The Spectator*, CLXI (July 1), p. 13.

C249 "In Search of a Miracle," *The Tablet*, CLXXII (July 2),
pp. 6-7.

C250 "High Wind in the Caribbean," *The Spectator*, CLXI
(July 8), p. 68.

Review of *In Hazard* by Richard Hughes.

C251   "Old Boy," *The Spectator*, CLXI (July 15), pp. 114, 116.

Review of *To You Mr. Chips!* by James Hilton.

C252   "Vive Le Roi," *The Spectator*, CLXI (July 22),
pp. 139-140.

C253   "To All Topographers," *The Spectator*, CLXI
(August 12), p. 271.

In *Collected Essays* as "The Lover of Leeds."

C254   "A Catholic Adventurer and His Mexican Journal,"
The Tablet, CLXXII (August 13), p. 200.

C255   "Twenty-four Hours to Metroland," *New Statesman and
Nation*, XVI (August 13), p. 250.

C256   "Men and Messages," *The Spectator*, CLXI (August 19),
pp. 310-311.

Review of *The History of the English Novel: The Day
Before Yesterday* by Ernest A. Baker.

C257   "Romance in Pimlico," *The Spectator*, CLXI
(September 2), p. 379.

Review of *The Polite Marriage and Other 18th Century
Essays* by J.M.S. Tompkins.

C258   "Short Stories," *The Spectator*, CLXI (September 9),
pp. 413-414.

Review of *Love, Here is My Hat* by William Saroyan;
A Character in Distress by Luigi Pirandello; *The
Money's All Right* by Leslie Halward; *Twenty-Four
Tales* by Gerald Bullett; *The Angle of Error* by Faith
Compton Mackenzie; *It Makes a Nice Change* by John
Gloag; and *The Smallways Rub Along* by Neil Bell.

C259   "A Lost Arcadia," *The Spectator*, CLXI (September 16),
p. 449.

Review of *The Old Century and Seven More Years* by
Siegfried Sassoon.

C260   "Trying to Connect You," *The Spectator*, CLXI
(September 16), p. 444.

Letter to the editor.

C261   "Voyage in the Dark," *The Spectator*, CLXI
         (September 16), p. 437.

C262   "Two Novels," *The Spectator*, CLXI (October 7),
         p. 578.

         Review of *The Death of the Heart* by Elizabeth Bowen
         and *Days of Hope* by André Malraux.

C263   "The Extraordinary Profession," *The Spectator*, CLXI
         (October 21), p. 666.

         Review of *History of the Film* by Maurice Bardeche
         and Robert Brasillach, translated and edited by Iris
         Barry.

C264   "The Saratoga Trunk," *The Spectator*, CLXI
         (November 4), p. 782.

         Review of *Pilgrimage* by Dorothy M. Richardson.

C265   "Conversation Piece," *The Spectator*, CLXI
         (November 18), pp. 26, 28 in "Literary Supplement."

         Review of *Trio* by Osbert, Edith and Sacheverell
         Sitwell.

C266   "Oxford Infelix," *The Spectator*, CLXI (December 16),
         p. 1053.

         Review of *An Oxford University Chest* by John Betjeman,
         with photographs by L. Moholy-Nagy.

C267   "The Dark Virgin," *The Tablet*, CLXXII (December 31),
         pp. 883-884.

C268   "The Good Life," *London Mercury*, XXXIX (December),
         pp. 217-218.

         Review of *Provence: From Minstrels to Machine* by
         Ford Madox Ford.

                              1939

C269   "The Escapist," *The Spectator*, CLXII (January 13),
         pp. 48-49.

C270   "Boy Loses Girl," *The Spectator*, CLXII (January 27),
        p. 141.

        Review of *A Heart for the Gods of Mexico* by Conrad
        Aiken.

C271   "The Real Thing," *The Spectator*, CLXII (February 3),
        p. 186.

        Review of *Jungle Trader* by H.R. Taylor.

C272   "Underworld," *London Mercury*, XXXIX (March),
        pp. 550-551.

        Review of *Christmas Holiday* by W. Somerset Maugham.

C273   "Mexico," *The Spectator*, CLXII (April 14), p. 642.

        Review of *Mexican Mosaic* by Rodney Gallop and *An
        Eye-Witness of Mexico* by R.H.K. Marrett.

C274   "Poetry from Limbo," *The Spectator*, CLXII (April 28),
        p. 720.

        Review of *Recusant Poets. With a Selection from
        Their Work. Vol. 1. St. Thomas More to Ben Jonson*
        by Louise Imogen Guiney.

C275   "Man Made Angry," *The Spectator*, CLXII (June 16),
        p. 1060.

        Review of *The Woman Who Was Poor* by Léon Bloy.

C276   "Ford Madox Ford," *The Spectator*, CLXIII (July 7),
        p. 11.

C277   "Book Market," *The Spectator*, CLXIII (July 14), p. 58.

        In *Lost Childhood* and *Collected Essays* as "George
        Moore and Others."

C278   "Bombing Raid," *The Spectator*, CLXIII (August 18),
        p. 249.

        In *Lost Childhood* as "Bombing Manoeuvre."

C279   "A Hoax on Mr. Hulton," *The Spectator*, CLXIII
        (August 25), p. 296.

C280   "Fiction," *The Spectator*, CLXIII (September 22),
        p. 420.

Review of *The Sea Tower* by Hugh Walpole; *Lives of Wives* by Laura Riding; and *The Arrogant History of White Ben* by Clemence Dane.

C281 "Fiction," *The Spectator*, CLXIII (September 29), p. 450.

Review of *Party Going* by Henry Green; *The Story of Mona Sheehy* by Lord Dunsany; and *The Red Centaur* by Marjorie Mack.

C282 "Fiction," *The Spectator*, CLXIII (October 6), p. 482.

Review of *The Blood of the Martyrs* by Naomi Mitchison; *Four-Part Setting* by Ann Bridge; and *Supercargo* by Earl Whitechorne.

C283 "Safety Area," *The Spectator*, CLXIII (October 13), p. 524.

Review of *The Flying Goat* by H.E. Bates.

C284 "Fiction," *The Spectator*, CLXIII (October 20), p. 556.

Review of *Night of the Poor* by Frederic Prokosch; *Wild Geese Overhead* by Neil M. Gunn; *Queen Anne Boleyn* by Francis Hackett; and *Old Home Week* by Minnie Hite Moody.

C285 "Fiction," *The Spectator*, CLXIII (October 27), p. 600.

Review of *Wickford Point* by John P. Marquand; *Parole D'Honneur* by Martin Freud; *Rejected Guest* by Richard Aldington; and *Gus and Ida* by Leslie Halward.

C286 "Fiction," *The Spectator*, CLXIII (November 10), p. 662.

Review of *Live and Kicking Ned* by John Masefield; *Let the People Sing* by J.B. Priestley; and *Flight from a Lady* by A.G. Macdonell.

C287 "Last Journey," *The Spectator*, CLXIII (November 17), p. 696.

Review of *The March of Literature. From Confucius to Modern Times* by Ford Madox Ford.

C288 "A Place in the Sun," *The Spectator*, CLXIII (November 24), p. 754.

Review of *Orchard's Bay* by Alfred Noyes.

C289   "Three Travellers," *The Spectator*, CLXIII
        (December 8), p. 838.

        Review of *Hinterland Liberia* by Etta Donner; *Wander-
        ings in the Peruvian Andes* by Dr. A.M. Renwick; and
        Unknown to the World - Haiti by Mabel Steedman.

                            1940

C290   "Orchard's Bay," *The Spectator*, CLXIV (January 26),
        p. 112.

        Letter to the editor.

C291   "Out of the Saddle," *The Spectator*, CLXIV (February
        23), p. 259.

        Review of *This Way Southward* by A.F. Tschiffely.

C292   "The Liberator," *The Spectator*, CLXIV (March 15),
        pp. 384, 386.

        Review of *Simón Bolivar* by Thomas Rourke.

C293   *"The Lieutenant Died Last," *Colliers*, CV (June 29),
        pp. 9-10.

C294   *"The News in English," *Strand Magazine*, XCIX (June),
        pp. 134-139.

C295   "Escape," *The Spectator*, CLXV (October 4), p. 344.

        Review of *Two Generations*, edited by Osbert Sitwell;
        and *More Than I Should* by Faith Compton Mackenzie.

C296   "Belloc on Chesterton," *The Spectator*, CLXV
        (October 11), p. 370.

        Review of *On the Place of Gilbert Chesterton in
        English Letters* by Hilaire Belloc.

C297   "The Second Deluge," *The Spectator*, CLXV
        (October 18), p. 398.

        Review of *All Aboard for Ararat* by H.G. Wells.

C298   "Notes on the Way," *Time and Tide*, XXI
        (October 19), pp. 1021-1022.

In *Lost Childhood* and *Collected Essays* as "At Home."

C299   "The Theatre," *The Spectator*, CLXV (November 1),
        p. 440.

        Review of "Diversion."

C300   "Great Dog of Weimar," *The Spectator*, CLXV
        (November 8), p. 474.

C301   "Don in Mexico," *The Spectator*, CLXV (November 22),
        pp. 538, 540.

        Review of *Mexico: A New Spain with Old Friends* by
        Prof. J.B. Trend.

C302   "The Unknown War," *The Spectator*, CLXV
        (November 29), p. 578.

C303   "One Man's War," *The Spectator*, CLXV (December 6),
        p. 614.

        Review of *My First War* by Captain Sir Basil
        Bartlett.

C304   "A Lost Leader," *The Spectator*, CLXV (December 13),
        p. 646.

        Review of *Postscripts* by J.B. Priestley.

C305   "The Austere Art," *The Spectator*, CLXV (December 20),
        p. 682.

        Review of *A Mathematician's Apology* by G.H. Hardy.

1941

C306   "The Theatre," *The Spectator*, CLXVI (January 3),
        p. 11.

        Review of "Jack and the Beanstalk" and "Aladdin."

C307   "Rebels and Eccentrics," *The Spectator*, CLXVI
        (January 10), p. 39.

        Review of *Autobiography* by Eric Gill; in *Lost Child-
        hood* and *Collected Essays* as "Eric Gill."

C308   "The Theatre," *The Spectator*, CLXVI (January 10),
        p. 35.
        Review of "Berkeley Square" and "Diversion No. 2."

C309   "The Theatre," *The Spectator*, CLXVI (January 24),
        p. 87.
        Review of "Dear Brutus."

C310   "The Theatre," *The Spectator*, CLXVI (January 31),
        p. 115.
        Review of "The Blue Goose" by Peter Blackmore.

C311   "In Easy Reach of Town," *The Spectator*, CLXVI
        (February 7), p. 154.
        Review of *Chiltern Country* by H.J. Massingham.

C312   "A Pride of Bombs," *The Spectator*, CLXVI (February 14),
        p. 178.
        Review of *Bomber's Moon* by Negley Farson and *England's
        Hour* by Vera Brittain.

C313   "Three Score Miles and Ten," *The Spectator*, CLXVI
        (February 14), p. 171.

C314   "The Theatre," *The Spectator*, CLXVI (February 21),
        p. 200.
        Review of "Revudeville" -- 141st Edition and "Strike
        Up the Music."

C315   "Through American Eyes," *The Spectator*, CLXVI
        (February 28), pp. 234-236.
        Review of *The White Cliffs* by Alice Duer Miller.

C316   "Mr. Hemingway's New Novel," *The Spectator*, CLXVI
        (March 7), p. 258.
        Review of *For Whom the Bell Tolls* by Ernest
        Hemingway.

C317   "The Theatre," *The Spectator*, CLXVI (March 7), p. 251.
        Review of "Thunder Rock" by Robert Ardrey and
        "Nineteen Naughty One."

C318   "Escape," *The Spectator*, CLXVI (March 14), p. 288.

Review of *Campden, xxiv Engravings after Pen Drawings* by F.L. Griggs, R.A.; in *Collected Essays* as "The Conservative."

C319   "The Theatre," *The Spectator*, CLXVI (March 14), p. 279.

Review of "Applesauce!"

C320   "The Theatre," *The Spectator*, CLXVI (March 21), p. 307.

Review of "New Faces."

C321   "Domestic War," *The Spectator*, CLXVI (March 28), pp. 348, 350.

Review of *Post D. Some Experiences of an Air Raid Warden* by John Strachey.

C322   "Herbert Read," *Horizon*, III (March), pp. 213-218.

Review of *Annals of Innocence and Experience* by Herbert Read.

C323   "The Theatre," *The Spectator*, CLXVI (April 11), p. 395.

Review of "Time for Comedy" by S.N. Behrman.

C324   "The Last Buchan," *The Spectator*, CLXVI (April 18), pp. 430, 432.

Review of *Sick Heart River* by John Buchan.

C325   "The Theatre," *The Spectator*, CLXVI (April 18), p. 424.

Review of "Wednesday After the War" and "Orchids and Onions."

C326   "The Theatre," *The Spectator*, CLXVI (April 25), p. 447.

Review of "Women Aren't Angels" by Vernon Sylvaine.

C327   "The Theatre," *The Spectator*, CLXVI (May 2), p. 472.

Review of "Under One Roof" by Kim Peacock and "Black Vanities."

C328   "The Theatre," *The Spectator*, CLXVI (May 16), p. 528.

Review of "Cottage to Let" by Geoffrey Kerr.

C329   "'Bed-Exhausted,'" *The Spectator*, CLXVI (May 23), p. 558.

Review of *Australia Visited 1940* by Noel Coward.

C330   "The Theatre," *The Spectator*, CLXVI (May 30), p. 580.

Review of "Up and Doing."

C331   "The Theatre," *The Spectator*, CLXVI (June 6), p. 607.

Review of "Revudeville"--144th Edition.

C332   "Lightning Tour," *The Spectator*, CLXVI (June 13), pp. 636, 638.

Review of *Report on England* by Ralph Ingersoll.

C333   "The Theatre," *The Spectator*, CLXVI (June 13), p. 630.

Review of "Dostigaeff and the Others" by Maxim Gorki.

C334   "The Theatre," *The Spectator*, CLXVI (June 20), p. 654.

Review of "Rise Above It" and "Actresses Will Happen" by Walter Ellis.

C335   "The Turn of the Screw," *The Spectator*, CLXVI (June 20), p. 657.

Review of *My Sister and I. The Diary of a Dutch Boy Refugee* by Dirk van der Heide.

C336   "The Theatre," *The Spectator*, CLXVI (June 27), p. 677.

Review of "Non-stop Vanities."

C337   "Mr. Cook's Century," *The Spectator*, CLXVII (July 4), p. 8.

C338   "The Theatre," *The Spectator*, CLXVII (July 11), p. 34.

Review of "Blithe Spirit" by Noel Coward.

C339   "Self-Portrait," *The Spectator*, CLXVII (July 18), pp. 66, 68.

Review of *The Chestertons* by Mrs. Cecil Chesterton; in *Collected Essays* as "G.K. Chesterton - 2."

C340   "The Theatre," *The Spectator*, CLXVII (July 18), p. 58.

Review of "King John" by William Shakespeare.

C341   "The Theatre," *The Spectator*, CLXVII (July 25), p. 82.

Review of "The New Ambassadors Revue."

C342   "Playboy," *The Spectator*, CLXVII (August 1), p. 114.

Review of *Richard Halliburton. His Story and His Life's Adventures.*

C343   "The Theatre," *The Spectator*, CLXVII (August 1), p. 106.

Review of "Lady Behave" by Stanley Lupino and "Quiet Weekend" by Esther McCracken.

C344   "The Theatre," *The Spectator*, CLXVII (August 29), p. 203.

Review of "Fun and Games."

C345   "The Theatre," *The Spectator*, CLXVII (September 5), p. 235.

Review of "The Cherry Orchard" by Anton Tchekhov and "Squaring the Circle" by Valentine Katayev.

C346   *"Men at Work," *The New Yorker*, XVII (October 25), pp. 50-54.

C347   *"When Greek Meets Greek," *Illustrated London News* (supplement), CXCIX (November 20), pp. 1-4ff.

1942

C348   "Her Uncle vs. His Father," *Esquire*, XVIII (July), pp. 30, 116, 118.

Also titled "When Greek Meets Greek"; reprinted in *Esquire* in October 1973, pp. 305-310.

1943

C349   "Wallis and Waugh," *Horizon*, VII (May), p. 362.

Letter to the editor.

C350   "The Poker-Face," *The Spectator*, CLXXI (October 15), p. 364.

Review of *Conan Doyle: His Life and Art* by Hesketh Pearson.

1944

C351   "G. K. Chesterton," *The Spectator*, CLXXII (April 21), p. 364.

Review of *Gilbert Keith Chesterton* by Maisie Ward.

C352   "The Maritains," *New Statesman and Nation*, XXVIII (September 9), p. 173.

Review of *We Have Been Friends Together* by Raissa Maritain.

C353   *"The News in English," *Ellery Queen's Mystery Magazine*, VII (November), pp. 111-118.

1945

C354   "François Mauriac vu par un Anglais," *La France Libre*, IX (April 16), pp. 418-420.

C355   "Graham Greene on Books," *The Evening Standard* (June 22), p. 6.

Review of *British Architects and Craftsmen* by Sacheverell Sitwell; *A Life of Music* by Norman O'Neill; and *Death of a Poet* by Leonid Grossman.

C356   "This Made Me Blush," *The Evening Standard* (June 29), p. 6.

Review of *Folly Bridge* by D.L. Murray; *Virginia Woolf* by David Daiches; and *Watering Place* by Robert Liddell.

C357   "The Apron Strings of Mrs. Moffat," *The Evening Standard* (July 6), p. 6.

Review of *Modern Explorations* by Kingdon Ward and *The Matabele Journals of Robert Moffat.*

C358   "From Crafts to the Conveyor Belt," *The Evening Standard* (July 13), p. 6.

Review of *Fifteen Craftsmen on Their Crafts*; *What Became of Anna Bottom* by Louis Bromfield; *The Barriers Are Down* by Jack Lindsay; *Subject to Authority* by Isabel C. Clarke; and *Time to Change Flats* by Margot Bennett.

C359   "No Wonder Woman Scared Him," *The Evening Standard* (July 20), p. 6.

Review of *A Forgotten Genius* by Lionel James.

C360   "Nobody Would Expect Revelations But--," *The Evening Standard* (July 27), p. 6.

Review of *Memoirs* by Lord Samuel; *Freedom Was Flesh and Blood* by Jose Antonio de Aguirre; *Chung King Diary* by Robert Payne; *Quiet Skies on Salween* by Ellen Thorp; and *Looming Lights* by George G. Carter.

C361   "A Mission and a Warning," *The Evening Standard* (August 3), p. 6.

Review of *Assize of Arms* by Brig. Gen. A.H. Morgan; *Bookman's Holiday* by Holbrook Jackson; and *Ha Ha Among the Trumpets* by Alun Lewis.

C362   "They Wanted to Use Another Name," *The Evening Standard* (August 10), p. 6.

Review of *Animal Farm* by George Orwell.

C363   "It May Be Dangerous," *The Evening Standard* (August 17), p. 6.

Review of *Most Secret* by Nevil Shute; *Equinox* by Allen Seager; *The Elderbrook Brothers* by Gerald Bullett; and *The Winds of Fear* by Hodding Carter.

C364   "Strange World," *The Evening Standard* (August 24), p. 6.

Review of *The Trial of Mrs. Duncan*, edited by C.E. Bechhofer; and *That Hideous Strength* by C.S. Lewis.

C365   "That Gay Deceiver Dickens," *The Evening Standard* (August 31), p. 6.

Review of *Charles Dickens* by Una Pope-Hennessy and *Forever Amber* by Kathleen Windsor.

C366   "Three Men in a Tank," *The Evening Standard* (September 7), p. 6.

Review of *Come To Dust* by Robin Maugham; *The Bridgehead* by Christopher Dilke; and *Vouza and the Solomon Islands* by Hector MacQuarrie.

C367   "Trollope in the Doldrums," *The Evening Standard* (September 14), p. 6.

Review of *Trollope: A Contemporary* by Michael Sadleir and *Rudyard Kipling* by Hilton Brown.

C368   "Civil War in the Village," *The Evening Standard* (September 20), p. 6.

Review of *Tales of a Devon Village* by Henry Williamson; *The Earth Remains* by Crichton Porteous; and *Peony* by Keith West.

C369   "Shape Between the Iron Curtains," *The Evening Standard* (September 27), p. 6.

Review of *A Coat of Many Colors* by Herbert Read and *A World Within a War* by Herbert Read.

C370   "The Doctor in the Limelight," *The Evening Standard* (October 4), p. 6.

Review of *Hotel Vesuvius* by John Fabricius; *The Weak and the Strong* by Gerald Kersh; *Thursday Afternoon* by Monica Dickens; *At Mrs. Lippincote's* by Elizabeth Taylor; and *To the Boating* by Inez Holden.

1946

C371   "The Two Maritains," *New Statesman and Nation*, XXXI
        (January 26), pp. 72-73.

        Review of *Adventures in Grace* by Raissa Maritain and
        Art in Poetry by Jacques Maritain.

C371a   *"The Innocent," *Tomorrow*, VI (November), pp. 21-23.

1947

C372   "Heroes Are Made in Childhood," *The Listener*, XXXVI
        (March 27), pp. 462-463.

C373   *"All But Empty," *Strand Magazine*, CXII (March),
        pp. 66-69.

C374   Letter, *The Listener*, XXXVII (April 10), p. 546.

        Re a word error in "Heroes Are Made in Childhood"
        published in the March 27 issue.

C375   *"The Lottery Ticket," *Strand Magazine*, CXIII (May-
        June), pp. 42-51.

C376   "Theatre," *New Statesman and Nation*, XXXIV
        (September 13), p. 20.

        Review of "Point Valaine" by Noel Coward.

C377   "Books in General," *New Statesman and Nation*, XXXIV
        (October 11), p. 292.

        Review of *A Treatise on the Novel* by Robert Liddell.

C378   *"Proof Positive," *Harper's Magazine*, CXCV
        (October), pp. 312-314.

C379   *"A Drive in the Country," *Harper's Magazine*, CXCV
        (November), pp. 450-457.

C380   *"The Lottery Ticket," *Cosmopolitan*, CXXIII
        (November), pp. 60-61, 194-198.

1948

C381   "From Feathers to Iron," *New Statesman and Nation*,
         XXXV (January 3), pp. 14-15.

         Review of *Robert Louis Stevenson* by Lettice Cooper.

C382   "La Civilisation Chrétienne est-elle en Péril?" *La
         Table Ronde*, No. 2 (February), pp. 211-223.

         Speech made to the Grande Conférence Catholique,
         Brussels, January 1948.

C383   "Dead Letter Office," *New Statesman and Nation*,
         XXXV (March 13), p. 221.

         Review of *The Letters of Eric Gill*, edited by Walter
         Shewring.

C384   "Kensington to Samoa," *New Statesman and Nation*,
         XXXVI (November 27), pp. 468-469.

         Review of *Henry James and Robert Louis Stevenson. A
         Record of Friendship and Criticism*, edited by Janet
         Adam Smith; in *Collected Essays* as "Two Friends."

C385   "The Creative Life in Our Time," *Partisan Review*,
         XV (November), pp. 1175-1189.

         Correspondence between Greene, Pritchett and Bowen
         later published in *Why Do I Write?*

1949

C386   "The Redemption of Mr. Joyboy," *The Month*, n.s. I
         (January), pp. 55-57.

         Review of *The Loved One* by Evelyn Waugh.

C387   *"The Hint of an Explanation," *Commonweal*, XLIX
         (February 11), pp. 438-442.

C388   *"The Hint of an Explanation," *The Month*, n.s. I
         (February), pp. 77-87.

C389   *"The Third Man," *American Magazine*, CXLVII (March), pp. 142-160.

An abridged version of the novel.

C390   Letter, *The Times* (June 21), p. 5.

Re dollars for British visitors to the U.S.

C391   Letter, *Times Literary Supplement* (June 24), p. 413.

Re Robert Louis Stevenson.

C392   "Simple Indices ...," *Études*, CCLXI (June), pp. 307-320.

C393   Letter, *The Times* (July 2), p. 5.

Re dollar allocations to visitors to the U.S.

C394   **"Behind the Tight Pupils," *The Month*, II (July), pp. 7-8.

C395   "Books in General," *New Statesman and Nation*, XXXVIII (August 20), pp. 198, 200.

Review of *The Journals of Francis Parkman* (2 vols.), edited by Mason Wade; in *Collected Essays* as "Francis Parkman."

C396   "The Ugly Act," *New Statesman and Nation*, XXXVIII (October 8), p. 388.

Review of *W. E. Henley* by John Connell.

C397   *"The Third Man," serialized in *The Daily Express* (December 8), p. 4; (December 9), p. 4; (December 10), p. 4; (December 12), p. 4; (December 13), p. 4; (December 14), p. 4; (December 15), p. 4; (December 16), p. 4; (December 17), p. 4; (December 19), p. 4; (December 20), p. 4; (December 21), p. 4; (December 22), p. 4; (December 23), p. 4; (December 24), p. 4; (December 28), p. 6.

C398   *"All But Empty," *Ellery Queen's Mystery Magazine*, XVII (December), pp. 114-116.

C399   "Dr. Oates of Salamanca," *The Month*, n.s. II (December), pp. 419-420.

Review of *Titus Oates* by Jane Lane.

C400   "Message aux Catholiques Français," *Dieu Vivant*,
        No. 14, pp. 31–35.

        Texte lu a la Semaine des Intellectuels Catholiques
        Français, May 15, 1949.

                              1950

C401   "Books in General," *New Statesman and Nation*, XXXIX
        (January 28), pp. 101–102.

        Review of *The Complete Plays of Henry James*, edited
        by Leon Edel.

C402   "The Third Man," *Ellery Queen's Mystery Magazine*,
        XVIII (April), pp. 103–144.

C403   "Mothering Sunday," *New Statesman and Nation*, XL
        (August 19), p. 205.

        Review of *Desert Calling. The Story of Charles de
        Foucauld* by Anne Fremantle.

C404   "The Catholic Church's New Dogma: The Assumption of
        Mary," *Life*, XXIX (October 30), pp. 50–52, 55–56, 58.

        Condensed in *Catholic Digest*, XV (January 1951),
        pp. 12–19, "The Assumption of Mary."

C405   "Letter, *Dieu Vivant*, No. 17, pp. 151–152.

        Re Scobie's actions in *The Heart of the Matter*.

                              1951

C406   "The Assumption of Mary," *Catholic Digest*, XV
        (January), pp. 12–19.

        Condensed from *Life*, XXIX (October 30, 1950), pp.
        50–52, 55–56, 58.

C407   "Our Lady and Her Assumption," *The Tablet*, CXCVII
        (February 3), pp. 87–89.

C408   Letter, *The Times* (April 17), p. 5.

        Re author's royalties.

C409   "The Badge of Courage," *New Statesman and Nation*,
        XLI (June 2), pp. 627-628.

        Review of *Stephen Crane* by John Berryman in the
        American Men of Letters Series.

C410   "Books in General," *New Statesman and Nation*, XLII
        (July 14), pp. 45-46.

        Review of *Allan's Wife*; *Allan Quartermain*; *Eric
        Brighteyes*; *Montezuma's Daughter*; *Nada the Lilly*;
        People of the Mist; *She* -- all reprints of novels
        from the publisher, Macdonald; and *The Cloak That I
        Left* by Lilias Rider Haggard.

C411   "Malaya, the Forgotten War," *Life*, XXXI (July 30),
        pp. 51-54, 59-62, 65.

C412   "The Sense of Apprehension," *The Month*, n.s. VI
        (July), pp. 49-51.

        Review of *Judgment on Deltchev* by Eric Ambler.

C413   "The Pope Who Remains a Priest," *Life*, XXXI
        (September 24), pp. 147-148, 151-152, 155-156, 160-
        162.

C414   "Simone Weil," *New Statesman and Nation*, XLII
        (October 6), pp. 372, 374.

        Review of *Waiting on God* by Simone Weil.

C415   "Malaya, the Forgotten War," *Reader's Digest*, LIX
        (November), pp. 119-123.

C416   "Pius XII, The Paradox of the Pope," *The Month*, n.s.
        VI (December), pp. 327-339.

C417   "The Pope Who Remains a Priest," *Catholic Digest*,
        XVI (December), pp. 86-96.

C418   "Les Paradoxes du Christianisme," *Dieu Vivant*, No. 18,
        pp. 35-42.

C419   "L'Aspect Religieux de Henry James," *Dieu Vivant*,
        No. 20, pp. 101-114.

1952

C420   "The Entertainments of A.E.W. Mason," *New Statesman and Nation*, XLIV "Autumn Books Supplement" (October 4), p. 381.

Review of *A. E. W. Mason* by Roger Lancelyn Green.

C421   "London Diary," *New Statesman and Nation*, XLIV (November 22), p. 593.

C422   "The Londoners: Notes from a Journal of the Blitz, 1940-41," *The Month*, n.s. VIII (November), pp. 278-287.

C423   "Books in General," *New Statesman and Nation*, XLIII (June 21), p. 745.

Review of *West African Explorers*, edited by C. Howard.

C424   "The Return of Charlie Chaplin, I. An Open Letter," *New Statesman and Nation*, XLIV (September 27), p. 344.

C425   "Dear Mr. Chaplin," *New Republic*, CXXVI (October 13), p. 5.

1953

C426   "A Stranger in the Theatre," *Picture Post*, LIX (April 18), pp. 19-20.

C427   "Character in Search of An Author," *New Statesman and Nation*, XLV (May 2), pp. 521-522.

Review of *Exploration Fawcett* by Lieut.-Col. P.H. Fawcett, edited by Brian Fawcett.

C428   "Books in General," *New Statesman and Nation*, XLVI (July 18), pp. 76-77.

Review of *Henry James. The Untried Years. 1843-70* by Leon Edel.

C429   "A Small Affair," *The Listener*, L (August 20), pp. 302-304.

Extract from *The Quiet American*.

C430   Letter, *The Times* (August 22), p. 7.
        Re Anglo-Texan Society.

C431   "Kenya As I See It," *The Sunday Times* (September 27
        and October 4).

C432   "Vengeance of Jenny's Case," *New Statesman and
        Nation*, XLVI (November 21), pp. 642, 644.
        Review of *To Beg I Am Ashamed* by Sheila Cousins.

C433   Letter, *The Times* (December 4), p. 9.
        Re Kenya.

C434   Letter, *The Times* (December 23), p. 7.
        Re Anglo-Texan Society.

                              1954

C435   Letter, *The Times* (March 25), p. 9.
        Re Dien Bien Phu.

C436   "Indo-China," *New Republic*, CXXX (April 5), pp. 13-15.

C437   "To Hope Till Hope Creates," *New Republic*, CXXX
        (April 12), pp. 11-13.

C438   "Before the Attack," *The Spectator*, CXCII (April 16),
        p. 456.

C439   "Catholics at War: Extracts from an Indo-China
        Journal," *The Tablet*, CCIII (April 17), pp. 366-367.

C440   "Indo-China Journal," *Commonweal*, LX (May 21),
        pp. 170-172.

C441   Letter, *The Times* (June 5), p. 7; also June 16, p. 9.
        Re obscene publications.

C442   *"The Destructors," *Picture Post*, LXIV: Part I (July
        24), pp. 36-38; Part II (July 31), pp. 29ff.

C443   "A Propos des Obsèques de Colette," *Le Figaro Lit-*
        téraire, VIII (August 14), p. 1.

        Re the refusal of the Cardinal Archbishop of Paris
        to bury Colette in consecrated ground.

C444   "Loser Takes All," *Picture Post*, LXIV: Part I
        (August 21), pp. 19-22ff.; Part II (August 28),
        pp. 25-27ff.; Part III (September 4), pp. 35-36ff.;
        Part IV (September 11), pp. 34-35ff.; Part V
        (September 18), pp. 35-36.

C445   "The General and the Spy, Extract from an Indo-
        China Journal," *London Magazine*, I (August), pp.
        26-29.

C446   *"Special Duties," *Punch*, CCXXVII (September 29),
        pp. 400-402.

C447   "Books in General," *New Statesman and Nation*, XLVIII
        (October 2), pp. 411-412.

        Review of *Livingstone's Travels*, edited by Dr. James
        I. Macnair.

C448   **"Song for Three Ageing Voices," *Punch*, CCXXVII
        (December 1), p. 697.

C449   "The Revenge," *Time and Tide*, XXXV (December 4),
        p. 1602.

C450   "A Few Pipes, Extract from an Indo-China Journal,"
        London Magazine, I (December), pp. 17-24.

                              1955

C451   "The Revenge," *Commonweal*, LXI (January 14), pp. 403-
        404.

C452   *"The Destructors," *Harper's Magazine*, CCX (January),
        pp. 68-75.

C453   Letter, *The Times* (February 13), p. 9.

        Re drinks at airports.

C454   "Diem's Critics," *America*, XCIII (May 28), p. 225.

C455   "Last Act in Indo-China," *New Republic*, CXXXII:
        Part I (May 9), pp. 9-11; Part II (May 16), pp. 10-12.

C456   *"Work Not in Progress," *Punch*, CCXXVIII (June 1),
        pp. 668-671.

C457   "A Memory of Indo-China," *The Listener*, LIV
        (September 15), p. 420.

C458   *"Loser Takes All," *Harper's Magazine*, CCXI: Part I
        (October), pp. 61-68; Part II (November), pp. 72-79;
        Part III (December), pp. 75-81.

        Conclusion, Part IV, published in January 1956.

C459   *"The Quiet American," *Picture Post*, LXIX: Part I
        (December 10), pp. 32-41; Part II (December 17),
        pp. 18-21; Part III (December 24), pp. 14-17ff.;
        Part IV (December 31), pp. 14-16ff.

        Conclusion, Part V and Part VI, of this abridged
        novel published in January 1956.

                              1956

C460   *"Church Militant," *Commonweal*, LXIII (January 6),
        pp. 350-352.

C461   *"The Quiet American," *Picture Post*, LXX: Part V
        (January 7), pp. 32-36; Part VI (January 14), pp.
        18-19ff.

C462   *"Church Militant," *New Statesman and Nation*, LI
        (January 21), pp. 66, 68.

C463   *"Loser Takes All," *Harper's Magazine*, CCXII: Part IV
        (January), pp. 74-80.

C464   "The John Gordon Society," *The Spectator*, CXCVI
        (March 9), p. 309.

C465   "Mad Hatters," *The Spectator*, CXCVI (March 30),
        p. 415.

Review of *Obscenity and the Law* by Norman St. John-
Stevas.

C466   Review, *London Magazine*, III (March), pp. 68-70.

Review of *Rudyard Kipling. His Life and Work* by
Charles Carrington.

C467   "The Catholic Temper in Poland," *Atlantic Monthly*,
CXCVII (March), pp. 39-41.

C468   **"Ballade for a Wedding," *Punch*, CCXXX (April 18),
p. 457.

C469   **"Ballade on a Press Conference," *New Statesman and
Nation*, LI (June 30), p. 755.

C470   "The Price of Faith," *New Statesman and Nation*, LII
(July 7), pp. 18-19.

Review of *Report on the Vatican* by Bernard Wall.

C471   *"The Destructors," *Ellery Queen's Mystery Magazine*,
XXXI (July), pp. 3-15.

C472   Letter, *The New York Times* (August 26), p. 8, sec. 7.

To Robert Clurman.

C473   Letter, *The Times* (September 3), p. 9; also
(September 6), p. 11.

Re Naga Hills.

C474   *"The Man Who Stole the Eiffel Tower," *Punch*, CCXXXI
(September 19), pp. 324-326.

C475   Letter, *The Times* (December 3), p. 11; also
(December 5), p. 11.

Re ban on *Pygmalion*.

1957

C476   *"A Visit to Morin," *London Magazine*, IV (January),
pp. 13-25.

C477   "Dickens and Dostoevsky," *New Statesman*, LIII
        (March 9), p. 309.

        Letter.

C478   "And the Other Writer," *New Statesman*, LIII
        (April 13), p. 478.

        Letter.

C479   *"Awful When You Think of It," *Punch*, CCXXXII
        (June 19), pp. 756-757.

C480   "Greene and Shaw," *New Statesman*, LIV (September 14,
        1957), p. 318; also (September 28), pp. 384-385.

        Letters.

C481   *"A Shocking Accident," *Punch*, CCXXXIII (November 6),
        pp. 526-528.

C482   "A Stranger in the Theatre," Bijou Theater *Playbill*
        for *The Potting Shed*, 1957.

        First American production, Bijou Theater, New York,
        January 29, 1957.

                              1958

C483   *"The Potting Shed," *Theatre Arts*, XLII (March),
        pp. 24-48.

C484   Letter, *The Times* (June 26), p. 11.

        Re theatre workshops.

                              1959

C485   Letter, *The Times* (January 3), p. 7; also (January 6),
        p. 9.

        Re Cuba.

C486   Letter, *Times Literary Supplement* (January 23), p. 47.

Re the private life of John Gordon.

C487   "John Gordon," *New Statesman*, LVII (April 24),
        p. 109.

        Letter.

C488   Letter, *The Times* (October 19), p. 11.

        Re Cuba.

C489   "The Man Who Built a Cathedral," *New Statesman*,
        LVIII (November 7), p. 628.

        Letter.

1960

C490   Letter, *The Times* (February 18), p. 13.

        Re pirated books.

C491   Letter, *The Times* (June 23), p. 10.

        To the French Minister of Cultural Affairs *re*
        Algerian Communist trial.

C492   Letter, *The Times* (December 23), p. 9.

        Re I.T.A. censorship of *The Complaisant Lover*.

1961

C493   Letter, *The Times* (January 4), p. 9.

        Re Laos.

C494   "The Greeneland Aboriginal," *New Statesman*, LXI
        (January 27), p. 139.

        Letter correcting a mistake in profile "The Greene-
        land Aboriginal."

C495   Letter, *New Statesman*, LXI (April 14), p. 585.

        Re Week-end competition.

C496 **"Lines on the Liberation of Cuba," *New Statesman*, LXI
(April 28), p. 671.

1962

C497 "In Search of a Character: A Congo Journal,"
Harper's Magazine, CCXXIV (January), pp. 66-74.

C498 *"When Greek Meets Greek," *Ava Maria*, XCV
(February 3), pp. 11-14, 24-25.

C499 Letter, *The Times* (February 21), p. 11.

Re Cuba.

C500 *"Across the Bridge," *Ellery Queen's Mystery Magazine*,
XLII (March), pp. 127-135.

C501 Letter, *Times Literary Supplement* (April 6), p. 233.

Re Tale of Mutiny.

C502 "An Unhappy Journal Produced a Great Novel," *Life
International*, XXXIII (September 10), pp. 77-79.

C503 "The Prefaces of Conrad and James," *The Listener*,
LXVIII (October 18), p. 598.

Excerpt from "Life and Letters."

C504 *"May We Borrow Your Husband?" *London Magazine*, II
(November), pp. 5-30.

1963

C505 *"Dear Dr. Falkenheim," *Vogue*, CXLI (January 1),
pp. 100-101.

C506 *"Dream of a Strange Land," *Saturday Evening Post*,
CCXXXVI (January 19), pp. 44-47.

C507 "Going Into Europe,"--Symposium II, *Encounter*, XX
(January), p. 54.

C508   *"May We Borrow Your Husband?" *Show*, III (February),
        pp. 72-75.

C509   *"Beauty," *The Spectator*, CCX (March 15), p. 324.

C510   *"A Discovery in the Woods," *Rogue*, VIII (March),
        pp. 68-72ff.

C511   *"Mortmain," *Playboy*, X (March), pp. 77, 110, 136-137.

C512   *"Mortmain," *New Statesman*, LXV (April 19), pp. 584-
        588.

C513   *"Beauty," *Esquire*, LIX (April), pp. 60, 142.

C514   "Letter to a West German Friend," *New Statesman*, LXV
        (May 31), pp. 824-825.

C515   *"A Discovery in the Woods," *London Magazine*, III
        (May), pp. 21-37.

C516   Letter, *The Times* (July 4), p. 13.

        Re opera adaptation of *Our Man in Havana*.

C517   "Return to Cuba," *The Sunday Telegraph* (September 22),
        pp. 4-5.

C518   "Nightmare Republic," *The Sunday Telegraph*
        (September 29), pp. 4-5.

C519   "Return to Cuba," *New Republic*, CXLIX (November 2),
        pp. 16-18.

C520   "Nightmare Republic," *New Republic*, CXLIX
        (November 16), pp. 18-20.

        Item C521 omitted.

                                    1964

C522   *"The Root of All Evil," *New Statesman*, LXVII
        (March 6), pp. 360-364.

C523   *"The Root of All Evil," *Saturday Evening Post*,
        CCXXXVII (March 7), pp. 56-61.

C524   Letter, *Times Literary Supplement* (March 26), p. 255.
        Re Cuba.

C525   "The Rude Mechanicals," *New Statesman*, LXVII (May 1),
        pp. 677-678.

C526   *"Cheap in August," *London Magazine*, IV (August),
        pp. 7-27.

C527   Letter, *The Times* (November 6).
        Re photographs of the tortures inflicted on Viet-
        Cong prisoners by Vietnamese army troops.

                        1965

C528   "The American Presence," *New Statesman*, LXIX
           (March 19), p. 448.
        Review of *South-East Asia in Turmoil* by Brian
        Crozier.

C529   Letter, *The Times* (April 26), p. 11.
        Re teacher's pay.

C530   Letter, *The Times* (May 12), p. 13.
        Re U.S. intervention in the Dominican Republic.

C531   *"Mortmain," *Argosy* (London), XXVI (June), pp. 4-13.

C532   *"The Over-Night Bag," *The Spectator*, CCXV (August 20),
        pp. 230-231.

C533   Letter, *Times Literary Supplement* (September 16),
        p. 801.
        Re Ford Madox Ford.

C534   Letter, *The Times* (September 24), p. 13.
        Re Viet Nam.

C535   Letter, *Times Literary Supplement* (September 30),
        p. 862.

        Re Ford Madox Ford.

C536   *"Doctor Crombie," *New Statesman*, LXX (October 8),
        pp. 518-519.

C537   *"The Over-Night Bag," *Status*, I (October), pp. 36-38.

C538   *"Invisible Japanese Gentlemen," *Saturday Evening
        Post*, CCXXXVIII (November 20), pp. 60-61.

C539   *"The Palace of Chance," *The Reporter*, XXXIII
        (December 2), pp. 41-42.

        Excerpt from *The Comedians*.

C540   *"Doctor Crombie," *Status*, I (December), pp. 36, 92,
        94.

C541   "John Hayward, 1904-1965: Some Memories," edited by
        John Carter. *Book Collector*, XIV (Winter), pp. 443-
        486.

        By Greene and others.

1966

C542   *"The Invisible Japanese Gentlemen," *The Spectator*,
        CCXVI (January 7), pp. 9-10.

C543   *"The Blessing," *New Statesman*, LXXI (February 25),
        pp. 254-255.

C544   *"The Blessing," *Harper's Magazine*, CCXXXII (March),
        pp. 91-94.

C545   "Poison Pen.--Introductory Note," *London Magazine*,
        V (March), pp. 70-73.

        Review of *Pinorman* by Richard Aldington.

C546   "Tribute to Evelyn Waugh," *The Times* (April 15),
        p. 15.

C547   Letter, *Times Literary Supplement* (July 28), p. 670.
       Re Gordon.

C548   *"Chagrin in Three Parts," *The Weekend Telegraph*
       (October 28), pp. 55, 57-58.

C549   "Tribute to M. Yves Allain," *The Times* (November 24),
       p. 14.

C550   "Fidel: An Impression," *The Weekend Telegraph*
       (December 2), pp. 9-10, 12.
       In *Collected Essays* as "The Marxist Heretic."

C551   Letter, *The Times* (December 29), p. 9.
       Re The Times.

C552   "Return of the Novelist," *Adam International Review*,
       Nos. 304-305-306, pp. 6-9.

                              1967

C553   *"Secret," *Vogue*, CXLIX (January 1), pp. 94-95, 144,
       151.

C554   *"Two Gentle People," *The Weekend Telegraph* (March 10),
       pp. 41-42, 45.

C555   *"Beauty," *Nova* (April), pp. 163, 166.

C556   *"A Shocking Accident," *Nova* (April), pp. 160-161.

C557   *"Awful When You Think of It," *Cosmopolitan*, CLXIII
       (August), p. 116.

C558   *"Chagrin in Three Parts," *Cosmopolitan*, CLXIII
       (August), pp. 114-115.

                              1968

C559   Letter, *The Times* (March 22), p. 11; also (March 25),
       p. 9.

Re Viet Nam demonstration.

C560   "And a Happy New Year: Remarks by Graham Greene at a
        PEN Meeting," *The Listener*, LXXIX (April 4), p. 442.

C561   "The Comic, Terrifying Mind of M. Leroux," *Life*, LXIV
        (April 12), p. 8.

        Review of *One for the Devil* by Etienne Leroux.

C562   "Graham Greene Revisits the Soupsweet Land," *The
        Observer* (colour supplement, May 19), p. 10.

C563   "The Mask Remover," *New Statesman*, LXXV (May 31),
        p. 728.

        Review of *The Years of the Week* by Patricia Cockburn.

C564   Statement recorded in the minutes of the International
        PEN Defence Committee for Soviet and Greek writers in
        prison, *Encounter*, XXX (June), p. 62.

C565   "Soupsweet Land," *Holiday*, XLIV (August), pp. 40-41.

C566   "Reflections on the Character of Kim Philby,"
        Esquire, LXX (September), pp. 110-111.

C567   Letter, *The Times* (November 13), p. 11.

        Re Nigeria.

                            1969

C568   "The Worm Inside the Lotus Blossom," *The Daily
        Telegraph Magazine* (January 3), pp. 6-7, 9, 11.

        Report on Paraguay.

C569   "Paraguay: Where the Living is Easy, So ...,"
        Holiday, XLV (April), pp. 68-71.

C570   Letter, *The Times* (July 5), p. 9.

        Re morality in international relations.

C571   "Dilemma Over Russia for Novelists," *The Times*
        (August 6), p. 9.

        Letter appealing to authors not to publish in Russia.

C572   Letter, *The Times* (August 15), p. 7.

        Re John Braine's suggestion that cultural links be
        severed.

C573   "Terror in Trinidad," *The Observer Review* (October
        26), p. 34.

        Review of *The Loss of Eldorado* by V.S. Naipaul.

C574   Reflection on the Funeral of Rudyard Kipling, *The
        Times* (October 28), p. 10.

C575   *"Crook's Tour," *Playboy*, XVI: Part I (November),
        pp. 114, 116, 192, 194, 196, 199-201, 203, 206-208;
        Part II (December), pp. 144, 146, 150, 339-340, 342,
        344-347.

        Conclusion, Part III, published in January 1970;
        selections from *Travels with My Aunt*.

                              1970

C576   Letter, *The Times* (January 12), p. 9.

        Re Haiti massacre.

C577   *"Crook's Tour," *Playboy*, XVII: Part III (January),
        pp. 142-143, 162, 224, 226, 228, 230-231.

C578   "Graham Greene Recollects," *The Daily Telegraph
        Magazine* (March 27), pp. 26-27, 29-30.

        Introductions to the Collected Edition of *It's a
        Battlefield*, *England Made Me* and *Brighton Rock*.

C579   "A Black Comedy in Havana," *The Daily Telegraph
        Magazine* (April 3), pp. 43, 46.

        Introduction to the Collected Edition of *Our Man in
        Havana*.

C580   "Lowdown from Our Man in Havana," *Vogue*, CLV
        (April 15), pp. 94-95.

C581   "Withdrawing from Cambodia," *The Times* (May 11),
        p. 9.

Letter *re* the effect of the monsoon on Cambodian operation.

C582   Letter, *The Times* (August 17), p. 7.

Re National Toy Museum.

C583   "Haggard Rides Again," *New Statesman*, LX (September 3), p. 310.

Letter.

C584   Letter, *The Times* (September 17), p. 11.

Re Concorde.

C585   "The Wrong Box," *Times Literary Supplement* (October 30), p. 1276.

Letter.

C586   "Books of the Year," *The Observer* (December 20), p. 17.

Remarks in symposium.

1971

C587   Letter, *The Times* (February 17), p. 15; also (February 23), p. 13.

Re war in Viet Nam.

C588   "Hints from an Unhappy Future," *The Daily Telegraph Magazine* (April 7), pp. 27-28.

Introduction to the Collected Edition of *The Confidential Agent*.

C589   "In the Footsteps of a Priest," *The Daily Telegraph Magazine* (April 16), pp. 45-46.

Introduction to the Collected Edition of *The Power and the Glory*.

C590   "Swamps, Rain and a Mad Cook," *The Daily Telegraph Magazine* (April 23), pp. 33-35.

Introduction to the Collected Edition of *The Heart of the Matter*.

C591   "On Becoming a Catholic," *Commonweal*, XCIV (September 3), pp. 451–453.

Excerpt from *A Sort of Life*.

C592   "Christ Came to Reconcile," *The Times* (September 10), p. 13.

Letter.

C593   "The Greenes of Berkhamsted," *Esquire*, LXXVI (September), pp. 126–129, 210, 212, 214.

Excerpt from *A Sort of Life*.

C594   Letter, *The Times* (November 26), p. 17; reprinted in *The New York Times* (December 2).

Re interrogation methods in Ulster.

1972

C595   "Chile: The Dangerous Edge," *The Observer* (colour supplement, January 2), pp. 4–5, 7–10.

C596   "Chile: The Dangerous Edge," *Harper's Magazine*, CCXLIV (March), pp. 32–34, 36.

C597   "It's a Battlefield," *Times Literary Supplement* (May 19), p. 576.

Letter.

C598   "Against Compromise," *The Listener*, LXXXVIII (September 21), p. 368.

Comments on Solzhenitsyn's Nobel Prize speech.

C599   Letter, *The Times* (October 17), p. 15.

Re the sinking of the Lusitania.

C600   "Edwardian Occasions," *Times Literary Supplement* (December 1), p. 1460.

Letter.

C601   Letter, *The Times* (December 11), p. 15.

        Re meeting places for visitors to London.

                            1973

C602   Letter, *The Times* (February 15), p. 19.

        Re Czech prisoners.

C603   "Disloyalty as a Virtue," *Vogue*, CLXI (March),
        pp. 147, 194.

C604   "Graham Greene on Film," *Intellectual Digest*, III
        (April), p. 25.

        Excerpt from *The Pleasure-Dome*.

C605   "Her Uncle vs. His Father," *Esquire*, LXXX (October),
        pp. 305-310, 497.

        Also titled "When Greek Meets Greek"; reprinted from
        Esquire, July 1942.

C606   "My Own Devil: the Experience of Opium Smoking,"
        Vogue, CLXII (October), pp. 188-189, 238.

        Excerpt from the Collected Edition of *The Quiet
        American*.

C607   "To Indochina With Love," *Travel and Leisure*, III
        (October-November), pp. 44-45, 87-89.

C608   Letter, *Times Literary Supplement* (November 16),
        p. 1401.

        Re viewpoint on language style.

C609   "A Memoir of Herbert Read," *The Times* (December 8),
        p. 8.

C610   **"Letter from the Workhouse," *Commonweal*, XCIX
        (December 28), p. 342.

1974

C611   *"Church Militant," *Critic*, XXXII (January-February),
        pp. 21-23.

C612   "Herbert Read, a Memoir," *Art News*, LXXIII
        (February), pp. 20-21.

        Excerpt from *Contrary Experience*.

C613   "Victim of Theology," *The Daily Telegraph Magazine*
        (July 5), pp. 33-34.

        Introduction to the Collected Edition of *A Burnt-Out
        Case*.

C614   "Pleasures of Deportation," *The Daily Telegraph
        Magazine* (October 11), pp. 65-66, 68.

C615   "The Lines on the Palm," *The Daily Telegraph Magazine*
        (November 15), pp. 55, 57.

C616   "A Thorn on the Yellow Rose," *The Daily Telegraph
        Magazine* (November 22), pp. 59-60.

C617   "Lord Jim," *Times Literary Supplement* (December 6),
        p. 1389.

C618   "Revolutionary Bystander," *The Daily Telegraph
        Magazine* (December 6), pp. 71, 73.

C619   "The Poet and the Gold," *The Daily Telegraph
        Magazine* (December 20), pp. 25-26.

1975

C620   "The Other ... Whom Only Others Know," *The Daily
        Telegraph Magazine* (January 10), pp. 23-24, 26.

C621   Letter, *The Times* (January 24), p. 18.

        Re the effect of increased mail charges on the
        publishing industry.

C622   "A Cheat Redressed," *Critic*, XXXIII (January–
        February), pp. 31–33.

        Introduction to the Collected Edition of *The End of
        the Affair*.

C623   Letter, *Times Literary Supplement* (May 30), p. 598.

        Re academics as book reviewers.

C624   "Odd Sound," *The New York Review of Books*
        (September 18), p. 60.

        Letter.

                              1976

C625   "A Young Man's Fancy," *The Daily Telegraph Magazine*
        (February 20), pp. 33–34.

        Introduction to the Collected Edition of *The Man
        Within*.

C626   "Film Books," *New Statesman*, XCI (February 27),
        p. 259.

        Letter *re* Shirley Temple libel suit, Korda and
        The Third Man.

C627   "Vagaries of Fortune," *The Daily Telegraph Magazine*
        (March 5), pp. 37–38.

        Introduction to the Collected Edition of *Loser
        Takes All*.

C628   "Black Humour in Haiti," *The Daily Telegraph
        Magazine* (March 12), pp. 39–40.

        Introduction to the Collected Edition of *The
        Comedians*.

C629   Letter, *The Times* (July 2), p. 17.

        Re July 4th.

1977

C630   Letter, *Times Literary Supplement* (February 4),
       p. 130.

       Re overrated authors.

C631   "The Country with Five Frontiers," *The New York
       Review of Books*, XXIV (February 17), pp. 10, 12-13.

C632   Discussion of Panama, *The Chicago Tribune* (March 27),
       sec. 2, p. 1.

1978

C633   "The Great Spectacular," *The New York Review of
       Books*, XXIV (January 26), p. 9.

C634   *"The Human Factor," *Playboy*, XXV (February),
       pp. 88, 90, 178-182.

       Excerpt from *The Human Factor*.

FILM CRITICISM

Certain book reviews appearing earlier in this list have been repeated in this section because they incorporate film criticism.

Note: Films marked with asterisks are not reviewed in *The Pleasure-Dome.*

1925

C635   "The Average Film," *The Oxford Outlook*, VII (February), pp. 96-97.

Review of *The Nibelungs*; *Mdlle. Midnight*; *Circus-mania*; *Cyrano de Bergerac*; *The Gay Corinthian*; *Zaza*; *Girl Shy*; and *The Call of the Wild*.

1934

C636   "Pigs, Be British," *The Spectator*, CLII (March 23), p. 455.

Review of *The Three Little Pigs* prepared by the Walt Disney Studios; in *Collected Essays* as "The British Pig."

1935

C637   "The Cinema," *The Spectator*, CLV (July 5), p. 14.

Review of *The Bride of Frankenstein*; *The Glass Key*; *No More Women*; *Abyssinia*; *Wings in the Dark*; and *Car 99*.

C638   "The Cinema," *The Spectator*, CLV (July 12), p. 54.

Review of *St. Petersburg*; *Paris Love Song*; and *The Phantom Light*.

C639   "The Cinema," *The Spectator*, CLV (July 19), p. 94.

Review of *Becky Sharp*; *Barcarole*; and *Public Hero No. 1*.

C640   "The Cinema," *The Spectator*, CLV (July 26), p. 150.

   Review of *Private Worlds*; *Living on Velvet*; and *Rome Express*.

C641   "The Cinema," *The Spectator*, CLV (August 2), p. 186.

   Review of *The Voice of Britain*; *Mimi*; and *Shanghai*.

C642   "The Cinema," *The Spectator*, CLV (August 9), p. 222.

   Review of *The Trunk Mystery*; *Hands of Orlac*; *Look up and Laugh*; *The Memory Expert*; and *Devil Dogs of the Air*.

C643   "The Cinema," *The Spectator*, CLV (August 16), p. 257.

   Review of *Der Schimmelreiter*; *Star of Midnight*; *False Faces*; and *All the King's Horses*.

C644   "The Cinema," *The Spectator*, CLV (August 23), p. 290.

   Review of *Where's George?*; *Boys Will Be Boys*; *The Murder Man*; and *The Great God Gold*.

C645   "The Cinema," *The Spectator*, CLV (August 30), p. 322.

   Review of *The Crusades*.

C646   "The Cinema," *The Spectator*, CLV (September 6), p. 353.

   Review of *Dood Water*; *Me and Marlborough*; and *The Barretts of Wimpole Street*.

C647   "The Cinema," *The Spectator*, CLV (September 13), p. 390.

   Review of *On Wings of Song*; *Peg of Old Drury*; and *Break of Hearts*.

C648   "The Cinema," *The Spectator*, CLV (September 20), p. 426.

   Review of *The Black Room* and *Gentlemen of the Navy*.

   "The Camera Eye," *The Spectator*, CLV (September 27), p. 472. (See C176.)

   Review of *A Grammar of the Film* by Raymond Spottiswoode.

C649   "The Cinema," *The Spectator*, CLV (September 27), p. 462.

   Review of *Jazz Comedy* and *Two for Tonight*.

C650   "The Cinema," *The Spectator*, CLV (October 4), p. 506.

Review of *Song of Ceylon*; *Musik im Blut*; and *The Dark Angel*.

C651 "The Cinema," *The Spectator*, CLV (October 11), p. 547.

Review of *Anna Karenina* and *The Informer*.

C652 "The Cinema," *The Spectator*, CLV (October 18), p. 606.

Review of *A Midsummer Night's Dream*.

C653 "The Cinema," *The Spectator*, CLV (October 25), p. 663.

Review of *Joan of Arc*; *Turn of the Tide*; *Top Hat*; and *She*.

C654 "The Cinema," *The Spectator*, CLV (November 1), p. 718.

Review of *Barbary Coast*; *Episode*; and *The Passing of the Third Floor Back*.

C655 "The Cinema," *The Spectator*, CLV (November 8), p. 774.

Review of *The March of Time*.

C656 "The Cinema," *The Spectator*, CLV (November 15), p. 814.

Review of *Last Love*; *Moscow Nights*; and *Oil for the Lamps of China*.

C657 "The Cinema," *The Spectator*, CLV (November 22), p. 863.

Review of *Arms and the Girl*; *Accent on Youth*; *The Tunnel*; and *New Babylon*.

C658 "The Cinema," *The Spectator*, CLV (November 29), p. 900.

Review of *The Last Outpost* and *The Irish in Us*.

C659 "The Cinema," *The Spectator*, CLV (December 6), p. 940.

Review of *La Bandéra*; *Woman Tamer*; and *Come Out of the Pantry*.

C660 "The Cinema," *The Spectator*, CLV (December 13), p. 984.

Review of *Page Miss Glory*; *A Fire Has Been Arranged*; *Here's to Romance*; and *The Port of Five Seas*.

C661 "The Cinema," *The Spectator*, CLV (December 20), p. 1028.

Review of *Riders to the Sea* and *Thanks a Million*.

C662 "The Cinema," *The Spectator*, CLV (December 27), p. 1068.

Review of *The Ghost Goes West* and **Foreign Affairs*.

1936

C663 "The Cinema," *The Spectator*, CLVI (January 3), p. 14.

Review of *The Guv'nor*; *Midshipman Easy*; and *Treasure Island*.

C664 "The Cinema," *The Spectator*, CLVI (January 10), p. 50.

Review of *Reifende Jugend*; *The Bride Comes Home*; and **King of the Damned*.

C665 "The Cinema," *The Spectator*, CLVI (January 17), p. 91.

Review of *Second Bureau* and *Sans Famille*.

C666 "The Cinema," *The Spectator*, CLVI (January 24), p. 129.

Review of **Koenigsmark*; **The Three Musketeers*; and **I Give My Heart*.

"Wings Over Wardour Street," *The Spectator*, CLVI (January 24), p. 137. (See C187.)

Review of *Documentary Film* by Paul Rotha and *Plan for Cinema* by Dallas Bower.

C667 "The Cinema," *The Spectator*, CLVI (January 31), p. 170.

Review of *The Case of the Lucky Legs*; *Charlie Chan in Shanghai*; and **The Amateur Gentleman*.

C668 "The Cinema," *The Spectator*, CLVI (February 7), p. 211.

Review of *Dr. Socrates*; *The Man Who Broke the Bank at Monte Carlo*; and *The Imperfect Lady*.

C669 "The Cinema," *The Spectator*, CLVI (February 14), p. 255.

Review of *Modern Times*.

C670 "The Cinema," *The Spectator*, CLVI (February 21), p. 300.

Review of *I Dream Too Much*; *Anything Goes*; *Faust*; *Hohe Schule*; and *Captain Blood*.

C671   "The Cinema," *The Spectator*, CLVI (February 28), p. 343.

       Review of *Things to Come* and *Bonne Chance*.

C672   "The Cinema," *The Spectator*, CLVI (March 6), p. 396.

       Review of *Rose of the Rancho* and *Jack of All Trades*.

C673   "The Cinema," *The Spectator*, CLVI (March 13), p. 467.

       Review of *Crime et Châtiment* and *Veille d'Armes*.

C674   "The Cinema," *The Spectator*, CLVI (March 20), p. 512.

       Review of *The Milky Way*; *Night Mail*; *Strike Me Pink*;
       and *Crime and Punishment*.

C675   "The Cinema," *The Spectator*, CLVI (March 27), p. 575.

       Review of *Rhodes of Africa* and *October*.

C676   "The Middle-Brow Film," *The Fortnightly (Review)*, CXLV
       (March), pp. 302-307.

C677   "The Cinema," *The Spectator*, CLVI (April 3), p. 616.

       Review of *Merlusse*; *The Day of the Great Adventure*; and
       Desire.

C678   "The Cinema," *The Spectator*, CLVI (April 10), p. 664.

       Review of *Liebesmelodie*; *Pot Luck*; *If You Could Only
       Cook*; and *One Way Ticket*.

C679   "The Cinema," *The Spectator*, CLVI (April 17), p. 703.

       Review of *Kliou the Tiger*.

C680   "The Cinema," *The Spectator*, CLVI (April 24), p. 744.

       Review of *Follow the Fleet* and *The Peace Film*.

C681   "The Cinema," *The Spectator*, CLVI (May 1), p. 791.

       Review of *These Three* and *The Student of Prague*.

C682   "The Cinema," *The Spectator*, CLVI (May 8), p. 835.

       Review of *Anne-Marie*; **La Belle au Bois Dormant*; and
       Tudor Rose.

C683   "The Cinema," *The Spectator*, CLVI (May 15), p. 879.

Review of *The Trail of the Lonesome Pine*; *Secret Agent*; and **A History of the Film, 1896-1936*.

C684   "The Cinema," *The Spectator*, CLVI (May 22), p. 931.

Review of *Klondyke Annie*; *Professional Soldier*; and **A History of the Film*.

C685   "The Cinema," *The Spectator*, CLVI (May 29), p. 978.

Review of *The Robber Symphony*; *The Emperor's Candlesticks*; and *The Littlest Rebel*.

C686   "The Cinema," *The Spectator*, CLVI (June 5), p. 1036.

Review of *The Marriage of Corbal*.

C687   "The Cinema," *The Spectator*, CLVI (June 12), p. 1080.

Review of *The Country Doctor*; **The Ex-Mrs. Bradford*; and **Thirteen Hours by Air*.

C688   "The Cinema," *The Spectator*, CLVI (June 19), p. 1131.

Review of *Dangerous*; *Big Brown Eyes*; and **Letzte Rose*.

C689   "The Cinema," *The Spectator*, CLVI (June 26), p. 1171.

Review of *Show Boat* and *The Moon's Our Home*.

C690   "The Cinema," *The Spectator*, CLVII (July 3), p. 15.

Review of *Fury* and *The Story of Louis Pasteur*.

C691   "The Cinema," *The Spectator*, CLVII (July 10), p. 56.

Review of *One Rainy Afternoon*; *Janosik*; and *The Phantom Gondola*.

C692   "The Cinema," *The Spectator*, CLVII (July 17), p. 97.

Review of *Poppy*; *Living Dangerously*; and *Charlie Chan at the Circus*.

C693   "The Cinema," *The Spectator*, CLVII (July 24), p. 139.

Review of *The Petrified Forest*.

C694   "The Cinema," *The Spectator*, CLVII (July 31), p. 199.

Review of *Laburnum Grove* and *Ourselves Alone*.

C695   "The Cinema," *The Spectator*, CLVII (August 7), p. 235.
        Review of *Under Two Flags* and *Captain January*.

C696   "The Cinema," *The Spectator*, CLVII (August 14), p. 270.
        Review of *Rhythm on the Range*.

C697   "The Cinema," *The Spectator*, CLVII (August 21), p. 307.
        Review of *Everything Is Thunder* and *Die Kirbbebijter*.

C698   "The Cinema," *The Spectator*, CLVII (August 28), p. 343.
        Review of *Mr. Deeds Goes to Town*.

C699   "The Cinema," *The Spectator*, CLVII (September 4), p. 379.
        Review of *The Man Who Could Work Miracles*.

C700   "The Cinema," *The Spectator*, CLVII (September 11), p. 416.
        Review of *As You Like It* and *Cover to Cover*.

C701   "The Cinema," *The Spectator*, CLVII (September 18), p. 455.
        Review of *The Great Ziegfeld*; *It's Love Again*; *March-
        land d'Amour*; and *East Meets West*.

C702   "The Cinema," *The Spectator*, CLVII (September 25), p. 495.
        Review of *The Song of Freedom* and *Anthony Adverse*.

C703   "The Cinema," *The Spectator*, CLVII (October 2), p. 543.
        Review of *Maria Bashkirtseff* and *My Man Godfrey*.

C704   "The Cinema," *The Spectator*, CLVII (October 9), p. 583.
        Review of *The Texas Rangers*; *Savoy Hotel 217*; and *The
        King Steps Out*.

C705   "The Cinema," *The Spectator*, CLVII (October 16), p. 632.
        Review of *Nutrition*.

C706   "The Cinema," *The Spectator*, CLVII (October 23), p. 679.
        Review of *Romeo and Juliet*.

C707   "The Cinema," *The Spectator*, CLVII (October 30), p. 747.
        Review of *La Kermesse Héroïque* and *The General Died at
        Dawn*.

C708   "The Cinema," *The Spectator*, CLVII (November 6), p. 808.

Review of *Dodsworth*; *Mayerling*; and *Fox Hunt*.

C709   "The Cinema," *The Spectator*, CLVII (November 13),
p. 851.

Review of *Fredlös* and *The Gay Desperado*.

C710   "The Cinema," *The Spectator*, CLVII (November 20),
p. 905.

Review of *Rembrandt*.

C711   "The Cinema," *The Spectator*, CLVII (November 27),
p. 945.

Review of *The New Gulliver*; *Bullets or Ballots*; and
The White Angel.

C712   "The Cinema," *The Spectator*, CLVII (December 4), p. 989.

Review of *The Green Pastures*.

C713   "The Cinema," *The Spectator*, CLVII (December 11),
p. 1037.

Review of *Sabotage* and *The Tenth Man*.

"Movie Memories," *The Spectator*, CLVII (December 11),
p. 1056. (See C207.)

Review of *Movie Parade* by Paul Rotha.

C714   "The Cinema," *The Spectator*, CLVII (December 18),
p. 1081.

Review of *Girls' Dormitory*; *Go West Young Man*; and
Hortobagy.

C715   "The Cinema," *The Spectator*, CLVII (December 25),
p. 1122.

Review of *The Garden of Allah*; *Confetti*; and *Walt
Disney Season*.

1937

C716   "The Cinema," *The Spectator*, CLVIII (January 1), p. 15.

Review of *The Jungle Princess* and *Windbag the Sailor*.

C717   "The Cinema," *The Spectator*, CLVIII (February 5),
        p. 219.

        Review of *Sensation* and *Mazurka*.

C718   "The Cinema," *The Spectator*, CLVIII (February 12),
        p. 267.

        Review of *The Plainsman* and *The Great Barrier*.

C719   "The Cinema," *The Spectator*, CLVIII (February 19),
        p. 312.

        Review of *The Deserter* and *Dreaming Lips*.

C720   "The Cinema," *The Spectator*, CLVIII (February 26),
        p. 356.

        Review of *We from Kronstadt*.

C721   "The Cinema," *The Spectator*, CLVIII (March 5), p. 403.

        Review of *Fire Over England*; *Maid of Salem*; and
        Theodora Goes Wild.

C722   "The Cinema," *The Spectator*, CLVIII (March 19), p. 516.

        Review of *The Luck of the Irish*; *The Sequel to Second
        Bureau*; *Thunder in the City*; and *Head Over Heels*.

C723   "The Cinema," *The Spectator*, CLVIII (March 26), p. 580.

        Review of *Three Smart Girls* and *For Valour*.

C724   "The Cinema," *The Spectator*, CLVIII (April 2), p. 619.

        Review of *The Good Earth* and *Dark Journey*.

C725   "The Cinema," *The Spectator*, CLVIII (April 9), p. 663.

        Review of *Winterset* and **After the Thin Man*.

C726   "The Cinema," *The Spectator*, CLVIII (April 16), p. 707.

        Review of *Elephant Boy*.

C727   "The Cinema," *The Spectator*, CLVIII (April 23), p. 759.

        Review of *Pépé le Moko* and *The Golem*.

C728   "The Cinema," *The Spectator*, CLVIII (April 30), p. 805.

Review of *Lost Horizon.*

C729   "The Cinema," *The Spectator*, CLVIII (May 7), p. 860.

Review of *Generation of Conquerors*; *Lloyds of London*; *The Gap*; and *Glamorous Night.*

C730   "The Cinema: Lenin and Lavender," *Night and Day*, I (July 1), p. 38.

Review of *We from Kronstadt*; *The Frog*; *Make Way for Tomorrow*; and *Der Herrscher.*

C731   "The Cinema: Horror for Adults," *Night and Day*, I (July 8), p. 30.

Review of *Black Legion*; *Night Must Fall*; *Top of the World*; and *The Last Train from Madrid.*

C732   "The Cinema: What Man Has Made of Man," *Night and Day*, I (July 15), p. 30.

Review of *God's Country and the Woman* and *Michael Strogoff.*

C733   "The Cinema: Without Beard or Bed," *Night and Day*, I (July 22), p. 30.

Review of *Parnell* and *Call It a Day.*

C734   "The Cinema: On the West Coast," *Night and Day*, I (July 29), pp. 30-31.

Review of **Secret Lives*; *The High Command*; *On the Avenue*; and *Yiddle with His Fiddle.*

C735   "The Cinema: Tribute to Harpo," *Night and Day*, I (August 12), pp. 30-31.

Review of *A Day at the Races* and *King Solomon's Mines.*

C736   "The Cinema: Pawn's Move and Knight's Move," *Night and Day*, I (August 19), p. 30.

Review of *Slave-Ship*; *Stradivarius*; *Woman Chases Man*; and **Easy Living.*

C737   "The Cinema: What's Left is Celluloid," *Night and Day*, I (August 26), p. 30.

Review of *Saratoga*; *High Wide and Handsome*; and *His Affair.*

C738   "The Cinema: More Song Than Dance," *Night and Day*, I
        (September 2), p. 30.

        Review of *A Castle in Flanders* and *For You Alone*.

C739   "The Cinema: A Flicker from the Flames," *Night and Day*,
        I (September 9), p. 30.

        Review of *Marked Woman*.

C740   "The Cinema: Two English Pictures," *Night and Day*, I
        (September 16), p. 30.

        Review of *Action for Slander* and *Brief Ecstasy*.

C741   "Film Lunch," *Night and Day*, I (September 16), pp. 14-16.

C742   "The Week's Films," *Night and Day*, I (September 30),
        pp. 38-39.

        Review of *Knight Without Armour* and *Café Metropole*.

C743   "The Films," *Night and Day*, I (October 7), p. 38.

        Review of *The Road Back* and *Gangway*.

C744   "The Films," *Night and Day*, I (October 14), p. 39.

        Review of *Big City*; *Tales from the Vienna Woods*; and
        Children at School.

C745   "The Films," *Night and Day*, I (October 21), p. 39.

        Review of *Les Perles de la Couronne* and *Exclusive*.

C746   "The Films," *Night and Day*, I (October 28), p. 31.

        Review of *Wee Willie Winkie* and *The Life of Emile Zola*.

C747   "The Films," *Night and Day*, I (November 4), p. 31.

        Review of *They Won't Forget* and *Nitchevo*.

C748   "Cinema: The Great and the Humble," *Night and Day*, I
        (November 18), p. 38.

        Review of *Land Without Bread* and *Personality Parade*.

C749   "Ideas in the Cinema," *The Spectator*, CLIX (November 19),
        pp. 894-895.

C750   "Cinema," *Night and Day*, I (November 25), p. 31.

        Review of *Dead End*.

C751   "Cinema," *Night and Day*, I (December 2), p. 31.

Review of *Lo Squadrone Bianco.*

C752   "The Films," *Night and Day*, I (December 9), p. 31.

Review of *Un Carnet de Bal* and *Underworld.*

C753   "Cinema," *Night and Day*, I (December 16), pp. 30-31.

Review of *Monica and Martin*; *Mademoiselle Docteur;* and *Eastern Valley.*

C754   "The Films," *Night and Day*, I (December 23), p. 31.

Review of *Marie Walewska* and *True Confession.*

C755   "Selection of Film Criticisms." *Garbo and the Night Watchman: a Selection from the Writings of British and American Film Critics.* Assembled and edited by Alistair Cooke. London: Jonathan Cape, pp. 207-239, 344-346.

Review of *Abyssinia*; *St. Petersburg*; *Song of Ceylon*; *The Case of the Lucky Legs*; *Rose of the Rancho*; *Kliou the Tiger*; *The Petrified Forest*; *Rhythm on the Range*; *Mr. Deeds Goes to Town*; *Nutrition*; *Romeo and Juliet*; *The New Gulliver*; *The Garden of Allah*; and *The Plainsman.*

C756   "Subjects and Stories." *Footnotes to the Film.* Edited by Charles Davy. London: Lovat Dickson, pp. 57-70; New York: Oxford University Press.

1938

C757   "The Cinema," *The Spectator*, CLX (June 10), p. 1056.

Review of *Orage.*

C758   "The Cinema," *The Spectator*, CLX (June 17), p. 1096.

Review of *L'Alibi* and *A Small Case of Murder.*

C759   "The Cinema," *The Spectator*, CLX (June 24), p. 1144.

Review of *From the Manger to the Cross*; *Swing, Sister, Swing*; *Sally, Irene and Mary*; *Sinners in Paradise*; and *The Devil's Party.*

C760   "The Cinema," *The Spectator*, CLXI (July 1), p. 16.

       Review of *L'Homme du Jour* and *You and Me*.

C761   "The Cinema," *The Spectator*, CLXI (August 5), p. 232.

       Review of *Kidnapped* and *I Cover the Waterfront*.

C762   "The Cinema," *The Spectator*, CLXI (August 12), p. 265.

       Review of *Little Tough Guy*; **Gold is Where You Find It*;
       and **Liszt Rhapsody*.

C763   "The Cinema," *The Spectator*, CLXI (August 19), p. 299.

       Review of *Son of Mongolia* and **Battle of Broadway*.

C764   "The Cinema," *The Spectator*, CLXI (August 26), p. 335.

       Review of *Fools for Scandal*; *Booloo*; and *Five Faces*.

       "The Extraordinary Profession," *The Spectator*, CLXI
       (October 21), p. 666. (See C263.)

       Review of *History of the Film* by Maurice Bardeche and
       Robert Brasillach, translated and edited by Iris Barry.

C765   "The Cinema," *The Spectator*, CLXI (November 4), p. 767.

       Review of *Katia*; *Sixty Glorious Years*; and **Old Iron*.

C766   "The Cinema," *The Spectator*, CLXI (November 11), p. 807.

       Review of *You Can't Take It with You* and **There Goes My
       Heart*.

C767   "The Cinema," *The Spectator*, CLXI (November 18), p. 858.

       Review of *Alerte en Méditerranée* and *Men with Wings*.

C768   "The Cinema," *The Spectator*, CLXI (November 25), p. 901.

       Review of *Lenin in October* and **Stranded in Paris*.

                              1939

C769   "The Cinema," *The Spectator*, CLXII (March 3), p. 349.

       Review of *The Dawn Patrol*; *Persons in Hiding*; *Never
       Say Die*; and *Kentucky*.

C770   "The Cinema," *The Spectator*, CLXII (April 7), p. 592.

Review of *Three Smart Girls Grow Up*; *Black Eyes*; and
Inspector Hornleigh.

C771   "The Cinema," *The Spectator*, CLXII (April 14), p. 632.

Review of *Hotel Imperial* and **The Three Musketeers*.

C772   "The Cinema," *The Spectator*, CLXII (April 21), p. 668.

Review of *Idiot's Delight*; *Beach Picnic*; and *They Drive
by Night*.

C773   "The Cinema," *The Spectator*, CLXII (April 28), p. 708.

Review of *The Four Feathers*; *The Sisters*; and *Thanks
for Everything*.

C774   "The Cinema," *The Spectator*, CLXII (May 5), p. 760.

Review of *Wuthering Heights* and *La Bête Humaine*.

C775   "The Cinema," *The Spectator*, CLXII (May 12), p. 804.

Review of *The Oklahoma Kid*; *The Lone Ranger*; and **Tail
Spin*.

C776   "The Cinema," *The Spectator*, CLXII (May 19), p. 852.

Review of *Jamaica Inn*; **J'Etais une Adventuriere*; and
*The Londoners.

C777   "The Cinema," *The Spectator*, CLXII (May 26), p. 901.

Review of New Documentaries by the G.P.O. Film Unit--
Men in Danger; *Spare Time*; *Health of a Nation* (all
privately shown); and *An Elephant Never Forgets*.

C778   "The Cinema," *The Spectator*, CLXII (June 2), p. 957.

Review of *Union Pacific*; *The Lone Ranger*; and
Episode 4.

C779   "The Cinema," *The Spectator*, CLXII (June 9), p. 997.

Review of *The Story of Vernon and Irene Castle* and *La
Femme du Boulanger*.

C780   "The Cinema," *The Spectator*, CLXII (June 16), p. 1036.

Review of *Goodbye, Mr. Chips!*; *Louise*; **You Can't Cheat
an Honest Man*; and **The Good Old Days*.

C781   "The Cinema," *The Spectator*, CLXII (June 23), p. 1088.

Review of *Confessions of a Nazi Spy* and *Hôtel du Nord*.

C782   "The Cinema," *The Spectator*, CLXII (June 30), p. 1128.

Review of *Beethoven*; *Peter the Great*; and *This Man in Paris*.

C783   "The Cinema," *The Spectator*, CLXIII (July 7), p. 15.

Review of *Boy Slaves* and *Captain Fury*.

C784   "The Cinema," *The Spectator*, CLXIII (July 14), p. 52.

Review of *The Hound of the Baskervilles* and *Man of Conquest*.

C785   "The Cinema," *The Spectator*, CLXIII (July 21), p. 92.

Review of *Hostages*; *Undercover Doctor*; *The Modern Miracle*; and *Man About Town*.

C786   "The Cinema," *The Spectator*, CLXIII (July 28), p. 144.

Review of *Le Drame de Shanghai* and *The Rebellious Son*.

C787   "The Cinema," *The Spectator*, CLXIII (August 4), p. 180.

Review of *The Rich Bride*.

C788   "The Cinema," *The Spectator*, CLXIII (August 11), p. 217.

Review of *Beau Geste* and *Un de la Légion*.

C789   "The Cinema," *The Spectator*, CLXIII (August 18), p. 252.

Review of *March of Time*; *Shipyard Sally*; *Blind Alley*; and *There Ain't No Justice*.

C790   "The Cinema," *The Spectator*, CLXIII (August 25), p. 289.

Review of *Les Disparus de St. Agil*; *Young Man's Fancy*; and *Golden Gloves*.

C791   "The Cinema," *The Spectator*, CLXIII (September 1), p. 325.

Review of *Professor Mamlock*; *Dodge City*; and *Five Came Back*.

C792   "The Cinema," *The Spectator*, CLXIII (September 22), p. 408.

Review of *Young Mr. Lincoln* and *I Was a Captive of Nazi Germany*.

C793 "The Cinema," *The Spectator*, CLXIII (September 29), p. 443.

Review of "News Reels"--playing at various cinemas.

C794 "The Cinema," *The Spectator*, CLXIII (October 6), p. 471.

Review of *An Englishman's Home*; *The Face at the Window*; and **L'Homme du Jour*.

C795 "The Cinema," *The Spectator*, CLXIII (October 13), p. 504.

Review of *Ignace*.

C796 "The Cinema," *The Spectator*, CLXIII (October 20), p. 544.

Review of *Stanley and Livingstone* and *Only Angels Have Wings*.

C797 "The Cinema," *The Spectator*, CLXIII (October 27), p. 584.

Review of *Nurse Edith Cavell*; *French Without Tears*; and *'Arf a Mo, Hitler*.

C798 "The Cinema," *The Spectator*, CLXIII (November 3), p. 619.

Review of *The Lion Has Wings*.

C799 "The Cinema," *The Spectator*, CLXIII (November 10), p. 648.

Review of *Daughters Courageous*; *Poison Pen*; and **The First Days*.

C800 "The Cinema," *The Spectator*, CLXIII (November 17), p. 683.

Review of *The Frozen Limits*.

C801 "The Cinema," *The Spectator*, CLXIII (November 24), p. 744.

Review of *Juarez* and **Rulers of the Sea*.

C802 "The Cinema," *The Spectator*, CLXIII (December 1), p. 776.

  Review of *Golden Boy*; *On the Night of the Fire*; and
  **Where's the Fire?*

C803 "The Cinema," *The Spectator*, CLXIII (December 8),
  p. 816.

  Review of **In Name Only*.

C804 "The Cinema," *The Spectator*, CLXIII (December 15),
  p. 864.

  Review of *The Marx Brothers at the Circus*; *Disputed
  Passage*; and *"Paramount News"--at various cinemas.

C805 "The Cinema," *The Spectator*, CLXIII (December 22),
  p. 900.

  Review of *First Love*; **Ducks and Drakes*; *Our Neighbors--
  the Carters*; and **Espionage Agent*.

C806 "The Cinema," *The Spectator*, CLXIII (December 29),
  p. 932.

  Review of **Remontons les Champs-Elysees* and **The Rains
  Came*.

1940

C807 "The Cinema," *The Spectator*, CLXIV (January 5), p. 16.

  Review of *Mr. Smith Goes to Washington* and **Each Dawn
  I Die*.

C808 "The Cinema," *The Spectator*, CLXIV (January 12), p. 44.

  Review of *The Real Glory* and *Twenty-One Days*.

C809 "The Cinema," *The Spectator*, CLXIV (January 19), p. 76.

  Review of *The Light That Failed* and *The Old Maid*.

C810 "The Cinema," *The Spectator*, CLXIV (January 26), p. 108.

  Review of *The Stars Look Down* and *Escape to Happiness*.

C811 "The Cinema," *The Spectator*, CLXIV (February 2), p. 144.

  Review of *The Arsenal Stadium Mystery* and *Pièges*.

C812 "The Cinema," *The Spectator*, CLXIV (February 9), p. 179.

Review of *The Wizard of Oz*; **Dust Be My Destiny*;
*Fifth Avenue Girl; and *African Skyway*.

C813 "The Cinema," *The Spectator*, CLXIV (February 16),
p. 213.

Review of *Dark Rapture*; *Destry Rides Again*; and *The
Hunchback of Notre-Dame*.

C814 "The Cinema," *The Spectator*, CLXIV (February 23),
p. 248.

Review of *Ninotchka*; *On Your Toes*; *A Chump at Oxford*;
and *These Children Are Safe*.

C815 "The Cinema," *The Spectator*, CLXIV (March 1), p. 284.

Review of **The Roaring Twenties*; **Prisons de Femmes*; and
*Hotel for Women.

C816 "The Cinema," *The Spectator*, CLXIV (March 8), p. 328.

Review of *Sherlock Holmes*.

C817 "The Cinema," *The Spectator*, CLXIV (March 15), p. 361.

Review of *The Proud Valley* and **Dead Man's Shoes*.

1958

C818 "The Novelist and the Cinema--A Personal Experience,"
International Film Annual No. 2. Edited by William
Whitebait. London: Calder, pp. 54-61.

1976

"Film Books," *New Statesman* (February 27), p. 259.

Letter *re* Shirley Temple libel suit, Korda and *The
Third Man*. (See C626.)

D

MISCELLANEA

This section lists manuscripts, typescripts, letters, cards
and annotated printed copies in collections. The reader
should note that in some cases the dates appended do not
necessarily reflect the date of composition but may instead
be a record of acquisition. In the case of the material at
the Humanities Research Center, the compiler has selected,
ordered and interpreted information in order that the list
will be of maximum benefit to researchers. Accordingly, this
list does not represent the complete collection, though it
does indicate the scope of the more important areas of the
collection. In the Humanities Research Center list, manuscripts of major works are arranged alphabetically, but all
other areas are arranged chronologically.

The second part of this section lists films with which
Greene has been involved either as screenplay writer or as
producer.

D1 MANUSCRIPTS IN THE COLLECTION OF THE HUMANITIES RESEARCH
CENTER AT AUSTIN, TEXAS

MAJOR WORKS

Brighton Rock

- Page proofs with A corrections (336pp), 1969 (for
  the Collected Edition).

A Burnt-Out Case

- Ams (ii, 122pp) with A inserts (4pp) and A revi-
  sions, June 26, 1959.
- Composite T and Tccms (ii, 182pp) with A revisions,
  nd (pub. 1961); first typescript.
- Tms (ii, 311pp) with A inserts (7pp) and A revi-
  sions, nd (pub. 1961); second typescript.
- Tms (iv, 327pp) with T insert (2pp) and A revisions,
  June 1960; final typescript.
- Proof copy with A emendations and corrections
  (264pp); 1961.

Carving a Statue

- Tms/inc (51pp) with A insert and A revisions,
  (1963-1964); Act I, Scene I missing.
- A play in three acts: Ams (34pp) with T insert and
  A revisions (1963-1964).
- A play in two acts: Tms/mimeo (81pp) with few A
  emendations (1963-1964).
- Act I: Tms (22pp) with A revisions (1964); "first
  corrections."
- Revisions: Tmss (18pp) with A insert and A revisions (1964); "2nd corrections."
- A Play in two acts: Act I: Tms (23pp) with A revisions (1964); "3rd corrections."
- A play in two acts: Tms (81pp) with A emendations,
  (1963-1964); final typescript.
- First page proof with A revisions and corrections
  and A, T and Tcc inserts with A revisions (approx.
  90pp); second page proof unmarked (82pp), 1964.
- First galley proofs with A revisions and corrections and Tcc inserts (39pp); second galley proofs
  unmarked (38pp); second galley proofs with A revisions and corrections and Tcc inserts (38pp), nd.

D1 (cont'd)

- A play in two acts: 1 duplicated production copy
  uncorrected (65pp); 3 duplicated production copies
  with A revisions and T and Tcc inserts with A emendations (66pp); 1 mimeo production copy with A
  revisions (81pp), nd.

Collected Essays

- A, T and Tcmss and printed/inc (approx. 200pp),
  various dates (includes drafts, copies and clippings
  assembled for collection).
- Tms, printed and Xerox (approx. 375pp), nd (printer's
  copy).
- Proof copy with A corrections (436pp), 1968 (included with this: earlier proof of front matter).
- Page proofs with A corrections (436pp), 1968.

Collected Stories

- Printed with A emendations S (3 books), nd (emen-
  dations made in Penguin editions of Greene's May We
  Borrow Your Husband?, A Sense of Reality, and
  Twenty-One Stories).
- Page proofs with A corrections (562pp), 1972 (in-
  cluded with this: corrected proofs of front matter).

The Comedians

- Journal and notes: 1 Ams (11pp); 40 A notes and T
  notes with A revisions, unarranged (August 6-
  August 23, 1963).
- AmsS/first draft with A revisions (194pp), nd.
- Tms/inc with A revisions (63pp), July 22, 1964.
- 2 Tccms with A emendations (487pp), nd; 1 Tccms in
  looseleaf binders.
- Tms with A revisions (421pp), nd.
- Proof copy with A emendations (194pp), nd.
- Blurb: 2Ams with A revisions (1p); 2 Tccms with A
  emendations (1p), nd.

The Complaisant Lover

- Tms/multilith script with Tccms insertion (77pp),
  nd.

The Confidential Agent

- AmsS (i, 118pp) with A insert (2pp) and A revisions,
  nd (pub. 1939).

D1 (cont'd)

> - Printed (Uniform Edition) S with A corrections for
>   Collected Edition (247pp), (1970).
> - Page proofs with A corrections, A and T insert
>   (297pp), 1970.

A Convoy to West Africa

> - Printed with A additions, emendations and notes
>   for reprinting in In Search of a Character (pp. 40-
>   55 of The Mint), nd.

England Made Me

> - Ams (i, 175pp) with A insert (1p) and A revisions,
>   November 16, 1933.
> - Page proofs with A corrections (285pp), 1969 (for
>   the Collected Edition).

A Gun for Sale

> - Ams (i, 132pp) with A revisions, nd (pub. 1936).
> - Page proofs with A corrections (238pp), 1972.
> - Introduction: Tms with A revisions (6pp); Tccms
>   with A emendations (7pp); Tccms/inc with A revi-
>   sions (6pp), October 4, 1972.

The Heart of the Matter

> - Printed with A corrections and T insert (340pp), nd
>   (corrections made in Uniform Edition of the novel
>   for Collected Edition).
> - Page proofs with A corrections (338pp), 1971 (in-
>   cluded with this: layout on front matter; 2 sets
>   of page proofs of front matter with A and T inserts
>   and A corrections. For Collected Edition).

The Honorary Consul

> - (Notes): Ams/notes (34pp in 2 notebooks), nd.
> - AmsS with A revisions (157pp), 1970.
> - Tms/inc with A revisions (154pp), 1970 (first
>   typescript).
> - Tms with A revisions (278pp), 1971 (second
>   typescript).
> - Tms/inc with A revisions (298pp), nd (third
>   typescript).
> - Tms/inc with A revisions (295pp), nd (fourth type-
>   script); included with this: map of, and newspapers
>   from, Corrientes, Argentina, with translation of
>   article.

D1 (cont'd)

- Tms/inc with A revisions (302pp), 1972 (fifth typescript).
- Tms with A revisions (350pp), 1972 (final typescript).
- Tms/inc with A revisions (98pp), nd (discarded pages from various typings).
- Page proofs with A corrections (335pp), 1973.
- Galley proofs with A corrections (212 sheets), 1973; included with these: ALS Raymond Greene to Graham Greene.

In Search of a Character: Two African Journals

- (Convoy to West Africa Journal): Ams/notebook (64pp), December 9 (1941)–March 8 (1942); notes and printed items loosely laid in.
- (Congo Journal): Ams (62pp) with A emendations, February–March, 1959.
- (Congo Journal): Tms (ii, 55pp) with A t.p. and A revisions, nd (pub. 1961).
- Page proofs (125pp) with A revisions, 1961.

It's a Battlefield

- Ams (i, 125pp) with A inserts (5pp) and A emendations, September 13, 1932–August 4, 1933.
- Tms/inc (135pp, including one A page) with A emendations, nd (pub. 1934).
- Page proofs with A corrections (237pp), 1969 (for the Collected Edition; includes 1st and 2nd proofs of front matter and introduction).

Journey Without Maps
- (notes): Ams (c. 80pp), January 11–March 11 (pub. 1936); cover sheet headed "Notes for 'Journey in the Dark.'"
- Ams (183pp) with A revisions, nd (pub. 1936).

The Lawless Roads

- Ams/inc (127pp) with printed inserts pasted on some pages and A revisions, nd (pub. 1939).

The Little Horsebus

- Ams/inc (18pp) with few A sketches, nd (pub. 1952); first draft.
- Ams (42pp) with few A sketches, nd (pub. 1952).

D1 (cont'd)

The Little Steamroller

- Ams (36pp) with few A sketches, nd (pub. 1953).

The Little Train

- Ams/inc (42pp, 4"x6"), nd (pub. 1947); pp. 32-33 missing.

The Living Room

- (Notes): Ams/notes (2pp), nd (first sketch out of the play).
- Mimeo script (80pp), June 19, 1952 (typing service stamp); not final version.

Lord Rochester's Monkey

- (Dorimant: A Restoration Portrait, Being the Life of John Wilmot, Second Earl of Rochester): Ams (160pp) with 2 tpp and A revisions, June 10, 1931.
- (Rochester: A Restoration Portrait: Notes): Amss (c. 150pp), nd.
- (Rochester: A Restoration Portrait; Being the Life of John Wilmot, Second Earl of Rochester): Tms (324pp in 4v.) with appendix and bibliography (65pp in 1v.) and A emendations, nd.
- A & Tms/miscellaneous pages with A revisions (15pp), nd (included with these: TLS/Xerox Greene's secretary to Texas. University. Humanities Research Center).
- (Bibliography): Ams (10pp); Tms/Xerox (11pp), nd.
- Tms with A revisions/Xerox (337pp), nd.
- TMS with A revisions (288pp), 1973 (retyping of Xerox copy; included with this: 28 discarded pages).
- Galley proofs with A revisions and corrections and T inserts (61 sheets), nd.
- Page proofs with A emendations and corrections (226pp), 1974.

The Man Within

- Ams (165pp) with A inserts (2pp) and A revisions, nd (pub. 1929).

D1 (cont'd)

May We Borrow Your Husband?

- Proof copy with A corrections and revisions (188pp), 1967.
- (May We Borrow Your Husband; short story): AmsS with revisions (25pp); Tms with A revisions (36pp), nd.
- (Chagrin in Three Parts; short story): Ams with A revisions (7pp); Tms with A revisions (11pp); Tccms with A emendations (11pp), nd.
- (Cheap in August; short story): Ams with A revisions (20pp); Tms with A revisions (34pp); Bound mimeo with A emendations (46pp), nd.
- (Cheap in August; London Magazine): Tms (47pp), nd.
- (Cheap in August): Galley proofs with A emendations and corrections (8pp), nd.
- (Doctor Crombie; short story): Ams with A revisions (8pp); Tms/inc with A revisions (pp 1-6, 8-9); Tccms with A emendations (9pp), nd.
- (The Invisible Japanese Gentlemen; short story): Ams with A revisions (5pp); Tms with A revisions (6pp), nd.
- (Mortmain; short story): Ams with A revisions (12pp); Tms with A emendations (12pp), nd.
- (The Over-Night Bag; short story): Ams with A revisions (7pp); Tms with A revisions and 1 extra page (8pp); Tccms with A emendations (8pp), nd.
- (Root of All Evil; short story): Tms with A revisions (16pp); Bound duplicated copy with A emendations (21pp), nd.

The Ministry of Fear

- Ams (136pp) with A inserts (4pp) and A revisions (1942).
- Page proofs with A corrections (271pp), 1972 (included with this: 2 galley proofs of introduction with A corrections, 3 sheets each).

The Name of Action

- Ams S with A revisions and illustrations (175pp), 1929-1930 (inscribed "For Vivienne" October 15, 1930).

D1 (cont'd)

Our Man in Havana

- (Novel): Ams/inc (76pp) with A inserts (13pp) and
  A revisions, nd (pub. 1958).
- (Novel): Composite A and Tms/working draft (331pp)
  with A revisions, nd (pub. 1958).
- (Blurb): Tms with A revisions (1p), nd.
- Page proofs with A corrections (280pp), 1969 (for
  the Collected Edition; includes 1st and 2nd proofs
  of front matter and introduction).

The Potting Shed

- (Play): Tms/mimeo (119pp) with Tms/mimeo inserts
  (4pp) and few A emendations, nd (pub. 1958).
- Tms/mimeo script (101pp), nd.

The Power and the Glory

- (A new novel): Ams (i, 137pp, [including one T page])
  with A revisions, nd (pub. 1940).
- Printed (Uniform Edition) S with A corrections for
  Collected Edition (290pp, 1970).
- Page proofs with A corrections (303pp), 1970–1971
  (for Collected Edition).

The Quiet American

- Page proofs with A corrections (221pp), 1972.

Rumour at Nightfall

- (A new novel): Ams/inc (i, 164pp) with A revisions,
  September 5, 1930–April 27, 1931 (pp. 129–130
  missing).

A Sense of Reality

- (Under the Garden; Dream of a Strange Land; A
  Discovery in the Woods): Amss (53, 10, 18pp) with
  A revisions, nd (pub. 1963).
- (Under the Garden; Dream of a Strange Land; A
  Discovery in the Woods): Tmss (67, 17, 25pp) with
  A revisions. No date. (and) A Sense of Reality.
  Page proofs (140pp) with A corrections, 1963.
- (Under the Garden; A Visit to Morin; Dream of a
  Strange Land; A Discovery in the Woods): Tmss
  (111, 27, 26, 38pp) with A emendations, nd (pub.
  1963).

D1 (cont'd)

     - (Under the Garden; Dream of a Strange Land; A
      Discovery in the Woods): Tmss (67, 17, 25pp) with
      A revisions, nd (pub. 1963).
     - Page proofs (140pp) with A corrections, 1963.
     - (Blurb): Tms with A revisions (1p), 1962.

A *Sort of Life*

     - A and Tms/inc with A revisions (85pp), nd (first
      version).
     - A, T and Tccms/inc with A revisions (50pp), nd
      (early miscellaneous draft pages).
     - T and Tccms/inc with A revisions (45pp), nd (first
      draft typescript).
     - A and Tms/inc with A revisions (101pp), nd
      (second typescript).
     - Tms/inc with A revisions and Ams page (142pp), nd
      (third typescript).
     - T and Tccms/inc with A revisions (187pp), nd (one
      page photocopy; fourth typescript).
     - Tccms and Tccms/photostat/inc with A revisions
      (176pp), nd (included with this: Tms/notes to
      typist; fifth typescript).
     - Tms with A revisions (182pp), nd (included with
      these: revision pages; sixth typescript).
     - Tms with A emendations and printer's marks (248pp),
      June 1970 (included with this: Tccms of new pages
      245-246; final typescript).
     - Tccms with A revisions and T insert (183pp), nd.
     - Page proofs with A corrections and T insert (256pp),
      1970 (contains duplicate pages and pulled pages for
      revision).
     - Galley proofs with A corrections and T inserts
      (129pp; 1970).
     - (Insert for future editions): Ams with A revisions
      (2pp; September 1971).

A *Spy's Bedside Book*

     - (Introduction): Ams with A revisions (2pp); TmsS
      with A revisions (3pp), nd.

Stamboul Train

     - Ams (i, 135pp) with A revisions, January 2, 1932.
     - TmsS with inscription to Rupert Hart-Davis (322pp),
      nd.

D1 (cont'd)

Travels with My Aunt

- (Notes): Ams (4pp), February 18, 1969.
- (Notes): Ams/notes (17pp in notebook), nd.
- AmsS with A revisions (147pp), nd.
- Tms with A revisions (291pp), nd.
- T and Tccms with A and T revisions (331pp), nd ("2nd revision").
- 2 Galley proofs with A corrections (197 sheets), 1969.
- (Blurb ?): Ams (1p), nd.

SCREENPLAYS

Brighton Rock

- (Screenplay): Tms/mimeo (114pp) with T insert and A emendations, nd (prod. 1947; 3rd shooting script, by Roy Boulting, from the screenplay by Graham Greene).
- (Screenplay): Tms (79pp) with T inserts (3pp) with A revisions, nd (prod. 1947; second film treatment).

The Comedians

- (Film play): T and Tccms/rough draft/inc with A revisions (91pp), nd.
- (Film play): A, T and Tccms/first version with A revisions (293pp), nd.
- (Film play: story line): A, T and Tccms/inc with A revisions (19pp); Tms/inc with A revisions and Tccms duplicate page (17pp), nd.
- (Film play: story line - No. 2): Tccms/inc with A revisions (14pp), nd.
- (Film play: story line - No. 3): Tccms/inc (28pp), nd.
- (Film play: story line - No. 4): Tccms/inc with A revisions (51pp), nd.
- (Screenplay [1]): Duplicated (165pp), nd.
- (Screenplay [2]): Duplicated with A revisions and A and Tcc revisions laid in (181pp), July 1, 1966.
- (Screenplay [3]): Duplicated with A revisions and A and Tcc revisions laid in (170pp), September 1, 1966.
- (Screenplay [4]): Duplicated with A revisions and A, Tcc and mimeo revisions laid in (165pp), December 1, 1966.

D1 (cont'd)

- (Motion picture version): 12 A.T. and Tccms/frag-
  ments with A revisions (192pp), nd.
- (Motion picture version): Tccms/screenplay/inc with
  A revisions (143pp), nd.
- (Motion picture version): Tccms/rough draft/inc
  with heavy A revisions (272pp), nd.
- (Motion picture version): Tccms/rough draft (2)/inc
  with heavy A revisions (227pp), nd.

The Living Room

- (Screenplay): 5 Ams/fragments and notes with A
  revisions (221pp), nd.
- (Screenplay): Duplicated (100pp), nd; Tccms revisions laid in (24 pp).
- (Screenplay): Xerox (107pp), nd.
- (Screenplay: Version A): Duplicated with A emendations (107pp), 1961.

No Man's Land

- (Film story): Ams with A revisions (30pp); Tms with
  A revisions (49pp), nd.

Our Man in Havana

- (Screenplay): Composite Ams (177pp) and proof
  sheets (?), (35pp) working draft with A revisions,
  nd ("1st draft").
- (Screenplay): Tms mimeo (iv, 143pp) with Tcc insert
  (1p) and few A emendations, January 12, 1959.
- (Screenplay): Scenes 18-22B. Tccms (4pp), nd.
- (Screenplay): Composite Ams (177pp) proof sheets
  (?), (35pp) working draft with A revisions, nd.
- (Screenplay: Notes): Ams (5pp), nd.

The Stranger's Hand

- (Story): Ams/fragment with A revisions (30pp), nd
  (film with Trevor Howard based on this story).
- (Commentary [?] on The Stranger's Hand): 2 Ams/
  drafts/unfinished (1p each); 1 A and Tccms/draft/
  unfinished (1p; 1954).

The Third Man

- (Story): Mimeo (127pp), June 2, 1948.
- (Treatment): Mimeo (120pp), nd.

D1 (cont'd)

>   - (Draft script 1): Mimeo (128pp), nd.
>   - (Draft script 2): Mimeo (98pp), September 20, 1948.
>   - (Release script): Mimeo (173pp), nd.

>   *Saint Joan*

>   - (Adapted for the screen by Graham Greene):
>   Composite A, Tcc and printed page Mss with A revi-
>   sions; 1st draft (107pp); 2nd draft (36pp); 3rd
>   draft (90pp), nd (prod. 1957).

INTRODUCTIONS

>   - *It's a Battlefield*: Tccms with A revisions (4pp), nd.

>   - *Brighton Rock*: Ams with A revisions (6pp): Tccms with
>   A revisions (8pp; 1962); included with this: 2 Tms
>   lists.

>   - *A Burnt-Out Case*: Ams with A revisions (4pp; 1963).

>   - *Collected Stories*: Ams/draft with A revisions (6pp);
>   Tms with A revisions (7pp), nd.

>   - *The Confidential Agent*: Ams with A revisions (4pp;
>   1962).

>   - *The Confidential Agent*: Tms with A revisions (6pp);
>   Tccms with A revisions (6pp), nd.

>   - *The End of the Affair*: Ams with A revisions (4pp;
>   1963).

>   - *England Made Me*: Ams with A revisions (4pp); Tccms
>   with A revisions (5pp; 1962).

>   - *A Gun for Sale*: Ams with A revisions (5pp; 1962).

>   - *The Heart of the Matter*: Ams with A revisions (4pp;
>   1963).

>   - *The Heart of the Matter* (for Collected Edition): A
>   and Tccms/draft with A revisions (9pp); Tms with A
>   revisions (8pp); Tccms/fragment (1p), 1970.

D1 (cont'd)

- *Journey Without Maps*: Ams with A revisions (5pp; 1963).

- *The Man Within*: Ams with A revisions (6pp; 1962).

- *The Ministry of Fear*: Ams with A revisions (7pp; 1962).

- *The Ministry of Fear*: Tms with A emendations (8pp); Tccms with A emendations (9pp); Tccms with A revisions (9pp), October 5, 1972.

- *Our Man in Havana*: Ams with A revisions (11pp); Tccms with A revisions (15pp; 1963).

- *The Pleasure-Dome*: Ams/draft with A revisions (5pp); Tms/draft with A revisions, 1972.

- *The Power and the Glory*: Tms with A emendations (5pp); Tccms with A revisions (5pp), nd.

- *The Quiet American*: Ams with A revisions (6pp); Tms with A revisions (19pp; 1963).

- *The Quiet American*: 1 Tms with A emendations (24pp); 2 Tccmss with A revisions (24pp each), October 10, 1972.

- *Stamboul Train*: Ams with A revisions (5pp; 1962).

INTRODUCTIONS TO BOOKS BY OTHER AUTHORS

- *Father Six* by Monsignor Olichon: Ams with A revisions (5pp; 1954).

- *God Protect Me from My Friends* by Gavin Maxwell: Ams/inc with A emendations (1p; 1956).

- *Cafe Royal Story*, Preface: Ams with A revisions (2pp); Tcc with A emendations (3pp; April 1962).

- *Parades' End* by Ford Madox Ford: A and Tms/draft with A revisions (7pp; 1962).

D1 (cont'd)

- *Les Oeuvres Choisis*: Ams with A revisions (2pp); Tms with A revisions (1p), 1964.

- *Papa Doc* by Bernard Diedrich: Ams with A revisions (3pp); Tms with A revisions (4pp), 1969.

- *The Snailwatcher and Other Stories* by Patricia Highsmith: Ams with A revisions (2pp); Tccms with A emendations (2pp; 1970).

- *Diplomat* by Gunnar Hagglof: Ams and printed/draft with A revisions (3pp); Tms/draft with A revisions (3pp), 1972.

- *With All Faults* by David Low: Ams/draft with A revisions (4pp); Tms/draft with A revisions (6pp); Tms/ printer's copy (6pp), 1972.

- Luciano d'Allesandro's book of Capri photographs: AmsS with A revisions (2pp), March 1972.

- *The Sign of the Four* by Conan Doyle: Ams with A revisions (3pp; 1973).

REVIEWS

- *Stephen Crane* by John Berryman: Ams with A revisions (2pp; 1951).

- *Obscenity and the Law* by Norman St. John Stevas: Ams with A revisions (3pp; 1956).

- *Desert Lore* by Henry de Montherlant: Ams with A revisions (3pp; 1957).

- *South-East Asia in Turmoil* by Brian Crozier: Ams/draft with A revisions (2pp); Tms/draft S with A revisions (3pp; 1965).

- *Pinorman*: a composite portrait by Richard Aldington: Tms (8pp); Galley proofs (3 sheets; 1966).

- *The Week* by Patricia Cockburn: Ams/draft with A revisions (2pp; 1968).

D1 (cont'd)

- *Judgment on Deltchev* by Eric Ambler; Ams/draft with A revisions (2pp; 1968).

- *One for the Devil* by Etienne Leroux; Ams/draft with A revisions (2pp); Tms/draft with A revisions (3pp; 1968).

- *The Loss of Eldorado* by V.S. Naipaul; Ams/draft with revisions (2pp); Tccms (2pp; 1969).

- *To Beg I Am Ashamed* by Sheila Cousins; Ams with A revisions (2pp), nd.

- *Desert Calling* by Anne Fremantle; Ams with A revisions (2pp), nd.

LETTERS

- to American Academy of Arts and Letters: AL/draft; TLS/draft (May 19, 1970).

- to Ernest F(rancis) Amy: 2 TLS; TLS "D. R. Tower" (secretary), October 21, 1955; October 28, 1955; March 20, 1956.

- to George Barker: 5 ALS; 1 TLS, 5 inc d (1967)-1968.

- to Edmund (Charles) Blunden: 4 TLS, August 3, 1944; January 24, 1955; March 21, 1957; August 18, 1957.

- to Elizabeth Bowen: ALS, April 13, ____.

- to John Carter: 1 TLS; 1 TL/copy, December 20, 1968; January 17, 1969 (included with these: TccL Carter to Greene, December 31, 1968).

- to Richard Church: TLS, July 16, 1945 (letterhead: Eyre & Spottiswoode).

- to Devis Cohen: TLS, February 2, 1955 (ANI Cohen to John Hayward at bottom).

- to Barbara Cooper: TLS (by secretary), November 5, 1946; May 29, 1947.

D1 (cont'd)

- to Nancy Cunard: TLS, February 19, 1945 (letterhead: Eyre & Spottiswoode).

- to The Editor, The Daily Telegraph: TL/draft, (August 1964; included with this: AL/draft).

- to The Editor, The Daily Telegraph: AL/draft S, (July 7, 1965).

- to The Editor, the Daily Telegraph: 2 TccL, May 27, 1966; June 4, 1966 (by secretary; included with these: AL/draft of May 27 letter).

- to Ronald Duncan: 2 TLS, October 21, 1957; October 24, 1957 (*re* Ezra Pound).

- to Constantine FitzGibbon: 3 TLS, November 4, 1965; November 21, 1966; December 12, 1966; 1 by secretary (included with these: TccL FitzGibbon to Greene).

- to Geoffrey Grigson: TLS, April 5, 1945 (letterhead: Eyre and Spottiswoode).

- to Vivien (Dayrell-Browning) Greene: 572 ALS; 3 ALS/inc; 6 ALI; 132 AL; 6 AL/inc; 47 Telegrams, 113 nd; 175 inc d 1925-1927 (most dates of letters added later).

- to Vivien (Dayrell-Browning) Greene: TLS from Hilary Trench (Greene pseudonym), nd.

- to John Hayward: 2 ALS; 3 TLS; 5 APCS; 2APC; 1 Printed PC; 1 Christmas card, 3 nd; 2 inc d 1931-1963.

- to John Hayward: TLS, August 26, 1952 (written on verso: notes *re The Living Room*).

- to John Hayward: TLS, December 15, 1952.

- to John Hayward: TLS, July 15, 1956.

- to John Hayward: TLS, June 19, 1959 (*re* his *The Complaisant Lover*).

- John Hayward: APCS, January 27, 1961 (postmark).

D1 (cont'd)

- (directed to Emmet Hughes) to Time-Life, Inc.: 3 ALS;
  10 TLS, 3 inc d 1950-1952.

- to Klaus W. Jonas: TLS, March 29, ____.

- to John Lehmann: 4 ALS; 8 TLS; 1 APCI, 3 nd; 3 inc d
  (1941-1946); 3 TLS by secretary.

- to John Lehmann: 2 TLS, July 28, 1952; August 1,
  1952 (enclosure).

- to John Lehmann: 21 TLS; 1 TL; 1 TPCS, 1954-1959;
  TPCS and TL by secretary (written on these: 5 ANI
  and 4 AN Lehmann to secretary and others; 1 AL/draft
  of reply by Lehmann).

- to John Lehmann: TLS, December 16, ____.

- to The London Magazine: TLS; TPCS D. R. Young
  (secretary), November 12, 1956; December 10 (1956).

- to Frederic Sawrey Lowndes: ALS, nd.

- to Mrs. Marie Adelaide (Belloc) Lowndes: 7 ALS; 1 TLS,
  5 nd; 2 inc d (c. 1930)-1945.

- to Faith Compton Mackenzie: TLS, October 30, ____.

- to Julian Maclaren-Ross: TLS, May 23, 1962.

- to André Malraux: TLS/draft; TccL (June 23, 1960;
  titled: An Open Letter to André Malraux).

- to Lady Ottoline (Violet Anne [Cavendish-Bentinck])
  Morrell: 10 ALS, 2 nd; 8 inc d (1930-1933).

- to Ferenc Munnich: A Telegram/draft; T Telegram/
  draft, September 26, 1957.

- to New Statesman: TL/draft (September 20, 1957;
  titled: Freedom and Justice in Ghana).

- to New Statesman: TL/draft (September 28, 1957;
  titled: Greene and Shaw).

- to The Editor, New Statesman: AL/draft (July 19, 1966).

D1 (cont'd)

- to Sylva Norman: ALS, June 22 (1933).

- (directed to Hermon Ould) to PEN: ALS, December 17 (1935).

- to Herbert Edward Palmer: ALS, nd (included with this: a note of explanation by Palmer on envelope and printed clipping of Greene poem The Unconquered).

- to A. D. Peters: 5 ALS (c. 1924-1925).

- to William (Charles Franklyn) Plomer: ALS, nd.

- to J(ohn) B(oynton) Priestley: TLS, September 10, 1954.

- to John Ramington: ALS/copy, October 17, 1974.

- (directed to Max Reinhardt) to The Bodley Head: 2 TLS, June 3, 1957; September 3, 1957.

- to Francis Warren Roberts: TLS "Josephine Reid" (secretary), April 29, 1963.

- to Francis Warren Roberts: TLS, May 8, 1963.

- (directed to Alan Ross) to London Magazine: 7 TLS, 1965-1971, 5 by or signed by secretary (included with these: TLS Laurence Pollinger Ltd. to London Magazine).

- to Rolfe Arnold Scott-James: ALS, October 6, ____.

- to Edith Sitwell: 2 ALS; 3 TLS; 1 ANS, 3 nd 1958; ANS co-signed by Sherman and Jeanne (included with these: TLS Josephine Reid [Greene's secretary] to Edith Sitwell, March 13, 1959).

- to The Editor, The Spectator: AL/draft (September 22, 1967).

- to The Spectator: AL/draft (September 19, 1970).

- to The Spectator: AL/draft, July 7, 1972.

- to The Spectator: ALI/draft (September 2, 1972).

D1 (cont'd)

- to Derek Stanford: TLS, October 25, 1954 (enclosed
  with this: TLS Greene to Muriel Spark; same date).

- to Noel Stock: TLS, December 18, 1964 (included in
  Noel Stock: correspondence concerning Pound
  Festschrift).

- to L(eonard) A(lfred) G(eorge) Strong: 3 ALS, 2 nd;
  December 20, _____ (included with 1 undated: sonnet).

- to Time, the weekly news-magazine: AL/draft, March 31,
  1973 (titled: A Question of Semantics).

- to The Times: TL/draft (July 20, 1964).

- to The Editor, The Times: TL/draft 5, October 29, 1964
  (included with this: AL/draft).

- to The Editor, The Times: AL/draft; TL/draft; Tele-
  gram/draft S, nd (September 4, 1967; August 15,
  1969; included with these: AL/draft of September 4,
  1967 letter).

- to The Editor, The Times: AL/draft (December 29, 1967).

- to The Editor, The Times: AL/draft S (January 12,
  1970).

- to The Times: ALS/draft (May 11, 1970).

- to The Times: ALS/draft (September 17, 1970).

- to The Times: AL/draft (February 23, 1971).

- to The Times: AL/draft (September 1971; included with
  this: TccL/version for The Telegraph, unpublished).

- to The Times: AL/draft (November 26, 1971).

- to The Times: AL/draft (October 17, 1972; included
  with this: ALS W. Graham Greene [his uncle] to Graham
  Greene referred to in the above letter).

- to The Times: AL/draft (January 10, 1973).

- to The Times: TL/draft (February 15, 1973; written
  with this: TL/draft to Ludek Pachman).

D1 (cont'd)

- to Times Literary Supplement: TL/draft, July 18, 1966.

- to Times Literary Supplement: AL/draft (October 26, 1970).

- to T(imes) L(iterary) S(upplement): AL/draft (December 1, 1972).

- to Mrs. Westerling: APCS, June 1934 ?

- to Wiadomosci: TLS, April 5, 1949 (*re* Joseph Conrad).

- to an unidentified editor: AL/draft, nd.

- to an unidentified editor: Ams with A revisions (3pp), nd (A Nation's Conscience: seemingly a letter to an editor).

- to an unidentified recipient: TL by I. A. Iversen with Ams/note in hand of Graham Greene, nd.

DIARIES/JOURNALS/NOTEBOOKS

- Diaries: 2 Ams/notebooks (367pp), 1932-1933 (few entries torn out).

- Notebook: Ams with paste-ins (22pp), 1936 (loosely laid in: 2 Ams, 2 printed items).

- Journal: The Defenders (Notes From a Journal of the Blitz 1940-1941), Ams with A revisions (13pp), 1940-1941.

- Notebook: Table Talk, Ams (3pp in notebook), nd (in Sierra Leone notebook [W.W. II]).

- Journal: During the Second Siege of London, Ams (15pp), June 22-July 18, 1944 (in bound notebook).

- Diaries: 54 small pocket diaries with A entries, 1957-1972 (each has a monthly list of books read by Greene).

- Journal: Saigon, Ams (26pp), December 30 (1962?)-January 15 (1963?).

D1 (cont'd)

- Journal: Mexico City, Bombay, etc., Ams (22pp),
  July 21 (1963?)-January 1 (1964?).

- Diary: Indo-China, Ams (5pp), nd.

- Places: Tms/thermofax copy with A revisions (9pp),
  nd (includes observations under the following additional headings: other writers, his own work, religion, politics, marriage, doctors, theatre).

MISCELLANEOUS

- For Vivienne: A Private Book, Which Will Never End.
  All the Verses, Indiscriminate of Value, Which You
  Caused: Ams/fair copies with subsequent copies and
  paste-ins (49pp); Christmas 1926 with additions to
  1932.

- The Empty Chair (detective story): Ams/inc with A
  revisions (56pp; 1926).
- Fantastic Arabia; a novel: Ams/fragment with A revisions (pp. 1, 8-14; 1933).

- Graham Greene's reply with replies by others, to
  Cyril Connolly Symposium and questionnaire (Horizon):
  A and TmssS replies (15 items). Replies by E.M.
  Forster, Osbert Sitwell, Lord David Cecil, Kathleen
  Raine, Clive Bell, Maurice Baring, Graham Greene,
  David Gascoyne, Philip Toynbee, Charles Morgan, C.W.
  Wedgwood, Enid Starkie, A.L. Rowse, John Lehmann,
  V.S. Pritchett, and Elizabeth Bowen (1945).

- Never, never continued: Ams/fragment with A revisions
  (1p; c. 1952).

- (Untitled article on Mrs. Newall): Ams with A revisions (4pp), 1954.

- Song for Three Ageing Voices: Tms (2pp; December 1,
  1954 publication); included with this: ALI/cover
  letter to typist.

- The Man Who Stole the Eiffel Tower (short story):
  Ams/draft with A revisions (8pp, the first page
  written on a picture postcard of the Eiffel Tower),
  September 19, 1956.

D1 (cont'd)

- The Horror Comic (a play): Ams/fragment with A revisions (3pp), November 1, 1956.

- (Greetings to Russia on 40th Anniversary of the Revolution): Ams with A revisions (2pp), 1957.

- The Writer and the Cinema: Ams with A revisions (9pp), 1958.

- Week-end Competition 1,621: AmsS (1p), 1961.

- May We Borrow Your Husband?: Tms (59pp; 1962).

- Mr. Conway's Congress (short story): Ams/inc with A revisions (23pp); Tms/inc with A revisions and T insert with A emendations (35pp; 1962).

- The Revenge: Ams with A revisions (3pp); proofs with Ams design (8pp), 1963.

- The Fall of Dien Bien Phu: Ams with A revisions (6pp); Tccms with A emendations (8pp; 1963).

- Week-end competition 1,709: 2 Tms/drafts with A revisions (1p each), 1963.

- A Birthday in October: Ams with A revisions (2pp); Tccms (4pp; 1964).

- A Birthday in October: Tccms (4pp; January 1964).

- Goa the Unique: Ams with A revisions (4pp); Tms/first draft with A revisions (8pp); Tccms/second draft/inc with A revisions (3pp), 1964; included with these: Tccms captions for illustrations.

- The Rude Mechanicals: Ams with A revisions (2pp); Tms with A revisions (4pp), 1964.

- Week-end Competition 1,850: AmsS with A revisions (2pp), 1965.

- Two Gentle People: Tms with A revisions and A note I on title page (12pp), August 17, 1966.

- Two Gentle People: Ams with A revisions (8pp), nd (included with this: A notes dated July 1966).

D1 (cont'd)

- (Address at University of Edinburgh): Ams with A
  revisions (5pp); Tms with A revisions (3pp); Tms
  (4pp; 1967).

- An Incident in Sinai: Ams with A revisions (7pp);
  Tccms with A revisions (12pp), 1967.

- (address Upon Receipt of Hamburg Shakespeare Prize):
  Ams/draft with A revisions (3pp); Tms/first version
  with A revisions (4pp); Tms/second version with A
  emendations (5pp); Tccms/second version (5pp);
  June 6, 1969.

- A Christmas Broadcast by Henry II: Ams/draft with A
  revisions (1p); Tccms (1p; 1970); for New Statesman
  competition (included with these: printed page of
  winning entries).

- Books of the Year: Ams/draft with A revisions (1p);
  Tccms (1p), 1970; for The Observer.

- New Statesman Week-end Competition 2,116: Ams/draft
  with A revisions (1p; 1970).

- The Dangerous Edge: Ams (16pp), 1971; diary of trip
  to Chile.

- Chile: The Dangerous Edge: Ams/draft with A revisions
  (5pp); Tms with A revisions (9pp); Tms/duplicated with
  A emendations (10pp); Tms/duplicated with A revisions
  (9pp; October 1971).

- S(olzhenitsyn)'s Nobel Speech: Ams/draft with A revisions (2pp on 1; 1972); for BBC foreign broadcasts.

- Go Slow at Clapham Junction: Ams/draft with A revisions (1p), June 19, 1972.

- A Personal Foreword: Ams with A revisions (4pp);
  Tms with A emendations (5pp), February 12, 1973.

- (The Assumption of Mary) The Mother of God: Ams with
  A revisions and A and T inserts with A revisions
  (7pp), nd.

D1 (cont'd)

- The Clever Twist; a melodrama in 3 acts: Ams/fragment
  with A revisions (8pp), nd (enclosed with this: A
  notes [3pp]).

- Dear Dr. Falkenheim ...: AmsS with A revisions (6pp);
  Tms (8pp), nd.

- Death of a Widow's Son: Tccms with A revisions (9pp),
  nd.

- The Destructors (short story): Ams with A revisions
  (13pp), nd.

- Epitaph for a Play: Ams with A revisions (5pp); Tccms
  (3pp), nd (concerns the play Carving a Statue).

- For a Home Sickness: Ams (1p), nd (for Vivien Dayrell-
  Browning).

- (The Heart of the Matter: dramatization): Ams/frag-
  ment (4pp); Tms/fragment with A revisions (3pp), nd.

- House of Reputation; a play in three acts: Ams/inc
  with A revisions and A inserts (43pp); Tms/inc (69pp),
  nd.

- (A Hundred Yards from Picadilly) The Strange West End:
  Ams with A revisions (3pp); Tms with A emendations
  (4pp), nd (original title: The Strange West End).

- John Hayward, Book Collector: Ams with A revisions
  (3pp); Tms with A revisions (3pp), nd.

- The Lotus Land: Ams with A revisions (4pp); Tms/
  second version with A revisions (9pp); Tms/third
  version with A revisions (10pp), nd (included with
  these: Ams list of illustrations).

- Lucius (a novel): Ams/fragment with A revisions
  (52pp), nd.

- (Untitled Story): Ams/inc with A revisions (11pp), nd
  (short story, Men at Work, extracted from this).

- Mr. Cinderella: Ams (1p); Tms (1p), nd.

D1 (cont'd)

- (The Nightmare Republic; article): Ams with A revisions (6pp); Tms with A revisions (10pp); Tms with A revisions (9pp), nd.

- Oh, Damn Your Morality; a comedy in three acts: Ams/fragment with A revisions (1p); A note (1p), nd.

- Paper on General Views and Opinions: Ams/answers (2pp), September 19__.

- The Paradox: Ams (2pp), nd (for Vivien Dayrell-Browning).

- Pius XII: The Paradox of the Pope (magazine article): Tms with A revisions (16pp); Tms with A revisions (7pp), nd.

- Prologue to Pilgrimage (novel): Tms with A emendations (243pp; c. 1924).

- Reading at Night: Tccms (9pp), nd.

- Reading at Night (short story): Ams with A revisions (5pp); Tms with A revisions (6pp); bound and duplicated copy with A revisions (10pp), nd.

- (Regina vs. Sir James Barrie): Ams with A revisions (3pp); Tms with A revisions (5pp), nd.

- Return to Havana (article): Ams with A revisions (7pp); Tms with A revisions (9pp); Tms with A revisions (6pp), nd.

- The Revolver in the Corner Cupboard: An Autobiographical Sketch: Ams with A revisions (3pp), nd.

- Secrets: Ams with A revisions (12pp), nd (title The Secret Society deleted).

- Security in Room 51: Ams with A revisions (3pp); Tms with A revisions (3pp), 1963.

- A Shocking Accident: Ams with A revisions (5pp); Tccms (11pp), nd.

- Song of the Cultivators: Ams (3pp), nd (written with this: Ams/notes 4pp).

D1 (cont'd)

- Sonnet: Ams, nd (enclosed with ALS to L.A.G. Strong, nd).

- The Tenth Man: Tccms (90pp), nd (included with this: TLS Laurence Pollinger Limited to Jill Phillips *re* copyright March 30, 1967).

- To You Being a Hideous Way Off: Ams (1p), nd (for Vivien Dayrell-Browning).

- Two Reasons for Not Writing Verse to You: Ams (1p), nd (for Vivien Dayrell-Browning).

- The Virtue of Disloyalty: Tms and printed with A revisions (5pp); Galley proofs/inc (5 sheets).

- A Visit to Poland (article): Ams with A revisions (5pp), nd.

- The Word PTERODACTYL or a Man of Extremes (novel); Ams/fragment with A revisions (27pp); A notes (4pp); nd (included with this: A Technique of Hypnosis by Griffith Edwards, Tms copy).

- (Paragraphs): 5 Amss with A revisions (2pp each), nd.

- (Quotations for Vivien Dayrell-Browning): 3 Ams/ quotations (1p each), nd.

- (Untitled Novel) Chapter One The Funeral of a Father; Chapter Two The Oldest Friend: Ams/fragment with A revisions (22pp), nd.

D2   THE LIBRARY OF THE UNIVERSITY OF ILLINOIS

SCREENPLAYS

Brighton Rock

- (Second shooting script by Roy Boulting from the screenplay by Graham Greene and Terrence Rattigan): Tms/mimeo (114pp), nd.

Lost Illusions

- Script: Shepperton (England), Reed Film Productions
  (19__): Tms/copy (110pp; title changed in manuscript
  to The Fallen Idol).

Our Man in Havana

- Release script: (111pp), nd (London, M. Harris).

D3   THE LIBRARY OF INDIANA UNIVERSITY

SCREENPLAYS

Saint Joan

- (Screenplay of the adaptation of George Bernard
  Shaw's play): Mimeo film script "dialogue
  continuity."

D4   THE LIBRARY OF THE BRITISH FILM INSTITUTE

SCREENPLAYS

Twenty-One Days

- Release script (film released in 1939).

D5   NEW YORK PUBLIC LIBRARY

PLAYS

The Complaisant Lover: A Comedy

(New York, Monica McCall 1961?): Typescript; Imprint
on mounted label.

The Potting Shed

(New York? 1956?): Typescript.

D6   BRITISH BROADCASTING CORPORATION

BROADCAST SCRIPTS

The British Broadcasting Corporation, Written Archives
Centre (Caversham Park, Reading, RG4 8TZ) has on file
numerous scripts of radio broadcasts in which Greene
was involved. The list of radio and television broadcasts in Section F accurately reflects the Centre's
holdings of scripts with the majority of them dated
between 1947 and 1962. The Centre also holds a file of
correspondence relating to Greene's talks and interviews between 1934 and 1954, a file relating to his
scriptwriting (1938-1954) and a file relating to the
use of his works in BBC programs (1938-1954).

FILMS WRITTEN OR PRODUCED
(WHOLLY OR IN PART) BY GRAHAM GREENE

D7   *Twenty-One Days* (1939) London Film Productions (*Twenty-One Days Together* in the U.S., distributed by Columbia Pictures). Screenplay adapted from a John Galsworthy story by Graham Greene and Basil Dean. Produced and directed by Basil Dean. Reviewed by Greene in *The Spectator*, January 12, 1940, p. 44; reprinted in *The Pleasure-Dome*, p. 362.

D8   *The Green Cockatoo* (1940) New World. Screenplay by Graham Greene and E.O. Berkman from Greene's story. Directed by William Cameron Menzies.

D9   *Brighton Rock* (1947) Associated British Pictures Corporation. Screenplay by Graham Greene and Terrence Rattigan. Directed by John Boulting. Produced by Roy Boulting.

D10   *The Fallen Idol* (1948) London Film Productions. Screenplay by Graham Greene. Produced and directed by Carol Reed.

D11   *The Third Man* (1949) London Film Productions. Screenplay by Graham Greene. Produced and directed by Carol Reed.

D12   *The Stranger's Hand* (1952) J. Arthur Rank Productions. Screenplay by Guy Elmes and Georgio Bassani from Greene's story. Directed by Mario Soldati. Co-produced by Graham Greene, Peter Moore and John Stafford.

D13   *Loser Takes All* (1956) J. Arthur Rank Productions. Screenplay by Graham Greene. Directed by Ken Annakin.

D14   *St. Joan* (1957) Wheel Productions. Screenplay by Graham Greene adapted from Shaw's play. Produced and directed by Otto Preminger.

D15   *Our Man in Havana* (1959) Columbia Pictures. Screenplay by Graham Greene. Produced and directed by Carol Reed.

D16   *The Comedians* (1967) Metro-Goldwyn-Mayer. Screenplay by Graham Greene. Produced and directed by Peter Glenville.

E

A BIBLIOGRAPHY OF WORKS ABOUT GRAHAM GREENE

This section is a selective list of books, pamphlets, theses,
dissertations, articles and parts of books about Greene.
However, the compiler has attempted to include all items
which seem of importance. For this reason the list does not
include all reviews. Rather, the compiler has sought those
review articles which mark significant points in Greene's
career. It is hoped that this list is as exhaustive as the
ordinary researcher on Greene should require.

This list is arranged in subsections and alphabetically.

BOOKS

E1 Allott, Kenneth and Miriam Farris. *The Art of Graham Greene.* London: Hamish Hamilton, 1951; Toronto: British Book Service, 1951; New York: Russell & Russell, 1963.

E2 Aoki, Yuzo, editor. *Gureamu Grin.* Tokyo: Kenkyusha, 1971.

E3 Atkins, John. *Graham Greene: A Biographical and Literary Study.* London: J. Calder, 1957; New York: Roy Publishers, 1958; New Revised Edition, London: Calder and Boyars, 1966.

E4 Bitterli, Urs. *Malraux, Conrad, Greene, Weiss: Echriftsteller und Kolonialismus.* Zurich, Cologne: Benziger, 1974.

E5 Boardman, Gwenn R. *Graham Greene: The Aesthetics of Exploration.* Gainesville: University of Florida Press, 1971.

E6 Cargas, Harry J., editor. *Graham Greene.* The Christian Critic Series. St. Louis: B. Herder Book Company, n.d. (1969).

E7 Charvat, Eva. *Die Religiosität und das Thema der Verfolgung in Sechs Romanen von Graham Greene.* European University Papers, XIV. Berne: Herbert Lang; Frankfurt/M.: Peter Lang, 1973.

E8 Dellevaux, Raymond. *Graham Greene et "Le Fond du Problème."* Brussels: Éditions "La Lecture au Foyer," 1951.

E9 DeVitis, A.A. *Graham Greene.* Twayne's English Authors Series - 3. New York: Twayne Publishers, 1964; New York: Grosset and Dunlap, n.d.

E10 Dubu, Jean. *La Poétique de Graham Greene dans la Puissance et la Gloire.* Paris: Lettres Modernes, 1972.

E11 Duran, Leopoldo. *La Crisis del Sacerdote en Graham Greene.* Madrid: La Editorial Catolica, 1974; Madrid: Biblioteca de Autores Christianos, 1976.

E12   Engel, Claire Élaine. *Esquisses Anglaises i Charles Morgan, Graham Greene, T.S. Eliot.* Paris: Editions "Je Sers," 1949.

E13   Evans, Robert Owen, editor. *Graham Greene: Some Critical Considerations.* Lexington: University of Kentucky Press, 1963.

E14   Fournier, R.P. Gaston, S.J. *Scobie, ou l'Homme Victime de sa Pitie: "Le Fond du Problème" de Graham Greene.* Toulouse: Imprimerie Parisienne, 1953.

E15   Fournier, R.P. Gaston, S.J. *Le Tourment de Dieu Chez les Amants de Graham Greene.* Toulouse: Imprimerie Parisienne, 1953.

E16   Hynes, Samuel L., editor. *Graham Greene: A Collection of Critical Essays.* Englewood Cliffs, N.J.: Prentice-Hall, Inc., 1973.

E17   Jonsson, Thorsten and Erik Lindegreen. *Tva Essayer on Graham Greene.* ("Ett Portraat au Scobie" and "Graham Greene"). Stockholm: Norstedt, 1950.

E18   Koga, Hideo. *Essays on Graham Greene and His Work.* Hiroshima: Hiroshima University Publication Society, 1977.

E19   Kohn, Lynette. *Graham Greene: The Major Novels.* Palo Alto: Stanford Honors Essays in Humanities, IV, 1961.

E20   Kunkel, F.L. *The Labyrinthine Ways of Graham Greene.* New York: Sheed and Ward, 1959; revised and expanded, Mamaroneck, N.Y.: Paul P. Appel, 1973.

E21   Langlois, José Miguel Ibáñez. *El Mundo Pecador de Graham Greene.* Santiago de Chile: Empressa Editora Zig-Zag, S.A., 1967.

E22   Lodge, David. *Graham Greene.* Columbia Essays on Modern Writers Series. New York: Columbia University Press, 1966.

E23   Madaule, Jacques. *Graham Greene.* Paris: Editions du Temps Présent, 1949.

E24   Matthews, Ronald. *Mon Ami Graham Greene.* Paris: Desclée De Brouwer, 1957.

E25 Mesnet, Marie-Beatrice. *Graham Greene and the Heart of the Matter: An Essay*. London: Cresset Press, 1954; Westport, Conn.: Greenwood Press, 1972.

E26 Noguchi, Keisuke, editor. *Guream Grin Kenkyu*. (A Study of Graham Greene). 2 vols. Tokyo: Nansosha, 1974.

E27 Pange, Victor de. *Graham Greene*. Preface by François Mauriac. Paris: Editions Universitaires, 1953; Barcelona: Editorial Fontanella, 1964.

E28 Phillips, Gene D. *Graham Greene: The Films of His Fiction*. Studies in Culture and Communication. New York: Teachers College Press, 1974.

E29 Price, Alan. *Brighton Rock (Graham Greene)*. Notes on English Literature. Oxford: Blackwell, 1969.

E30 Pryce-Jones, David. *Graham Greene*. Writers and Critics Series. London: Oliver and Boyd, 1963; 2nd ed. Edinburgh: Oliver and Boyd, 1973.

E31 Rillo, Lila E. *The Power and the Glory*. English Pamphlet #12. Buenos Aires: The Argentine Association of English Culture, 1946.

E32 Rischik, Josef. *Graham Greene und sein Werk*. Schweizer Anglistische Arbeiten 28. Bern: A Francke, 1951.

E33 Rostenne, Paul. *Graham Greene: Témoin des Temps Tragiques*. Prefatory letter by Graham Greene. Paris: Julliard, 1949.

E34 Roy, Gregor. *Graham Greene's The Power and the Glory and Other Works: A Critical Commentary*. Monarch Notes and Study Guide. New York: Simon & Schuster, 1966.

E35 Ryan, John Sprott, editor. *Gleanings from Greeneland*. Armidale, New South Wales (Australia): University of New England, 1972.

E36 Stratford, Philip. *Faith and Fiction: Creative Process in Greene and Mauriac*. Notre Dame, Indiana: University of Notre Dame Press, 1964.

E37 Sturzl, Erwin. *Von Satan zu Gott: Religiöse Probleme bei Graham Greene*. Vienna: Graph. Lerh. und Versuchs-Anstalt, 1954.

E38   Turnell, Martin. *Graham Greene: A Critical Essay.*
       Contemporary Writers in Christian Perspective. Grand
       Rapids, Mich.: Eerdmans, 1967.

E39   Wolfe, Peter. *Graham Greene the Entertainer.* Cross-
       Currents/Modern Critiques. Carbondale: Southern
       Illinois University Press, 1972.

E40   Wyndham, Francis. *Graham Greene.* British Book News on
       Writers and Their Work, No. 67, British Council. London:
       Longmans Green, 1955; rpt. 1962.

E41   Unsigned. *Graham Greene Demasque, Finally Exposed.*
       Republic of Haiti: Bulletin of the Department of Foreign
       Affairs, n.d.

       An attack on Graham Greene by various Haitians following
       the publication of *The Comedians.*

                       THESES AND DISSERTATIONS
                  (DA indicates *Dissertation Abstracts*)

E42   Adamson, Judith Emily. "Greene on Film." University
       of Montreal (Canada) doctoral dissertation, 1977.

E42a   Baker, M.A. "A Study of the Use of Environment in the
       Novel with Particular Reference to Some of the Novels
       of Graham Greene." University of London, Institute of
       Education M.Phil. thesis, 1972.

E43   Barratt, Harold. "Existentialism in Graham Greene's
       *The Name of Action, The Heart of the Matter, A Burnt-
       Out Case*: The Theme of Betrayal." Windsor (Canada)
       M.A. thesis, 1964.

E44   Beckles, William Anthony. "Catholicism in the Fiction
       of Graham Greene." University of Alberta (Canada)
       doctoral dissertation, 1972.

E45   Bedard, Bernard John. "The Thriller Pattern in the
       Major Novels of Graham Greene." University of Michigan
       doctoral dissertation, 1959. DA, XX, pp. 1779-1780.

E46   Bell, Martha F. "Graham Greene and the Idea of Child-
       hood." North Texas State University M.A. thesis, 1966.

E47 Boardman, Gwenn Rosina. "Graham Greene: The Aesthetics of Exploration." Claremont Graduate School doctoral dissertation, 1963. DA, XXIV, p. 2474.

E48 Bowen, Valerie F. "Graham Greene and the Roman Liturgy." University of Hawaii M.A. thesis, 1962.

E49 Bowes, Sr. Saint Martin of Lima. "Graham Greene: Religious Dramatist." Villanova University M.A. thesis, 1964.

E50 Brannon, Lilian Borop. "Iconology of the Child Figure in Graham Greene's Fiction." East Texas State University doctoral dissertation, 1977. DA, XXXVIII, p. 4155A.

E51 Brooks, Sammy K. "Graham Greene and Mexico: A Critical Study of *The Power and the Glory* and *Another Mexico*." University of Texas at Austin M.A. thesis, 1966.

E52 Cardinale, Vincent G. "Graham Greene's Conception of Evil." Boston College M.A. thesis, 1950.

E53 Cawthon, Daniel D. "The Themes of Alienation in the Major Novels of Graham Greene." University of Tulsa M.S. thesis, 1966.

E54 Christman, Elizabeth Ann. "Hell Lay About Them: Childhood in the Work of Graham Greene." New York University doctoral dissertation, 1972. DA, XXXIII, p. 6345A.

E55 Clines, Patrick. "The Child and Being: Key to the Novels of Georges Bernanos and Graham Greene." Fresno State College M.A. thesis, 1966.

E56 Conroy, Esther A. "American Critics on Four Novels of Graham Greene." Rivier College M.A. thesis, 1961.

E57 Consolo, Dominick Peter. "The Technique of Graham Greene: A Stylistic Analysis of Five Novels." University of Iowa doctoral dissertation, 1959. DA, XX, p. 297.

E58 Coroneou, Marianthi. "Suffering as Part of the Human Condition in the Fiction of Graham Greene, Albert Camus, and Nikos Kazantzakis." University of Kentucky doctoral dissertation, 1967. DA, XXX, p. 3454A.

E59 Crull, Mary E. "Down the Labyrinthine Ways: A Study of Graham Greene's Novels." Colorado State College M.A. thesis, 1959.

E60   Currie, John Sheldon. "Supernaturalism in Graham
       Greene: A Comparison of Orthodox Catholicism with the
       Religious Vision in the Major Novels." University of
       Alabama doctoral dissertation, 1967. DA, XXVIII,
       pp. 3176-3177A.

E61   Davidson, Arnold C. "Graham Greene: A Writer of the
       Cross Rather Than the Resurrection." Kansas State
       Teachers College M.A. thesis, 1966.

E62   DeVitis, Angelo Anthony. "The Religious Theme in Rex
       Warner, Evelyn Waugh, and Graham Greene." University
       of Wisconsin doctoral dissertation, 1954. DA, XV
       (1955), pp. 605-606.

E63   Duffy, William Robert. "Graham Greene: Entertainer and
       Novelist." University of Chicago doctoral dissertation,
       1973.

E63a   Duran, Justo L. "The Priesthood in the Writings of
       Graham Greene." University of London, Kings College
       doctoral dissertation, 1972.

E64   Duran, Leopoldo. "El Substrato Teológico en la Obra
       de Graham Greene." University of Madrid doctoral dis-
       sertation, 1973.

E65   Eberly, Ralph Stephens. "Joyce Cary's Theme of Freedom
       and a Comparison with James Joyce and Graham Greene."
       University of Michigan doctoral dissertation, 1970.
       DA, XXXI, p. 6601A.

E66   Eigner, Franz. "Der Symbolcharokter der Landschafts-
       bildes in den Werken Graham Greenes." University of
       Vienna doctoral dissertation, 1952.

E67   Enn, Josef. "Graham Greenes Romane: Eine Neuinterpre-
       tation ihres Religiösen Gehaltes." University of
       Vienna doctoral dissertation, 1972.

E68   Elson, John T. "The Concept of Order in the Novels and
       Entertainments of Graham Greene." Columbia University
       M.A. thesis, 1954.

E69   Fay, Marguerite Mary. "Graham Greene: A Study of Five
       Major Novels." Purdue University doctoral dissertation,
       1973. DA, XXXIV, p. 5965A.

E70   Fitzgerald, Ellen F. "Difficulty Squared: Is Graham
       Greene a Great Catholic Novelist?" Columbia University
       M.A. thesis, 1959.

E71   Flake, Elaine M. "Graham Greene's Obsession with the
       Lost Childhood Theme in His Novels, Short Stories and
       Essays." Brigham Young University M.A. thesis, 1968.

E72   Flynn, Sr. M. Robert of Citeaux. "The Utility of Suf-
       fering in the Novels of Graham Greene." Boston College
       M.A. thesis, 1965.

E73   Galen, Ruth E. "Graham Greene: A Study of Absolute
       and Relative Concepts of Morality." University of New
       Mexico M.A. thesis, 1953.

E74   Gaston, George M. "Forms of Salvation in the Novels
       of Graham Greene." Auburn University doctoral disser-
       tation, 1974. DA, XXXV, p. 1655A.

E75   Geist, Joseph E. "The Critical Reception of Graham
       Greene in Selected American Catholic Periodicals, 1930-
       1970." University of Kansas doctoral dissertation,
       1972. DA, XXXIII, p. 2933A.

E76   Ginn, Regis C. "The Imaginary World Created by Graham
       Greene." University of Arizona M.A. thesis, 1961.

E77   Gonzales, Ramond Joseph. "The Latin American Dictator
       in the Novel." University of Southern California doc-
       toral dissertation, 1971. DA, XXXII, pp. 5787A-5788A.

E78   Groven, John O. "The Influence of Religion on the Works
       of Graham Greene." University of Colorado M.A. thesis,
       1966.

E79   Guest, Lawrence A. "Christian Tragedy and the Works of
       Graham Greene: A Redefinition as Applied to *Brighton
       Rock*, *The End of the Affair*, *A Burnt-Out Case* and *The
       Power and the Glory*." Fresno State College M.A. thesis,
       1969.

E80   Gusdorf, Barbara Neuroth. "Concepts of Sainthood in the
       Novels of Albert Camus and Graham Greene." Michigan
       State University doctoral dissertation, 1968. DA,
       XXIX, pp. 1895A-1896A.

E81   Hanlon, Robert Michael. "Graham Greene's Religious
       Sense." University of Massachusetts doctoral disser-
       tation, 1971. DA, XXXII, p. 4001A.

E82   Harmer, Ruth Mulvey. "Mexico, Modern Literature, and
       the Search for Soul." University of Southern California
       doctoral dissertation, 1972. DA, XXXV, pp. 452A–453A.

E83   Hoodecheck, Donald J. "The Theme of Purgation in
       Graham Greene's *The Power and the Glory*." Mankato State
       College M.A. thesis, 1965.

E84   Hooper, Walter D. "The Peguy Motif in the 'Catholic'
       Novels of Graham Greene." University of Rhode Island
       M.A. thesis, 1966.

E85   Horne, Sandra G. "Imagery as Exposition: A Study of
       Selected Novels by Graham Greene." University of Rhode
       Island M.A. thesis, n.d.

E86   Ingersoll, Earl George. "Imagery in the Novels of
       Graham Greene." University of Wisconsin doctoral dis-
       sertation, 1971. DA, XXXII, p. 3308A.

E87   Jean–de–la Charity, Sr. "Structure and Theme in Graham
       Greene's *The Potting Shed*." Rivier College M.A. thesis,
       1959.

E88   Kambeitz, Clemens G. "The Pessimistic Realism of
       Graham Greene." University of Toronto (Canada) M.A.
       thesis, 1965.

E89   Keegan, Maureen Therese. "The Man–God Relationship: A
       Comparative Study of the Fiction of Rabindranath
       Tagore and Graham Greene." Catholic University of
       America doctoral dissertation, 1973. DA, XXXIV,
       p. 7324A.

E90   Kelleher, James Patrick. "The Orthodoxy and Values of
       Graham Greene." Boston University doctoral disserta-
       tion, 1966. DA, XXVII, p. 1825A.

E91   Koban, Charles. "Theme, Character and Style in the Work
       of Graham Greene." Columbia University M.A. thesis,
       1960.

E92   Koithara, James Aggaeus. "The Pattern of Border Struggle
       in Graham Greene." University of Montreal (Canada)
       doctoral dissertation, 1963.

E93   Korn, Frederick Benjamin. "Condemned to Consequences:
        A Study of Tragic Process in Three Works by Joseph Con-
        rad and Graham Greene." University of Illinois at
        Urbana-Champaign doctoral dissertation, 1973. DA,
        XXXIV, p. 5977A.

E94   Kreuzer, Wilhelm. "Die Auswirkung der Weltanschaulicher
        Grundhaltung auf Charackterzeichnung und Stoffgestal-
        tung in Greenes Werken." University of Graz doctoral
        dissertation, 1952.

E95   Kunkel, Francis Leo. "A Critical Study of Graham
        Greene." Columbia University doctoral dissertation,
        1959. DA, XX, pp. 670-671.

E96   LaChance, Louis. "Types of Fantasy in the Fiction of
        Graham Greene." University of Montreal (Canada) M.A.
        thesis, 1966.

E97   LaChance, Paul Richard. "Man and Religion in the
        Novels of William Golding and Graham Greene." Kent
        State University doctoral dissertation, 1970. DA,
        XXXI, p. 6062A.

E97a   Lamble, M.D. "A Critical Study of the Later Novels of
        Graham Greene." University of Liverpool (England) M.A.
        thesis, 1965.

E98   Lattinville, Ronald Edward. "Comic Characterization in
        the Fiction of Graham Greene." University of Southern
        California doctoral dissertation, 1974. DA, XXXV,
        p. 3750A.

E99   Ledeboer, Leroy D. "The Despair That Leads to Faith:
        A Study of the Major Religious Novels of Graham Greene."
        Moorhead State College M.A. thesis, 1965.

E100   Lenore, Mary. "From Fiction to Film: A Critical Analy-
        sis of Graham Greene's *The Fallen Idol*, *The Third Man*,
        and *Our Man in Havana*, Directed by Carol Reed." Uni-
        versity of Southern California doctoral dissertation,
        1976. DA, XXXVII, p. 5405A.

E101   Longree, Georgia A. "The Concepts of Belief and Non-
        Belief in the Writings of Graham Greene." Texas
        Christian University M.A. thesis, 1968.

E102   Love, Frances A. "Graham Greene's Use of the Christian
        Concept of Descent." Texas Agricultural and Mechani-
        cal University M.A. thesis, 1969.

E103   Lynes, Charles M. "The Whiskey Priest, an Atypical
        Martyr: An Examination of the Whiskey Priest of *The
        Power and the Glory* as a Reworking of the Standard
        Martyr Story." Fresno State College M.A. thesis, 1967.

E104   MacDonald, Sara Jane. "The Aesthetics of Grace in
        Flannery O'Connor and Graham Greene." University of
        Illinois at Urbana-Champaign doctoral dissertation,
        1972. DA, XXXIII, p. 5734A.

E105   Manly, Jane Burt. "Graham Greene: The Insanity of
        Innocence." University of Connecticut doctoral disser-
        tation, 1969. DA, XXX, p. 3016A.

E106   Marlowe, Jeanne A. "A Comparison of Relgious Themes
        in the Fiction of Graham Greene and Flannery O'Connor."
        Bowling Green State University M.A. thesis, 1969.

E107   McCarthy, David R. "The Priest in Graham Greene: His
        Use and Failure." Columbia University M.A. thesis,
        1961.

E108   McClendon, Margaret A. "God in a Godless World: A
        Study of Graham Greene 1929-1951." University of
        Texas at Austin M.A. thesis, 1961.

E109   McCullagh, James Charles. "Aesthetics and the Reli-
        gious Mind: François Mauriac, Graham Greene, and Flan-
        nery O'Connor." Lehigh University doctoral disser-
        tation, 1975. DA, XXXV, p. 7316A.

E110   McDonald, Ann Gilbert. "A Bibliography of the Periodi-
        cal Contributions of Graham Greene." George Washing-
        ton University doctoral dissertation, 1969.

E111   McDonald, Horace Thelton. "Africa as a Fictive World:
        Seven Modern Responses from Joseph Conrad to Graham
        Greene." University of Southern Louisiana doctoral
        dissertation, 1975. DA, XXXVI, p. 7440A.

E112   McDonald, Marjorie M. "Sacred and Profane Love as
        Depicted in the Writings of Graham Greene." Saint
        Mary's (Canada) M.A. thesis, 1965.

E113   McLeod, Sr. Madelene S. "An Indexed Synthesis of the
        Critical Thought of Graham Greene and Patrick Bray-
        brooke." Siena Heights College M.A. thesis, 1958.

E113a   Mensah, A.N. "The Treatment of Private Codes of Con-
        duct and Religious Themes in the Novels of Graham
        Greene." University of Leeds (England) M.Phil. thesis,
        1968.

E114   Miller, Helen M. "The Eschatology of Graham Greene."
        Stetson University M.A. thesis, 1965.

E115   Mills, Joseph L. "Plutchik's Emotive Theory as Applied
        to Eschatology Elements in Key Works of Graham Greene."
        Morehead State University M.A. thesis, 1967.

E116   Moore, Karen Rae. "The Comic Technique in Graham
        Greene." Georgia State University doctoral disser-
        tation, 1976. DA, XXXVI, pp. 5322A-5323A.

E117   Morrison, Patrick John. "The Quest Motif in the Fic-
        tion of Graham Greene." University of Toronto
        (Canada) doctoral dissertation, 1975. DA, XXXVIII,
        p. 5464A.

E117a   Muller, C.H. "The Novels of Graham Greene: A Critical
        Study with Particular Reference to the Religious
        Themes." University of Wales at Aberystwyth (United
        Kingdom) M.A. thesis, 1968.

E118   Nee, James M. "Graham Greene's *The Power and the
        Glory*: A Source of Study." Boston College M.A. thesis,
        1964.

E119   Omibiya, A.A. "The Treatment of Pain and Death in
        Five Novels of Graham Greene: *The Man Within*, *It's a
        Battlefield*, *Brighton Rock*, *The Power and the Glory*,
        and *The Heart of the Matter*." University of London
        (England) M.Phil. thesis, 1967.

E120   O'Grady, Walter Anthony. "Political Contexts in the
        Novels of Graham Greene and Joyce Cary." University
        of Toronto (Canada) doctoral dissertation, 1971. DA,
        XXXII, p. 6995A.

E121   Patten, Karl Watson, Jr. "The Relationship Between
        Form and Religious Ideas in the Fiction of Graham

Greene." Boston University doctoral dissertation, 1956.

E122   Pearson, Sheryl Marie Sherman. "The Anglo-American Novel of the Mexican Revolution, 1910-1940: D.H. Lawrence, B. Traven, Graham Greene." University of Michigan doctoral dissertation, 1976. DA, XXXVII, p. 1543A.

E123   Pepin, Sr. Lucienne. "The Function of Imagery in Graham Greene's Fiction." Rivier College M.A. thesis, 1957.

E124   Perez Lapuente, Felix. "The Sense of Failure in Graham Greene." Deusto M.A. thesis, 1973.

E124a   Priems, C.W.L. "The Moral Problem in the Works of Graham Greene." National University (Ireland) M.A. thesis, 1955.

E125   Quirk, Frank B. "Graham Greene and the Human Condition." University of Massachusetts M.A. thesis, 1965.

E125a   Ragheb, G.A.A.M. "The Vision of Life Presented in Graham Greene's Fiction and the Presentation of Some of His Novels to University Students in Egypt." London University, Institute of Education M. Phil. thesis, 1976.

E126   Read, Donald R. "Pattern and Meaning in the Novels of Graham Greene." Trinity College M.A. thesis, 1965.

E127   Rosenkranz, Joel Harris. "Graham Greene's Travel Writings: Sources of His Fiction." New York University doctoral dissertation, 1978. DA, XXXIX, p. 2262A.

E128   Rottino, Joseph F. "Despair in the Novels of Graham Greene." Long Island University M.A. thesis, n.d.

E129   Rozsnafszky, Jane S. "The Search for Meaning of the Characters of Graham Greene: The Necessity of Suffering." Drake University M.A. thesis, 1965.

E130   Rusyn, Br. August S. "Ambiguity as a Literary Technique in Selected Novels of Graham Greene." University of Rhode Island M.A. thesis, 1969.

E131   Sabine, Francisco J. "Graham Greene's Heroes: Regeneration Through Experience." University of British Columbia (Canada) M.A. thesis, 1969.

E132   Sanders, Marvin C. "The Use of Ambiguity and Paradox in the Catholic Novels of Graham Greene." University of Idaho M.A. thesis, 1962.

E133   Sauer, Josef. "Die Darstellung des Katholischen Menschen bei Archibald Joseph Cronin und Graham Greene." University of Erlangen doctoral dissertation, 1953.

E134   Sheehan, Thomas M. "Graham Greene and the Problem of Good and Evil." University of Louisville M.A. thesis, 1956.

E135   Sheehan, Thomas M. "The Catholic Treatment of Sin and Redemption in the Novels of Graham Greene." University of Ottawa (Canada) doctoral dissertation, 1960.

E136   Siecke, Gerda. "Das Romanwerk Graham Greenes in Seinem Verhältnis zu den Romanen von Georges Bernanos und François Mauriac." Friedrich-Alexander University of Erlangen doctoral dissertation, 1955.

E137   Siferd, Nancy K. "Graham Greene's Attitudes Toward Love and Marriage." Bowling Green State University M.A. thesis, 1964.

E138   Slate, Audrey Nelson. "Technique and Form in the Novels of Graham Greene." University of Wisconsin doctoral dissertation, 1960. DA, XXI, pp. 629-630.

E139   Stahl, Norma M. "The Novels of Graham Greene: A Discussion of the Themes of Love and Pity and the Novelist's Technique." Columbia University M.A. thesis, 1953.

E140   Stenberg, Carl Edward. "The Quest for Justice in the Fiction of Graham Greene." University of Connecticut doctoral dissertation, 1969. DA, XXX, p. 3024A.

E141   Stine, Norma Contryman. "As It Is and As It Ought to Be: Graham Greene on the Cinema." University of Nebraska M.A. thesis, c. 1969.

E142   Stowe, Mary L. "The Significance of Interpersonal Re-
        lationships in the Novels of Graham Greene." Washing-
        ton State University at Pullman M.A. thesis, 1965.

E143   Strasill, Edmund. "Die Kunst der Personenbeschreibung
        in Romanen Galsworthys, Maughams und Graham Greenes."
        University of Graz doctoral dissertation, 1949.

E144   Suarez, Ralph P. "The Application of Catholic Criteria
        to the Works of Graham Greene." C.W. Post College M.A.
        thesis, 1963.

E145   Sullivan, Virginia M. "The Heart of Darkness in
        Graham Greene: Some Critical Considerations of Greene's
        Vision of the World as It Relates to His Preoccupation
        with Death in His Novels and Entertainments, with Par-
        ticular Emphasis on *It's a Battlefield*." Columbia
        University M.A. thesis, 1966.

E146   Tolbert, Evelyn O. "The Greene Priest." University
        of Houston M.A. thesis, 1965.

E147   Veitch, Douglas W. "The Fictional Landscape of
        Mexico: Readings in D.H. Lawrence, Graham Greene and
        Malcolm Lowry." University of Montreal (Canada)
        doctoral dissertation, 1974.

E148   Villaneuva, Rev. Rodolfo E. "The Ethic of Graham
        Greene's Novels." Mankato State College M.A. thesis,
        1967.

E149   Wagner, Nora E. "The Foundations of Graham Greene's
        Thought, with Particular Emphasis on the Concepts of
        Evil and Redemption as Presented in His Early Work."
        George Washington University M.A. thesis, 1964.

E150   Walters, Dorothy Jeanne. "The Theme of Destructive
        Innocence in the Modern Novel: Greene, James, Cary,
        Porter." University of Oklahoma doctoral disserta-
        tion, 1960. DA, XXI, p. 2300.

E151   Whidden, Sr. Mary B. "The Prophetic Artistry of
        Graham Greene." University of New Hampshire M.A.
        thesis, 1968.

E152   Willig, Charles Lloyd. "The Short Fiction of Graham
        Greene." University of Tulsa doctoral dissertation,
        1970. DA, XXXI, pp. 2945A-2946A.

E153   Wobbe, R.A. "The Name of Power: An Analysis of Its
        Use in the Fiction of Graham Greene." University of
        Exeter (England) doctoral dissertation, 1971.

E154   Zerman, Malvyn B. "The Writer as Technician: A Study
        of the Literary Methods of Graham Greene." Columbia
        University M.A. thesis, 1953.

                        BIBLIOGRAPHIES

E155   Beebe, Maurice. "Criticism of Graham Greene: A Selec-
        ted Checklist with an Index to Studies of Separate
        Works." *Modern Fiction Studies*: Graham Greene Special
        Number, III (Autumn 1957), pp. 281-288.

E156   Birmingham, William. "Graham Greene Criticism: A
        Bibliographical Study." *Thought*, XXVII (Spring 1952),
        pp. 72-100.

E157   Brennan, Neil. "Bibliography." *Graham Greene: Some
        Critical Considerations*. Edited by Robert O. Evans.
        Lexington: University of Kentucky Press, 1963, pp.
        245-276.

E158   Cargas, Harry J. "Graham Greene: 100 Articles Through
        1965: An Annotated Checklist." *Catholic Library
        World*, XL, No. 8 (April 1969), pp. 488-490; No. 9
        (May-June 1969), pp. 566-569.

E159   Costello, Donald P. "Graham Greene and the Catholic
        Press." *Renascence*: Graham Greene Special Number,
        XII (Fall 1959), pp. 3-28.

E160   Davis, Robert Murray. "Contributions to *Night and Day*
        by Elizabeth Bowen, Graham Greene, and Anthony
        Powell." *Studies in the Novel*: Special Number,
        Twentieth Century British Novel, III (Winter 1971),
        pp. 401-404.

E161   Hargreaves, Phylis. "Graham Greene: A Selected Bib-
        liography." *Bulletin of Bibliography and Magazine
        Notes*, XXII (January-April 1957), pp. 45-48.

        Reprinted and expanded in *Modern Fiction Studies*:
        Graham Greene Special Number, III (Autumn 1957),
        pp. 269-280.

E162   Remords, G. "Graham Greene: Notes Biographiques et
        Bibliographiques." *Bulletin de la Faculté des Lettres
        de Strasbourg*, XXIX (May-June 1951), pp. 393-399.

E163   Vann, Jerry Don. *Graham Greene: A Checklist of
        Criticism*. Kent, Ohio: Kent State University Press,
        1970.

E164   Wobbe, R.A. "Graham Greene's Literary and Theater
        Reviews and Articles in *The Spectator*, 1932-1941."
        Bulletin of Bibliography and Magazine Notes, XXXIV,
        (January-March 1977), pp. 21-28.

E165   Unsigned. "A Bibliography of Graham Greene."
        Marginalia, II (April 1951), pp. 16-19.

                              ARTICLES

E166   Abirached, R. "Le Paria de Graham Greene." *Études*,
        No. 11 (November 1963), pp. 241-244.

E167   Adam, George. "Graham Greene Établit son Panthéon
        des Littératures Anglaise et Française." *Figaro
        Littéraire* (May 2, 1959), p. 4.

E168   Adamson, Judy. "Graham Greene as Film Critic."
        Sight and Sound, XLI (Spring 1972), pp. 104-106.

E169   Adamson, Judy and Philip Stratford. "Looking for
        The Third Man: On the Trail in Texas, New York,
        Hollywood." *Encounter*, L (June 1978), pp. 39-46.

E170   Aguirre De Carcer, Nuno. "La Novela en la Inglaterra
        Actual: II. Graham Greene." *Arbor*, XIV (September-
        October 1949), pp. 99-113.

E171   Allen, W. Gore. "Evelyn Waugh and Graham Greene."
        Irish Monthly, LXXVII (January 1949), pp. 16-22.

E172   Allen W. Gore. "The World of Graham Greene." *Irish
        Ecclesiastical Record*, LXXI (January 1949), pp. 42-49.

E173   Allen, W. Gore. "Another View of Graham Greene."
        Catholic World, CLXIX (April 1949), pp. 69-70.

E174   Allen, Walter. "Awareness of Evil: Graham Greene."
       Nation, CLXXXII (April 21, 1957), pp. 344-346.

E175   Allen, Walter. Untitled. *London Magazine*, V (March
       1966), pp. 73-80.
       Re The Comedians.

E176   Allen, Walter. "An Interview in New York with Walter
       Allen by Walter Sale." *Studies in the Novel*: Special
       Number: Twentieth Century British Novel, III (Winter
       1971), pp. 405-429.

E177   Alloway, Lawrence. "Symbolism in *The Third Man*."
       World Review, n.s. No. 13 (March 1950), pp. 57-60.

E178   Alvarez, A. "In the Gloomy Country of Graham Greene's
       Heart." *Saturday Review*, LIV (September 25, 1971),
       pp. 33-35, 49.

E179   Alves, Leonard. "The Relevance of Graham Greene."
       English Language and Literature (Tokyo), XI (1974),
       pp. 47-76.

E180   Anisimov, I. "Romany Grexema Grina." *Inostrannaya
       Literatura*, X (October 1964), pp. 221-226.

E181   Antip, Felicia. "Greeneland." *România Literaǎ*, VI
       (October 1973), p. 30.

E182   Arnesen, Axel. "Graham Greenes Idéverden." *Samtiden*,
       LXXII (November 1963), pp. 636-644.

E183   Astier, C. "La Tentation du Roman Policier dans Deux
       Romans: *Un Crime*, de Georges Bernanos, *Le Rocher de
       Brighton*, de Graham Greene." *Revue de Littérature
       Comparée*, XLIV (1970), pp. 224-243.

E184   Auden, W.H. "The Heresy of Our Time." *Renascence*, I
       (Spring 1949), pp. 223-224.

       Reprinted in *The Wind and the Rain*, VI (Summer 1949),
       pp. 53-54 and in *Renascence*, XXV (Summer 1973),
       pp. 181-182.

E185   Avvisati, Marilena. "Graham Greene Contra Se."
       Revista di Letterature Moderne e Comparate, XXVI
       (1973), p. 30.

E186   Baker, Denys Val. "My Favorite Forgotten Book."
        Tomorrow, VII (July 1948), pp. 63-64.

E187   Barbour, Thomas. "The Living Room." *Hudson Review*,
        VII (Autumn 1954), pp. 470-471.

E188   Barker, Paul. "The Masks of Graham Greene: *The
        Comedians*." *New Society* (January 27, 1966), p. 29.

E189   Barlow, G. "L'Art de Graham Greene." *Esprit*, XXVII
        (March 1959), pp. 517-525.

E190   Barnes, Robert J. "Two Modes of Fiction: Hemingway
        and Greene." *Renascence*, XIV (Summer 1962), pp. 193-
        198.

E191   Barra, Giovanni. "La Conversione di Graham Greene."
        Vita e Pensiero, XXXVI (July 1953), pp. 310-315.

E192   Barrat, R.G. "Greenes Bekehrung." *Neues Abendland*
        (Augsburg), IV, No. 11 (1949), p. 388.

E193   Barratt, Harold. "Adultery as Betrayal in Graham
        Greene." *Dalhousie Review*, XLV (Autumn 1965), pp.
        324-332.

E194   Barthelme, D. "Tired Terror of Graham Greene."
        Holiday, XXXIX (April 1966), pp. 146ff.

E195   Battock, Marjorie. "The Novels of Graham Greene."
        The Norseman, XIII (January-February 1955), pp. 45-52.

E196   Bayley, John. "The Greening of Graham Greene." *The
        Listener*, LXXXVI (September 16, 1971), pp. 375-376.

E197   Beary, Thomas John. "Religion and the Modern Novel."
        Catholic World, CLXVI (December 1947), pp. 203-211.

E198   Bechner, Hubert. "Priestegestalten in der Roman-
        literatur der Gegenwart." *Stimmen der Zeit*, CLIII
        (1953), pp. 345-355.

E199   Bechner, Hubert. "*Der Stille Amerikaner*." *Stimmen
        der Zeit*, CLX (April 1957), pp. 68-72.

E200   Bedard, B.J. "Reunion in Havana." *Literature/Film
        Quarterly*, II (Fall 1974), pp. 352-358.

E201   Bedford, Sybille. "Tragic Comedians." *New York Review of Books* (March 3, 1966), pp. 25-27.

E202   Bedient, C. "Nihilism of Boredom." *New Republic*, CLXV (October 2, 1971), pp. 23-24.

E203   Bedoyere, Michael de la. "From My Window in Fleet Street." *Catholic World*, CLXXIV (October 1951), pp. 56-61.

E204   Beirnaert, Louis. "Die Menschliche Armseligkeit und die Gnade: Zu Graham Greenes Gestalten." *Universitas*, V (November 1950), pp. 395-397.

E205   Beirnaert, Louis. "Does Sanctification Depend on Psychic Structure?" *Cross Currents*, No. 2 (Winter 1951), pp. 39-43.

E206   Beltzikoff, Boris. "Kaj Munk och Graham Greene: En Studie i Kristen Kriminologi." *Ord och Bild*, LXVI (1957), pp. 248-258.

E207   Bentley, P. "Is the British Novel Dead?" *Saturday Review of Literature*, XIX (January 28, 1939), p. 4.

E208   Bergonzi, Bernard. "Greeneland Revisited." *New Society* (November 20, 1969), pp. 824-825.

E209   Bergonzi, Bernard. "Graham Greene Supplied the Lyrics: A Footnote to the Thirties." *Encounter*, XLVII (December 1976), pp. 67-71.

E210   Bertram, Anthony. "The Stirrup and the Ground." *The Tablet*, CXCVII (May 26, 1951), pp. 417-418.

E211   Bertram, Anthony. "Another Part of the Wood." *The Tablet*, CXCVIII (September 8, 1951), p. 156.

E212   Binyon, T.J. "Graham Greene: The Human Factor." *Times Literary Supplement* (March 17, 1978), p. 301.

E213   Bitterli, Urs. "Graham Greene und der Kolonialismus." *Neue Zürcher Zeitung*, IV (April 1971), p. 52.

E214   Blajot, J. "La Renuncia a la fe de Father William Callifer." *Razon y Fe*, CLX (December 1959), pp. 441-450.

E215   Blanchet, Andre. "Un Nouveau 'Type' de Prêtre dans le
        Roman Contemporain." *Études*, No. 279 (February 1954),
        pp. 145-164 and No. 280 (March 1954), pp. 303-310.

E216   Blöcker, Günter. "Der Befreite Graham Greene."
        Merkur Deutsche Zeitschrift für Europäisches Denken
        (Stuttgart), XXVI (1972), pp. 195-197.

E217   Boardman, Gwenn Rosina. "Greene's 'Under the Garden';
        Aesthetic Explorations." *Renascence*, XVII (Summer
        1965), pp. 180-190, 194.

E218   Bogan, L. "Good Beyond Evil." *New Republic*, CXXV
        (December 10, 1951), p. 29.

E219   Böker, Uwe. "Henry James, Graham Greene und das
        Problem der Form." *Literatur in Wissenschaft und
        Unterricht*, VII (1974), pp. 16-33.

E220   Bouscaren, Anthony T. "France and Graham Greene ver-
        sus America and Diem." *Catholic World*, CLXXXI
        (September 1955), pp. 414-417.

E221   Bowen, Elizabeth. "Story, Theme, and Situation."
        The Listener, LVI (October 25, 1956), pp. 651-652.

E222   Boyd, John D. "Earth Imagery in Graham Greene's
        The Potting Shed." *Modern Drama*, XVI (June 1973),
        pp. 69-80.

E223   Boyle, Alexander. "Graham Greene." *Irish Monthly*,
        LXXVII (November 1949), pp. 319-325.

E224   Boyle, Alexander. "The Symbolism of Graham Greene."
        Irish Monthly, LXXX (March 1952), pp. 98-102.

E225   Boyle, Raymond M. "Man of Controversy." *The Grail*,
        XXXV (July 1952), pp. 1-7.

E226   Boyle, Ted E. and Terence Brown. "The Serious Side
        of Kingsley Amis's *Lucky Jim*." *Criticism*, IX (1966),
        pp. 100-107.

        Lucky Jim compared to *The Heart of the Matter*.

E227   Brady, Charles A. "Melodramatic Cousin of R.L.S."
        America, LXIV (January 25, 1941), pp. 439-440.

E228   Brady, Charles A. "Contemporary Catholic Authors:
        Graham Greene, Novelist of Good and Evil." *Catholic
        Library World*, XVI (December 1944), pp. 67-74, 89.

E229   Brandstrup, Ole. "Til Helvede med Succesen."
        Perspektiv (Det Danske Magasin), VIII, No. 7 (1961),
        pp. 47-50.

E230   Braybrooke, Neville. "Graham Greene." *Envoy*, III
        (September 1950), pp. 10-23.

E231   Braybrooke, Neville. "Graham Greene." *English
        Journal*, XXXIX (October 1950), pp. 415-423.

E232   Braybrooke, Neville. "Graham Greene: A Pioneer Novel-
        ist." *College English*, XII (October 1950), pp. 1-9.

E233   Braybrooke, Neville. "Péguy: The Radiance of His Art."
        Commonweal, LIII (November 10, 1950), pp. 114-115.

E234   Braybrooke, Neville. "Graham Greene as Critic."
        Commonweal, LIX (July 6, 1951), pp. 312-314.

        Reprinted in *New Adelphi*, XXVIII (Fourth Quarter 1951),
        pp. 425-430 and the *Irish Monthly*, LXXX (October 1953),
        pp. 383-388.

E235   Braybrooke, Neville. "Graham Greene and the Double
        Man: An Approach to *The End of the Affair*." *Dublin
        Review*, CCXXVI (First Quarter 1952), pp. 61-73.

        Reprinted in *Graham Greene*. Edited by Harry J. Car-
        gas. The Christian Critic Series. St. Louis: B.
        Herder Book Company, n.d. (1969), pp. 114-129.

E236   Braybrooke, Neville. "End to Anguish?" *Commonweal*,
        LXIII (January 20, 1956), pp. 406-407.

E237   Braybrooke, Neville. "Graham Greene--the Double Man."
        Twentieth Century (Melbourne), XXIII (1969), pp. 293-
        304.

E238   Braybrooke, Neville. "Graham Greene--The Double Man:
        An Approach to his Novel, *The End of the Affair*."
        Queen's Quarterly, LXXVII (Spring 1970), pp. 29-39.

E239   Breit, Harvey. "The Quiet Englishman." *The New York
        Times Book Review* (August 26, 1956), p. 8.

E240   Brennan, Neil. "Coney Island Rock." *Accent*, XVI
        (Spring 1956), pp. 140-142.

E241   Brion, Marcel. "Les Romans de Graham Greene." *Revue
        des Deux Mondes*, No. 6 (March 15, 1950), pp. 367-375.

E242   Brissaud, André. "C'est un Champ de Bataille/C'est
        un Homme Traqué/C'est l'univers de Graham Greene."
        Arts, No. 434 (October 22, 1953), p. 5.

E243   Brock, D. Heyward and James M. Welsh. "Graham Greene
        and the Structure of Salvation." *Renascence*, XXVII
        (1974), pp. 31-39.

E244   Bröger, Niels Chr. "Gudsforholdet i Graham Greenes
        Menneskeskildring." *Kirke og Kultr*, LVIII (1953),
        pp. 275-283.

E245   Brown, John Mason. "Parish Greene." *Saturday Review*,
        XXXVII (December 18, 1954), pp. 24-25.

E246   Browne, E. Martin. "Graham Greene: Theatre's Gain."
        Theatre Arts, XLV (November 1961), pp. 20-24.

E247   Bryden, Ronald. "Graham Greene, Alas." *The
        Spectator*, CCIX (September 28, 1962), pp. 441-442.

E248   Burgess, Anthony. "Politics in the Novels of Graham
        Greene." *Journal of Contemporary History*, II (April
        1967), pp. 93-99.

E249   Burgess, Anthony. "Graham Greene as Monsieur Vert."
        The Tablet, CCXXIX (March 15, 1975), pp. 259-260.

E250   Byatt, A.S. "Evil is Commonplace." *Encounter*, XXI
        (June 1966), pp. 64-66.

E251   Caillet, G. "Un Roman n'est pas une Histoire."
        France Illustration, VII (March 17, 1951), p. 291.

E252   Calder-Marshall, Arthur. "The Works of Graham
        Greene." *Horizon*, I (May 1940), pp. 367-375.

        Reprinted as "Graham Greene." *Little Reviews
        Anthology*. London: Allen and Unwin, 1943, pp. 197-
        204.

E253   Camaño Rencoret, Maria Esther. "El Triple Asendio en
        Sarah Miles, Heroina de *El Fin de la Aventura* de
        Graham Greene." *Kãnina* (San José, Costa Rica), I,
        No. 1 (1977), pp. 15-21.

E254   Cameron, J.M. "The Catholic Novelist and European
        Culture." *Twentieth Century Studies*, No. 1 (March
        1969), pp. 79-94.

E255   Camilucci, Marcello. "Saggi Cattolici di Graham
        Greene." *Studium*, LIV (December 1958), pp. 823-830.

E256   Carter, Rev. G. Emmett. "Greene's Latest Novel is
        Written for Sinners." *The Ensign* (October 13, 1951),
        p. 14.

E257   Cartmell, Canon Joseph. "Canon Joseph Cartmell
        Writes." *The Tablet*, CXCI (June 5, 1948), p. 354.

        Reprinted as "A Postscript to Evelyn Waugh," *Common-
        weal*, XLVIII (July 16, 1948), pp. 325-326 and in
        Graham Greene: A Collection of Critical Essays. Edited
        by Samuel L. Hynes. Englewood Cliffs, N.J.: Prentice-
        Hall, Inc., 1973, pp. 103-104.

E258   Cassidy, John. "America and Innocence: Henry James
        and Graham Greene." *Blackfriars*, XXXVIII (June 1957),
        pp. 261-267.

E259   Cassis, A.F. "Dream as Literary Device in Graham
        Greene's Novels." *Literature and Psychology*, XXIV,
        No. 3 (1974), pp. 99-108.

E260   Castelli, Fernando. "Graham Greene Alle Prese con Gli
        Antichi Amori." *La Civiltà Cattolica* (Rome), CXXV,
        No. 1 (1974), pp. 240-249.

E261   Castelli, Fernando. "Graham Greene, un Romanziere che
        Afascina e Sconcerta." *Letture*, XVII (1962), pp. 563-
        580.

E262   Cayrol, Jean. "Autour de l'oeuvre de Graham Greene."
        Revue de la Pensée Française, X (April 1951), pp. 68-72.

E263   Céleste, Sister Marie. "Bernanos and Graham Greene,
        or the Role of the Priest in *The Diary of a Country
        Priest* and *The Power and the Glory*." *Culture*, XXX
        (December 1969), pp. 287-298.

E264   Chaigne, Louis.   "Graham Greene." *Vies et Oeuvres
        d'écrivains*, III (1950), pp. 193-237.

E265   Chapman, Raymond. "The Vision of Graham Greene."
        Forms of Extremity, No. 19 (1965), pp. 75-94.

E266   Chaudhury, M.K. "Graham Greene's *Travels with My Aunt*:
        A Picaresque Novel." *Panjab University Research Bulle-
        tin* (Arts), III, No. 2 (1972), pp. 79-85.

E267   Chavardes, Maurice. "Graham Greene, ou la Nudité de
        Dieu." *Vie Intellectuelle*, No. 7 (July 1950), pp. 113-
        117.

E268   Cheney, Lynne. "Joseph Conrad's *The Secret Agent* and
        Graham Greene's *It's a Battlefield*: A Study in Struc-
        tural Meaning." *Modern Fiction Studies*, XVI (Summer
        1970), pp. 117-131.

E269   Choisy, Maryse. "Psychoanalysis and Catholicism."
        Cross Currents, No. 3 (1951), pp. 75-90.

E270   Clancy, L.J. "Graham Greene's Battlefield." *Melbourne
        Critical Review*, No. 10 (1967), pp. 99-108.

E271   Clancy, W. "The Moral Burden of Mr. Greene's Parable."
        Commonweal, LXIII (March 16, 1956), p. 622.

E272   Clurman, Robert. "The Quiet Englishman: Greene's
        Answer to Critics of *The Quiet American*." *The New
        York Times Book Review* (August 26, 1956), p. 8.

E273   Codey, Regina. "Notes on Graham Greene's Dramatic
        Technique." *Approach*, No. 17 (1955), pp. 23-27.

E274   Connolly, Francis X. "The Heart of the Matter."
        Newsletter: Catholic Book Club, XL (Midsummer 1948),
        pp. 1-2.

E275   Connolly, Francis X. "Inside Modern Man: The Spiritual
        Adventures of Graham Greene." *Renascence*, I (Spring
        1949), pp. 16-24.

E276   Consolo, Dominick P. "Music as Motif: The Unity of
        Brighton Rock." *Renascence*, XV (Fall 1962), pp. 12-20.

        Reprinted in *Graham Greene*. Edited by Harry J. Cargas.
        The Christian Critic Series. St. Louis: B. Herder Book
        Company, n.d. (1969), pp. 75-87.

E277 Cooney, T.E. "Author as Traveler." *Saturday Review*, XXXIX (March 10, 1956), p. 12.

E278 Cosman, Max. "An Early Chapter in Graham Greene." *Arizona Quarterly*, XI (Summer 1955), pp. 143-147.

E279 Cosman, Max. "Disquieted Graham Greene." *Colorado Quarterly*, VI (Winter 1958), pp. 319-325.

E280 Costello, Donald P. "Graham Greene and the Catholic Press." *Renascence*: Graham Greene Special Number, XII (Fall 1959), pp. 3-28.

E281 Costello, Donald P. "The Latest in Greene Criticism." *Renascence*: Graham Greene Special Number, XII (Fall 1959), pp. 38-40.

E282 Cottrell, Beekman W. "Second Time Charm: The Theatre of Graham Greene." *Modern Fiction Studies*: Graham Greene Special Number, III (Autumn 1957), pp. 249-255.

E283 Coulthard, A.R. "Graham Greene's 'The Hint of an Explanation': A Reinterpretation." *Studies in Short Fiction*, VIII (Fall 1971), pp. 601-605.

E284 Cox, Gerald H., III. "Graham Greene's Mystical Rose in Brighton." *Renascence*, XXIII (Autumn 1970), pp. 21-30.

E285 Christopher, Michael. "Troubled Priests in Fiction." *U.S. Catholic and Jubilee*, XXXIV (June 1969), pp. 48-50.

E286 Cronin, Vincent. "Graham Greene's First Play." *Catholic World*, CLXXVII (September 1953), pp. 406-410.

E287 Crubellier, Maurice. "Graham Greene: La Tragedie de la Pitié." *Vie Intellectuelle*, No. 12 (December 1951), pp. 57-58.

E288 Cunningham, Lawrence. "The Alter Ego of Greene's 'Whiskey Priest.'" *English Language Notes* (University of Colorado), VIII, No. 1 (1970), pp. 50-52.

E289 Curtis, Jean-Louis. "Impressions de Londres." *La Table Ronde*, No. 1 (1948), pp. 155-158.

E290 Davenport, John. "The Last Albigensian." *The Spectator*, CCXV (January 28, 1966), pp. 110-111.

E291   Davidson, Arnold C. "Graham Greene's Spiritual Lepers."
       Iowa English Yearbook, XV (Fall 1970), pp. 50-55.

E292   Davidson, Richard Allen. "Graham Greene and L.P.
       Hartley: *The Basement Room* and *The Go-Between*." *Notes
       and Queries*, n.s. XIII (March 13, 1966), pp. 101-102.

E293   Davies, H. "Catching the Conscience: Graham Greene's
       Plays." *Religion in Life*, XXXVI (Winter 1967), pp.
       605-614.

E294   Davis, Robert Murray. "From Standard to Classic:
       Graham Greene in Transit." *Studies in the Novel*, V
       (Winter 1973), pp. 530-546.

E295   Davis, Robert Murray. "More Graham Greene on Film:
       Uncollected Reviews and Fragments of Reviews."
       Literature/Film Quarterly, II (Fall 1974), pp. 384-385.

E296   Day-Lewis, Sean. "The Dominant Shades of Greene."
       The Daily Telegraph (September 15, 1975), p. 7.

E297   Decap, Roger. "La Tradition Puritaine dans la Litéra-
       ture Anglaise: John Bunyan et Graham Greene." *Caliban*,
       n.s. I, No. 2 (1965), pp. 129-145.

E298   Déchet, Ferruccio. "Suggestioni e Limiti della Tema-
       tica di Graham Greene." *Giornale di Metafisica* (Turin),
       XIX (1964), pp. 75-89.

E299   Deedy, J. "News and Views." *Commonweal*, CIII (April 23,
       1976), p. 260.

E300   DeHegedus, Adam. "Graham Greene: The Man and His Work."
       World Review, XV (August 1948), pp. 57-61.

E301   DeHegedus, Adam. "Graham Greene and the Modern Novel."
       Tomorrow, VIII (October 1948), pp. 54-56.

E302   Delbanco, Nicholas. "The Human Factor." *New Republic*,
       CLXXVIII (March 11, 1978), pp. 32-33.

E303   Delpech, Jeanie. "Graham Greene à Paris." *Nouvelles
       Litéraires* (December 19, 1946), pp. 1-2.

E304   Delteil, F. "Romanciers Catholiques Anglais: II.
       Graham Greene." *Livres et Lecteurs*, No. 17 (1948),
       pp. 433-435.

E305   Desmond, John F.   "Graham Greene and the Eternal Dimension."   *American Benedictine Review*, XX (September 1969), pp. 418-427.

E306   DeVitis, A.A.   "Notes on *The Power and the Glory*."   *The Annotator*, No. 5 (May 1955), pp. 7-10.

E307   DeVitis, A.A.   "Allegory in *Brighton Rock*."   *Modern Fiction Studies*: Graham Greene Special Number, III (Autumn 1957), pp. 216-224.

E308   DeVitis, A.A.   "The Church and Major Scobie."   *Renascence*, X (Spring 1958), pp. 115-120.

E309   DeVitis, A.A.   "The Entertaining Mr. Greene."   *Renascence*, XIV (Autumn 1961), pp. 8-24.

E310   DeVitis, A.A.   "Greene's *The Comedians*: Hollower Men."   *Renascence*, XVIII (Spring 1966), pp. 129-136, 146.

E311   Dhoeve, Andries.   "Graham Greene."   *De Periscoop*, (January 1, 1953), p. 1.

E312   Didion, J.   "Marks of Identity."   *National Review*, X (March 25, 1961), pp. 190-191.

E313   Dinkins, Paul.   "Graham Greene: The Incomplete Version."   *Catholic World*, CLXXVI (November 1952), pp. 96-102.

E314   Dneprov, V.   "Vera i Bezverie" (Faith and Unbelief).   *Zvezda* (Moscow), IV (1969), pp. 202-210; V, pp. 204-215.

E315   Dombrowski, T.Q.   "Graham Greene: Techniques of Intensity."   *Ariel*, VI (October 1975), pp. 29-38.

E316   Domenichelli, Mario.   "L'incredible Messia: Il Primo Greene fra Eliot e James Joyce."   *Lettore di Provincia*, XXV-XXVI (1976), pp. 117-131.

E317   Donoghue, D.   "Visit to Greeneland."   *Commonweal*, XCIX (November 30, 1973), pp. 241-242.

E318   Dooley, D.J.   "*A Burnt-Out Case* Reconsidered."   *Wiseman Review*, No. 496 (Summer 1963), pp. 168-178.

E319   Dooley, D.J.   "The Suspension of Disbelief: Greene's *A Burnt-Out Case*."   *Dalhousie Review*, XLIII (Autumn 1963), pp. 343-352.

E320 Downing, Francis. "The Art of Fiction." *Commonweal*,
      LV (December 28, 1951), pp. 297-299.

E321 Downing, Francis. "Graham Greene and the Case for Dis-
      loyalty." *Commonweal*, LV (March 14, 1952), pp. 564-566.

E322 Doyle, Louis F., S.J. "Graham Greene as Moralist."
      America, XCI (September 18, 1954), p. 604.

E323 Drążkiewicz, Joanna. "Understanding Suspense."
      Zagadnienia Rodzajów Literackich, XVII, No. 2 (1974),
      pp. 21-30.
      Re novels of Graham Greene, Arthur Conan Doyle and
      Joseph Conrad.

E324 Duché, Jean. "Je n'écrivai Plus de Romans Policiers,
      nous dit Graham Greene." *Figaro Littéraire* (December
      20, 1947), p. 6.

E325 Duché, Jean. "Du Rocher de Sysyphe au Rocher de
      Brighton." *La Table Ronde*, No. 2 (February 1948),
      pp. 306-309.

E326 Duesberg, Jacques. "Un Épigone du 'Misérabilisme':
      Graham Greene." *Synthèses*, No. 69 (February 1952),
      pp. 348-353.

E327 Duffy, Joseph M., Jr. "The Lost World of Graham
      Greene." *Thought*, XXXIII (Summer 1958), pp. 229-247.

E328 Dunlevy, Maurice. "He Couldn't Win at Russian Rou-
      lette." *Canberra Times* (September 25, 1971), p. 14.

E329 DuParc, Robert. "Saint ou Maudit? Le Prêtre dans
      La Puissance et la Glorie." *Études*, CCLX (March 1949),
      pp. 368-381.

E330 Duran, Justo Leopoldo. "La Última Gran Novela Católica
      de Graham Greene." *Filologia Moderna*, No. 29-30 (1968),
      pp. 167-178.

E331 Duran, Justo Leopoldo. "Graham Greene's 'A Visit to
      Morin.'" *Clergy Review*, LIX (October 1974), pp. 643-647.

E332 Duran, Justo Leopoldo. "The Essential Priesthood as
      Portrayed by Graham Greene." *Clergy Review*, LX
      (February 1975), pp. 103-116.

E333 Duran, Justo Leopoldo. "The Hint of an Explanation of Graham Greene." *Contemporary Review*, CCXXVI (March 1975), pp. 152-155.

E334 Duran, Justo Leopoldo. "A Priest Reads *The Honorary Consul.*" *Clergy Review*, LXI (September 1976), pp. 343-349.

E335 Eishiskina, N. "Graham Greene's Novels." *Voprosi Literaturi*, VI (June 1961), pp. 149-169.

E336 Elistratova, Anna. "Graham Greene and His New Novel." *Soviet Literature*, VIII (1956), pp. 149-155.

E337 Elliott, D. "Graham Greene's Singular Success in the Perilous Switch from Print to Film." *Biography News*, I (June 1974), p. 648.

E338 Ellis, William D., Jr. "The Grand Theme of Graham Greene." *Southwest Review*, XLI (Summer 1956), pp. 239-250.

E339 Elsen, Claude. "Graham Greene ou la Geste de l'homme Traqué." *La Table Ronde*, No. 14 (February 1949), pp. 297-301.

E340 Engel, Claire Elaine. "Einige Englische Romanciers von Heute." *Du*, VIII (January 1948), p. 28.

E341 Engelborghs, Maurits. "Hoogtepunten in het Werk van Graham Greene." *Dietsche Warande en Belfort* (Antwerp), (June 1951), pp. 564-566.

E342 Engelborghs, Maurits. "Beschouwingen bij de Laatste Roman van Graham Greene" (*The Quiet American*). *Dietsche Warande en Belfort* (Antwerp), III (1956), pp. 433-444.

E343 Engelborghs, Maurits. "Graham Greene." *Dietsche Warande en Belfort* (Antwerp), IV (1957), pp. 236-239.

E344 Engelborghs, Maurits. "Graham Greene: *The Potting Shed.*" *Dietsche Warande en Belfort* (Antwerp), V (1958), pp. 308-310.

E345 Engelborghs, Maurits. "De Nieuwe Roman van Graham Greene." *Kultuur Leven*, XXVI (February 1959), pp. 119-122.

E346   Engelborghs, Maurits. "Engelse Letteren: *The Complaisant Lover*: Een Blijspel van Graham Greene." *Dietsche Warande en Belfort* (Antwerp), VIII (October 1959), pp. 497-501.

E347   Engelborghs, Maurits. "Graham Greene: *A Burnt-Out Case*." *Kultuur Leven*, XXVIII (October 1961), pp. 610-615.

E348   Engelborghs, Maurits. "Dagboek van een Romancier." *Dietsche Warande en Belfort* (Antwerp), CVII (May-June 1962), p. 372.

E349   Engelborghs, Maurits. "Graham Greene op de Terug Weg?" *Dietsche Warande en Belfort* (Antwerp), CIX (1964), pp. 55-63.

E350   Engelborghs, Maurits. "De Opuatting van Roman en Romanschrijver bij Graham Greene." *Dietsche Warande en Belfort* (Antwerp), CIX (1964), pp. 172-198.

E351   Enright, D.J. "Edge of Danger." *New Society* (September 16, 1971), pp. 524-525.

E352   Erba, Luciano. "Incontro con Graham Greene." *Vita e Pensiero*, XXXII (September 1949), pp. 507-509.

E353   Escarpit, Robert. "L'Arriére-plan Mexicain dans Lawrence et dans Greene." *Langues Modernes*, XLV (February 1951), pp. 44-46.

E354   Esslin, M. Review of *The Return of A. J. Raffles*. *Plays and Players*, XXIII (February 1976), p. 30.

E355   Evans, Robert O. "Existentialism in Graham Greene's *The Quiet American*." *Modern Fiction Studies*: Graham Greene Special Number, III (Autumn 1957), pp. 241-248.

E356   Fadiman, Clifton. "The Decline of Attention." *Saturday Review of Literature*, XXXII (August 6, 1949), pp. 20-24.

E357   Fagin, Steven. "Narrative Design in *Travels with My Aunt*." *Literature/Film Quarterly*, II (Fall 1974), pp. 379-383.

E358   Fay, Teresita and Michael G. Yetman. "Scobie the Just: A Reassessment of *The Heart of the Matter*." *Renascence*, XXIX (1977), pp. 142-156.

E359 Fielding, Gabriel. "Graham Greene: The Religious
      Englishman." *The Listener*, LXXII (September 24, 1964),
      pp. 465-466.

E360 Filyushkina, S.N. "Roman Grema Grina *Chelovek Vnutri*"
      (*Graham Greene's Novel The Man Within*). *Permskii
      Universitet* (Perm'.), CLXXXVIII (1968), pp. 3-18.

E361 Filyushkina, S.N. "Iskusstvo Grina—Romanista" (The
      Art of Greene, the Novelist). *Vestnik Moskovskogo
      Universiteta*. *Filologiya*, IV (1969), pp. 18-29.

E362 Findlater, Richard. "Graham Greene as Dramatist."
      Twentieth Century, CLIII (June 1953), pp. 471-473.

E363 Finn, J. "Obsession with Failure." *New Republic*,
      CLXI (July 5, 1969), pp. 30-31.

E364 Finn, J. "*A Sort of Life*." *Commonweal*, XCV (October
      29, 1971), pp. 113-114.

E365 Flint, R.W. "Recent Fiction." *Hudson Review*, I (1948-
      1949), pp. 590-596.

E366 Flood, Ethelbert, O.F.M. "Christian Language in Modern
      Literature." *Culture*, XII (1961), pp. 28-42.

E367 Foote, Timothy. "Man Without." *Time*, XCVIII
      (September 27, 1971), p. 94.

E368 Foote, Timothy. "Our Man in Gehenna." *Time*, CII
      (September 17, 1973), p. 99.

E369 Fouchet, Max-Pol. "Graham Greene." *Revue de Paris*,
      LVII (July 1950), pp. 59-68.

E370 Fowler, Alastair. "Novelist of Damnation." *Theology*,
      LVI (July 1953), pp. 259-264.

E371 Freedman, Ralph. "Novel of Contention: *The Quiet
      American*." *Western Review*, XXI (Autumn 1956), pp. 76-
      81.

E372 Fremantle, Anne. "The Hunted Men of Graham Greene."
      Saturday Review, XXXVI (January 10, 1953), pp. 15-16.

E373 French, Philip. "Screen Greene." *London Magazine*,
      VIII (April 1968), pp. 54-57.

E374 Friedman, Melvin. "The Vision Obscured" (A Graham
      Greene Symposium). *Renascence*, XXIII (Fall 1970),
      pp. 3-54.

E375 Frykman, Erik. "Some Notes on the Theme of Self-
      Realization in English and Scandinavian Literature of
      the Nineteenth and Twentieth Centuries." *Aberdeen
      University Review*, XLIV (September 1972), pp. 241-255.

E376 Fulford, R. "On Graham Greene: Slippers, Pipe and Raw
      Terror." *Maclean's Magazine*, LXXVI (September 7, 1963),
      pp. 69-70.

E377 Fytton, Francis. "Graham Greene: Catholicism and Con-
      troversy." *Catholic World*, CLXXX (December 1954),
      pp. 172-175.

E378 Gainham, Sarah. "Grim Grin." *The Spectator*, CCX
      (May 31, 1963), p. 694.

E379 Gallagher, Michael P. "Human Values in Modern Litera-
      ture." *Studies*, LVII (Summer 1968), pp. 142-153.

E380 Gardiner, Harold C., S.J. "Taste and Worth."
      America, LXXV (April 20, 1946), p. 53.

E381 Gardiner, Harold C., S.J. *"Heart of the Matter*:
      Greene's Greatest?" *America*, LXXIX (July 17, 1948),
      pp. 350-351.

E382 Gardiner, Harold C., S.J. "Graham Greene, Catholic
      Shocker." *Renascence*, I (Spring 1949), pp. 12-15.

E383 Gardiner, Harold C., S.J. "Second Thoughts on
      Greene's Latest." *America*, LXXVI (December 15, 1951),
      pp. 312-313.

      Reprinted in *In All Conscience*. New York: Hanover
      House, 1959, pp. 98-102.

E384 Gardiner, Harold C., S.J. "Nature and Grace."
      America, XCIV (March 10, 1956), p. 639.

E385 Garrigue, Jean. "Six Writers of Crisis." *Commentary*,
      XXVII (March 1959), pp. 270-272.

E386 Gassner, John. "Broadway in Review." *Educational
      Theatre Journal*, XI (March 1959), pp. 29-39.

E387   Gilbert, Rafael.   "La Crisis del Sacerdote en Graham
       Greene." *Arbor*, CCCLXXV (1977), pp. 81-86.

E388   Gilman, Richard.   "Up from Hell with Graham Greene."
       New Republic, CLIV (January 29, 1966), pp. 25-29.

E389   Ginna, R.E.   "Carol Reed Directs *Our Man in Havana*."
       Horizon, II (November 1959), pp. 26-31, 122, 126.

E390   Glicksberg, Charles I.   "Graham Greene: Catholicism in
       Fiction." *Criticism*, I (Fall 1959), pp. 339-353.

E391   Golden, Janet.   "Graham Greene and the Sense of Sin."
       St. Joseph Magazine (June 1953), pp. 8-9, 26.

E392   Göller, Karl Heinz.   "Graham Greene: *The Power and the
       Glory*." *Der Moderne Englische Roman*, LI (1966),
       pp. 245-261.

E393   Gomez, Joseph A.   "*The Third Man*." *Literature/Film
       Quarterly*, II (1974), pp. 332-340.

E394   Gonzalez Salas, Carlos.   "Tres Libros y Tres Autores
       Discutidos: Graham Greene contra Mejico." *Abside*,
       XXIV (1960), pp. 358-361.

E395   Gordon, Caroline.   "Some Readings and Misreadings."
       Sewanee Review, LXI (Summer 1953), pp. 393-396.

E396   Graef, Hilda.   "Marriage and Our Catholic Novelists."
       Catholic World, CLXXXIX (June 1959), pp. 185-190.

E397   Graude, Luke.   "Gabriel Fielding, New Master of the
       Catholic Classic?" *Catholic World*, CXCVII (June 1964),
       pp. 172-179.

E398   Gražyte, Ilona.   "Graham Greene." *Aidai*, CLXXXVI
       (May 1966), pp. 200-205.

E399   Gregor, Ian.   "The New Romanticism: A Comment on *The
       Living Room*." *Blackfriars*, XXXIV (September 1953),
       pp. 403-406.

E400   Gregor, Ian.   "The Greene Baize Door." *Blackfriars*,
       XXXVI (September 1955), pp. 327-333.

E401   Gregor, Ian.   "A Sort of Fiction?" *Blackfriars*, LIII
       (March 1972), pp. 120-124.

E402   Greisch, J.R.   "Patterns of Evil and How to Break Them."
       Christianity Today, XIX (June 20, 1975), pp. 13-14.

E403   Grenzmann, Wilhelm.   "Das Leiden der Literatur--Das
       Leiden an der Literatur."   *Begegnung*, XIX (July-August
       1964), pp. 5-10.

E404   Grob, A.   "Power and the Glory: Graham Greene's Argu-
       ment from Design."   *Criticism*, XI (Winter 1969),
       pp. 1-30.

E405   Grubbs, Henry A.   "Albert Camus and Graham Greene."
       Modern Language Quarterly, X (March 1949), pp. 33-42.

E406   Grunt, Olav Paus.   "Grunntrekk i Graham Greenes For-
       tellerkunst."   *Samtiden*, LXIII (1954), pp. 341-349.

E407   Guerrero Zamora, Juan.   "Graham Green su Cuarto de
       Estar contra la Muerte."   *Indice*, VIII (September 30,
       1953), p. 24.

E408   H., T.   *"The Potting Shed*: Figmentum Fidei."   *Dublin
       Review*, CCXXXII (Spring 1958), pp. 71-73.

E409   Haber, Herbert R.   "The Two Worlds of Graham Greene."
       Modern Fiction Studies: Graham Greene Special Number,
       III (Autumn 1957), pp. 256-268.

E410   Hahn, Karl J.   "Graham Greene."   *Hochland* (München),
       XLI (July 1949), pp. 455-465.

E411   Hamilton, Alex.   "Graham Greene."   *The Guardian*
       (September 11, 1971), p. 8.

E412   Hanlon, Robert M., S.J.   "The Ascent to Belief in
       Graham Greene's *A Burnt-Out Case*."   *Christianity and
       Literature*, XXVI, No. 4 (1977), pp. 20-26.

E413   Hanlon, Robert M., S.J.   "Pity of Treachery: Graham
       Greene's *The Human Factor*."   *America*, CXXXVI (June 17,
       1978), pp. 486-488.

E414   Happel, Nikolaus.   "Formbetrachtung an Graham Greens
       Short Story 'The Hint of an Explanation.'"   *Die
       Neueren Sprachen*, IX (1960), pp. 81-86.

E415   Harmer, Ruth Mulvey.   "Greene World of Mexico: The Birth
       of a Novelist."   *Renascence*, XV (Summer 1963), pp. 171-
       182.

E416 Harris, Wendell V. "Molly's 'Yes': The Transvaluation of Sex in Modern Fiction." *Texas Studies in Literature and Language*, X (1968), pp. 107-118.

E417 Hawton, Hector and Roger Manvell. "A Sort of Roman." *Humanist*, LXXXVI (October 1971), pp. 303-305.

E418 Hayes, Richard. "*The Living Room*." *Commonweal*, LXI (December 24, 1954), pp. 333-334.

E419 Hayman, Ronald. "Le Roman Anglais d'Après-Guerre, III." *Revue de Lettres Modernes*, III (April 1954), pp. 88-93.

E420 Hays, H.R. "A Defense of the Thriller." *Partisan Review*, XII (Winter 1945), pp. 135-137.

E421 Heilpern, John. "On the Dangerous Edge." *The Observer Magazine* (December 7, 1975), p. 17.

E422 Herling, Gustav. "Two Sanctities: Graham Greene and Camus." *Adam International Review*, No. 201 (December 1949), pp. 10-19.

E423 Herzog, Bert. "Welt unter Geschlossenem Himmel: Zu den Büchern von Graham Greene." *Stimmen der Zeit*, CLI (March 1952), pp. 420-426; (October 1952), pp. 20-25.

E424 Hess, M. Whitcomb. "Graham Greene's Travesty on *The Ring and the Book*." *Catholic World*, CXCIV (October 1961), pp. 37-42.

E425 Hewes, H. "Resurrection Will Out." *Saturday Review*, XL (February 16, 1957), pp. 26-27.

E426 Hicks, Granville. "In a Novel It's the Life, Not the Politics, That Counts." *The New York Times Book Review* (August 12, 1956), p. 5.

E427 Hicks, Granville. "Gestation of a Brain Child." *Saturday Review*, XLV (January 6, 1962), p. 62.

E428 Higdon, David Leon. "Graham Greene's Second Thoughts: The Text of *The Heart of the Matter*." *Studies in Bibliography* (University of Virginia Bibliographical Society), III (1977), pp. 249-256.

E429 Highet, Gilbert. "Our Man in Purgatory." *Horizon*, III
      (May 1961), pp. 116-117.

E430 Hill, Roland. "Graham Greene, Die Stunde der *Komödian-
      len*." *Hochland* (München), LIX (1966), pp. 90-94.

E431 Hillig, Franz, S.J. "Die Kraft und die Herrlichkeit."
      Stimmen der Zeit (Freiburg), CLXIII (February 1949),
      pp. 354-366.

E432 Hinchliffe, A.P. "The Good American." *Twentieth
      Century*, CLXVIII (December 1960), pp. 529-539.

E433 Hobson, L.Z. "Innocent Abroad." *Good Housekeeping*,
      CXVII (March 1956), p. 13.

E434 Hoggart, Richard. "The Force of Caricature: Aspects of
      the Art of Graham Greene, with Particular Reference to
      The Power and the Glory." *Essays in Criticism*, III
      (October 1953), pp. 447-462.

      Reprinted in *Graham Greene: A Collection of Critical
      Essays*. Edited by Samuel L. Hynes. Englewood Cliffs,
      N.J.: Prentice-Hall, Inc., 1973, pp. 79-94.

E435 Hollis, Carroll C. "Nathanael West and the 'Lonely
      Crowd.'" *Thought*, XXXIII (Autumn 1958), pp. 398-416.

E436 Horst, Karl August. "Argernis der Schöptung, zur
      Theologie Graham Greenes." *Merkur*, V (February 1951),
      pp. 184-187.

E437 Hortmann, Wilhelm. "Graham Greene: The Burnt-Out
      Catholic." *Twentieth Century Literature*, X (July
      1964), pp. 64-76.

E438 Houle, Sheila. "The Subjective Theological Vision of
      Graham Greene." *Renascence*, XXIII (Autumn 1970),
      pp. 3-13.

E439 Howes, Jane. "Out of the Pit." *Catholic World*,
      CLXXI (April 1950), pp. 36-40.

E440 Hughes, Catharine. "Innocence Revisited." *Renascence*:
      Graham Greene Special Number, XII (Fall 1959), pp. 29-
      34.

E441 Hughes, Catharine. "Growing Up As Greene." *America*, CXXV (October 2, 1971), pp. 230-232.

E442 Hughes, Riley E. *"The End of the Affair."* *Catholic World*, CLXXIV (January 1952), p. 312.

E443 Hughes, Riley E. *"The Quiet American*: The Case Reopened." *Renascence*: Graham Greene Special Number, XII (Fall 1959), pp. 41-42, 49.

E444 Hynes, Joseph. "The Facts at 'The Heart of the Matter.'" *Texas Studies in Literature and Language*, XIII (1972), pp. 711-726.

E445 Hynes, Samuel. "Religion in the West End." *Commonweal*, LIX (February 12, 1954), pp. 475-478.

E446 Igoe, W.J. "London Letter." *America*, XCII (December 23, 1954), pp. 99-101.

E447 Igoe, W.J. "Graham Greene." *John O'London's*, IV (July 6, 1961), pp. 24-25.

E448 Ihlenfeld, Kurt. "Kann ein Sünder ein Heiliger Sein? Ueber G. Greenes Buch *Die Kraft und die Herrlichkeit*." *Evangelische Welt* (Bethel), III (1947), pp. 636-637.

E449 Isaacs, Rita. "Three Levels of Allegory in Graham Greene's *The End of the Affair*." *Linguistics and Literature*, I, No. 1 (1975), pp. 29-52.

E450 Ivănescu, Mircea. "Virtutile Divertismentului" (The Virtues of *The Confidential Agent*). *România Literară* (Bucharest), III (July 1970), p. 20.

E451 Ivaschova, Valentina. "Legende und Wahrheit über Graham Greene." *Zeitschrift für Anglistik und Amerikanistik* (East Berlin), X (1962), pp. 225-258.

E452 Jacobsen, Josephine. "A Catholic Quartet." *Christian Scholar*, XLVII (Summer 1964), pp. 139-154.

Re Greene, Muriel Spark, J.F. Powers and Flannery O'Connor.

E453 Jameson, Storm. "British Literature: Survey and Critique." *Saturday Review*, XXXIV (October 13, 1951), pp. 24-26, 47.

E454   Jans, Adrien. "Graham Greene, Entre le Péché et
       l'amour." *Empreintes*, IV (February-April 1948),
       pp. 46-49.

E455   Jefferson, Mary Evelyn. "*The Heart of the Matter*: The
       Responsible Man." *The Carolina Quarterly*, IX (Summer
       1957), pp. 23-31.

       Reprinted in *Graham Greene*. Edited by Harry J. Cargas.
       The Christian Critic Series. St. Louis: B. Herder Book
       Company, n.d. (1969), pp. 88-100.

E456   Jerrold, Douglas. "Graham Greene, Pleasure-Hater."
       Picture Post, LIV (March 15, 1952), pp. 51-53.

       Reprinted in *Harper's*, CCV (August 1952), pp. 50-52.

E457   Johnston, J.L. "Graham Greene--The Unhappy Man." *The
       Central Literary Magazine* (Birmingham), XXXVIII (July
       1954), pp. 43-49.

E458   Jones, Grahame C. "Graham Greene and the Legend of
       Péguy." *Comparative Literature*, XXI (Spring 1969),
       pp. 138-145.

E459   Jones, Grahame C. "Léon Bloy et Graham Greene:
       L'influence de *La Femme Pauvre* sur *The End of the
       Affair*." *Revue de Littérature Comparée*, XLIV (October-
       December 1970), pp. 540-546.

E460   Jones, James Land. "Graham Greene and the Structure of
       the Moral Imagination." *Phoneix*, No. 2 (1966), pp.
       34-56.

E461   Joselyn, Sister M., O.S.B. "Graham Greene's Novels:
       The Conscience of the World." *Literature and Society*,
       XII (1964), pp. 153-172.

E462   Joseph, Brother. "Greene's 'The Hint of an Explana-
       tion.'" *Explicator*, XIX (January 1961), Item 21.

E463   Jouve, Raymond. "La Damnation de Scobie?" *Études*,
       No. 263 (November 1949), pp. 164-177.

E464   Kähler, Klaus. "Die Syntax des Dialogs im Modernen
       Englisch Untersucht an Werken von Harold Pinter und
       Graham Greene." *Zeitschrift für Anglistik und
       Amerikanistik* (East Berlin), XXIII (1975), pp. 41-63.

E465   Kauffman, Stanley. "With Graham Greene in Havana."
       New Republic, CXLII (February 15, 1960), pp. 22-23.

E466   Keily, Robert. "The Craft of Despondency--the Tradi-
       tional Novelists." *Daedalus*, XCII (Spring 1963), pp.
       220-237.
       Re Greene, Waugh and Porter.

E467   Kellogg, J.D. "Burnt-Out Case?" *America*, CXXII
       (March 14, 1970), pp. 273-274.

E468   Kennedy, W. "Let Us All Now Be Thankful for Mr.
       Greene's Deadly Boredom." *Look*, XXXV (October 19,
       1971), p. 64.

E469   Kenny, Herbert A. "Graham Greene." *Catholic World*,
       CLXXXV (August 1957), pp. 326-329.

E470   Kermode, Frank. "Mr. Greene's Eggs and Crosses."
       Encounter, XVI (April 1961), pp. 69-75.

E471   Kevin, Neil. "Fiction Priests." *Irish Ecclesiastical
       Record*, LX (October 1940), pp. 253-257.

E472   Keyser, Les. "England Made Me." *Literature/Film
       Quarterly*, II (Fall 1974), p. 364.

E473   Khatchadourian, Haig. "Some Major Trends in Twentieth-
       Century English Literature." *Visva-Bharati Quarterly*,
       XXVII (Autumn 1961), pp. 140-149.

E474   King, Bruce. "Graham Greene's Inferno." *Études
       Anglaises*, XXI (January-March 1968), pp. 35-51.

E475   King, James. "In the Lost Boyhood of Judas: Graham
       Greene's Early Novels of Hell." *Dalhousie Review*,
       XLIX (Summer 1969), pp. 229-236.

E476   Klein, Luce A. "La Première Piece de Graham Greene
       Sera Jouée à Paris." *Arts*, No. 388 (December 5, 1952),
       p. 3.

E477   Knipp, Thomas R. "Gide and Greene: Africa and the
       Literary Imagination." *Serif*, VI (June 1969),
       pp. 3-14.

E478   Kort, Wesley. "The Obsession of Graham Greene."
       Thought, LXV (Spring 1970), pp. 20-44.

E479   Koster, Wilhelm. "Dennoch Nicht." *Frankfurter Hefte*,
       VIII (April 1953), pp. 314-315.

E480   Kubal, David L. "Graham Greene's *Brighton Rock*: the
       Political Theme." *Renascence*, XXIII (Autumn 1970),
       pp. 46-54.

E481   Kunkel, Francis Leo. "The Priest as Scapegoat in the
       Modern Catholic Novel." *Ramparts*, I (January 1963),
       pp. 72-78.

E482   Lambert, J.W. "Graham Greene: The Next Move." *The
       Sunday Times* (January 16, 1966), pp. 41-42.

E483   Langlois, José Miguel Ibáñez. "Catolicismo y Protestan-
       tismo en la Novela de Graham Greene." *Atlántida*,
       No. 22 (1966), pp. 381-397.

E484   Lanina, T. "Paradoxes of Graham Greene." *Inostrannaja
       Literatura*, No. 3 (April 1959), pp. 188-196.

E485   Larsen, Eric. "*The Quiet American*." *New Republic*
       (August 7-14, 1976), pp. 40-42.

E486   Laski, Margharita. "How Well Have They Worn?--
       Brighton Rock." *The Times* (February 17, 1966), p. 15.

E487   Las Vergnas, Raymond. "A Propos de Graham Greene."
       Hommes et Mondes, IX (May 1949), pp. 147-151.

E488   Las Vergnas, Raymond. "Une Curiosité Affamée."
       Nouvelles Littéraires, XVII (September 1971), p. 9.

E489   Lauder, R.E. "Catholic Novel and the Inside God."
       Commonweal, CI (October 25, 1974), pp. 78-81.

E490   Lauras, Antoine. "Sommes-nous des Comediens?" *Études*,
       No. 324 (April 1966), pp. 510-513.

E491   Laurens, A. "Comment j'ai Introduit Graham Greene en
       France." *France-Asie* (Saigon), III (April 1948),
       pp. 455-459.

E492   Lees, F.N. "Graham Greene: A Comment." *Scrutiny*,
       XIX (October 1952), pp. 31-42.

E493   Lehane, J.C., C.M.   "*The Heart of the Matter* is a
       Superior Example of the Craftsmanship of Fiction."
       The New World, (July 23, 1948), p. 15.

E494   Lehmann, J.   "The Blundering, Ineffectual American."
       New Republic, CXXXIV (March 12, 1956), pp. 26-27.

E495   Lemaitre, Henri.   "Un Romancier Chrétien de l'absurde:
       Graham Greene."   *Culture Catholique*, IV (September
       1949).

E496   Lenfest, David S.   "'*Brighton Rock*' '*Young Scarface.*'"
       Literature/Film Quarterly, II (Fall 1974), pp. 373-378.

E497   Lennon, Peter.   "The French Honour Graham Greene."
       The Guardian (January 2, 1969), p. 9.

E498   Lerner, Lawrence.   "Graham Greene."   *Critical Quar-
       terly*, V (Autumn 1963), pp. 217-231.

E499   Levin, Gerald.   "The Rhetoric of Graham Greene's *The
       Heart of the Matter.*"   *Renascence*, XXIII (Autumn 1970),
       pp. 14-20.

E500   Levine, N.   "Mr. Greene Mellowed."   *Atlantic Advocate*,
       LVI (February 1966), p. 72.

E501   Lewis, R.W.B.   "The 'Trilogy' of Graham Greene."
       Modern Fiction Studies: Graham Greene Special Number,
       III (Autumn 1957), pp. 195-215.

       Reprinted in *Graham Greene: A Collection of Critical
       Essays*. Edited by Samuel L. Hynes.   Englewood Cliffs,
       N.J.:   Prentice-Hall, Inc., 1973, pp. 49-74.

E502   Lewis, R.W.B.   "The Fiction of Graham Greene: Between
       the Horror and the Glory."   *Kenyon Review*, XIX (Winter
       1957), pp. 56-75.

       Reprinted as "Graham Greene: The Religious Affair," in
       *The Picaresque Saint: Representative Figures in Con-
       temporary Fiction*.   Philadelphia and New York: J.B.
       Lippincott Co., 1959, pp. 220-274.

E503   Lewis, Theophilus.   "Post Mortem Report."   *America*,
       XCII (January 8, 1955), pp. 386-387.

E504 Liberman, M.M. "The Uses of Anti-fiction: Greene's
      'Across the Bridge.'" *Georgia Review*, XXVII (1973),
      pp. 321-328.

E505 Liebling, A.J. "Talkative Something-or-Other." *New
      Yorker*, XXXII (April 7, 1956), pp. 148-154.

E506 Lindman-Stafford, Kerstin. "En Sorts Komedi."
      Horisont (Vasa), XIII, No. 3 (1966), pp. 27-30.

      Re The Comedians.

E507 Link, Joseph. "Der Schnapspriester." *Die Seele*
      (Regensburg), XXV (1949), p. 271.

E508 Lodge, David. "Use of Key Words in the Novels of
      Graham Greene: Love, Hate and *The End of the Affair*."
      Blackfriars, XLII (November 1961), pp. 468-474.

E509 Lodge, David. "Graham Greene's Comedians." *Commonweal*,
      LXXXIII (February 25, 1966), pp. 604-606.

E510 Lohf, Kenneth A. "Graham Greene and the Problem of
      Evil." *Catholic World*, CLXXIII (June 1951), pp. 196-
      199.

E511 Lord, Daniel A., S.J. "Tragedy and Graham Greene" (in
      his syndicated column "Along the Way"). *The New World*
      (October 1, 1948), p. 4.

E512 MacInnes, Colin. "Involved and Aloof: A Sense of
      Reality." *The Spectator*, CCX (June 21, 1963), p. 812.

E513 Maclaren-Ross, J. "Excursion in Greeneland." *London
      Magazine*, IV (December 1964), pp. 56-65.

E514 MacSween, R.J. "Exiled from the Garden: Graham
      Greene." *Antigonish Review*, I (Summer 1970), pp. 41-
      48.

E515 Madaule, Jacques. "El Misterio del Amor en la Obra de
      Graham Greene." *Sur*, No. 226 (January-February 1954),
      pp. 48-65.

E516 Madden, Joan. "With Crooked Lines: Greene's *The Living
      Room*." *America*, XC (March 6, 1954), pp. 600-602.

E517 Magid, N.L. "Tantalizing Two-Way Mirrors of Graham
      Greene." *Commonweal*, XC (September 19, 1969), pp. 567-
      568.

E518 Magny, Claude-Edmonde. "Graham Greene." *Poésie 46*, No. 32 (May 1946), pp. 32-37.

E519 Magny, Claude-Edmonde. "De Benito Cereno au Rocher de Brighton." *Guilde du Livre*, XVI (July 1951), pp. 150-153.

E520 Maguire, Mother C.E. "Grace and the Play." *America*, XCIII (July 30, 1955), pp. 433-435.

E521 Majid, S.D. "The Existential Concern in Graham Greene." *Indiana Journal of English Studies*, XII (December 1971), pp. 75-85.

E522 Marian, Sister, I.H.M. "Graham Greene's People: Being and Becoming." *Renascence*, XVIII (Autumn 1965), pp. 16-22.

E523 Marie-Céleste, Sister. "Georges Bernanos et Graham Greene: Le Prêtre dans *Le Journal d'un Curé de Campagne* et *La Puissance et la Gloire*." *Revue des Lettres Modernes*, No. 5 (1965), pp. 43-70.

E524 Markovic, Vida E. "Graham Greene in Search of God." *Texas Studies in Literature and Language*, V (Summer 1963), pp. 271-282.

E525 Marshall, Bruce. "Graham Greene and Evelyn Waugh." *Commonweal*, LI (March 3, 1950), pp. 551-553.

Reprinted in Italian in *Vita e Pensiero*, XXXV (August 1952), pp. 471-474.

E526 Martin, Christopher. "Power Without Glory." *Journal of Ecumenical Studies* (Pittsburgh, Pennsylvania), IV, No. 3 (1967), pp. 469-472.

E527 Mason, H.A. "A Note on Contemporary 'Philosophical' Literary Criticism in France." *Scrutiny*, XVI (March 1949), pp. 54-60.

E528 Mass, Roslyn. "The Presentation of the Character of Sarah Miles in the Film Version of *The End of the Affair*." *Literature/Film Quarterly*, II (Fall 1974), pp. 347-351.

E529 Maudit, Jean. "*Le Living Room* de Graham Greene." *Études*, No. 283 (November 1954), pp. 365-371.

E530   Mauriac, François. "*La Puissance et la Gloire.*"
       Figaro Littéraire (October 30, 1948), pp. 1, 3.

       Reprinted in *Renascence*, I (Spring 1949), pp. 25-27.

E531   Maxwell, J.C. "'The Dry Salvages': A Possible Echo of
       Graham Greene." *Notes and Queries*, n.s. XI (October
       1964), p. 387.

E532   May, John R. "Images of the Apocalypse in the Black
       Novel." *Renascence*, XXIII (Autumn 1970), pp. 30-45.

E533   Mayhew, Alice. "*The Comedians.*" *The National Catholic
       Reporter* (March 30, 1966).

       Reprinted in *Graham Greene*. Edited by Harry J. Cargas.
       The Christian Critic Series. St. Louis: B. Herder Book
       Company, n.d. (1969), pp. 134-141.

E534   Mayne, Richard. "Where God Makes the Scenery." *New
       Statesman*, LXVI (August 2, 1963), p. 144.

E535   Mayne, Richard. "TLS Commentary: Second Innings."
       Times Literary Supplement (December 12, 1975), p. 1486.

E536   McCall, Dan. "*Brighton Rock*: The Price of Order."
       English Language Notes, III (June 1966), pp. 290-294.

E537   McCann, Janet. "Graham Greene: The Ambiguity of Death."
       Christian Century, XCII (April 30, 1975), pp. 432-435.

E538   McCarthy, Mary. "Graham Greene and the Intelligentsia."
       Partisan Review, XI (Spring 1944), pp. 228-230.

E539   McCarthy, Mary. "Sheep in Wolves' Clothing." *Partisan
       Review*, XXIV (Spring 1957), pp. 270-274.

       Reprinted in *Sights and Spectacles: 1937-1958*. London:
       Heinemann, 1959, pp. 177-183.

E540   McConnell, Frank. "Reconsideration: *The End of the
       Affair.*" *New Republic*, CLXXVIII (March 11, 1978),
       pp. 35-37.

E541   McCormick, John O. "The Rough and Lurid Vision: Henry
       James, Graham Greene and the International Theme."
       Jahrbuch für Amerikastudien, II (1957), pp. 158-167.

E542   McDonald, James L. "Graham Greene: A Reconsideration."
       Arizona Quarterly, XXVII (1971), pp. 197-210.

E543 McDonnell, Lawrence V. "The Priest-Hero in the Modern Novel." *Catholic World*, CXCVI (February 1963), pp. 306-311.

E544 McDougal, Stuart Y. "Visual Tropes: An Analysis of *The Fallen Idol*." *Style*, IX (1975), pp. 502-513.

E545 McGowan, F.A. "Symbolism in *Brighton Rock*." *Renascence*, VIII (Autumn 1955), pp. 25-35.

E546 McGugan, Ruth E. "*The Heart of the Matter*." *Literature/Film Quarterly*, II (Fall 1974), pp. 359-363.

E547 McInerny, R. "The Greene-ing of America." *Commonweal*, XCV (October 15, 1971), pp. 59-61.

E548 McLaughlin, J.J. "*The Potting Shed* and the Potter's Wheel." *America*, XCVII (August 17, 1957), pp. 505-506, 508.

E549 McLaughlin, Richard. "Graham Greene: Saint or Cynic?" *America*, LXXIX (July 24, 1948), pp. 370-371.

E550 McLaughlin, Richard. "I've Been Reading...." *Theatre Arts*, XXXV (December 1951), pp. 34-35.

E551 McMahon, J. "Graham Greene and *The Quiet American*." *Jammu and Kashmir University Review*, I (November 1958), pp. 64-73.

E552 McNamara, E. "Prospects of the Catholic Novel." *America*, XCVII (August 17, 1957), pp. 505-506ff.

E553 Mehoke, James S. "Sartre's Theory of Emotion and Three English Novelists: Waugh, Greene and Amis." *Wisconsin Studies in Literature*, No. 3 (1966), pp. 105-113.

E554 Melchiori, Giorgio. "The English Novelist and the American Tradition." *Sewanee Review*, LXVIII (July 1960), pp. 502-515.

E555 Mesnet, Marie Beatrice. "*Le Potting Shed* de Graham Greene." *Études*, CCXCVI (September 1958), pp. 238-247.

E556 Mesnet, Marie Beatrice. "La Vision Politique de Graham Greene." *Études*, CCCIII (December 1970), pp. 686-705.

E557 Mewshaw, Michael. "Staying Power and the Glory."
      Nation, CCXXIV (April 16, 1977), pp. 469-472.

E558 Michener, Richard L. "Apocalyptic Mexico: *The Plumed
      Serpent* and *The Power and the Glory*." *University
      Review* (Kansas City), XXXIV (June 1968), pp. 313-316.

E559 Miller, Bruce. "Graham Greene." *Meanjin*, V (Spring
      1946), pp. 193-197.

E560 Miller, Karl. "Father, Son, and Holy Ghost." *New
      York Review of Books* (July 20, 1972), pp. 12-15.

E561 Miller, R.H. "Graham Greene, *The Potting Shed*, Act
      III." *Bibliographical Society of America. Papers*,
      LXXI (January 1977), pp. 105-107.

E562 Miller, R.H. "Textual Alterations in Graham Greene's
      Stamboul Train." *Bibliographical Society of America.
      Papers*, LXXI (July 1977), pp. 378-381.

E563 Milner, Ian. "Values and Irony in Graham Greene."
      Prague Studies in English, XIV (1971), pp. 65-73.

E564 Mitchell, Julian. "Grim Grin in the Gloom." *New
      Statesman*, LXXVIII (November 21, 1969), p. 733.

E565 Molnar, Thomas. "Anatomy of Evil." *Commonweal*, LXV
      (December 7, 1956), pp. 246-248.

E566 Mondrone, Domenico, S.J. "Uno Sguardo su Graham Greene
      da l'Ultima Stanza." *Civiltà Cattolica*, CVIII (May
      1957), pp. 279-293.

E567 Monge Rudín, Patricia E. "Elementos Descriptivos Evo-
      cadores de Muerte en *The Power and the Glory*." *Revista
      de la Universidad de Costa Rica*, XLI (1975), pp. 193-
      198.

E568 Monroe, N. Elizabeth. "The New Man in Fiction."
      Renascence, VI (August 1953), pp. 9-17.

E569 Montesi, Gotthard. "Tragödie der Nächstenliebe."
      Wort und Wahrheit, III (August 1948), pp. 610-615.

E570 Mookerjee, R.N. "Graham Greene on the Art of Fiction."
      Rajasthan University Studies in English, VI (1972),
      pp. 91-101.

E571 Moré, Marcel. "Les Deux Holocaustes de Scobie." *Dieu Vivant*, No. 16 (1950), pp. 77-105.

Reprinted as "The Two Holocausts of Scobie," in *Cross Currents*, I (Winter 1951), pp. 44-63.

E572 Moré, Marcel. "A Propos de Newman." *Dieu Vivant*, No. 15 (1950), pp. 63-81.

E573 Moré, Marcel and Père Jouve. "Propos de Table avec Graham Greene." *Dieu Vivant*, No. 16 (1950), pp. 127-137.

E574 Mosley, Nicholas. "A New Puritanism." *The European* (May 1953), pp. 28-40.

E575 Mudrick, Marvin. "The Offending Member." *Hudson Review*, XXVIII (1975), pp. 271-278.

E576 Muggeridge, Malcolm. "Books." *Esquire*, LXXII (August 1969), pp. 16ff.

E577 Muller, C.H. "Graham Greene and the Justification of God's Ways." *Unisa English Studies*, X, No. 1 (1972), pp. 23-35.

E578 Muller, C.H. "Graham Greene and the Absurd." *Unisa English Studies*, X, No. 2 (1972), pp. 34-44.

E579 Munzar, Jiří. "Graham Greene, Essayist." *Philologica Pragensia*, XIV (1971), pp. 30-38.

E580 Murphy, John P., S.J. "*The Potting Shed* and Catholic Critics." *The Tablet*, CCXI (March 1, 1958), p. 210.

E581 Murphy, John P., S.J. "*The Potting Shed*--Dogmatic and Dramatic Effects." *Renascence*: Graham Greene Special Number, XII (Fall 1959), pp. 43-49.

E582 Natan, Alex. "Neuer Graham Greene: *The Comedians*." *Christ und Welt* (Stuttgart), XIX (1966), p. 27.

E583 Neis, Edgar. "Zum Sprachstil Graham Greenes." *Die Neueren Sprachen*, n.s. VI (April 1957), pp. 166-173.

E584 Nichita, Radu. "Măsură Pentru Măsură." *Luceafărul*, XVI (February 1973), p. 9.

E585   Nichol, Davidson. "Our Critics and Lovers--Three Re-
       assessments." *Transition*, V, No. 22 (1955), pp. 32-37.
       Re Albert Schweitzer, Graham Greene and Joyce Cary.

E586   Nicholson, Jenny. "Graham Greene--A Third Man of Real
       Life." *Picture Post*, LXIV (August 14, 1954), pp. 18-19.

E587   Nolan, Jack Edmund. "Graham Greene's Films."
       Literature/Film Quarterly, II (Fall 1974), pp. 302-309.

E588   North, Roy. "Graham Greene." *Visvabharati Quarterly*,
       XXI (Spring 1956), pp. 376-399.

E589   Noxon, James. "Kierkegaard's Stages and *A Burnt-Out
       Case*." *Review of English Literature* (Leeds), III
       (January 1962), pp. 90-101.

E590   Nye, Robert. "How to Read Graham Greene Without Kneel-
       ing." *Books and Bookmen*, XIX (October 1973), pp. 18-
       21.

E591   O'Brien, Conor Cruise. Review of *The Human Factor*.
       New York Review of Books (June 1, 1978), pp. 3-5.

E592   O'Donnell, Donat (pseud. Conor Cruise O'Brien). "An
       Epic of the Thirties: Graham Greene." *The Bell*, XIII
       (February 1947), pp. 7-16.
       Expanded in *Chimera*, V (Summer 1947), pp. 18-30.

E593   O'Donnell, Donat (pseud. Conor Cruise O'Brien).
       "Graham Greene's Lost Childhood." *A.D. 52*, III
       (Winter 1952), pp. 43-47.

E594   O'Donnell, Donat (pseud. Conor Cruise O'Brien). "Our
       Men in Africa." *The Spectator*, CCVI (January 20,
       1961), p. 80.

E595   O'Donovan, P. "Graham Greene's Leper Colony." *New
       Republic*, CXLIV (February 20, 1961), pp. 21-22.

E596   O'Fáolain, Seán. "The Novels of Graham Greene: *The
       Heart of the Matter*." *Britain Today*, No. 148 (August
       1948), pp. 32-36.

E597   O'Grady, Emmett. "Graham Greene, Écrivain Eschatolo-
       gique." *Revue de l'Université d'Ottawa*, XXII (April
       1952), pp. 156-170.

E598 Ogude, S.E. "In Search of Misery: A Study of Graham Greene's Travels in Africa." *Odù*, XI (1975), pp. 45-60.

E599 Ogude, S.E. "Graham Greene's Africa." *Odù*, XIV (1976), pp. 41-65.

E600 Ower, John. "Dark Parable: History and Theology in Graham Greene's 'The Destructors.'" *Cithara*, XV (November 1975), pp. 69-78.

E601 Paleivskij, P. "Fantomy: Burǔaznyj mir v Romanax Grema Grina." *Nouyj mir*, XXXVIII, No. 6 (1962), pp. 229-243.

E602 Parinaud, André. "La Leçon de Vengeance de Graham Greene." *Arts*, No. 565 (April 25, 1956), pp. 1, 6.

E603 Parsons, L. "Graham Greene." *Fortnightly*, CLXXVI (October 1951), pp. 704-705.

E604 Patten, Karl. "The Structure of *The Power and the Glory*." *Modern Fiction Studies*: Graham Greene Special Number, III (Autumn 1957), pp. 225-234.

      Reprinted in *Graham Greene*. Edited by Harry J. Cargas. The Christian Critic Series. St. Louis: B. Herder Book Company, n.d. (1969), pp. 101-113.

E605 Peters, S.J. "*A Burnt-Out Case*, Een Mislukte Roman." *Streven* (November 1961), pp. 161-166.

E606 Peters, W. "The Concern of Graham Greene." *The Month*, n.s. X (November 1953), pp. 281-290.

E607 Pfleger, Karl. "Religiöse Wirklichkeit...." *Wort und Wahrheit*, IV (June 1949), pp. 473-478.

E608 Phillips, Gene D. "On the Perils of Being Tagged a Catholic Novelist." *National Catholic Reporter*, XIII (September 23, 1977), pp. 7-8.

E609 Phillips, W. "The Pursuit of Good and Evil." *American Mercury*, LXXIV (May 1952), pp. 102-106.

E610 Pitts, Arthur W., Jr. "Greene's 'The Basement Room.'" *Explicator*, XXIII (October 1964), Item 17.

E611   Plomer, William. "Mr. Greene's New Novel." *The
       Spectator*, CLIV (June 28, 1935), p. 1116.

       Re England Made Me.

E612   Plomer, William. "Fiction." *The Spectator*, CLVII
       (July 17, 1936), pp. 110-111.

       Re A Gun for Sale.

E613   Plomer, William. "Pinkie and Rose." *The Spectator*,
       CLXI (July 15, 1938), p. 116.

       Re Brighton Rock.

E614   Podlipskaya, E.I. "O Roli Obraza-simvola v Raskrytii
       Ideinogo Soderzhaniya Romana Grema Grina *Komedianty*."
       UZ Tashkentskogo Pedagogicheskogo Instituta, LXXXVI
       (1972), pp. 168-181.

E615   Poole, Roger C. "Graham Greene's Indirection."
       Blackfriars, XLV (June 1964), pp. 257-268.

       Reprinted in *Graham Greene*. Edited by Harry J. Cargas.
       The Christian Critic Series. St. Louis: B. Herder
       Book Company, n.d. (1969), pp. 29-44.

E616   Poole, Roger. "Those Sad Arguments: Two Aspects of
       Graham Greene." *Renaissance and Modern Studies*
       (Nottingham), XIII (1969), pp. 148-160.

       Re The Quiet American and A Burnt-Out Case.

E617   Poulson, Bruce. "Graham Greene's *A Burnt-Out Case*."
       Diogenes (Hobart), (September 1961), pp. 71-73.

E618   Powell, Dilys. "A Trio of Thrillers." *Britain Today*,
       No. 178 (February 1951), p. 36.

E619   Prescott, P.S. "Ice in the Heart." *Newsweek*, LXXVIII
       (September 20, 1971), pp. 94ff.

E620   Pritchett, V.S. "A Modern Mind." *The Spectator*,
       CLII (February 9, 1934), p. 206.

       Re It's a Battlefield.

E621   Pritchett. V.S. "Graham Greene's Appreciation of
       Oliver Twist." *New Statesman and Nation*, XXXIX
       (March 25, 1950), p. 344.

E622 Pritchett, V.S. "A Literary Letter from London."
The New York Times Book Review (November 4, 1951),
p. 41.

E623 Pritchett, V.S. "The World of Graham Greene." *New
Statesman and Nation*, LV (January 4, 1958), pp. 17-18.

E624 Pritchett, V.S. "Brown's Hotel, Haiti." *New Statesman*, LXXI (January 28, 1966), p. 129.

E625 Pritchett, V.S. "The Shadow of Unease." *New Statesman*, LXXXII (September 17, 1971), pp. 366-367.

E626 Pritchett, V.S. "Man of Disappearances." *Atlas World
Press Review*, XXV (July 1978), pp. 27-29.

E627 Pryce-Jones, David. "Graham Greene's Human Comedy."
Adam International Review, Nos. 301-2-3 (1966),
pp. 21-38.

E628 Puentevella, Renato, S.J. "Ambiguity in Greene."
Renascence: Graham Greene Special Number, XII (Fall
1959), pp. 35-37.

E629 Pujals, Esteban. "The Globe Theatre, Londres."
Filologia Moderna, I (1960), pp. 59-63.

Re Greene's *The Complaisant Lover* and Robert Bolt's
A Man for All Seasons.

E630 Rahv, Philip. "Wicked American Innocence." *Commentary*,
XXI (May 1956), pp. 488-490.

Reply with rejoinder by D. Trilling (July 1956),
pp. 66-71.

E631 Raphael, Frederick. "Bonds Honoured." *The Sunday
Times* (September 16, 1973), p. 40.

E632 Raphael, Frederick. "Dishing the Dirt." *The Sunday
Times Magazine* (May 15, 1977), p. 78.

E633 Remords, G. "Graham Greene: Notes Biographiques et
Bibliographiques." *Bulletin de la Faculté des Lettres
de Strasbourg*, XXIX (May-June 1951), pp. 393-399.

E634 Rewak, William J., S.J. "*The Potting Shed*: Maturation
of Graham Greene's Vision." *Catholic World*, CLXXXVI
(December 1957), pp. 210-213.

E635　Reynolds, Louise T.　"Our Spies and Their Spies."
　　　　New Renaissance, I (Winter 1969), pp. 52-63.

　　　　Brief discussion of the following authors:　Rebecca
　　　　West, Oleg Penkovskiy, Gordon Lonsdale, Kurt Singer,
　　　　Rudyard Kipling, John Buchan, E. Phillips Oppenheim,
　　　　Edgar Wallace, W. Somerset Maugham, Graham Greene, Eric
　　　　Ambler, Manning Coles, Mickey Spillane, Mladin Zarubica
　　　　and John Bingham.

E636　Rimaud, Jean.　"Psychologists versus Morality."　*Cross
　　　　Currents*, No. 2 (1951), pp. 26-38.

E637　Robertson, Roderick.　"Toward a Definition of Religious
　　　　Drama."　*Educational Theatre Journal*, IX (1957), pp.
　　　　99-105.

E638　Rodriguez Monegal, Emir.　*"El Revés de la Trama* o la
　　　　Màscara del Realismo."　*Sur*, No. 183 (January 1950),
　　　　pp. 57-60.

E639　Rolo, Charles J.　"Graham Greene: The Man and the Mes-
　　　　sage."　*Atlantic Monthly*, CCVII (May 1961), pp. 60-65.

E640　Rosenthal, Raymond.　"Over the Border to Haiti."　*The
　　　　New Leader*, XLIX (February 14, 1966), pp. 19-20.

E641　Rosewald, Robert.　"Graham Greene op Nieuwe Paden."
　　　　De Periscoop (February 1, 1956), p. 7.

E642　Rossani, Wolfango.　"Graham Greene fra Grazia e
　　　　Peccato."　*Osservatore Romano*, XXVI (April 1972), p. 3.

E643　Rostenne, Paul.　"Introduction à Graham Greene: Roman-
　　　　cier Catholique."　*Revue Nouvelle*, VI (September 15,
　　　　1947), pp. 193-204.

E644　Routh, Michael.　"Greene's Parody of Farce and Comedy
　　　　in *The Comedians*."　*Renascence*, XXVI (Spring 1974),
　　　　pp. 138-151.

E645　Roy, Jean-Henri.　"L'oeuvre de Graham Greene ou un
　　　　Christianisme de la Damnation."　*Les Temps Modernes*,
　　　　LII (1950), pp. 1513-1519.

E646　Ruck, Heribert.　"Graham Greene: Die Stunde der Komö-
　　　　dianten."　*Neu Deutsche Hefte Beitrage zur Europäischen
　　　　Gegenwart* (Gütersloh), XIV (1967), pp. 170-173.

E647 Rudman, Harry W. "Clough and Graham Greene's *The Quiet American.*" *Victorian Newsletter*, No. 19 (1961), pp. 14-15.

E648 Ruotolo, Lucio P. "*Brighton Rock*'s Absurd Heroine." *Modern Language Quarterly*, XXV (December 1964), pp. 425-433.

E649 Sackville-West, Edward. "The Electric Hare: Some Aspects of Graham Greene." *The Month*, VI (September 1951), pp. 141-147.

E650 Sackville-West, Edward. "Time-Bomb." *The Month*, XXV (March 1961), pp. 175-178.

Sale, Richard B. "An Interview in New York with Walter Allen." *Studies in the Novel*, III (Winter 1971), pp. 405-429. (See E176.)

E651 Salter, James. "Bio." *People*, V (January 19, 1976), pp. 64-67.

E652 Sandra, Sister Mary, S.S.A. "The Priest-Hero in Modern Fiction." *The Personalist*, XLVI (Autumn 1965), pp. 527-542.

Re Edward O'Connor, J.F. Powers, Georges Bernanos and Graham Greene.

E653 Schellenberg, Johannes. "Graham Greene: *Unser Mann in Havanna.*" *Der Bibliothekar* (Leipsig), XIX (1965), pp. 966-969.

E654 Schmidthues, K. "G. Greene." *Die Neue Heimat* (Berlin), IV, No. 5 (1949), pp. 429-433.

E655 Schmidthus, Karlheinz. "Graham Greenes Katholizismus: Die Religiöse Erfahrung der Welt in Seinem Romanen." *Wort und Wahrheit*, XII (January 1957), pp. 39-51.

E656 Schoonderwoerd, N. "Heeft Graham Greene Ons Weer Teleurgesteld?" *Kultuur Leven*, XXVI (November 1959), pp. 703-704.

E657 Schumann, Hildegard. "Zum Problem des Anti-Helden in Graham Greenes Neuren Romanen." *Wissenschaftliche Zeitschrift der Universität Rostock*, XII (1963), pp. 71-77.

E658   Scott, Nathan A., Jr. "Christian Novelist's Dilemma."
       Christian Century, LXXIII (August 1, 1956), pp. 901-902.

E659   Scott-Kilvert, Ian. "English Fiction, 1969-1970."
       British Book News (June 1971), pp. 425-430.

E660   Scruton, Roger. "Graham Greene." *The Spectator*,
       CCXXVI (May 15, 1971), pp. 667-668.

E661   Servotte, Herman. "Bij de Jongste Roman van Graham
       Greene." *Dietsche Warande en Belfort* (Antwerp), VI
       (1955), pp. 367-370.

       Re Loser Takes All.

E662   Servotte, Herman. "Bedenkingen bij *A Burnt-Out Case*,
       Graham Greene's Jongste Roman." *Dietsche Warande en
       Belfort* (Antwerp), CVI (June 1961), pp. 371-375.

E663   Seward, Barbara. "Graham Greene: A Hint of an Expla-
       nation." *Western Review*, XXII (Winter 1958), pp. 83-
       95.

E664   Sewell, Elizabeth. "Graham Greene." *Dublin Review*,
       CCXXVIII (First Quarter 1954), pp. 12-21.

E665   Sewell, Elizabeth. "The Imagination of Graham Greene."
       Thought, XXIX (March 1954), pp. 51-60.

       Reprinted in *Wort und Wahrheit*, IX (April 1954),
       pp. 281-288.

E666   Sharrock, R. "Graham Greene: The Tragic Comedian."
       The Tablet, CCIII (January 4, 1969), p. 8.

E667   Sheed, Wilfrid." "Enemies of Catholic Promise."
       Commonweal, LXXVII (1963), pp. 560-563.

E668   Sheed, Wilfrid. "Greene-ing of Graham Greene." *Life*,
       LXXI (September 24, 1971), p. 10.

E679   Sheed, Wilfrid. "Report." *Book-of-the-Month Club News*
       (Fall 1973), pp. 2-3.

E670   Shenker, Israel. "Graham Greene at Sixty-six." *The
       New York Times Book Review* (September 12, 1971), p. 26.

E671   Shen'ko, I.V. and N.V. Gurova. "Nekotorye Osobennosti
       Upotrebleniya Sravnenii v Romane Grema Grina *Vlast i*

Slava" (Some Features of the Use of Comparisons in Graham Greene's Novel *The Power and the Glory*). *Nekotorye Voprosy Angliiskoi Filologii Chelyabinskii Pedagogicheskii Institut, Chelyabinsk,* II (1971), pp. 102-109.

E672 Sheridan, John D. "Graham Greene and the Irish." *The Irish Monthly,* LXXXI (1953), pp. 211-216.

E673 Shor, Ira Neil. "Greene's Later Humanism: *A Burnt-Out Case.*" *Literary Review* (Fairleigh Dickinson University), XVI (Summer 1973), pp. 397-411.

E674 Shpektorova, N. Yu. "Opyt Lingvostilistcheskogo Analiza Individual 'nogo Stilya G. Grina" (An Attempt at a Linguo-stylistic Analysis of Greene's Style, based on *The Quiet American*). *Trudy Samarkanskogo Universitea,* CCXLIII (1973), pp. 89-97.

E675 Sigaux, Gilbert. "Un Cas Désespéré." *Preuves,* No. 121 (March 1961).

      Re A Burnt-Out Case.

E676 Silva Delgado, Adolfo. "La Carrera Literaria de Graham Greene." *Marcha,* XIII (November 23, 1951), pp. 14-15, 71.

E677 Silveira, Gerald E. "Greene's 'The Basement Room.'" *Explicator,* XV (December 1965), Item 13.

E678 Simon, Rev. John K. "*Off the Voie Royale*: The Failure of Greene's *A Burnt-Out Case.*" *Symposium,* XVIII (Summer 1964), pp. 163-169.

E679 Simons, J.W. "Salvation in the Novels." *Commonweal,* LVI (April 25, 1952), pp. 74-76.

E680 Simons, Katherine. "Graham Greene." *Book-of-the-Month Club News* (June 1948), pp. 6-7.

E681 Sissman, L.E. "Evergreen." *The New Yorker,* XLVI (February 28, 1970), pp. 110-114.

E682 Sissman, L.E. "Graham Greene Begins." *The New Yorker,* XLVII (October 2, 1971), pp. 126-130.

E683 Smith, A.J.M. "Graham Greene's Theological Thrillers." *Queen's Quarterly,* LXVIII (Spring 1961), pp. 15-33.

E684   Smith, Francis J. "The Anatomy of *A Burnt-Out Case*."
       America, CV (September 9, 1961), pp. 711-712.

E685   Snow, Royall. "Oxford: Thin Smoke and Thin Fire."
       Poetry (Chicago), XXVIII (May 1926), pp. 112-114.

E686   Sokolov, R.A. "Short Greene." *Newsweek*, LXXIII
       (May 19, 1969), pp. 110ff.

E687   Solomon, Petre. "Eseurile lui Graham Greene" (Graham
       Greene's Essays). *Romônia Literară*, No. 19 (May 1969),
       p. 20.

E688   Solov'Eva, N. "Gumanizum Grèkhema Grina" (The Humanism
       of Graham Greene). *Raduga*, IV (1969), pp. 153-161.

E689   Sonnenfield, Albert. "Twentieth Century Gothic: Re-
       flections on the Catholic Novel." *Southern Review*,
       n.s. I, No. 2 (Spring 1965), pp. 388-405.

E690   Sordet, Etienne. "Signification de Graham Greene."
       Cahiers Protestants, XXXVII (1953), pp. 239-250.

E691   Spaventa Filippi, Lia. "Produzione Poliziesca di
       Graham Greene." *L'Italia che Scrive*, XLV (1962), p. 87.

E692   Spier, Ursula. "Melodrama in Graham Greene's *The End of
       the Affair*." *Modern Fiction Studies*: Graham Greene
       Special Number, III (Autumn 1957), pp. 235-240.

E693   Spinucci, Pietro. "L'Ultimo Dramma di Graham Greene."
       Humanitas (Brescia), XV (November 1960), pp. 820-825.

E694   Stanford, Derek. *"The Potting Shed."* *Contemporary
       Review*, No. 1110 (June 1958), pp. 301-303.

E695   Stanford, Derek. *"The Complaisant Lover."* *The Critic*,
       XVIII (December 1959), pp. 16-18; (January 1960), pp.
       79-80.

E696   Stanley, John. "Life in the Living Room." *Commonweal*,
       LXI (December 31, 1954), pp. 354-355.

E697   Stanley, John. "Life in the Living Room." *Commonweal*,
       LXXI (October 30, 1959), pp. 123-124.

E698   Steiner, George. Review of *Lord Rochester's Monkey*.
       The New Yorker, L (October 28, 1974), pp. 185-186ff.

E699 Steiner, George. Review of *The Human Factor*. *The New Yorker*, LIV (May 8, 1978), pp. 149-154.

E700 Sternlicht, Sanford. "The Sad Comedies: Graham Greene's Later Novels." *Florida Quarterly*, I (1968), pp. 65-77.

E701 Sternlicht, Sanford. "Two Views of the Builder in Graham Greene's *A Burnt-Out Case* and William Golding's *The Spire*." *Calcutta Review*, I (January-March 1970), pp. 401-404.

Reprinted in *Studies in the Humanities*, II (Fall-Winter 1970), pp. 17-19.

E702 Sternlicht, Sanford. "Prologue to the Sad Comedies: Graham Greene's Major Early Novels." *Midwest Quarterly*, XII (Summer 1971), pp. 427-435.

E703 Stinson, J. "Graham Greene's 'The Destructors': Fable for a World Far East of Eden." *American Benedictine Review*, XXIV (December 1973), pp. 510-518.

E704 Strange, Roderick. "Graham Greene: The Writer." *New Blackfriars*, LIV (January 1973), pp. 29-35.

E705 Stratford, Philip. "Graham Greene: Master of Melodrama." *Tamarack Review*, No. 19 (Spring 1961), pp. 67-86.

E706 Stratford, Philip. "The Uncomplacent Dramatist: Some Aspects of Graham Greene's Theatre." *Wisconsin Studies in Contemporary Literature*, II (Fall 1961), pp. 5-19.

Reprinted in *Graham Greene: A Collection of Critical Essays*. Edited by Samuel L. Hynes. Englewood Cliffs, N.J.: Prentice-Hall, Inc., 1973, pp. 138-153.

E707 Stratford, Philip. "Unlocking the Potting Shed." *Kenyon Review*, XXIV (Winter 1962), pp. 129-143.

E708 Stratford, Philip. "Chalk and Cheese: A Comparative Study of *A Kiss for the Leper* and *A Burnt-Out Case*." *University of Toronto Quarterly*, XXXIII (January 1964), pp. 200-218.

Stratford, Philip and Judy Adamson. "Looking for the Third Man: On the Trail in Texas, New York, Hollywood." *Encounter*, L (June 1978), pp. 39-46. (See E169.)

E709   "Strix." "Their Man in Habarovsk." *The Spectator*, CCI
       (November 14, 1958), p. 650.

       Re Our Man in Havana.

E710   Strong, L.A.G. "The Book of the Month." *The Specta-
       tor*, CXLIX (December 9, 1932), p. 842.

       Re Stamboul Train.

E711   Sullivan, Dan. "The Theater: Graham Greene's *Carving
       A Statue.*" *The New York Times* (May 1, 1968), p. 43.

E712   Sullivan, Walter. "Where Have All the Flowers Gone?
       Part Two: The Novel in the Gnostic Twilight."
       Sewanee Review, LXXVIII (Autumn 1970), pp. 654-664.

E713   Sultan, Stanley. "An Old-Irish Model for *Ulysses.*"
       James Joyce Quarterly, V (1968), pp. 103-109.

E714   Sutherland, James. "Hedonism in Control." *Times
       Literary Supplement* (September 20, 1974), p. 992.

       Re Lord Rochester's Monkey.

E715   Sylvester, Harry. "Graham Greene." *Commonweal*,
       XXXIII (October 25, 1940), pp. 11-13.

E716   Symons, Julian. "Waiting for the War." *The Sunday
       Times* (April 5, 1970), p. 32.

E717   Taber, Robert. "Castro's Cuba." *Nation*, CXC
       (January 23, 1960), pp. 63-64.

E718   Tanazhko, L.G. "Angliiskii Antkolonial 'nyi Roman i
       Poslevoennye Romany G. Grina" (The English Anticolonial
       Novel and G. Greene's Postwar Novels). *Permskii Uni-
       versitet* (Perm'), CCLXX (1973), pp. 310-326.

E719   Tarnawski, Wit. "Przemiany Grahama Greeña." *Kultura*,
       CXXXVIII, No. 4 (April 1959), pp. 131-137.

E720   Taylor, Marion A. and John Clark. "Further Sources for
       'The Second Death' by Graham Greene." *Papers on
       English Language and Literature*, I (Autumn 1965),
       pp. 378-380.

E721   Thale, Jerome and Rose Marie Thale. "Greene's Literary
       Pilgrimage: Allusions in *Travels with My Aunt.*" *Papers*

on *Language and Literature*, XIII (Spring 1977), pp. 207-212.

E722 Thomas, D.P. "Mr. Tench and Secondary Glory in *The Power and the Glory*." *English Language Notes*, VII, No. 2 (1969), pp. 129-133.

E723 Thoorens, Leon. "Graham Greene: Une Sorte de Vie." *Revue Génerale* (Belge), X (1971), pp. 102-103.

E724 Tracy, Honor. "The Life and Soul of the Party." *New Republic*, CXL (April 20, 1959), pp. 15-16.

E725 Tracy, Honor. "Two Voices Are There." *New Republic*, CXLVI (February 5, 1962), pp. 20-21.

E726 Traversi, Derek. "Graham Greene: I. The Earlier Novels." *Twentieth Century*, CXLIX (March 1951), pp. 231-240; "Graham Greene: II. The Later Novels" (April 1951), pp. 318-328.

"Graham Greene: The Earlier Novels," reprinted in *Graham Greene: A Collection of Critical Essays*. Edited by Samuel L. Hynes. Englewood Cliffs, N.J.: Prentice-Hall, Inc., 1973, pp. 17-29.

E727 Tressin, Deanna. "Toward Understanding." *English Journal*, LV (1966), pp. 1170-1174.

E728 Trifu, Sever. "Graham Greene." *Tribuna*, No. 40 (October 1969), p. 8.

E729 Trifu, Sever. "Graham Greene, Contemporanul Nostru" (Graham Greene, Our Contemporary). *Studia Universitatis Babes-Bolyai*, series philologia, XIX, No. 1 (1974), pp. 59-60.

E730 Trifu, Sever. "Un Contemporan Nelinistit: Graham Greene" (A Restless Contemporary: Graham Greene). *Steaua*, n.s. XXV, No. 10 (1974), pp. 52-54.

E731 Trifu, Sever. "Greene in România." *Steaua*, n.s. XXVI, No. 5 (1975), pp. 53-55.

E732 Trifu, Sever. "Language and Style in Graham Greene's Novels." *Studia Universitatis Babes-Bolyai*, series philologia, XX (1975), pp. 57-70.

E733 Trilling, Diana and Philip Rahv. "America and *The
      Quiet American.*" *Commentary*, XXII (July 1956), pp.
      66-71.

E734 Tsuchiya, Tetsu. "Kindai Utopia No Shumatsu--Graham
      Greene No Baai." *Eigo Seinen* (Tokyo), CXVIII (1972),
      pp. 126-128.

E735 Turnell, Martin. "Baroque Art and Poetry." *Commonweal*,
      LV (October 26, 1951), pp. 55-57.

E736 Turnell, Martin. "Graham Greene: The Man Within."
      Ramparts, IV (June 1965), pp. 54-64.

E737 Turnell, Martin. Review of *La Crisis del Sacerdote* en
      Graham Greene by Leopoldo Duran." *Times Literary
      Supplement* (February 13, 1976), p. 170.

E738 Tynan, Kenneth. "An Inner View of Graham Greene."
      Harper's Bazaar, LXXXVI (February 1953), pp. 128-129,
      209-210, 214-215.

      Abridged in *Persona Grata*. London: Wingate, 1953,
      pp. 53-56.

E739 Tysdhl, Bjørn. "Graham Greene--Fluktens og Forfølgel-
      sens dikter." *Kirke og Kultur*, LXVII (1962), pp. 293-
      298.

E740 Vallette, Jacques. "La Jeunesse de Graham Greene."
      Mercure de France, No. 1058 (October 1951), pp. 326-327.

E741 Van Wert, William F. "Narrative Structure in *The
      Third Man.*" *Literature/Film Quarterly*, II (Fall 1974),
      pp. 341-346.

E742 Vargo, Edward P., S.V.D. "Struggling with a Bugaboo:
      The Priest Character in Achebe and Greene and Keneally."
      Fu Jen Studies (Republic of China), IX (1976), pp. 1-
      17.

E743 Viatte, A. "Graham Greene, Romancier de la Grâce."
      Revue de l'Université Laval, IV (April 1950), pp. 753-
      758.

E744 Vieira, Manuel. "Notas Para um Estudo Sobre Graham
      Greene." *Tempo Presente*, No. 20 (1960), pp. 46-52.

E745 Vilangiyil, Sebastian O. "The Demonic Heroes of Graham
      Greene." *Saint Louis University Research Journal*, IV
      (June 1973), pp. 201-211.

E746 Viola, André. "Graham Greene et 'Le Tombeau de l'homme Blanc.'" *Études Anglaises*, XXIX (1976), pp. 167-178.

E747 Voorhees, Richard J. "The World of Graham Greene." *South Atlantic Quarterly*, L (July 1951), pp. 389-398.

E748 Voorhees, Richard J. "Recent Greene." *South Atlantic Quarterly*, LXII (Spring 1963), pp. 244-255.

E749 Walbridge, E. Letter discussing Graham Greene and Beatrix Potter. *Saturday Review of Literature*, XXVII (February 12, 1944), p. 36.

E750 Walker, Ronald C. "Seriation as Stylistic Norm in Graham Greene's *The Heart of the Matter*." *Language and Style: An International Journal* (Southern Illinois University), VI (1973), pp. 161-175.

E751 Wall, Barbara. "London Letter." *America*, LXXVII (August 9, 1947), pp. 521-522.

E752 Wall, Barbara. "London Letter." *America*, LXXIX (August 28, 1948), pp. 470-471.

E753 Wansbrough, John. "Graham Greene: The Detective in the Wasteland." *Harvard Advocate*, CXXXVI (December 1952), pp. 11-13, 29-31.

E754 Wassmer, Thomas A., S.J. "Graham Greene: Literary Artist and Philosopher-Theologian." *Homiletic and Pastoral Review*, LVIII (March 1958), pp. 583-589.

E755 Wassmer, Thomas A., S.J. "Faith and Reason in Graham Greene." *Studies* (Dublin), XLVIII (Summer 1959), pp. 163-167.

E756 Wassmer, Thomas A., S.J. "The Sinners of Graham Greene." *Dalhousie Review*, XXXIX (Autumn 1959), pp. 326-332.

E757 Wassmer, Thomas A., S.J. "Reason and Faith as Seen by Graham Greene." *Drama Critique*, II (November 1959), pp. 126-130.

E758 Wassmer, Thomas A., S.J. "Faith and Belief: A Footnote to Greene's 'Visit to Morin.'" *Renascence*, XI (1959), pp. 84-88.

E759   Wassmer, Thomas A., S.J. "Graham Greene: A Look at His
       Sinners." *Critic*, XVIII (December 1959--January 1960),
       pp. 16-17, 72-74.

E760   Wassmer, Thomas A., S.J. "The Problem and Mystery of
       Sin in the Works of Graham Greene." *The Christian
       Scholar*, XLIII (Winter 1960), pp. 309-315.

E761   Wasson, John. "Hamlet's Second Chance." *Research
       Studies* (Washington State University), XXVIII
       (September 1960), pp. 117-124.

E762   Waugh, Auberon. Authors Comment on Living Authors They
       Most Admire--Waugh Comments on Greene. *The New York
       Times* (December 4, 1977), sec. 7, p. 3.

E763   Waugh, Evelyn. "Felix Culpa?" *The Tablet*, CXCI
       (June 5, 1948), pp. 352-354.

       Reprinted in *Commonweal*, XLVIII (July 16, 1948), pp.
       322-325 and in *Graham Greene: A Collection of Critical
       Essays*. Edited by Samuel L. Hynes. Englewood Cliffs,
       N.J.: Prentice-Hall, Inc., 1973, pp. 95-102.

E764   Waugh, Evelyn. Letter to the Editor. *The Tablet*,
       CXCII (July 17, 1948), p. 41.

E765   Waugh, Evelyn. "The Heart's Own Reasons." *Commonweal*,
       LIV (August 17, 1951), pp. 458-459.

E766   Waugh, Evelyn. "The Point of Departure." *The Month*,
       n.s. VI (September 1951), pp. 174-176.

       Re The End of the Affair.

E767   Weales, Gerald. "There Are Demons at the Bottom of the
       Garden." *Kenyon Review*, XXXI, No. 4 (1969), pp. 554-
       560.

E768   Weeks, E. "Peripatetic Reviewer." *Atlantic*, CCXXVIII
       (October 1971), p. 132.

E769   Welse, James M. and Gerald R. Barrett. "Graham Greene's
       Ministry of Fear: The Transformation of an Entertain-
       ment." *Literature/Film Quarterly*, II (Fall 1974),
       pp. 310-323.

E770   Weseliński, Andrzej. "Irony and Melodrama in *The Heart of the Matter.*" *Studia Anglica Posnaniensia, an International Review of English Studies*, VIII (1976), pp. 167-173.

E771   West, Anthony. "Saint's Progress." *The New Yorker*, XXVII (November 10, 1951), pp. 154ff.

E772   Weyergans, Franz. "La Saison des Pluies de Graham Greene." *Revue Nouvelle*, XXXIII (April 1961), pp. 417-420.

E773   White, W.D. "*The Power and the Glory*: An Apology to the Church." *University of Portland Review*, XXI (Spring 1969), pp. 14-22.

E774   Wichert, Robert A. "The Quality of Graham Greene's Mercy." *College English*, XXV (November 1963), pp. 99-103.

E775   Willig, Charles L. "Greene's 'The Basement Room.'" *Explicator*, XXXI (February 1973), Item 48.

E776   Wilshire, A.D. "Conflict and Conciliation in Graham Greene." *Essays and Studies*, n.s. XIX (1966), pp. 122-137.

E777   Wilson, Angus. "An Interview in London with Angus Wilson." *Studies in the Novel*, II (Spring 1970), pp. 76-87.

E778   Wilson, Colin. "Graham Greene's Autobiography." *The Spectator*, CCXXVII (September 18, 1971), pp. 413-414.

E779   Wolfe, Peter. "Graham Greene and the Art of Entertainment." *Studies in the Twentieth Century*, No. 6 (Fall 1970), pp. 35-61.

E780   Wolfe, Peter. "*Travels with My Aunt*." *Studies in the Twentieth Century*, No. 6 (Fall 1970), pp. 119-123.

E781   Wolfe, Peter. "*The Honorary Consul*." *Studies in the Twentieth Century*, No. 14 (Fall 1974), pp. 117-120.

E782   Woodcock, George. "Mexico and the English Novelist." *Western Review*, XXI (Autumn 1956), pp. 21-32.

E783   Wright, Andrew. "A Note on Joyce Cary's Reputation."
       Modern Fiction Studies, IX (Autumn 1963), pp. 207-209.

E784   Wyatt, E. van R. "God in a Garden." *Critique*, I
       (February 1958), pp. 45-58.

E785   Wyndham, Francis. "A Burnt-Out Case." *London Maga-
       zine*, VIII (March 1961), pp. 62-63.

E786   Wyndham, Francis. "A Pitiable God." *The Listener*
       (September 13, 1973), pp. 350-351.

E787   Young, Vernon. "Hollywood: Lost Moments." *Accent*,
       IX (Winter 1949), pp. 120-128.

E788   Young, Vernon. "Hell on Earth: Six Versions." *Hudson
       Review*, II (Summer 1949), pp. 311-317.

E789   Young, Vernon. "The Friends of Graham Greene."
       Hudson Review, XXVII (1974), pp. 245-251.

E790   Zabel, Morton Dauwen. "Graham Greene." *Nation*, CLVII
       (July 3, 1943), pp. 18-20.

E791   Zambrano, Ana Laura. "Greene's Vision of Childhood:
       'The Basement Room' and 'The Fallen Idol.'"
       Literature/Film Quarterly, II (Fall 1974), pp. 324-331.

E792   Zimmermann, Peter. "Graham Greenes Auseinandersetzung
       Mit der Imperialistigschen Vietnamaggression in dem
       Roman *The Quiet American*." *Zeitschrift für Anglistik
       und Amerikanistik* (Berlin, E. Germany), XXI (1973),
       pp. 34-49.

E793   Unsigned. Portrait. *Bookman* (London), LXXVI
       (September 1929), p. 289.

E794   Unsigned. Biographical Note. *Wilson Bulletin*, IV
       (November 1929), p. 98.

E795   Unsigned. "Problems of the Catholic Writer."
       Catholic World, CLXVI (March 1948), pp. 481-486.

E796   Unsigned. Biographical Note. *Saturday Review of
       Literature*, XXXI (July 10, 1948), p. 9.

E797   Unsigned. "*The Heart of the Matter*." *Catholic Review
       Service* (July 26, 1948), entire issue.

E798 Unsigned. Biographical Note. *Time*, LII (August 9, 1948), p. 85.

E799 Unsigned. "Bishop Attacks Greene's New Novel." *London Universe* (September 3, 1948).

E800 Unsigned. "Group Loyalties." *Times Literary Supplement* (January 15, 1949), p. 41.

E801 Unsigned. "Profile--Graham Greene." *The Observer* (November 27, 1949), p. 2.

E802 Unsigned. "Adam's Tree." *Twentieth Century*, CL (October 1951), pp. 334-342.

E803 Unsigned. "Novelist Graham Greene: Adultery Can Lead to Sainthood." *Time*, LVIII (October 29, 1951), pp. 98-104.

E804 Unsigned. "Shocker." *Time*, LVIII (October 29, 1951), pp. 98-104.

E805 Unsigned. "Greene, Not Red." *Newsweek*, XXXIX (February 11, 1952), p. 28.

E806 Unsigned. Biographical Note. *Publishers Weekly*, CLXIII (January 3, 1953), p. 30.

E807 Unsigned. "Colette's Burial." *Commonweal*, LX (September 17, 1954), p. 573.

E808 Unsigned. "This is Graham Greene." *Newsweek*, XLIV (November 29, 1954), pp. 92-93.

E809 Unsigned. "Diem's Critics: Graham Greene and Father O'Conner's Reply." *America*, XCIII (May 28, 1955), p. 225.

E810 Unsigned. "Men Who Fascinate Women." *Look*, XIX (September 6, 1955), p. 43.

E811 Unsigned. "Greene's Disservice to the Church." *America*, XCIV (February 11, 1956), p. 518.

Editorial.

E812 Unsigned. "Américain Tranquille." *Nouvelles Littéraires* (March 8, 1956), p. 7.

E813   Unsigned. Portrait. *Saturday Night*, LXXI (May 12,
       1956), p. 18.

E814   Unsigned. "When Greene is Red." *Newsweek*, XLVIII
       (October 1, 1956), pp. 94, 96.

E815   Unsigned. "To Get Rave Reviews, Write an Anti-U.S.A.
       Novel!" *Saturday Evening Post*, CCXXIX (October 6,
       1956), p. 10.

E816   Unsigned. "Engelse Letteren: Beschouwingen bij de
       Laatste Roman van Graham Greene." *Dietsche Warande en
       Belfort* (Antwerp, 1956), pp. 443-444.

E817   Unsigned. "A Spiritual Suspense Story." *Life*, XLII
       (April 1, 1957), pp. 65-66.

E818   Unsigned. "Graham Greene vs. Selwyn Lloyd." *Time and
       Tide*, XL (January 17, 1959), p. 65.

E819   Unsigned. "Whose Man in Havana?" *Commonweal*, LXX
       (July 3, 1959), p. 342.

E820   Unsigned. "Further Adventures of Mr. Greene."
       Commonweal, LXX (September 11, 1959), p. 486.

E821   Unsigned. Portrait. *Times Literary Supplement*
       (September 9, 1960), p. vii.

E822   Unsigned. "The Greeneland Aboriginal." *New Statesman*,
       LXI (January 13, 1961), pp. 44-45, 139.

E823   Unsigned. "Our Man in Havana." *Newsweek*, LXII
       (July 15, 1963), p. 50.

E824   Unsigned. "Novelist Whitewashes Castro Regime."
       Christian Century, LXXX (November 27, 1963), pp. 1457-
       1458.

E825   Unsigned. "New Year's Honours." *London Illustrated
       News*, CCXLVIII (January 8, 1966), p. 13.

E826   Unsigned. "New Honor and New Novel." *Life*, LX
       (February 4, 1966), pp. 43-44.

E827   Unsigned. "The Dark Truster in God and the Thwarted
       Believer in Man." *Times Literary Supplement* (March 3,
       1969), pp. 257-258.

E828   Unsigned. "Portrait of No Lady." *Times Literary
       Supplement* (December 20, 1969), p. 1329.

E829   Unsigned. "Hamlet's Aunt." *Time*, XCV (January 19,
       1970), p. 68.

E830   Unsigned. "Graham Greene in Adversity." *Bookseller*
       (September 4, 1971), p. 1470.

E831   Unsigned. "Graham Greene: The Man Within." *Times
       Literary Supplement* (September 17, 1971), pp. 1101-
       1102.

       Reprinted in *Graham Greene: A Collection of Critical
       Essays*. Edited by Samuel L. Hynes. Englewood Cliffs,
       N.J.: Prentice-Hall, Inc., 1973, pp. 8-16.

E832   Unsigned. "The Cost of Caring." *Times Literary
       Supplement* (September 14, 1973), pp. 1055-1056.

E833   Unsigned. "TLS--Commentary: Second Impressions."
       Times Literary Supplement (March 26, 1976), p. 346.

       Re Greene's prefaces in the Collected Edition.

                REFERENCES TO GREENE IN BOOKS

E834   Albérès, R.M. (pseud. Rene Marill). "Graham Greene et
       la Responsabilité." *Les Hommes Traqués*. Paris: La
       Nouvelle Editions, 1953, pp. 157-185.

E835   Alder, Jacob H. "Graham Greene's Plays: Technique
       Versus Value." *Graham Greene: Some Critical Con-
       siderations*. Edited by Robert O. Evans. Lexington:
       University of Kentucky Press, 1963, pp. 219-230.

E836   Allen, Walter. "The Novels of Graham Greene." *Penguin
       New Writing, 18*. Harmondsworth: Penguin Books, 1943,
       pp. 148-160.

E837   Allen, Walter. "The Novels of Graham Greene." *Writers
       of Today*. Edited by Denys Val Baker. London: Sedg-
       wick, 1946, pp. 15-28.

E838   Allen, Walter. "Seven Novels Discussed." *Reading a
       Novel*. London: Phoenix House, 1949, pp. 34-39; rpt.
       1956, pp. 37-42.

E839   Allen, Walter. "The Thirties: British--3." *Tradition
       and Drama: The English and American Novel from the
       Twenties to Our Time*. London: Phoenix House, 1964,
       pp. 202-207.

       Reprinted in *The Modern Novel in Britain and the United
       States*. New York: E.P. Dutton & Co., 1964, pp. 202-
       207.

E840   Allott, Miriam. "The Moral Situation in *The Quiet
       American*." *Graham Greene: Some Critical Considerations*.
       Edited by Robert O. Evans. Lexington: University of
       Kentucky Press, 1963, pp. 188-206.

E841   Atkins, John. "Altogether Amen: A Reconsideration of
       The Power and the Glory." *Graham Greene: Some Critical
       Considerations*. Edited by Robert O. Evans. Lexington:
       University of Kentucky Press, 1963, pp. 181-187.

E842   Atkins, John. "The Curse of the Film." *Graham Greene:
       Some Critical Considerations*. Edited by Robert O.
       Evans. Lexington: University of Kentucky Press, 1963,
       pp. 207-218.

E843   Atkinson, F.K. "Floreat Augusta--or, On First Looking
       Into *Travels with My Aunt*." *Gleanings from Greeneland*.
       Edited by J.S. Ryan. Armidale, New South Wales (Aus-
       tralia): University of New England, 1972, pp. 81-90.

E844   Beaton, Cecil and Kenneth Tynan. *Persona Grata*.
       London: Wingate, 1953, pp. 53-55; New York: Putnam,
       1954, pp. 53-56.

E845   Bentley, Eric. "A Real Writer." *What Is Theatre?*
       New York: Horizon Press, 1956, pp. 25-29.

E846   Bernoville, Gáetan. "Introduction." *Le Catholicisme
       dans L'Oeuvre de François Mauriac*. Edited by Robert
       J. North. Paris: Editions du Conquistador, 1950.

E847   Booth, Wayne C. *The Rhetoric of Fiction*. Chicago:
       University of Chicago Press, 1963, pp. 156, 160,
       186-187, 277-278, 389.

E848   Browne, E.M. "Contemporary Drama in the Catholic
       Tradition." *Christian Faith and the Contemporary Arts*.
       Edited by F. Eversole. New York: Abingdon, 1962,
       pp. 132-141.

E849 Buckler, William E. and Arnold B. Sklare. *Stories from Six Authors.* New York: McGraw-Hill, 1960.

E850 Burgess, Anthony. "The Greene and the Red: Politics in the Novels of Graham Greene." *Urgent Copy, Literary Studies.* London: Cape, 1968, pp. 13-20.

E851 Burgess, Anthony. "The Politics of Graham Greene." *Page 2: The Best of "Speaking of Books" from the New York Times Book Review.* Edited by E.F. Brown. New York: Holt, 1969, pp. 284-291.

E852 Burgess, Anthony. *The Novel Now: A Student's Guide to Contemporary Fiction.* London: Faber & Faber, 1971, pp. 61-64.

E853 Calder-Marshall, Arthur. "Graham Greene." *Little Reviews Anthology.* London: Allen and Unwin, 1943, pp. 197-204.

E854 Calder-Marshall, Arthur. "Graham Greene." *Living Writers: Being Critical Studies Broadcast in the B.B.C. Third Programme.* Edited by Gilbert H. Phelps. London: Sylvan Press, 1947, pp. 39-47.

E855 Cargas, Harry J. "Introduction." *Graham Greene.* The Christian Critic Series. Edited by Harry J. Cargas. St. Louis: B. Herder Book Company, n.d. (1969), p. vii.

E856 Cartmell, Canon Joseph. "A Postscript to Evelyn Waugh." *Graham Greene: A Collection of Critical Essays.* Edited by Samuel Hynes. Englewood Cliffs, N.J.: Prentice-Hall, Inc., 1973, pp. 103-104.

E857 Chaigne, Louis. "Graham Greene." *Vies et Oeuvres d'Ecrivains, III.* Paris: Fernand Lanore, 1950, pp. 195-237.

E858 Chapman, Raymond. "The Vision of Graham Greene." *Forms of Extremity in the Modern Novel.* Edited by Nathan A. Scott, Jr. Richmond, Virginia: John Knox Press, 1965, pp. 75-94.

E859 Church, Richard. "Graham Greene." *British Authors.* London: Longmans, Green, 1948, pp. 137-140.

E860   Clurman, Harold. "Graham Greene 1957." *Lies Like
       Truth*. New York: Macmillan, 1958, pp. 176-178.

E861   Connolly, Francis. *The Types of Literature*. New York:
       Harcourt, Brace, 1955, pp. 706-707.

E862   Consolo, Dominick P. "Graham Greene: Style and Stylis-
       tics in Five Novels." *Graham Greene: Some Critical
       Considerations*. Edited by Robert O. Evans. Lexington:
       University of Kentucky Press, 1963, pp. 61-95.

E863   Consolo, Dominick P. "Music as Motif: The Unity of
       Brighton Rock." *Graham Greene*. The Christian Critic
       Series. Edited by Harry J. Cargas. St. Louis: B.
       Herder Book Co., n.d. (1969), pp. 75-87.

E864   Croft, J.C. "Graham Greene and Africa (*Journey Without
       Maps* and *The Heart of the Matter*)." *Gleanings from
       Greeneland*. Edited by J.S. Ryan. Armidale, New South
       Wales (Australia): University of New England, 1972,
       pp. 70-80.

E865   Davies, Horton. "The Confessional and the Altar."
       A Mirror of the Ministry in Modern Novels. New York:
       Oxford University Press, 1959, pp. 100-110.

E866   DeVitis, A.A. "The Catholic as Novelist: Graham Greene
       and François Mauriac." *Graham Greene: Some Critical
       Considerations*. Edited by Robert O. Evans. Lexington:
       University of Kentucky Press, 1963, pp. 112-126.

E867   Eagleton, Terry. "Reluctant Heroes: The Novels of
       Graham Greene." *Exiles and Emigrés: Studies in Modern
       Literature*. London: Chatto & Windus, 1970, pp. 108-137.

E868   Engel, Claire Élaine. "Graham Greene." *Esquisses
       Anglaises i Charles Morgan, Graham Greene, T.S. Eliot*.
       Paris: Editions "Je Sers," 1949, pp. 57-98.

E869   Enright, D.J. "The Man Within: The Memoirs of Graham
       Greene." *Man is an Onion: Reviews and Essays*. London:
       Chatto & Windus, 1972, pp. 16-19.

E870   Evans, Robert O. "The Satanist Fallacy of *Brighton
       Rock*." *Graham Greene: Some Critical Considerations*.
       Edited by Robert O. Evans. Lexington: University of
       Kentucky Press, 1963, pp. 151-168.

E871 Fraser, G.S. *The Modern Writer and His World.*
Baltimore: Pelican Books, 1964, pp. 133-138.

E872 Frederiksen, Emil. "Graham Greene." *Fremmede Digtere
i Det 20. Århundrede.* Edited by Sven M. Kristensen.
Copenhagen: G.E.C. Grad., 1968, III pp. 199-213.

E873 Fricker, Robert. "Graham Greene." *Christliche Dichter
im 20. Jahrhundert.* Bern: Francke, 1968, pp. 253-269.

E874 Friedman, Melvin. *The Vision Obscured: Perceptions of
Some Twentieth-Century Catholic Novelists.* New York:
Fordham University Press, 1970.

E875 Gable, Sister Mariella. *This is Catholic Fiction.*
New York: Sheed and Ward, 1948, passim.

E876 Gardiner, Harold C., S.J. "Mr. Greene Does It Again"
and "Second Thoughts on Greene's Latest." *In All
Conscience.* New York: Hanover House, 1959, pp. 96-102.

E877 Gassner, J. "Points of Return: Religion and Graham
Greene's *The Potting Shed.*" *Theatre at the Crossroads.*
New York: Holt, Rinehart & Winston, 1960, pp. 155-157.

E878 Gillie, Christopher. "The Critical Decade, 1930-1940."
Movements in English Literature, 1900-1940. London,
New York: Cambridge University Press, 1975, pp. 122-
149.

E879 Gilman, R. "Mixture Almost As Before." *Common and
Uncommon Masks: Writings on Theater, 1961-1970.* New
York: Random House, pp. 249-251.

E880 Goad, Kathleen M. *Twentieth-Century Short Stories:
Notes on Chosen English Texts.* Bath, Somerset: James
Brodie, Ltd., n.d. pp. 35-39.

Re "The Destructors."

E881 Graff, Hilda. "Graham Greene." *Modern Gloom and
Christian Hope.* Chicago: Regnery, 1959, pp. 84-97.

E882 Gregor, Ian and Brian Nicholas. "Grace and Morality:
Thérèse Desqueyroux (1927), *The End of the Affair*
(1951)." *The Moral and the Story.* London: Faber &
Faber, 1962, pp. 185-216.

Reprinted as "*The End of the Affair*" in *Graham Greene:
A Collection of Critical Essays*. Edited by Samuel L.
Hynes. Englewood Cliffs, N.J.: Prentice-Hall, Inc.,
1973, pp. 110-125.

E883   Gregor, Ian and David Lodge. "Graham Greene." *The
English Novel: Questions in Literature*. Edited by
Cedric Watts. London: Sussex, 1976, pp. 152-171.

Dialogue.

E884   Guitton, Jean. "Ya-t-il Encore une Nature Humaine?"
L'Humanisme et la Grâce. Paris: Editions de Flore,
1950, pp. 125-142.

E885   Gusev, E.A. Russian Foreword to English Edition of
Greene's Stories. Moscow: Uysshaya Shkola, 1970.

E886   Haber, Herbert R. "The End of the Catholic Cycle:
The Writer Versus the Saint." *Graham Greene: Some
Critical Considerations*. Edited by Robert O. Evans.
Lexington: University of Kentucky Press, 1963,
pp. 127-150.

E887   Hall, James. "Efficient Saints and Civilians: Graham
Greene." *The Lunatic Giant in the Drawing Room: The
British and American Novel Since 1930*. Bloomington:
Indiana University Press, 1968, pp. 111-123.

E888   Hardwick, Elizabeth. "Loveless Love: Graham Greene."
A View of My Own: Essays in Literature and Society.
London: Heinemann, 1964, pp. 92-102.

E889   Havinghurst, Walter. "Study of 'Across the Bridge.'"
Instructor's Manual: Masters of the Modern Short Story.
New York: Harcourt, Brace, 1955, pp. 27-28.

E890   Heilpern, John. "Graham Greene: End of the Affair."
Authors in the News, II. New York: Gale, 1976, pp.
122-124.

E891   Hesla, David H. "Theological Ambiguity in the 'Catholic Novels.'" *Graham Greene: Some Critical Considerations*. Edited by Robert O. Evans. Lexington: University of Kentucky Press, 1963, pp. 96-111.

E892   Hoehn, Matthew, editor. "Graham Greene." *Catholic
Authors*. St. Mary's Abbey, 1948, pp. 289-290.

E893   Hoggart, Richard. "The Force of Caricature." *Speaking*
       to Each Other. II . London: Chatto & Windus, 1970.
       pp. 40-55.

       Reprinted in *Graham Greene: A Collection of Critical*
       Essays. Edited by Samuel Hynes. Englewood Cliffs,
       N.J.: Prentice-Hall, Inc., 1973, pp. 79-94.

E894   Hughes, Riley E. "*The Quiet American*: The Case Re-
       opened." *Graham Greene.* The Christian Critic Series.
       Edited by Harry J. Cargas. St. Louis: B. Herder Book
       Co., n.d. (1969), pp. 130-133.

E895   Hynes, Samuel L. "Introduction." *Graham Greene: A*
       Collection of Critical Essays. Edited by Samuel L.
       Hynes. Englewood Cliffs, N.J.: Prentice-Hall, Inc.,
       1973, pp. 1-7.

E896   Jefferson, Mary Evelyn. "*The Heart of the Matter*: The
       Responsible Man." *Graham Greene.* The Christian Critic
       Series. Edited by Harry J. Cargas. St. Louis: B.
       Herder Book Co., n.d. (1969), pp. 88-100.

E897   Jonsson, Thorsten Georg. "Ett Portrait av Scobie."
       Tva Essayer om Graham Greene. Stockholm: Norstedts,
       1950, pp. 1-8.

E898   Joselyn, Sister M., O.S.B. "Graham Greene's Novels:
       The Conscience in the World." *Literature and Society.*
       A Selection of Papers Delivered at the Joint Meeting
       of the Midwest Modern Language Association and the
       Central Renaissance Conference, 1963. Edited by B.
       Slote. Lincoln: University of Nebraska Press, 1964,
       pp. 153-172.

E899   Karl, F.R. "Graham Greene's Demoniacal Heroes." *The*
       Contemporary English Novel. Revised Edition. New
       York: Farrar, Straus, 1972, pp. 85-106; "Postscript,"
       pp. 335-338.

E900   Kazin, Alfred. "Graham Greene and the Age of Absurdity."
       Contemporaries: Essays on Modern Life and Literature.
       Boston: Little, Brown & Co., 1962; London: Secker &
       Warburg, 1963, pp. 158-161.

E901   Kellogg, Gene. "Graham Greene." *The Vital Tradition:*
       The Catholic Novel in a Period of Convergence. Chicago:
       Loyola University Press, 1970, pp. 111-136.

E902   Kennedy, Alan. "Inconsistencies of Narration in Graham
       Greene." *The Protean Self: Dramatic Action in Contem-*
       porary Fiction. New York: Columbia University Press,
       1974, pp. 231–249.

E903   Kermode, J. Frank. "Mr. Greene's Eggs and Crosses."
       Puzzles and Epiphanies. London: Routledge & Kegan
       Paul, 1962; New York: Chilmark Press, 1963, pp. 176–187.

E904   Kerr, Walter. "Playwrights." *Pieces at Eight.* New
       York: Simon & Schuster, 1957, pp. 117–149.

E905   Kerr, Walter. *"The Complaisant Lover."* *The Theater*
       in Spite of Itself. New York: Simon & Schuster, 1963,
       pp. 157–160.

E906   Kettle, Arnold. *An Introduction to the English Novel.*
       II. London: Hutchinson, 1953, pp. 170–177; 2nd ed.
       1967, pp. 153–159; New York: Harper & Row, 1968, pp.
       48–50, 335–341.

E907   Knaak Peuser, Angélica. "La Novela de Graham Greene."
       El Espiritu y la Carne en las Grandes Creaciones
       Literarias. Buenos Aires: Ediciones Peuser, 1952,
       pp. 161–179.

E908   Kunkel, Francis L. "The Theme of Sin and Grace in
       Graham Greene." *Graham Greene: Some Critical Considera-*
       tions. Edited by Robert O. Evans. Lexington: Univer-
       sity of Kentucky Press, 1963, pp. 49–60.

E909   Kuntz, Stanley J., editor. "Graham Greene." *Twentieth*
       Century Authors. First Supplement. New York: Wilson,
       1942, pp. 572–573; rpt. 1955, pp. 387–388.

E910   Laitinen, Kai. "The Heart of the Novel: The Turning
       Point in *The Heart of the Matter.*" *Graham Greene:*
       Some Critical Considerations. Edited by Robert O.
       Evans. Lexington: University of Kentucky Press, 1963,
       pp. 169–180.

E911   Lambert, Gavin. "The Double Agent." *The Dangerous*
       Edge. London: Barrie & Jenkins, 1975, pp. 132–170.

E912   László, Passuth. "Graham Greene." *Az Angol Irodalom a*
       Huszadik Században (*English Literature in the Twentieth*
       Century). II. Budapest: Gondolat, 1973, pp. 31–56.

E913   Levi, Albert William. *Literature, Philosophy and the
       Imagination*. Bloomington: Indiana University Press,
       1969, pp. 261, 266-268, 270-272.

E914   Lewis, R.W.B. "Graham Greene: The Religious Affair."
       *The Picaresque Saint: Representative Figures in Con-
       temporary Fiction*. Philadelphia, New York: J.B. Lippin-
       cott, 1959, pp. 220-274.

E915   Lewis, R.W.B. "Introduction." *Graham Greene, The
       Power and the Glory, Text and Criticism*. The Viking
       Critical Library. Edited by R.W.B. Lewis and Peter J.
       Conn. New York: Viking Press, 1970, pp. vii-xvi.

E916   Lewis, R.W.B. "The Trilogy." *Graham Greene: A Col-
       lection of Critical Essays*. Edited by Samual L. Hynes.
       Englewood Cliffs, N.J.: Prentice-Hall, Inc., 1973,
       pp. 49-74.

E917   Lichtheim, George. "Adam's Tree." *Collected Essays*.
       New York: Viking Press, 1973, pp. 477-482.

E918   Lichtheim, George. "Anglo-American." *Collected Essays*.
       New York: Viking Press, 1973, pp. 490-492.

E919   Lindegren, Erik. "Graham Greene." *Tva Essayer om
       Graham Greene*. Stockholm: Norstedts, 1950, pp. 9-16.

E920   Lodge, David. *About Catholic Authors*. London, New
       York: St. Paul Publications, 1957.

E921   Lodge, David. "Graham Greene." *The Novelist at the
       Crossroads, and Other Essays on Fiction and Criticism*.
       London: Routledge & Kegan Paul, 1971; Ithaca, New
       York: Cornell University Press, 1971, pp. 87-118.

       Lodge, David and Ian Gregor. "Graham Greene." *The
       English Novel: Questions in Literature*. Edited by
       Cedric Watts. London: Sussex, 1976, pp. 152-171. (See
       E883.)

       Dialogue.

E922   Lodge, David. "Graham Greene." *Six Contemporary
       British Novelists*. Edited by George Slade. New York:
       Columbia University Press, 1976, pp. 1-56.

E923 Lumley, Frederick. "Britain." *New Trends in 20th
      Century Drama: A Survey Since Ibsen and Shaw.* London:
      Barrie & Rockliff, 1967; New York: Oxford University
      Press, 1967, pp. 255-316.

E924 Lynskey, Winifred. *Reading Modern Fiction: 30 Stories
      with Study Aids.* New York: Scribners, 1952, pp. 245-
      246.

E925 Maclaren-Ross, J. "Excursions in Greeneland." *Memoirs
      of the Forties.* London: Alan Ross, 1965, pp. 13-28.

E926 Manners, Penelope J., editor. *Novels of Today.* London:
      University of London Press, 1967.

E927 Manvell, Roger and R.K. Neilson Baxter. "Carol Reed
      Talks to Roger Manvell" (followed by a short extract
      from the post-production script of *The Third Man*). *The
      Cinema 1952.* Harmondsworth: Penguin Books, 1952;
      Pelican Books A260, pp. 67-87.

E928 Martin, Graham. "Novelists of Three Decades: Evelyn
      Waugh, Graham Greene, C.P. Snow." *The Pelican Guide to
      English Literature: 7. The Modern Age.* Edited by
      Boris Ford. Baltimore: Penguin Books, 1961; Revised
      Edition, 1967, pp. 394-414.

E929 Mauriac, François. "Graham Greene." *Mes Grandes Hommes.*
      Monaco: Editions de Rocher, 1949.

      Reprinted as *Men I Hold Great.* New York: Philosophical
      Library, 1951, pp. 124-128, and as "Graham Greene," in
      Graham Greene: A Collection of Critical Essays. Edited
      by Samuel L. Lynes. Englewood Cliffs, N.J.: Prentice-
      Hall, Inc., 1973, pp. 75-78. Also published in *Great
      Men.* London: Rockliff, 1952, pp. 117-121.

E930 Maurois, André. *Points of View: From Kipling to Graham
      Greene.* New York: Frederick Ungar, 1968, pp. 383-409.

E931 Mayhew, Alice. "The Comedians." *Graham Greene.* The
      Christian Critic Series. Edited by Harry J. Cargas.
      St. Louis: B. Herder Book Co., n.d. (1969), pp. 134-
      141.

E932 McCarthy, Mary. "Sheep in Wolves' Clothing." *Sights
      and Spectacles: 1937-1958.* London: Heinemann, 1959,
      pp. 177-183.

E933 McInherny, Frances C. *"It's a Battlefield*--A World of Chaos." *Gleanings from Greeneland.* Edited by J.S. Ryan. Armidale, New South Wales (Australia): University of New England, 1972, pp. 20-30.

E934 McInherny, Frances C. "Some Thoughts Occasioned on Re- reading *The Power and the Glory." Gleanings from Greeneland.* Edited by J.S. Ryan. Armidale, New South Wales (Australia): University of New England, 1972, pp. 31-43.

E935 Mesnet, Marie-Beatrice. "Graham Greene." *The Politics of Twentieth-Century Novelists.* Edited by George A. Panichas. New York: Hawthorn Books, 1971, pp. 100-123.

E936 Miller, Alexander. "Great Britain: Graham Greene." *The Renewal of Man: A Twentieth-Century Essay on Justi- fication by Faith.* London: Victor Gollancz, 1956, pp. 28-34.

E937 Moeller, Charles. "Graham Greene ou le Martyre de l'Esperance." *Literature du XXe Siècle et Christi- anisme: I: Silence de Dieu.* Tournai, Belgium: Cas- terman, 1953, pp. 259-301.

E938 Moré, Marcel. "The Two Holocausts of Scobie." *Cross Currents of Psychiatry and Catholic Morality.* Edited by William Birmingham and Joseph E. Cunneen. New York: Pantheon Books, 1964.

E939 Mueller, W.R. "Theme of Love: Graham Greene's *The Heart of the Matter." Prophetic Voice in Modern Fiction.* New York: Association Press, 1959, pp. 136- 157.

E940 Murray, Edward. "Graham Greene and the Silver Screen." *The Cinematic Imagination: Writers and the Motion Pictures.* New York: Frederick Ungar, 1972, pp. 244-260.

E941 Nakando, Kii. "G. Greene to Gendaissi." *Kirisutokoyo to Bungaku (Dai 3 Shu) (Christianity and Literature 3).* Edited by Tomoichi Sasabuchi. Tokyo: Kasama Shoin, 1975, pp. 155-172.

E942 Newby, P.H. "Character and Situation: Graham Greene, Joyce Cary and L.P. Hartley." *The Novel, 1945-1950.* London: Longmans, Green, 1951, pp. 33-36.

E943 O'Donnell, Donat (pseud. Connor Cruise O'Brien).
      "Graham Greene: The Anatomy of Pity." *Maria Cross:*
      Imaginative Patterns in a Group of Modern Catholic
      Writers. New York: Oxford University Press, 1952,
      pp. 61-94.

E944 O'Faoláin, Seán. "Graham Greene: I Suffer; Therefore,
      I Am." *The Vanishing Hero: Studies in Novelists of the*
      Twenties. London: Eyre & Spottiswoode, 1956, pp. 71-
      97; Boston: Little Brown, 1957, pp. 45-72.

E945 Orwell, George. "Letter to T.R. Fyvel." *The Collected*
      Essays, Journalism and Letters of George Orwell, IV.
      Edited by Sonia Orwell and Ian Angus. London: Secker
      & Warburg, 1968, pp. 496-497.

E946 Orwell, George. "The Sanctified Sinner." *The Col-*
      lected Essays, Journalism and Letters of George Orwell.
      Edited by Sonia Orwell and Ian Angus. London: Secker &
      Warburg, 1968, pp. 439-443.

      Reprinted in *Graham Greene: A Collection of Critical*
      Essays. Edited by Samuel L. Hynes. Englewood Cliffs,
      N.J.: Prentice-Hall, Inc., 1973, pp. 105-109.

E947 Patten, Karl. "The Structure of *The Power and the*
      Glory." *Graham Greene.* Christian Critic Series.
      Edited by Harry J. Cargas. St. Louis: B. Herder Book
      Co., n.d. (1969), pp. 101-113.

E948 Poole, Roger C. "Graham Greene's Indirection."
      Graham Greene. Christian Critic Series. Edited by
      Harry J. Cargas. St. Louis: B. Herder Book Co., n.d.
      (1969), pp. 29-44.

E949 Prescott, Orville. "Comrades of the Coterie: Henry
      Green, Compton-Burnett, Elizabeth Bowen, Graham
      Greene." *In My Opinion.* Indianapolis: Bobbs-Merrill,
      1952, pp. 92-109.

E950 Quennell, Peter. *The Sign of the Fish.* London:
      Collins, 1960, pp. 60-61.

E951 Reed, Henry. *The Novel Since 1939.* London: Longmans,
      Green, 1946, pp. 15-18.

E952 Reinhardt, Kurt F. "Graham Greene: Victory in Failure."
      The Theological Novel of Modern Europe: An Analysis of

Eight Authors. New York: Frederick Ungar, 1969,
pp. 170-202.

E953 Ruotolo, Lucio P. "Rose Wilson." *Six Essential Heroes:
The Politics of Faith.* Cambridge, Mass.: Harvard University Press, 1973, pp. 39-53; 147-148.

E954 Ryan, J.S. "Men of Affairs--the Greenes of Berkham-
sted." *Gleanings from Greeneland.* Edited by J.S. Ryan.
Armidale, New South Wales (Australia): University of
New England, 1972, pp. 1-19.

E955 Ryan, J.S. "Structure, Imagery and Theme in *The Power
and the Glory.*" *Gleanings from Greeneland.* Edited by
J.S. Ryan. Armidale, New South Wales (Australia):
University of New England, 1972, pp. 44-69.

E956 Sale, William M., Jr., James Hall and Martin Steinmann,
Jr. *Critical Discussions for Teachers Using 'Short
Stories: Tradition and Direction.'* Norfolk, Conn.: New
Directions, 1949, pp. 62-64.

E957 Schorer, Mark. *The Story: A Critical Anthology.* New
York: Prentice-Hall, 1950, pp. 183-185.

E958 Scott, Carolyn D. "The Witch at the Corner: Notes on
Graham Greene's Mythology." *Graham Greene: Some
Critical Considerations.* Edited by Robert O. Evans.
Lexington: University of Kentucky Press, 1963, pp.
231-244.

E959 Scott, Carolyn D. "The Urban Romance: A Study of
Graham Greene's Thrillers." *Graham Greene.* The
Christian Critic Series. Edited by Harry J. Cargas.
St. Louis: B. Herder Book Co., n.d. (1969), pp. 1-28.

E960 Scott, Nathan A., Jr. "Graham Greene: Christian Tra-
gedian." *Graham Greene: Some Critical Considerations.*
Edited by Robert O. Evans. Lexington: University of
Kentucky Press, 1963, pp. 25-48.

Reprinted in *Craters of the Spirit: Studies in the
Modern Novel* by Nathan A. Scott, Jr. Washington:
Corpus Books, 1968, pp. 201-232.

E961 Shakhova, K. "Afterword" to the Ukranian translations
of *The Quiet American* and *Our Man in Havana.* Kiev:
Dnipro, 1971.

E962   Sheed, Wilfrid. "Racing the Clock with Greene and
       Pritchett." *The Morning After: Selected Essays and
       Reviews*. New York: Farrar, Straus & Giroux, 1971,
       pp. 66-75.

E963   Sinclair, Andrew. *"Introduction."* *The Third Man* by
       Graham Greene and Carol Reed. London: Lorrimer, 1968,
       pp. 5-6.

E964   Solomon, Petre. "Romanelle lui Graham Greene" (Graham
       Greene's Novels). Introduction. *Graham Greene. Un
       Caz de Mulitare* (*A Burnt-Out Case*). Bucuresti: Editura
       Pentru Literatură, 1968, pp. v-xxxvi.

E965   Sonnenfeld, A. "Children's Faces: Graham Greene." *The
       Vision Obscured*. Edited by Melvin J. Friedman. New
       York: Fordham University Press, 1970, pp. 109-128.

E966   Stevenson, Lionel. "Traditionalists Between Wars."
       History of the English Novel, XI. Yesterday and After.
       New York: Barnes & Noble, 1967, pp. 333-344.

E967   Stewart, Douglas. "Catholicism." *The Ark of God*.
       London: Carey Kingsgate Press, 1961, pp. 71-98.

E968   Strong, L.A.G. *English Novelists Today*. Radiotjänst,
       1955, pp. 115-116.

E969   Takeuchi, Masao. *"The Heart of the Matter* no Kosei,
       Shuho Oyobi Buntai ni Tsuite." *Gengo to Buntai:
       Higashida Chiaki Kyoja Kanreki Kinen Ronbonshu*. Edited
       by Chiaki Higashida. Osaka: Osaka Kyoiku Tosho, 1975,
       pp. 239-251.

E970   Tracy, H.L.W. "Graham Greene." *The Critic as Artist:
       Essays on Books 1920-1970*. Edited by G.A. Harrison.
       New York: Liveright, 1972, pp. 315-320.

E971   Traversi, Derek. "Graham Greene: The Earlier Novels."
       Graham Greene: A Collection of Critical Essays. Edited
       by Samuel L. Hynes. Englewood Cliffs, N.J.: Prentice-
       Hall, Inc., 1973, pp. 17-29.

       Tynan, Kenneth and Cecil Beaton. *Persona Grata*.
       London: Wingate, 1953, pp. 53-55; New York: Putnam,
       1954, pp. 53-56. (See E844.)

E972 Tynan, Kenneth. *"The Living Room* by Graham Greene, at Wyndham's." *Curtains: Selections from the Drama Criticism and Related Writings.* New York: Atheneum, 1961, pp. 47-49.

E973 Tynan, Kenneth. *"The Potting Shed* by Graham Greene, at the Globe." *Curtains: Selections from the Drama Criticism and Related Writings.* New York: Atheneum, 1961, pp. 207-209.

E974 Tynan, Kenneth. *"The Power and the Glory,* adapted by Denis Cannan and Pierre Bost from Graham Greene's Novel, at the Phoenix." *Curtains: Selections from the Drama Criticism and Related Writings.* New York: Atheneum, 1961, pp. 124-125.

E975 Waugh, Evelyn. "Felix Culpa?" *Graham Greene: A Collection of Critical Essays.* Edited by Samuel L. Hynes. Englewood Cliffs, N.J.: Prentice-Hall, Inc., 1973, pp. 95-102.

E976 Webster, Harvey Curtis. "The World of Graham Greene." *Graham Greene: Some Critical Considerations.* Edited by Robert O. Evans. Lexington: University of Kentucky Press, 1963, pp. 1-24.

E977 Webster, Harvey Curtis. "Graham Greene: Stoical Catholic." *After the Trauma: Representative British Novelists Since 1920.* Lexington: University of Kentucky Press, 1970, pp. 97-123.

E978 West, Anthony. "Graham Greene." *Principles and Persuasions.* New York: Harcourt, Brace, 1957, pp. 174-178.

E979 West, Paul. "Graham Greene." *The Wine of Absurdity: Essays on Literature and Consolation.* University Park: Pennsylvania State University Press, 1966, pp. 174-185.

E980 Wilshire, A.D. "Conflict and Conciliation in Graham Greene." *Essays and Studies, 1966.* Edited by R.M. Wilson. New York: Humanities Press, 1966, pp. 122-137.

E981 Wilson, Colin. "The Implications of Realism: Evelyn Waugh and Graham Greene." *The Strength to Dream: Literature and the Imagination.* Boston: Houghton Mifflin, 1962, pp. 42-55.

E982   Woodcock, George.   "Graham Greene."   *The Writer and*
       Politics.   London: Porcupine Press, 1948, pp. 125-153.

E983   Woodward, Anthony.   "Graham Greene: The War Against
       Boredom."   *Seven Studies in English for Dorothy*
       Cavers.   Edited by Robert Gildas.   Cape Town: Purnell,
       1971, pp. 64-105.

E984   Zabel, Morton Dauwen.   "Graham Greene."   *Forms of Modern*
       Fiction.   Edited by W. Van O'Connor.   Minneapolis:
       University of Minnesota Press; London: Geoffrey Cumber-
       lege, 1948, pp. 287-293.

       Also reprinted with some changes in *Critiques and*
       Essays on Modern Fiction 1920-1951.   Edited by J.W.
       Albridge.   New York: Ronald Press, 1952, pp. 518-525;
       Craft and Character in Modern Fiction.   New York:
       Viking Press, 1957, pp. 276-296; and as "The Best and
       the Worst," in *Graham Greene: A Collection of Critical*
       Essays.   Edited by Samuel L. Hynes.   Englewood Cliffs,
       N.J.: Prentice-Hall, Inc., 1973, pp. 30-48.

F

GRAHAM GREENE'S RADIO AND TELEVISION BROADCASTS
AND FILM APPEARANCES

Most of the information in this section has been provided by
the BBC Written Archives Centre (Claversham Park, Reading,
RG4 8TZ). A description of additional holdings at the Centre
can be seen in D6.

F1   "Oxford Poets Symposium." BBC–Radio. January 25, 1925.

Readings from their own works by Harold Acton, Graham Greene, B. Howard, G.G. MacLeod, Patrick Monkhouse and A.L. Rowse.

F2   "A Day Saved." BBC–National Service. June 22, 1934.

Short story read by Harcourt Williams.

F3   "The Cinema." BBC–National Service. August 29, 1937.

Talk.

F4   "Fortnightly Review of Literature, Art and the Theatre." (S/Writer). BBC–Spanish Service. March 28, 1941.

F5   "Fortnightly Review of Literature, Art and the Theatre." (S/Writer). BBC–Spanish Service. April 12, 1941.

F6   "Fortnightly Review of Literature, Art and the Theatre." (S/Writer). BBC–Spanish Service. April 26, 1941.

F7   "Fortnightly Review of Literature, Art and the Theatre." (S/Writer). BBC–Spanish Service. May 10, 1941.

F8   "Fortnightly Review of Literature, Art and the Theatre." (S/Writer). BBC–Spanish Service. May 28, 1941.

F9   "Fortnightly Review of Literature, Art and the Theatre." (S/Writer). BBC–Spanish Service. June 18, 1941.

F10 "Fortnightly Review of Literature, Art and the Theatre." (S/Writer). BBC–Spanish Service. July 3, 1941.

F11 "Fortnightly Review of Literature, Art and the Theatre." (S/Writer). BBC–Spanish Service. July 16, 1941.

F12 "Fortnightly Review of Literature, Art and the Theatre." (S/Writer). BBC–Spanish Service. July 29, 1941.

F13 "Fortnightly Review of Literature, Art and the Theatre." (S/Writer). BBC–Spanish Service. August 14, 1941.

F14 "The Crisis." BBC–Third Programme. March 9, 1947.

One of a series of talks.

F15 "The Artist in Society." BBC–Third Programme. July 10, 1948.

Scripted discussion with V.S. Pritchett and Elizabeth Bowen.

F16   "Picture Parade." London Transcription Service, No. 13, (recorded). September 22, 1948.

F17   "London West Central." BBC-English European Service. November 6, 1948.

Interview.

F18   "Robert Louis Stevenson." BBC-English European Service. August 17, 1949.

Based on *New Statesman* article.

F19   "Stage, Screen and Studio." BBC-General Overseas Service. July 27, 1953.

Interview by Therese Denny.

F20   "A Small Affair." BBC-Third Programme. August 10, 1953; repeated August 13, 1953.

Extract from novel then in progress, based on an incident in Indo-China in 1951.

F21   "Anglo Texan Society." BBC-North American Service. December 23, 1953.

Interview.

F22   "On Indo-China." BBC-General Overseas Service. May 10, 1954.

Interview by Brian Crozier.

F23   "We Write Novels." BBC-General Overseas Service. June 30, 1955.

Discussion with Walter Allen.

F24   "A Memory of Indo-China." BBC-Third Programme. September 8, 1955.

Reading extract from unpublished novel.

F25   "Asia and the West." BBC-London Calling Asia. June 11, 1957.

Discussion on the novel.

F26 "The World We Live In." BBC–General Overseas Service. September 5, 1959.

Discussion with Colin Willis.

F27 "Life and Letters." BBC–General Overseas Service. January 29, 1961.

Interview by Peter Duval Smith.

F28 "Life and Letters." BBC–General Overseas Service. November 19, 1961. Repeated as "The World of Books" on the Home Service, January 13, 1962.

Readings by Greene from *In Search of a Character*.

F29 "Myth, Reality and Fiction." BBC–Third Programme. April 2, 1962.

Conversation with Frank Kermode.

F30 "Life and Letters." BBC–General Overseas Service. Early October, 1962.

Re the prefaces of Conrad and James.

F31 "The Masters – Conrad." BBC–Home Service. December 21, 1962.

Reading extracts from *Remembering Mr. Jones*.

F32 "Words, Words, Words." The World We Live In. BBC–Home Service. April 5, 1963.

F33 "The Masters: Graham Greene." BBC–Home Service. Introduced by Francis Watson. September, 1964.

F34 "Who, What, Where, When." The Masters. BBC–Radio 4. December 15, 1967.

F35 "Late Night Extra." BBC–Radio 1. February 7, 1968.

Interview by Gerry Monte *re* University Rag in Cardiff.

F36 "Ten to Eight." BBC–Radio 4. February 15, 1968.

Re private collection.

F37 "World at One." BBC–Radio 4. March 29, 1968.

Interview *re* Russian writers and Russia in general.

F38   "Pick of the Week." BBC-Radio 4.   July 18, 1969.

      Extract from *Omnibus*, November 17, 1968.

F39   "Confirmation: A Writer at Work." BBC-Radio 4.
      August 14, 1969.

      Extract from *Omnibus*, November 17, 1968.

F40   "Now Read On." BBC-Radio 4.   April 8, 1970; also "Pick
      of the Week." April 10, 1970.

      Interview by Ronald Bryden *re Brighton Rock, England
      Made Me, It's a Battlefield* and *Our Man in Havana*.

F41   "Now Read On." BBC-Radio 4.   April 21, 1971.

      Interview *re* Collected Edition.

F42   "Now Read On." BBC-Radio 4.   September 15, 1971.

      Interview *re A Sort of Life*.

F43   "With Jimmy Young." BBC-Radio 2.   February 12, 1974.

F44   "World at One." BBC-Radio 4.   February 13, 1974.

      Re his reaction to Solzhenitsyn's expulsion from
      Russia.

F45   "P.M." BBC-Radio 4.   February 15, 1974.

      Re his interests outside writing.

F46   "You and Yours." BBC-Radio 4.   February 16, 1974.

      Re illiteracy.

F47   "Kaleidescope." BBC-Radio 4.   December 3, 1975; repeated
      on BBC-Radio 3 on March 4, 1976.

      Interview *re Return of A.J. Raffles*.

F48   "Recollections of Herbert Read," with others. BBC-
      Radio 3.   December 4, 1977.

F49   "Late Night Line Up." BBC-TV.   November 8, 1964.

      Interview.

F50   "Omnibus." The Hunted Man. BBC-TV.   November 17, 1968;
      repeated July 13, 1969 and August 17, 1969.

      Interview by Christopher Burstall.

F51 *Day for Night* (1974), a film directed by François
     Truffaut.

     Greene appeared incognito in the role of an English
     insurance investigator.

G

PUBLISHED OR BROADCAST INTERVIEWS WITH GRAHAM GREENE

G1   Bryden, Ronald. "Now Read On." BBC-Radio 4 (April 8,
      1970). Also "Pick of the Week" (April 10, 1970).

      Re Brighton Rock, England Made Me, It's a Battlefield,
      and *Our Man in Havana.*

G2   Bryden, Ronald. "Graham Greene Discusses With Ronald
      Bryden the Collected Edition of His Novels Which Was
      Published Not Long Ago." *The Listener,* LXXXIII
      (April 23, 1970), pp. 544–545.

G3   Burstall, Christopher. "Graham Greene Takes the Orient
      Express." *The Listener,* LXXX (November 21, 1968), pp.
      672–674, 676–677.

      Transcript of Greene's conversation which forms the
      basis of the *Omnibus* production "The Hunted Man."
      which was transmitted on BBC-1 TV.

G4   Burstall, Christopher. "A Writer at Work." Broadcast
      on BBC-Radio 4 (August 14, 1969).

G5   Chamberlain, Greg. With Greene in Haiti. *Manchester
      Guardian* (March 21, 1976), p. 7.

G6   Crozier, Brian. "On Indo China." BBC-General Overseas
      Service (May 10, 1954).

G7   Denny, Therese. "Stage, Screen and Studio." BBC-
      General Overseas Service (July 27, 1953).

G8   Dennys, Louise and Amanda Todd. "The Greene Factor."
      The Sunday Telegraph (March 12, 1978), p. 14.

G9   Easton, Elizabeth. "A Conversation with Graham Greene."
      Book-of-the-Month Club News (Fall 1973), pp. 4, 20.

G10   Emerson, Gloria. "Our Man in Antibes: Graham Greene."
      Rolling Stone, No. 260 (March 9, 1978), pp. 45–49.

G11   Harwood, Ronald. "Time and the Novelist – Graham Greene
      Interviewed." *The Listener,* XCIV (December 4, 1975),
      pp. 747, 749.

G12   Hewes, Henry. "Resurrection Will Out--Broadway Post-
      script." *Saturday Review,* XL (February 16, 1957),
      pp. 26–27.

      Re The Potting Shed.

G13   Kermode, Frank. "The House of Fiction: Interviews with
      Seven English Novelists." *Partisan Review*, XXX (Spring
      1963), pp. 61-82.

G14   Kermode, Frank. "Myth, Reality, and Fiction." *The
      Listener*, LXVIII (August 30, 1962), pp. 311-313.

      Summary of a symposium which he compiled and presented
      in the Third Programme which included contributions from
      a number of distinguished novelists -- Iris Murdoch,
      Graham Greene, Angus Wilson, Ivy Compton-Burnett, C.P.
      Snow, John Wain, Muriel Spark -- from conversations
      with each.

G15   Kingsmill, Hugh and Hesketh Pearson. *Talking of Dick
      Whittington*. London: Eyre & Spottiswoode, 1947, pp. 10-
      11, 98-99, 125-126.

      Records several short conversations with Greene.

G16   Lambert, J.W. "The Private World of Graham Greene."
      The Sunday Times (March 5, 1978).

G17   Maddocks, Melvin. "Greene, 'the Funny Writer,' on
      Comedy." *Life*, LXVIII (January 23, 1970), p. 10.

G18   Magnusson, Magnus. "Tabasco." *The Listener*, LXXXV
      (May 6, 1971), p. 584.

      Greene talks about his novels and about Mexico, recorded
      for the BBC-Radio 4 series, "Now Read On."

G19   Mewshaw, Michael. "Greene in Antibes." *London Maga-
      zine*, XVII (June-July 1977), pp. 35-45.

G20   Monte, Gerry. "Late Night Extra." BBC-Radio 1
      (February 7, 1968).

      Re University Rag in Cardiff.

G21   Naipaul, V.S. "Graham Greene." *The Daily Telegraph
      Magazine*, No. 179 (March 8, 1968), pp. 28-32.

G22   Oaks, Philip. "Greene Screen." *The Sunday Times*
      (March 1, 1970), p. 58.

      Re Greene's visit to the British Film Institute to
      discuss the problems of writing for movies.

G23   Osterman, Robert. "Interview with Graham Greene."
      Catholic World, CLXX (February 1950), pp. 356-361.

G24 Perrott, Roy. "Graham Greene: A Brief Encounter." *The Observer Review* (November 16, 1969), p. 25.

G25 Phillips, Gene D. "Graham Greene: On the Screen." *Catholic World*, CCIX (August 1969), pp. 218-221.

Reprinted in *Graham Greene: A Collection of Critical Essays*. Edited by Samuel L. Hynes. Englewood Cliffs, N.J.: Prentice-Hall, Inc., 1973, pp. 168-175.

G26 Phillips, Gene D. "Graham Greene Interviewed by Gene D. Phillips." *The Month*, I (June 1970), pp. 362-367.

G27 Phillips, Gene D. "Graham Greene Interview." *Twentieth Century*, XXV (Summer 1970), pp. 111-117.

G28 Pritchett, V.S. "The Human Factor in Graham Greene." *The New York Times Magazine* (February 26, 1978), pp. 33-36, 38, 40-42, 44, 46; also *The New York Times Biographical Service*, IX (February 1978), pp. 188-193.

G29 Pritchett, V.S. Interview/article about Greene. *San Francisco Chronicle* (March 4, 1978), p. 13.

G30 Pritchett, V.S. Interview with Greene. *The Times* (March 18, 1978), p. 6.

G31 Shuttleworth, Martin and Simon Raven. "The Art of Fiction: Graham Greene." *The Paris Review*, No. 3 (Autumn 1953), pp. 24-41.

Reprinted in *Graham Greene: A Collection of Critical Essays*. Edited by Samuel L. Hynes. Englewood Cliffs, N.J.: Prentice-Hall, Inc., 1973, pp. 154-167.

G32 Smith, Peter Duval. "Life and Letters." BBC-General Overseas Service (January 29, 1961).

G33 Toynbee, Philip. "Literature and Life - 2: Graham Greene on 'The Job of the Writer.'" *The Observer* (September 15, 1957), p. 3.

G34 Wills, Colin. "Interview with Graham Greene." On BBC series, "The World We Live In" (September 5, 1959).

G35 Unsigned. "London West Central." BBC-English European Service (November 6, 1948).

G36   Unsigned. "The Angry Man Within." *The Sunday Times*
      (April 12, 1953), p. 5.

G37   Unsigned. "Anglo Texan Society." BBC–North American
      Service (December 23, 1953).

G38   Unsigned. "Greene on the Permissive Novel." Associated
      Press Wire Service (November 23, 1973).

G39   Unsigned. "Mr. Greene Promises No More Miracles."
      Life, XLII (April 1, 1957), p. 68.

G40   Unsigned. "Late Night Line Up." BBC–TV (November 8,
      1964).

G41   Unsigned. "New Honor and a New Novel." *Life*, LX
      (February 4, 1966), pp. 43–44.

G42   Unsigned. "World at One." BBC–Radio (March 29, 1968).
      Re Russian writers and Russia in general.

G43   Unsigned. "Now Read On." BBC–Radio 4 (April 21, 1971).
      Re Collected Edition.

G44   Unsigned. Interview. *The New York Times* (September 12,
      1971), sec. 7, p. 2.

G45   Unsigned. "Now Read On." BBC–Radio 4 (September 15,
      1971).
      Re A Sort of Life.

G46   Unsigned. "Kaleidescope." BBC–Radio 4 (December 3,
      1975); repeated on BBC–Radio 4 (March 4, 1976).
      Re Return of A.J. Raffles.

G47   Unsigned. Greene interviewed about his life and
      career. *Washington Post* (April 4, 1976), sec. 11, p. 1.

G48   Unsigned. Interview with Greene upon the publication
      of *The Human Factor*. *The New York Times* (February 26,
      1978), sec. 6, p. 33.

BOOKS AND PAMPHLETS

Another Mexico, A14b
Babbling April, A1
The Basement Room, A10
The Bear Fell Free, A9
The Best of Saki, A25
The Bodley Head Ford Madox
  Ford, A43
Brighton Rock, A13
British Dramatists, A17
A Burnt-Out Case, A41
Carving A Statue, A47
Collected Essays, A52
Collected Stories, A56
The Comedians, A48
The Complaisant Lover, A39
The Confidential Agent,
  A15
The End of the Affair, A27
England Made Me, A8
Essais Catholiques, A32
The Fallen Idol, A23
Graham Greene on Film,
  A57b
A Gun for Sale, A12
The Heart of the Matter,
  A21
The Honorary Consul, A59
The Human Factor, A63
An Impossible Woman, A61
In Search of a Character,
  A42
Introductions to Three
  Novels, A44
It's a Battlefield, A6

Journey Without Maps, A11
The Labyrinthine Ways, A16b
The Lawless Roads, A14
The Little Fire Engine, A24
The Little Horse Bus, A28
The Little Red Fire Engine,
  A24b
The Little Steamroller, A30
The Little Train, A19
The Living Room, A29
Lord Rochester's Monkey,
  A60
Loser Takes All, A34
The Lost Childhood, A26
The Man Within, A2
May We Borrow Your Husband?,
  A50
The Ministry of Fear, A18
The Name of Action, A3
Nineteen Stories, A20
Nino Caffé, A31
The Old School, A7
Orient Express, A5b
Our Man in Havana, A38
The Pleasure-Dome, A57
The Potting Shed, A37
The Power and the Glory,
  A16
The Quiet American, A35
The Return of A.J. Raffles,
  A62
The Revenge, A46
Rumour at Nightfall, A4
A Sense of Reality, A45
A Sort of Life, A55

The Spy's Bedside Book, A36
Stamboul Train, A5
The Third Man, A23
The Third Man, Modern Film
    Scripts, A51
This Gun for Hire, A12b
Travels with My Aunt, A53

Twenty-One Stories, A33
Victorian Detective Fic-
    tion, A49
The Virtue of Disloyalty,
    A40
Why Do I Write?, A22

PERIODICAL AND NEWSPAPER CONTRIBUTIONS

Across the Bridge, C500
The Adventurer, C38
Adventures in Four Con-
    tinents, C89
After Strange Gods, C137
Against Compromise, C598
Airport, C159
Alfred Tennyson Intervenes,
    C236
All But Empty, C373, C398
All the Facts of Fiction,
    C148
The American Presence, C528
Analysis of a Journey, C175
And a Happy New Year:
    Remarks by Graham Greene
    at a PEN Meeting, C560
And the Other Writer, C478
Anthony à Wood, C92
Apologia, C17
Apres Vous, C35
The Apron Strings of Mrs.
    Moffat, C357
A Propos des Obsèques de
    Colette, C443
Arabia Deserta, C182
L'Aspect Religieux de
    Henry James, C419
The Assumption of Mary,
    C406
Atmosphere, C9
At the Theatre, C15
The Austere Art, C305
Awful When You Think of It,
    C479, C557
Background for Heroes, C210

Background to Henry James,
    C156
The Back Porch, C54
The Badge of Courage, C409
Ballade for a Wedding, C468
Ballade on a Press Con-
    ference, C469
Beatrix Potter: A Critical
    Estimate, C96
Beauty, C509, C513, C555
Bed-Exhausted, C329
Before Breakfast, C57
Before the Attack, C438
Behind the Tight Pupils,
    C394
Belloc on Chesterton, C296
Bird Alone, C198
A Black Comedy in Havana,
    C579
Black Humour in Haiti, C628
The Blessing, C543, C544
The Blind Eye, C248
A Boat-Load of Politicians,
    C184
Bombing Raid, C278
Book Market, C277
Books in General, C377, C395,
    C401, C410, C423, C428,
    C447
Books of the Year, C586
Bow Street Nights, C94
Boy Loses Girl, C270
Brother, C161
The Byronic East, C222
The Camera Eye, C176
Casanova, C100

Casanova and Others, C87
Casual Myrrh, C60
A Catholic Adventurer and
  His Mexican Journal,
  C254
The Catholic Church's New
  Dogma: The Assumption
  of Mary, C404
Catholics at War: Extracts
  from an Indo-China
  Journal, C439
The Catholic Temper in
  Poland, C467
Caesar's Ghost, C71
Chagrin in Three Parts,
  C548, C558
A Chance for Mr. Lever, C188
Character in Search of an
  Author, C427
Charles II, C101
Cheap in August, C526
A Cheat Redressed: Intro-
  duction to *The End of
  the Affair*, C622
Childishness, C36, C45
Chilean Adventure, C231
Chile: The Dangerous Edge,
  C595, C596
Christ Came to Reconcile,
  C592
Church Militant, C460, C462,
  C611
La Civilisation Chrétienne
  est-elle in Péril?, C382
Civil War in the Village,
  C368
The Comic, Terrifying Mind
  of M. Leroux, C561
The Coming, C16, C23
Comments on Auden, C252
Conversation Piece, C265
The Country with Five
  Frontiers, C631
Cowardice, C63
The Creative Life in Our
  Time, C385
Creative Reading, C164
Crook's Tour, C575, C577

Daniel Defoe, C77
The Dark Backward: A Foot-
  note, C179
The Dark Enemy, C200
The Dark Virgin, C267
A Day at the Generals, C242
A Day with Cedillo, C247
Dead Letter Office, C383
Dear Dr. Falkenheim, C505
Dear Mr. Chaplin, C425
Death and Cosmetics, C48
Death in the Cotswolds, C98
The Destructors, C442, C452,
  C471
Devil-Blacksmith, C190
Dickens and Dostoevsky, C477
The Dictator of Grand Bassa,
  C186
Diem's Critics, C454
Dilemma Over Russia for
  Novelists, C571
A Discovery in the Woods,
  C510, C515
Discussion of Panama, C632
Disloyalty as a Virtue, C603
Doctor Crombie, C536, C540
The Doctor in the Limelight,
  C370
Dr. Oates of Salamanca, C399
The Domestic Background, C171
Domestic War, C321
Don in Mexico, C301
Dream of a Strange Land, C506
A Drive in the Country, C379
Edwardian Inferno, C132
Edwardian Occasions, C600
Eight More Harvard Poets:
  Bretano's, C21
Elephant Boy, C219
The End of the Party, C78
The Entertainments of A.E.W.
  Mason, C420
An Epic Fragment from "The
  Dish Pioneers" Attributed
  to A__F___D N__Y__S, C4
Escape, C79, C295, C318
The Escapist, C269
The Extraordinary Profession,
  C263

The Facts of Fiction, C76
Fears, C18
A Few Pipes, Extract from an
    Indo-China Journal, C450
Fiction, C97, C102, C104,
    C106, C107, C108, C109,
    C110, C111, C112, C113,
    C115, C117, C119, C120,
    C122, C124, C126, C135,
    C136, C138, C139, C141,
    C143, C144, C145, C146,
    C150, C151, C154, C155,
    C157, C158, C160, C280,
    C281, C282, C284, C285,
    C286
Fiction Chronicle, C116,
    C201, C203, C204, C209,
    C211, C213, C216
Fidel: An Impression, C550
Film Books, C626
The Final Pepys, C121
Ford Madox Ford, C276
The Fortnightly Library,
    C195
Fragment from 'Angina Pec-
    toris': A Long Poem, C61
François Mauriac vu par un
    Anglais, C354
The French Peace, C26
From Crafts to the Conveyor
    Belt, C358
From Feathers to Iron, C381
From the Devil's Side, C163
From the Mantlepiece, C245
The Furies in Mississippi,
    C217
The General and the Spy,
    C445
George Darley, C72
G.K. Chesterton, C351
Gladstone Bags and Marma-
    lade, C206
The Godly Distance, C46
Going into Europe, C507
Gold Bricks, C99
The Good Life, C268
Graduates of Douai, C180
Graham Greene on Books, C355
Graham Greene on Film, C604

Graham Greene Recollects,
    C578
Graham Greene Revisits the
    Soupsweet Land, C562
A Grand Little Horse, C208
Great Dog of Weimar, C300
The Great Spectacular, C633
Greene and Shaw, C480
The Greeneland Aboriginal,
    C494
The Greenes of Berkhamsted,
    C593
Haggard Rides Again, C583
Harkaway's Oxford, C241
Herbert Read, C322
Herbert Read, a Memoir, C612
The Heritage, C39
Heroes Are Made in Childhood,
    C372
Her Uncle vs. His Father,
    C348, C605
High Wind in the Caribbean,
    C250
The Hint of an Explanation,
    C387, C388
Hints from an Unhappy Future,
    C588
The History Schools, C30
A Hoax on Mr. Hulton, C279
Homage to the Bombardier,
    C238
The Horoscopic Approach, C95
The Human Factor, C634
If You Were Dead, C49
I.M., C32
The Improbable Tale of the
    Archbishop of Canterbridge,
    C33
Indo-China, C436
Indo-China Journal, C440
In Easy Reach of Town, C311
Inflation, C85
The Innocent, C371a
In Search of a Character: A
    Congo Journal, C497
In Search of a Miracle, C249
Inside Oxford, C246
In the Footsteps of a Priest,
    C589

In the Occupied Area. An Oxford Undergraduate's Impressions, C24
Invisible Japanese Gentlemen, C538, C542
Irish Short Stories, C234
The Irrational Age, C84
Isis Idol, C174
It May Be Dangerous, C363
It's a Battlefield, C597
A Jacobite Poet, C103
John Drinkwater, C22
John Evelyn, C128
John Gordon, C487
The John Gordon Society, C464
John Hayward, 1904-1965: Some Memories, C541
Jubilee, C178
The Judgement, C25
Kensington to Samoa, C348
Kenya As I See It, C431
Lamb's Testimonials, C134
The Landowner in Revolt, C214
Last Act in Indo-China, C455
The Last Buchan, C324
Last Journey, C287
Legend, C192
The Lesson of the Master, C167
Letter from the Workhouse, C610
Letter to a West German Friend, C514
Letters, Untitled, C75, C181, C194, C235, C244, C374, C390, C391, C393, C405, C408, C430, C433, C434, C435, C441, C453, C472, C473, C475, C484, C485, C486, C488, C490, C491, C492, C493, C495, C499, C501, C516, C524, C527, C529, C530, C533, C534, C535, C547, C551, C559, C567, C570, C572,

C576, C581, C582, C584, C587, C594, C599, C601, C602, C608, C621, C623, C629, C630
The Liberator, C292
The Lieutennant Died Last, C293
Lightning Tour, C332
Lines on the Liberation of Cuba, C496
The Lines on the Palm, C615
Lippens, C58
London Diary, C421
The Londoners: Notes from a Journel of the Blitz, 1940-41, C422
Lord Jim, C617
The Lord Knows, C62
Loser Takes All, C444, C458, C463
A Lost Arcadia, C259
A Lost Leader, C304
The Lottery Ticket, C375, C380
Lowdown from Our Man in Havana, C580
Mad Hatters, C465
Magic, C3
Malaya, the Forgotten War, C411, C415
Man Made Angry, C275
Manoeuvres in Kent, C177
The Man of Mode, C172
The Man Who Built a Cathedral, C489
The Man Who Stole the Eiffel Tower, C474
The Maritains, C352
The Mask Remover, C563
Matured in Bottle, C233
May We Borrow Your Husband?, C504, C508
A Medium of Exchange, C197
A Memoir of Herbert Read, C609
A Memory of Indo-China, C457
Men and Messages, C256
Men at Work, C346

Message aux Catholiques
  Français, C400
Mexican Sunday, C243
Mexico, C273
A Mission and a Warning,
  C361
Mr. Cook's Century, C337
Mr. Hemingway's New Novel,
  C316
Mr. Maugham's Pattern, C240
Mr. Maugham's Short Stories,
  C152
Mr. Priestley in Search of
  the Comic, C64
The Mitre, C34
Mortmain, C511, C512, C531
Mothering Sunday, C403
Movie Memories, C207
Murder for the Wrong Reason,
  C73
Myers and Myers, C166
My New Books, C5
My Own Devil: the Experience
  of Opium Smoking, C606
The Newgate Calendar, C82
The New House, C14
The News in English, C294,
  C353
Nightmare Republic, C518,
  C520
1930, C41
Nobody Would Expect Revela-
  tions But--, C360
The Norwegian Way, C142
A Note on Hans Andersen,
  C123
Notes on the Way, C298
A Novelist's Notebook, C229
No Wonder Women Scared Him,
  C359
The Nudest Book of the
  Week, C230
Oberammergau, C74
Odd Sound, C624
Old Age of a Georgian, C8
Old Boy, C251
Old Love, C13
On a Walking Tour, C51

On Becoming a Catholic, C591
One Man's War, C303
Orchard's Bay, C290
Oslo and Stockholm, C129
The Other ... Whom Only
  Others Know, C620
Our Lady and Her Assumption,
  C407
Out of the Saddle, C291
The Overnight Bag, C532,
  C537
Oxford Infelix, C266
Paint and Wood, C11
The Palace of Chance, C539
Paradisal Tea, C19, C50
Les Paradoxes du Christian-
  isme, C418
Paraguay: Where the Living
  is Easy, So ..., C569
A Pauper's Wealth, C12
Pius XII, The Paradox of the
  Pope, C416
A Place in the Sun, C288
Playboy, C342
Pleasures of Deportation,
  C614
The Poet and the Gold, C619
Poetry by Wireless, C47
Poetry from Limbo, C274
The Poets Fight, C59
Poison Pen. - Introductory
  Note, C545
The Poker-Face, C350
The Pope Who Remains a
  Priest, C413, C417
Portrait by G. Wylde, C239
Portrait of a Lady, C196
The Potting Shed, C483
The Prefaces of Conrad and
  James, C503
The Price of Faith, C470
A Pride of Bombs, C312
A Prisoner of the Forsytes,
  C91
Proof Positive, C378
The Public Life, C189
The Quiet American, C459,
  C461

The Rash Act, C114
The Real Thing, C271
Rebel Manqué, C127
Rebels and Eccentrics, C307
The Redemption of Mr. Joy-
   boy, C386
Reflection on the Funeral
   of Rudyard Kipling, C574
Reflections on the Character
   of Kim Philby, C566
Remembering Mr. Jones, C226
A Restoration Fantasia, C173
The Return of Charlie Chap-
   lin, I. An Open Letter,
   C424
Return of the Novelist, C552
Return to Cuba, C517, C519
The Revenge, C449, C451
Reviews, Untitled, C20, C27,
   C28, C29, C40, C43, C44,
   C52, C55, C56, C466
Revolutionary Bystander,
   C618
R.L.S. for Adults, C218
Rochester's Poems, C125
Romance in Pimlico, C257
The Root of All Evil, C522,
   C523
The Rude Mechanicals, C525
Sad Cure, C68
Safety Area, C283
Samuel Butler, C130
The Saratoga Trunk, C264
The Second Deluge, C297
Secret, C553
The Secret Room, C31, C69
The Seed Cake and the Lovely
   Lady, C153
Selfdom, C10
Self-Portrait, C339
The Sense of Apprehension,
   C412
Servants of the Novel, C90
Seventeenth-Century Verse,
   C105
Shape Between the Iron Cur-
   tains, C369

A Shocking Accident, C481,
   C556
Short Stories, C133, C162,
   C169, C183, C191, C193,
   C202, C205, C212, C237,
   C258
Simone Weil, C414
Simple Indices ..., C392
A Small Affair, C429
Small Talk, C37
Song for Three Ageing Voices,
   C448
Sonnet, C42, C53, C70
Soupsweet Land, C565
Spanish Gold, C170
Spawn, C67
Special Duties, C446
A Spoiled Priest, C185
Statement by Graham Greene
   Recorded in the Minutes of
   the International PEN De-
   fence Committee for Soviet
   and Greek Writers in Pri-
   son, C564
Stendahl, C66
Stepping Stones, C6
Strange Prisons, C80
A Stranger in the Theatre,
   C426, C482
Strange Worlds, C83, C364
Strike in Paris, C131
Swamps, Rain and a Mad Cook,
   C590
Taking Stock, C81
Terror in Trinidad, C573
The Thatched Cottagers, C222
That Gay Deceiver Dickens,
   C365
The Theatre, C147, C149,
   C227, C299, C306, C308,
   C309, C310, C314, C317,
   C319, C320, C323, C325,
   C326, C327, C328, C330,
   C331, C333, C334, C336,
   C338, C340, C341, C343,
   C344, C345
Theatre, C376

They Wanted to Use Another
  Name, C362
The Third Man, C389, C397,
  C402
This Made Me Blush, C356
A Thorn on the Yellow Rose,
  C616
Three Men in a Tank, C366
Three Poets, C93
Three Score Miles and Ten,
  C313
Three Travellers, C289
Through American Eyes, C315
Thunder in the Air, C223
The Tick of the Clock, C1
To All Topographers, C253
To Hope Till Hope Creates,
  C437
To Indochina with Love, C607
The Traveller's Library,
  C140
Tread Softly, C215
The Trial of Pan, C7
Tribute to Evelyn Waugh,
  C546
Tribute to M. Yves Allain,
  C549
Trollope in the Doldrums,
  C367
Trying to Connect You, C260
The Turn of the Screw, C335
Twenty-four Hours to Metro-
  land, C255
Two Capitals, C118
Two Gentle People, C554
The Two Maritains, C371
Two Novels, C262

Two Tall Travellers, C199
A Typewriter in the Desert,
  C220
The Tyranny of Realism, C2
The Ugly Act, C396
The Unconquered, C65
Underworld, C272
An Unhappy Journal Produced
  a Great Novel, C502
An Unheroic Dramatist, C224
The Unknown War, C302
The Unsentimental Journey,
  C86
Vagaries of Fortune, C627
Vengeance of Jenny's Case,
  C432
A Vestryman for St. Pancras,
  C228
A Veteran at Play, C225
Victim of Theology, C613
Victoriana, C88
A Visit to Morin, C476
Vive Le Roi, C252
Voyage in the Dark, C261
Wallis and Waugh, C349
The Waste Land, C168
West Coast, C165
When Greek Meets Greek, C347,
  C498
Wings Over Wardour Street,
  C187
Work Not in Progress, C456
The Worm Inside the Lotus
  Blossom, C568
The Wrong Box, C585
A Young Man's Fancy, C625

INDEX OF WORKS REVIEWED BY GREENE

BOOKS

About Levy, C126
Absalom, Absalom!, C217
Across Lapland, C86
Adventures in Grace, C371
Adventures of an Alpine
    Guide, C86
A.E.W. Mason, C420
Africa Dances, C165
After Strange Gods, C137
After Such Pleasures, C133
After the Party, C106
Alanna Autumnal, C122
Albert Goes Through, C126
Alice James. Her Brothers
    Her Journal, C156
All Aboard for Ararat, C297
Allan Quartermain, C410
Allan's Wife, C410
Altogether. The Collected
    Stories of W. Somerset
    Maugham, C152
Anatomy of Oxford. An An-
    thology, C246
And Lastly the Fireworks,
    C183
And Quiet Flows the Don,
    C135
Andrew's Harvest, C144
And Then You Wish, C203
Angel-Face, C102
Angel Making Music, C157
Angels on Horseback, C89
The Angle of Error, C258
Animal Farm, C362

Annals of Innocence and Ex-
    perience, C322
Ann and Aurelia, C145
Anthony Hope and His Books,
    C174
Antigua, C204
Arnold Bennett's Letters to
    His Nephew, C189
The Arrogant History of White
    Ben, C280
The Artificial Silk Girl,
    C117
Art in Poetry, C371
The Art of the Novel, C167
The Art of the Novel from
    1700 to the Present Time,
    C164
Aspects of Seventeenth-
    Century Verse, C105
Assize of Arms, C361
At Mrs. Lippincote's, C370
At Sea, C154
At the Shrine of St. Charles,
    C134
Australia Visited 1940, C329
Autobiography (Eric Gill),
    C307
The Bachelor of Arts, C216
The Balcony, C108
The Balliols, C143
Barnham Rectory, C154
The Barriers Are Down, C358
Beany-Eye, C177
The Beginning, C183

Best Short Stories of 1936.
  English and American, C205
Best Short Stories of 1937,
  C237
The Big Money, C209
Bird Alone, C198
Black Exchange, C139
The Black Mountain, C112
Blasting and Bombardiering,
  C238
Blind Men Crossing a Bridge,
  C151
Blockade. The Diary of an
  Austrian Middle-Class
  Woman, 1914-24, C85
The Blood of the Martyrs,
  C282
The Blue Bed, C212
Bomber's Moon, C312
Bonfire, C120
Bookman's Holiday, C361
Bread and Wine, C211
The Bridgehead, C366
British Architects and
  Craftsmen, C355
The Burning Cactus, C192
But for the Grace of God,
  C81
By-Road, C213
Cactus Land, C141
The Cage Bird, C112
The Camberwell Miracle, C120
Campden, xxiv Engravings
  after Pen Drawings, C318
Candelabra: Selected Essays
  and Addresses, C91
Captain Nicholas, C155
Casanova, C100
A Case of Conscience and
  Other Tales, C212
Cathedral Carol Service,
  C162
Chances and Mischances, C81
A Character in Distress,
  C258
Charles Dickens, C365

Charles Lamb. His Life Re-
  corded by his Contemporar-
  ies, C134
Charles II, C101
A Chaste Polygamy, C202
The Chestertons, C339
The Chevalier D'Eon, C87
The Children Triumphant, C143
Children with Fire, C133
Chiltern Country, C311
Christmas Holiday, C272
Christmas Tree, C126
Chung King Diary, C360
The Cloak That I Left, C410
The Coat of Many Colors,
  C369
Collected Poems (Edwin Ar-
  lington Robinson), C93
Collected Poems (John Drink-
  water), C22
The Collected Poems of D.H.
  Lawrence, C93
Collected Short Stories
  (Stella Benson), C205
Come in at the Door, C151
Come to Dust, C366
Company K, C102
Company Parade, C136
The Complete Plays of Henry
  James, C401
Conan Doyle: His Life and
  Art, C350
Concert Pitch, C144
Conrad's Prefaces to His
  Works, C226
Cosmopolitans, C191
The Cosy Room, C191
the Cotswolds, C221
A Cotswold Year, C221
Crack of Whips, C145
Crossings: A Fairy Play, C34
The Cross of Peace, C122
The Cuban Farm, C117
The Curate's Wife, C154
The Curse of the Wise Woman,
  C119

Cut and Come Again, C183

The Dandy Hun, C87

Dark Windows, C154

A Date with a Duchess and Other Stories, C229

Daughter to Phillip, C111

Dawn of Darkness, C124

Daylight and Champaign, C233

Days of Hope, C262

Dead Woman's Shoes, C158

Death of a Poet, C355

The Death of the Heart, C262

Deep Streets, C151

Delicate Monster, C213

Desert Calling. The Story of Charles de Foucauld, C403

The Desire and Pursuit of the Whole, C163

Dew in April, C155

Dew on the Grass, C150

The Ding Dong Bell, C27

Dinosaur Tracks and Other Stories, C216

Discovery by Torchlight, C111

Doctor Gion, C104

Documentary Film, C187

Don Fernando, C170

Durbar, C107

The Earth Remains, C368

Earth Stopped, C160

Edmund Campion, C180

The Education Outlook, C20

Eggs and Baker, C211

EGO 2: Being a Second Installment of a Contemporary Diary, C208

Eight More Harvard Poets, C21

The Elderbook Brothers, C363

The Endless Furrow, C158

The Enemy at the Gate, C107

England's Hour, C312

Entertaining the Islanders, C136

Equinox, C363

Eric Brighteyes, C410

The Escapes of Captain O'Brien, R.N. 1804-1808, C80

Escape to Life, C119

Eve in the Sunlight, C230

Exploration Fawcett, C427

An Eye-Witness of Mexico, C273

The Faber Book of Modern Stories, C237

The Facts of Fiction, C76

Falling Star, C141

Family Parade, C139

Farewell, My Muse, C93

Fellow Countrymen, C237

Fellow Mortals, C202

Fierce and Gentle, C183

Fifteen Craftsmen on Their Crafts, C358

The First Wife, C115

Five Silver Daughters, C135

The Fleshy Screen, C216

Flight from a Lady, C286

Flo, C106

Flowering Judas, C192

The Flowering Thorn, C113

The Flying Goat, C283

Folly Bridge, C356

Fontamara, C160

Fools and Philosophers, C64

Forever Amber, C365

A Forgotten Genius, C359

For Whom the Bell Tolls, C316

Four-Part Setting, C282

Freedom Was Flesh and Blood, C360

From Death to Morning, C191

A Froward Child, C162

Further Extracts from the Note-Books of Samuel Butler, C130

The Gates of Hell, C124

Gay Pagan, C144

General Buntop's Miracle, C133

Gentlemen-The Regiment, C110
Ghosts, C237
Gilbert Keith Chesterton,
  C351
The Ginger Griffin, C143
The Golden Net, C126
Gold Fever, C197
Good Merchant, C158
The Goose-Man, C150
A Grammar of the Film, C176
Grand Canary, C107
Granville the Polite: The
  Life of George Granville
  Lord Lansdowne, C103
Great Circle, C117
Great Trade Route. A Senti-
  mental Journey, C214
Green Hills of Africa, C195
Gus and Ida, C285
Hag's Harvest, C113
Ha Ha Among the Trumpets,
  C361
Half Way East, C169
Halfway House, C93
Hans Christian Andersen,
  C123
Hardy Perennial, C108
Harpoon, C80
A Heart for the Gods of
  Mexico, C270
Henry Airbubble in Search of
  a Circumference to His
  Breath, C206
Henry James and Robert Louis
  Stevenson. A Record of
  Friendship and Criticism,
  C384
Henry James. The Untried
  Years. 1843-70, C428
Here To-day and Gone To-
  morrow, C141
Hindu Heaven, C106
Hinterland Liberia, C289
The History of the Bow
  Street Runners, 1729-
  1829, C94
The History of the English
  Novel: The Day Before
  Yesterday, C256

The History of the English
  Novel. The Novel of Senti-
  ment and the Gothic Romance,
  C148
History of the Film, C263
His Worship the Mayor, C155
Honeymoon, C162
Hordubal, C146
Hotel Vesuvius, C370
Hot-House, C113
Hubert's Arthur, C185
Human Nature, C106
Hungaria, C205
I Claudius, C138
Ilonka Speaks of Hungary,
  C209
I Lost My Memory. The Case as
  the Patient Saw It, C83
An Indian Ass, C55
India's Coral Strand, C146
In Hazard, C250
In the Line. 1914-1918, C83
It Makes a Nice Change, C258
Ivar Kreuger, C99
John Evelyn, C128
Joseph Conrad and His Circle,
  C171
The Journals of Francis Park-
  man, C395
The Journey of 'The Flame,'
  C122
Juan in Mexico, C216
Judgment on Deltchev, C412
Julian Grant Loses His Way,
  C104
Jungle Trader, C271
The Kaiser Goes: the Generals
  Remain, C106
Kaleidoscope, C145
Kensington Gardens, C28
King Coffin, C182
Kissing the Rod, C237
Klengenberg of the Arctic. An
  Autobiography, C89
Kneel to the Rising Sun, C193
Knight Without Armour, C109
Known Signatures, C93
The Laburnum Tree, C183
The Ladies, C120

Lamb in His Bosom, C146
The Last Cargo, C144
Laughter in Heaven, C104
The Law and the McLaughlins,
  C209
Legion of the Rearguard,
  C145
The Letters of Eric Gill,
  C383
Let the People Sing, C286
The Life and Letters of
  George Darley Poet and
  Critic, C72
The Life and Times of
  Anthony à Wood, C92
Life in a Noble Household.
  1641-1700, C210
The Life of Daniel Defoe,
  C77
The Life of Henri Brulard,
  C66
A Life of Music, C355
Little Children, C237
Little Friend, C110
Little Man What Now, C104
Little Mexican, C29
Live and Kicking Ned, C286
Lives of Wives, C280
Livingstone's Travels, C447
London Bridge is Falling,
  C141
Looming Lights, C360
The Lord of Life, C108
The Loss of Eldorado, C573
Lost Paradise, C122
The Loved One, C386
Love, Here is My Hat, C258
Love on the Dole, C110
Manassas, C102
Mandoa, Mandoa!, C97
The Maniac, C87
The Marchesa, C191
The March of Literature.
  From Confucius to Modern
  Times, C287
The Matabele Journals of
  Robert Moffat, C357
A Mathematician's Apology,
  C305

Mediterranean Blues, C120
Memoirs, C360
Men on the Horizon, C89
Mexican Mosaic, C273
Mexico: A New Spain with Old
  Friends, C301
Midnight, C203
Midnight on the Desert, C220
Miracle on Sinai, C119
Mirth and Mocking of Sinner
  Stocking, C88
The Missing Miniature, C204
Mr. J. Jay, C113
Mr. Jorkens Remembers Africa,
  C162
Mr. White, The Red Barn, Hell
  and Bridewater, C212
Mrs. Ritchie, C111
Mrs. Van Kleek, C107
Modern Explorations, C357
The Money's All Right, C258
Montezuma's Daughter, C410
Moods and Tenses, C104
More Than I Should, C295
Most Secret, C363
Movie Parade, C207
Mutiny!, C106
My First War, C303
My Flesh and Blood, A Lyric
  Autobiography, C84
My Life and Adventures, C87
My Sister and I. The Diary of
  a Dutch Boy Refugee, C335
Nada the Lilly, C410
Name of Gentlemen, C112
A Nest of Simple Folk, C116
The Newgate Calendar or Male-
  factors' Bloody Register,
  C82
The Newgate Garland, C88
New Joy in Heaven, C183
News from Havre, C139
Night of the Poor, C284
Nightwood, C204
No Castle in Spain, C117
No Place Like Home, C196
No Second Spring, C115
Novel on Yellow Paper, C203
No. 2 Joy Street, C43

Obscenity and the Law, C465
Of Mortal Love, C204
O. Henry Memorial Award
  Prize Stories, C169
O. Henry Memorial Award
  Prize Stories of 1935,
  C193
The Old Century and Seven
  More Years, C259
Old Home Week, C284
The Old Man Dies, C111
One for the Devil, C561
One Lives to Tell the Tale,
  C79
On the Place of Gilbert
  Chesterton in English
  Letters, C296
The Orators, C93
Orchard's Bay, C288
Original Design, C108
Orrery, C224
An Oxford Tragedy, C107
An Oxford University Chest,
  C266
Panorama with Music, C109
Parent or Pedagogue, C40
Parody Party, C204
Parole D'Honneur, C285
Party Going, C281
Pavements at Anderby, C237
Peace Broke Out, C85
Penny, Puce, C204
Peony, C368
People Are Fascinating, C212
People of the Mist, C410
Picaro, C139
The Pieces of a Fan, C237
Pie in the Sky, C211
Pilgrimage, C264
Pinorman, C545
The Plebeian's Progress,
  C108
The Poetical Works of John
  Wilmot Earl of Rochester,
  C125
The Polite Marriage and
  Other 18th Century Essays,
  C257

The Popular Novel in England,
  1770-1800, C90
The Porch, C213
Post D. Some Experiences of an
  Air Raid Warden, C321
Postscripts, C304
Pretty Witty Nell, C95
The Progress of Julius, C102
The Progress to the Lake,
  C160
Provence: From Minstrels to
  Machine, C268
A Purse of Coppers, C234
Queen Anne Boleyn, C284
The Quest for Corvo, C132
Quiet Skies on Salween, C360
Rabble in Arms, C124
The Rash Act, C114
Recusant Poets. With a Selec-
  tion from Their Work. Vol 1.
  St. Thomas More to Ben
  Jonson, C274
The Red Centaur, C281
Regiment Reichstag, C89
Rejected Guest, C285
Report on England, C332
Report on the Vatican, C470
The Rest is Lies, C81
Resurrection, C157
Revolt, C97
Revolt on the Pampas, C231
Rhondda Roundabout, C143
Richard Halliburton. His
  Story and His Life's Ad-
  ventures, C342
Ricochets, C162
The Rivet in Grandfather's
  Neck: A Comedy of Limita-
  tions, C34
R.L. Stevenson, C218
The Road to Oblivion, C80
The Road to Oxiana, C222
Robert Louis Stevenson, C381
Robert Southwell the Writer,
  C180
Rochester, C173
Rochester: Portrait of a Re-
  storation Poet, C172

The Root and the Flower, C166

Round About "The Mitre" at Oxford: Episodes of the University City and Hotel, C34

Rubber, C109

Rudyard Kipling, C367

Rudyard Kipling. His Life and Work, C466

Saga of Saints, C142

Salah and His American, C112

Salvin, C209

Samuel Pepys: The Man in the Making, C121

Sard Harker, C44

The Sea Tower, C280

Selected Short Stories (Hjalmar Söderberg), C169

Semi-Precious Stones, C135

Seven Gothic Tales, C158

Seven Stars and Orion, C155

The Shadow Across the Page, C215

Shadows of Ecstasy, C97

Shake Hands with the Devil, C115

Shaw: George Versus Bernard, C228

She, C410

Short Stories (Per Hallström), C109

The Short Stories of Liam O'Flaherty, C234

Sick Heart River, C324

Silver Collar Boy, C162

Simón Bolívar, C292

Singing Out of Tune, C109

Single Combat, C138

The Smallways Rub Along, C258

The Smith of Smiths, C127

Something Short and Sweet, C223

The Song in the House, C205

Songs of the Affections, C88

Sophy Cassmajor, C162

South-East Asia in Turmoil, C528

The Splendour Falls, C203

Steam Packet, C201, C202

Stephen Crane, C409

Stories of Three Decades (Thomas Mann), C201

The Story of a Country-Town, C110

The Story of Mona Sheehy, C281

The Strange River, C97

Subject to Authority, C358

Summing Up, C240

Sun Circle, C111

The Sun in Capricorn, C160

Supercargo, C282

Swallows, C138

Tales of a Devon Village, C368

Tandem, C109

Tea on Sunday, C192

That Hideous Strength, C364

That Was the End, C136

Theatre, C216

The Things Men Do, C202

Thirteen Such Years, C84

Three Guineas, C245

365 Days, C202

Three Men Die, C157

This Way Southward, C291

Thursday Afternoon, C370

Tiger Juan, C97

Time to Change Flats, C358

Tinker's Wind, C116

Titus Oates, C399

Tobacco Road, C116

To Beg I am Ashamed, C432

To Blush Unseen, C183

Tops and Bottoms, C112

To the Boating, C370

A Tower of Skulls, C86

To You Mr. Chips!, 251

The Tramp, C205

Traveller's Pack, C115

A Treatise on the Novel, C377

The Trial of Mrs. Duncan, C364

Trio, C265
Trollope: A Contemporary,
   C367
The Trouble I've Seen, C193
Twenty-Four Tales (Gerald
   Bullett), C258
Two Black Sheep, C115
Two Generations, C295
Two Loves I Have, C113
Under the Fifth Rib. A Bel-
   ligerent Autobiography, C84
Unfinished Cathedral, C150
Unknown Liberia, C199
Unknown to the World-Haiti,
   C289
The Valiant Wife, C116
Verse in Bloom, C56
Virginia Woolf, C356
Vive Le Roy, C225
Vouza and the Solomon
   Islands, C366
Waiting on God, C414
The Wake of the Southern
   Cross, C86
Wanderings in the Peruvian
   Andes, C289
War with the Newts, C213
Watering Place, C356
Water on the Brain, C113
The Weak and the Strong,
   C370

We Have Been Friends To-
   gether, C352
W.E. Henley, C396
West African Explorers, C423
What Became of Anna Bottom,
   C358
What the Sweet Hell, C169
The Wheel of Life, C104
The White Cliffs, C315
Wickford Point, C285
Wild Geese Overhead, C284
Wild Oats, C83
Wild Strawberries, C144
The Wind Blows Over, C200
The Winds of Fear, C363
The Woman Who Had Imagina-
   tion, C133
The Woman Who Was Poor, C275
Women Must Work, C157
A World Can End, C79
The World His Pillow, C102
The World Over, C193
The World Went Mad, C146
A World Within a War, C369
The Years of the Week, C563
Yet in My Flesh, C110
Yonder Lies Jericho, C119
You Must Break Out Sometimes,
   C193
Youth Can't Be Served, C119
Zulu Paraclete, C168

DRAMA

Actresses Will Happen, C334
Aladdin, C306
Applesauce, C319
Beaux Strategem, C52
Berkeley Square, C308
Black Vanities, C327
Blithe Spirit, C338
The Blue Goose, C310
The Cherry Orchard, C345
Cottage to Let, C328
Dear Brutus, C309
Diversion, C299

Diversion No. 2, C308
Dostigaeff and the Others,
   C333
Fun and Games, C344
Jack and the Beanstalk, C306
King John, C340
Lady Behave, C343
A Man's House, C147
The Moon in the Yellow River,
   C149
Mutiny, C149
The New Ambassadors Review,
   C341

New Faces, C320
Nineteen Naughty One, C317
Non-Stop Vanities, C336
Oberammergau, passion play,
    C74
Orchids and Onions, C325
Point Valaine, C376
Quiet Weekend, C343
Revudeville-141st Edition,
    C314
Revudeville-144th Edition,
    C331

Rise Above It, C334
Sir Martin Marr-All, C227
Squaring the Circle, C345
Strike Up the Music, C314
Thunder Rock, C317
Time for Comedy, C323
Under One Roof, C327
Up and Doing, C330
Wednesday After the War,
    C325
Women Aren't Angels, C326

FILM

Abyssinia, C637, C755
Accent on Youth, C657
Action for Slander, C740
African Skyway, C812
After the Thin Man, C775
Alerte en Méditerranée, C767
L'Alibi, C758
All the King's Horses, C643
The Amateur Gentleman, C667
Anna Karenina, C651
Anne-Marie, C682
Anthony Adverse, C702
Anything Goes, C670
'Arf a Mo, Hitler, C797
Arms and the Girl, C657
The Arsenal Stadium Mystery,
    C811
As You Like It, C700
La Bandéra, C659
Barbary Coast, C654
Barcarole, C639
The Barretts of Wimpole
    Street, C646
Battle of Broadway, C763
Beach Picnic, C772
Beau Geste, C788
Becky Sharp, C639
Beethoven, C782
La Belle au Bois Dormant,
    C682
La Bête Humaine, C774

Big Brown Eyes, C688
Big City, C744
Black Eyes, C770
Black Legion, C711
The Black Room C648
Blind Alley, C789
Bonne Chance, C671
Booloo, C764
Boy Slaves, C783
Boys Will Be Boys, C644
Break of Hearts, C647
The Bride Comes Home, C664
Brief Ecstasy, C740
The Bride of Frankenstein,
    C637
Bullets or Ballots, C711
Café Metropole, C742
Call It a Day, C733
The Call of the Wild, C635
Captain Blood, C670
Captain Fury, C783
Captain January, C695
Un Carnet de Bal, C752
Car 99, C637
The Case of the Lucky Legs,
    C667, C755
A Castle in Flanders, C738
Charlie Chan at the Circus,
    C692
Charlie Chan in Shanghai,
    C667

Children at School, C744
A Chump at Oxford, C814
Circusmania, C635
Come Out of the Pantry, C659
Confessions of a Nazi Spy,
   C781
Confetti, C715
The Country Doctor, C687
Cover to Cover, C700
Crime and Punishment, C674
Crime et Châtiment, C673
The Crusades, C645
Cyrano de Bergerac, C635
Dangerous, C688
The Dark Angel, C650
Dark Journey, C724
Dark Rapture, C813
Daughters Courageous, C799
The Dawn Patrol, C769
A Day at the Races, C735
The Day of the Great Adven-
   ture, C677
Dead End, C750
Dead Man's Shoes, C817
The Deserter, C719
Desire, C677
Destry Rides Again, C813
Devil Dogs of the Air,
   C642
The Devil's Party, C759
Les Disparus de St. Agil,
   C790
Disputed Passage, C804
Dr. Socrates, C668
Dodge City, C791
Dodsworth, C708
Dood Water, C646
La Drame de Shanghai, C786
Dreaming Lips, C719
Ducks and Drakes, C805
Dust Be My Destiny, C812
Each Dawn I Die, C807
Eastern Valley, C753
East Meets West, C701
Easy Living, C736
Elephant Boy, C726
An Elephant Never Forgets,
   C777

The Emperor's Candlesticks,
   C685
An Englishman's Home, C794
Episode, C654
Episode 4, C778
Escape to Happiness, C810
Espionage Agent, C805
Everything Is Thunder, C697
Exclusive, C745
The Ex-Mrs. Bradford, C687
The Face at the Window, C794
False Faces, C643
Faust, C670
La Femme du Boulanger, C779
Fifth Avenue Girl, C812
A Fire Has Been Arranged,
   C660
Fire Over England, C721
The First Days, C799
First Love, C805
Five Came Back, C791
Five Faces, C764
Follow the Fleet, C680
Fools for Scandal, C764
Foreign Affairs, C662
For Valour, C723
For You Alone, C738
The Four Feathers, C773
Fox Hunt, C708
Fredlös, C709
French Without Tears, C797
The Frog, C730
From the Manger to the Cross,
   C759
The Frozen Limits, C800
Fury, C690
Gangway, C743
The Gap, C729
The Garden of Allah, C715,
   C755
The Gay Corinthian, C635
The Gay Desperado, C709
The General Died at Dawn,
   C707
Generation of Conquerors,
   C729
Gentlemen of the Navy, C648
The Ghost Goes West, C662

Girl's Dormitory, C714
Girl Shy, C635
Glamorous Night, C729
The Glass Key, C637
God's Country and the Woman,
  C732
Golden Boy, C802
Golden Gloves, C790
Gold is Where You Find It,
  C762
The Golem, C727
Goodbye, Mr. Chips!, C780
The Good Earth, C724
The Good Old Days, C780
Go West Young Man, C714
The Great Barrier, C718
The Great God Gold, C644
The Great Ziegfeld, C701
The Green Pastures, C712
The Guv'nor, C663
Hands of Orlac, C642
Head Over Heels, C722
Health of a Nation, C777
Here's to Romance, C660
Der Herrscher, C730
The High Command, C734
High Wide and Handsome, C737
His Affair, C737
A History of the Film, 1896–
  1936, C683, C684
Hohe Schule, C670
L'Homme du Jour, C760, C794
Hortobagy, C714
Hostages, C785
Hôtel du Nord, C781
Hotel for Women, C815
Hotel Imperial, C771
The Hound of the Basker-
  villes, C784
The Hunchback of Notre-
  Dame, C813
I Cover the Waterfront,
  C761
Idiot's Delight, C772
I Dream Too Much, C670
If Only You Could Cook, C678
I Give My Heart, C666
Ignace, C795
The Imperfect Lady, C668

The Informer, C651
In Name Only, C803
Inspector Hornleigh, C770
Irene and Mary, C759
The Irish in Us, C658
It's Love Again, C701
I Was a Captive of Nazi
  Germany, C792
Jack of All Trades, C672
Jamaica Inn, C776
Janosik, C691
Jazz Comedy, C649
J'Etais une Adventuriere,
  C776
Joan of Arc, C653
Juarez, C801
The Jungle Princess, C716
Katia, C765
Kentucky, C769
La Kermesse Héroïque, C707
Kidnapped, C761
King of the Damned, C664
King Solomon's Mines, C735
The King Steps Out, C704
Kliou the Tiger, C679, C755
Klondyke Annie, C684
Knight Without Armour, C742
Koenigsmark, C666
Die Kribbebijter, C697
Laburnum Grove, C694
Land Without Bread, C748
Last Love, C656
The Last Outpost, C658
The Last Train from Madrid,
  C731
Lenin in October, C768
Letzte Rose, C688
Liebesmelodie, C678
The Life of Emile Zola, C746
The Light That Failed, C809
The Lion Has Wings, C798
The Littlest Rebel, C685
Little Tough Guy, C762
Living Dangerously, C692
Living on Velvet, C640
Lloyds of London, C729
The Londoners, C776
The Lone Ranger, C775, C778

Look Up and Laugh, C642
Lost Horizon, C728
Louise, C780
The Luck of the Irish, C722
Mademoiselle Docteur, C753
Mdlle. Midnight, C635
Maid of Salem, C721
Make Way for Tomorrow, C730
Man About Town, C785
Man of Conquest, C784
The Man Who Broke the Bank
  at Monte Carlo, C668
The Man Who Could Work
  Miracles, C699
Marchland d'Amour, C701
The March of Time, C655,
  C789
Maria Bashkirtseff, C703
Marie Walewska, C754
Marked Woman, C739
The Marriage of Corbal, C686
The Marx Brothers at the
  Circus, C804
Mayerling, C708
Mazurka, C717
Me and Marlborough, C646
The Memory Expert, C642
Men in Danger, C777
Men with Wings, C767
Merlusse, C677
Michael Strogoff, C732
Midshipman Easy, C663
A Midsummer Night's Dream,
  C652
The Milky Way, C674
Mimi, C641
Mr. Deeds Goes to Town,
  C698, C755
Mr. Smith Goes to Washing-
  ton, C807
The Modern Miracle, C785
Modern Times, C669
Monica and Martin, C753
The Moon's Our Home, C689
Moscow Nights, C656
The Murder Man, C644
Musik im Blut, C650
My Man Godfrey, C703

Never Say Die, C769
New Babylon, C657
The New Gulliver, C711, C755
News Reels, playing at
  various cinemas, C793
The Nibelungs, C635
Night Mail, C674
Night Must Fall, C731
Ninotchka, C814
Nitchevo, C747
No More Women, C637
Nurse Edith Cavell, C797
Nutrition, C705, C755
October, C675
Oil for the Lamps of China,
  C656
The Oklahoma Kid, C775
Old Iron, C765
The Old Maid, C809
One Rainy Afternoon, C691
One Way Ticket, C678
Only Angels Have Wings, C796
On the Avenue, C734
On the Night of the Fire,
  C802
On Wings of Song, C647
On Your Toes, C814
Orage, C757
Our Neighbors - the Carters,
  C805
Ourselves Alone, C694
Page Miss Glory, C660
Paramount News, at various
  cinemas, C809
Paris Love Song, C638
Parnell, C733
The Passing of the Third
  Floor Back, C654
The Peace Film, C680
Peg of Old Drury, C647
Pépé le Moko, C777
Les Perles de la Couronne,
  C745
Personality Parade, C748
Persons in Hiding, C769
Peter the Great, C782
The Petrified Forest, C693,
  C755
The Phantom Gondola, C691

The Phantom Light, C638
Pièges, C811
The Plainsman, C778, C755
Poison Pen, C799
Poppy, C692
The Port of Five Seas, C660
Pot Luck, C678
Prisons de Femmes, C815
Private Worlds, C640
Professional Soldier, C684
Professor Mamlock, C791
The Proud Valley, C817
Public Hero No. 1, C639
The Rains Came, C806
The Real Glory, C808
The Rebellious Son, C786
Reifende Jugend, C664
Rembrandt, C710
Remontons les Champs-
  Elysees, C806
Rhodes of Africa, C675
Rhythm on the Range, C696,
  C755
The Rich Bride, C787
Riders to the Sea, C661
The Road Back, C743
The Roaring Twenties, C815
The Robber Symphony, C685
Rome Express, C640
Romeo and Juliet, C706,
  C755
Rose of the Rancho, C672,
  C755
Rulers of the Sea, C801
Sabotage, C713
St. Petersburg, C638, C755
Sans Famille, C665
Saratoga, C737
Savoy Hotel 217, C704
Der Schimmelreiter, C643
Second Bureau, C665
Secret Agent, C683
Secret Lives, C734
Sensation, C717
The Sequel to Second Bureau,
  C722
Shanghai, C641
She, C653

Sherlock Holmes, C816
Shipyard Sally, C789
Show Boat, C689
Sinners in Paradise, C759
The Sisters, C773
Sixty Glorious Years, C765
Slave-Ship, C736
A Small Case of Murder, C758
Song of Ceylon, C650, C755
The Song of Freedom, C702
Son of Mongolia, C763
Spare Time, C777
Lo Squadrone Bianco, C751
Stanley and Livingstone,
  C796
Star of Midnight, C643
The Stars Look Down, C810
The Story of Louis Pasteur,
  C690
The Story of Vernon and Irene
  Castle, C779
Stradivarius, C736
Stranded in Paris, C768
Strike Me Pink, C674
The Student of Prague, C681
Swing, Sister, Swing, C759
Tail Spin, C775
Tales from the Vienna Woods,
  C744
The Tenth Man, C713
The Texas Rangers, C704
Thanks a Million, C661
Thanks for Everything, C773
Theodora Goes Wild, C721
There Ain't No Justice, C789
There Goes My Heart, C766
These Children Are Safe, C814
These Three, C681
They Drive By Night, C772
They Won't Forget, C747
Things to Come, C671
Thirteen Hours by Air, C684
This Man in Paris, C782
The Three Little Pigs, C636
The Three Musketeers, C666,
  C771
Three Smart Girls, C723
Three Smart Girls Grow Up,
  C770

Thunder in the City, C722
Top Hat, C653
Top of the World, C731
The Trail of the Lonesome
  Pine, C683
Treasure Island, C663
True Confession, C754
The Trunk Mystery, C642
Tudor Rose, C682
The Tunnel, C657
Turn of the Tide, C653
Twenty-One Days, C808
Two for Tonight, C649
Un de la Légion, C788
Undercover Doctor, C785
Under Two Flags, C695
Underworld, C752
Union Pacific, C778
Veille d'Armes, C673
The Voice of Britain, C641
Walt Disney Season, C715
Wee Willie Winkie, C746

We from Kronstadt, C720,
  C730
Where's George?, C644
Where's the Fire?, C802
The White Angel, C711
Windbag the Sailor, C716
Wings in the Dark, C637
Winterset, C725
The Wizard of Oz, C812
Woman Chases Man, C736
Woman Tamer, C659
Wuthering Heights, C774
Yiddle with His Fiddle,
  C734
You and Me, C760
You Can't Cheat an Honest
  Man, C780
You Can't Take It with You,
  C766
Young Man's Fancy, C790
Young Mr. Lincoln, C792
Zaza, C635